Ultimate UI/UX Design for Professionals

Create Impactful, User-Centric Designs with Research and Collaboration Techniques for Seamless Responsive Web Interfaces

Sharanpreet Kaur

www.orangeava.com

First Published: December 2024

Published By: Orange Education Pvt Ltd, AVA®

Address: 9, Daryaganj, Delhi, 110002, India

275 New North Road Islington Suite 1314 London,
N1 7AA, United Kingdom

ISBN (PBK): 978-93-48107-38-1
ISBN (E-BOOK): 978-93-48107-30-5

Scan the QR code to explore our entire catalogue

www.orangeava.com

Dedicated To

My Sister, Harjit Kaur

and

My Daughter, Evleen Kaur

Your Support and Love Inspire Every Page of This Book

About the Author

With more than 14 years of experience in creating user-friendly, intuitive digital experiences, Sharanpreet Kaur is an accomplished UI/UX designer. She began her career with a strong foundation in technology, earning a Bachelor of Science in Information Technology (BSc IT) from GNDU University, which she later complemented with an MBA and a specialization in User Experience Design from London University. This unique blend of technical expertise and strategic understanding has equipped her with the skills to navigate and innovate in the complex world of user experience design.

Throughout her career, Sharanpreet has had the chance to work for both product-focused and service-based IT firms, gaining a broad range of expertise and insights into various design issues and methods. Her diverse portfolio, which includes admin panels, Android and iOS apps, websites, and more, demonstrates her versatility across different digital platforms. Her expertise, however, lies in UX design, where she excels at understanding user behavior and transforming insights into streamlined, meaningful experiences.

Sharanpreet combines logic and empathy in her design approach, focusing on users' needs and their interaction with technology. She believes that great design can make digital products easy and enjoyable to use. By blending technical skills with human-centered design, she aims to create solutions that are both practical and visually appealing.

Beyond her professional life, Sharanpreet is also an artist who brings her love for creativity into her work as a UI/UX designer. Passionate about staying updated with latest design trends and tools, she constantly pushes herself to learn more. Her talent for sketching gives her a unique edge, allowing her to bring ideas to life and visualize concepts from the very start. This blend of art and design helps her to create solutions that are both visually appealing and user-friendly.

This book brings together Sharanpreet's experience and passion to guide designers through the challenges of the field, covering basic concepts to advanced techniques. She hopes her insights will inspire a new generation of designers to not only create, but innovate and make a lasting impact in the digital world.

About the Technical Reviewer

Sidharth Khurana is a Senior UX Designer based in New Delhi, India, with a passion for creating user-centered, data-driven experiences that make an impact. Over the years, he has worked on diverse projects – from building design systems and crafting end-to-end user journeys to designing immersive experiences in cloud security, education, and crypto trading platforms. He excels at using storytelling to bring complex ideas to life through intuitive and visually engaging interfaces. Currently, he leads design initiatives at Averlon Inc., where he ensures the delivery of cohesive and impactful experiences for users.

Acknowledgements

I would like to express my heartfelt gratitude to everyone who supported and encouraged me in the creation of this book on UI/UX design. First and foremost, I am deeply thankful to my family for their unwavering support and patience throughout this journey. Their encouragement and understanding allowed me the time and space to focus on writing and research.

I am also immensely grateful to the organizations where I had the privilege of working and learning. These experiences provided me with valuable insights into UI/UX design, fostering my growth and shaping my perspective on creating effective and user-centric design.

Moreover, I extend my sincere thanks to my publishers for believing in this project and guiding me through the publication process. Their expertise, attention to detail, and commitment to quality have been invaluable in bringing this book to life. Everyone's contributions are reflected in my work, and I sincerely appreciate all the support I received along the way.

Preface

It is impossible to overestimate the importance of good UI/UX design in the digital age, where experience frequently takes position over everything else. This book bridges the knowledge gap between those who are new to the subject and those who want to improve their current abilities, making it suitable for both aspiring designers and seasoned professionals. In ten chapters, we break down the fundamental ideas, patterns, and methodologies that power intuitive, impactful design.

Each chapter delves deeply into a unique facet of UI/UX design– from foundational concepts to advanced practices. Each idea is given life by real-world examples, which demonstrate how theory may be translated into workable design solutions. Important topics including information architecture, user psychology, and the craft of seamless experience creation will be covered. Additionally, we emphasize tools, practical advice, and best practices that are appropriate for a range of skill levels.

A snapshot of key insights and skills covered throughout the book is listed as follows:

Chapter 1. The Design Thinking Process: This chapter introduces UI/UX and the design process–a problem-solving approach with stages like research, ideation, prototyping, testing, and implementation. This framework helps designers understand users, coming up with innovative concepts, refine solutions, and deliver products that benefit both users and businesses.

Chapter 2. Fundamentals of UX Design: This chapter covers the fundamentals of UX design, focusing on how Context, Content, Communication, and Community shape digital experiences. We will tackle the challenges of applying these elements and learn about the Seven-Step Method used by UX designers to solve design problems creatively.

Chapter 3. Research and Analysis for UX Design: The UX research methods are covered in this chapter, which will help you with everything from goal-setting to collecting, evaluating, and using user insights. You will learn qualitative and quantitative methods, like interviews and analytics, to inform user-centered, impactful design decisions

Chapter 4. The Art of UX Mapping: This chapter discusses the fundamentals of UX mapping, including how to better understand user interactions using empathy maps, journey maps, and user personas, as well as tools to improve the clarity and efficacy of mapping.

Chapter 5. Mastering Information Architecture and Sitemaps: Sitemaps and information architecture, two essential components for creating user-friendly websites, are covered in this chapter. In addition to exploring IA systems and learning about IA concepts like organization and clarity, you will also discover how sitemaps facilitate efficient website planning.

Chapter 6. The Power of Wireframes and Prototypes: With practical examples, this chapter emphasizes the value of wireframes in structuring ideas for design. Additionally, you will explore prototypes and discover how interactive elements bring wireframes to life. You will earn about the best tools for creating and testing prototypes and wireframes.

Chapter 7. Visual Design and UI Patterns: A key concept for focusing user attention and designing user-friendly interfaces is visual hierarchy, which is covered in this chapter. You will examine UI design patterns, industry-standard solutions for common issues and find top UI pattern libraries to streamline your design process.

Chapter 8. The Power of Mockups: This chapter covers the role of mockups in UI design, key tools for creating them, and the importance of microcopy and microinteractions. We will explore how AI affects UI design, highlighting both its advantages and disadvantages.

Chapter 9. Responsive Web Design: The fundamentals of responsive web design (RWD), such as media queries, flexible grids, and responsive pictures, are covered in this chapter. The distinctions between responsive and adaptive design will also be covered, with an emphasis on the Mobile-First methodology.

Chapter 10. Mastering in Design Handoff: This chapter covers the design handoff process, where UX designers deliver assets and documentation to developers. You will discover how a seamless transition from design to development is ensured by efficient cooperation and communication between designers and developers.

Chapter 11. Interview Preparation for UI/UX Designer: This last section offers advice on how to effectively present design skills to prospective employers, prepare for frequently asked interview questions, and create an engaging portfolio.

This book will lead you through a careful journey in user-centered design, regardless of your goals–whether you want to start a new career or hone your skills. By the end of the chapter, you will not only know how to create aesthetically pleasing and useful interfaces, but you will also know why both businesses and users find them important. Welcome to your toolkit for shaping the future of digital experience–let us create something remarkable together.

Get a Free eBook

We hope you are enjoying your recently purchased book! Your feedback is incredibly valuable to us, and to all other readers looking for great books.

If you found this book helpful or enjoyable, we would truly appreciate it, if you could take a moment to leave a short review with a 5 star rating on Amazon. It helps us grow, and lets other readers discover our books.

As a thank you, we would love to send you a free digital copy of this book, and a **30%** discount code on your next cart value on our official websites:

www.orangeava.com

www.orangeava.in (For Indian Subcontinent)

☑ **Here's how:**

Leave a review for the book on Amazon.

Take a screenshot of your review, and send an email to **info@orangeava.com** (it can be just the confirmation screen).

Once, we receive your screenshot, we will send you the digital file, within 24 hours.

Thank you so much for your support – it means a lot to us!

Colored Images

Please follow the links or scan the QR codes to download the ***Images*** of the book:

You can find code bundles of our books on our official Github Repository. Go to the following link to and QR code to explore the further:

https://github.com/orgs/ava-orange-education/repositories

Please follow the link to download the Colored Images of the book: ***https://rebrand.ly/a1214d***

In case there's an update to the code, it will be updated on the existing GitHub repository.

Errata

We take immense pride in our work at **Orange Education Pvt Ltd,** and follow best practices to ensure the accuracy of our content to provide an indulging reading experience to our subscribers. Our readers are our mirrors, and we use their inputs to reflect and improve upon human errors, if any, that may have occurred during the publishing processes involved. To let us maintain the quality and help us reach out to any readers who might be having difficulties due to any unforeseen errors, please write to us at :

errata@orangeava.com

Your support, suggestions, and feedback are highly appreciated.

DID YOU KNOW

Did you know that Orange Education Pvt Ltd offers eBook versions of every book published, with PDF and ePub files available? You can upgrade to the eBook version at **www.orangeava.com** and as a print book customer, you are entitled to a discount on the eBook copy. Get in touch with us at: **info@orangeava.com** for more details.

At **www.orangeava.com**, you can also read a collection of free technical articles, sign up for a range of free newsletters, and receive exclusive discounts and offers on AVA® Books and eBooks.

PIRACY

If you come across any illegal copies of our works in any form on the internet, we would be grateful if you would provide us with the location address or website name. Please contact us at **info@orangeava.com** with a link to the material.

ARE YOU INTERESTED IN AUTHORING WITH US?

If there is a topic that you have expertise in, and you are interested in either writing or contributing to a book, please write to us at **business@orangeava.com**. We are on a journey to help developers and tech professionals to gain insights on the present technological advancements and innovations happening across the globe and build a community that believes Knowledge is best acquired by sharing and learning with others. Please reach out to us to learn what our audience demands and how you can be part of this educational reform. We also welcome ideas from tech experts and help them build learning and development content for their domains.

REVIEWS

Please leave a review. Once you have read and used this book, why not leave a review on the site that you purchased it from? Potential readers can then see and use your unbiased opinion to make purchase decisions. We at Orange Education would love to know what you think about our products, and our authors can learn from your feedback. Thank you!

For more information about Orange Education, please visit **www.orangeava.com**.

Table of Contents

1. The Design Thinking Process **1**
Introduction 1
Structure 1
History of UI and UX 2
Understanding UX and UI Design 3
Understanding the Difference Between UX and UI 3
The Design Thinking Process 4
Here is How it Works 5
Importance of Design Thinking 6
The Five Stages of the Design Thinking Process 7
1. Empathize 8
2. Define 9
3. Ideate 12
Popular Ideation Methods 13
4. Prototype 14
Different Methods for Making Prototypes 15
5. Test 16
User Testing Methods 16
Iterative and Non-Linear Process 17
Big Brands' Design Thinking Success Stories 18
UberEats 18
Achievement 20
AirBnb 20
Achievement 22
Workshop 22
Solving the Gift Dilemma for 7–12-Year-Olds 22
Empathize 23
Define 23
Ideate 25

Prototype 25

Test 26

Iterate - Iterate - Iterate 27

Additional Considerations 28

Future of Design Thinking 29

Design Thinking Tools: A Quick Guide 30

Creating Personas 30

User Mapping 31

Empathy Maps 31

Brainstorming 31

Benefits of Design Thinking Tools 31

Cost-Free Design Thinking Resources 32

Conclusion 32

Key Terms 33

2. Fundamentals of UX Design 35

Introduction 35

Structure 35

User Experience (UX) 36

The Story Behind UX 37

Importance of UX Design 37

The 4 Cs of UX Design 39

Consistency 39

Power of Design Consistency 40

Continuity 41

Power of Continuity 42

Context 43

Power of Context 44

Complementary 45

Power of Complementary 46

Wrap-Up the 4 C's 47

Difficulties in Implementing the 4 Cs 47

C-P-S Hypothesis 47

The Seven-Step Method 48
1. Identify the Problem 49
2. Research the Problem 50
3. Formulate Creative Challenge 50
4. Explore Ideas 50
5. Evaluate the Ideas 51
6. Draw Up an Action Plan 52
7. Take Action 52
Purpose Behind Designers' Use of CPS 53
Creative Problem Solving (CPS) versus the Design Thinking Process 53
Introduction to UX Designer 54
Roles of UX designers 55
User-Centered Design 56
User-Centered Design Examples 56
Benefits of User Centered Design 58
User-Centered Design Process 59
User-Centered Design versus Design Thinking Process 60
Factors that Influence User Experience 61
Useful 62
Usable 64
Findable 65
Credible 66
Desirable 67
Accessible 68
Valuable 70
Wrapping Up 71
Conclusion 71
Key Terms 72
3. Research and Analysis for UX Design 74
Introduction 74
Structure 74

Introduction to UX Research 75
Goal of UX Research 75
Importance of UX Research 76
Benefits of UX Research 77
UX Research Process 78
1. Setting Clear Research Goals 78
Conducting Stakeholder Interviews 79
2. Selecting Your Research Methods 79
3. Preparing a Strategic User Research Plan 80
4. Recruiting Participants 82
Designing a Screening Survey 82
5. Exploring Research Opportunities 83
6. Analyzing and Integrating Results 84
7. Sharing Your Research Findings 84
Iterate and Improve 85
UX Research Methods 85
Qualitative versus Quantitative 86
Behavioral versus Attitudinal 86
Generative versus Evaluative 87
User Interviews 88
Effective Timing for User Interview Sessions 89
Effective Techniques for User Interview 89
Downsides of User Interviews 90
Focus Groups 90
Effective Timing for Holding Focus Groups 90
Effective Technique to Conduct Focus Groups 91
Downsides of Focus Groups 92
Surveys 92
Effective Timing to Conduct Surveys 93
Effective Technique to Conduct Surveys 93
Downsides of Surveys 94
Card Sorting 94

Effective Timing to Conduct Card Sorting ... 95
Effective Technique to Conduct Card Sorting ... 96
Downsides of Card Sorting ... 96
Diary Studies ... 97
Effective Timing to Conduct Diary Studies ... 97
Effective Technique to Conduct Diary Studies ... 98
Downsides of Diary Studies ... 98
Usability Testing ... 99
Effective Timing to Conduct Usability Tests ... 100
Effective Technique to Conduct Usability Tests ... 100
Downsides of Usability Tests ... 101
Field Studies ... 101
Effective Timing to Conduct Field Studies ... 102
Effective Technique to Conduct Field Studies ... 103
Downsides of Field Studies ... 104
Tree Testing ... 104
Effective Timing to Conduct Tree Testing ... 104
Effective Technique to Conduct Tree Testing ... 105
Downsides of Tree Testing ... 106
Eye Tracking ... 106
Effective Timing to Conduct Eye Tracking ... 107
Effective Technique to Conduct Eye Tracking ... 108
Downsides of Eye Tracking ... 109
A/B Testing ... 109
Effective Timing to Conduct A/B Testing ... 110
Effective Technique to Conduct A/B Testing ... 110
Downsides of A/B Testing ... 111
Five-Second Tests ... 112
Effective Timing to Conduct Five-second Testing ... 112
Effective Technique to Conduct Five-second Testing ... 113
Key Questions to Consider During a Five-second Test ... 113
Downsides of Five-second Testing ... 114

Quick Guide - Categories of Methods 115
UX Research Tools 116
Real-World UX Research Case Studies 117
Google Search's Mobile Optimization 117
UX Research Methods Used 117
Key Changes Implemented 118
Outcome 119
Amazon's Checkout Process Improvement 119
UX Research Methods Used 120
Key Changes Implemented 120
Outcome 121
Conclusion 121
Key Terms 122
4. The Art of UX Mapping 125
Introduction 125
Structure 125
Introduction to UX Mapping 126
Importance of UX Mapping 126
Fundamentals of UX Mapping 127
Point of View 128
Scope 128
Focus 128
Structure 129
Selecting the Format 129
Create a User Experience Map 129
Step 1: Developing a Persona 130
Step 2: Performing User Research 131
Step 3: Define the Journey Stages 131
Step 4: Define Customer Interactions 132
Step 5: Pinpoint Friction Points 133
Step 6: Resolve Issues 133
User Persona 134

Benefits of Creating a Persona 134
Tools to Create Persona 135
Types of User Persona 136
Goal-Directed Personas 136
Role-Based Personas 137
Fictional Personas 138
Engaging Personas 140
Other Types of User Persona 142
Comparing Key Persona Types 142

Key Components of a User Persona 144
Personal Information 144
Background 144
Goals and Needs 144
Behavior Patterns 145
Pain Points and Challenges 145
Motivations 146
Quotes 146
Scenarios 146
Example of Persona 147

Types of User Experience Mapping 149
Customer Journey Maps 149
Importance of Customer Journey Mapping 149
Customer Journey Stages 150
Key Elements of Customer Journey Map 152
Creating a Customer Journey Map 154
Using Customer Journey Map Templates 154
1. Clearly Define the Map's Goals 154
2. Describe Your Personalities and Set Their Objectives 154
3. Highlight Your Target Customer Personas 155
4. List Every Touchpoint 155
5. Assess the Resources You Now Have and Those You will Require 158

6. Go on the Customer Journey by Yourself.....158
7. Examine Your Findings.....158
8. Update Your Map Over Time.....158
Example of Customer Journey Map.....159
Empathy Maps.....159
Structure of Empathy Maps.....160
Importance of Empathy Maps.....161
Creating Empathy Maps.....161
Empathy Maps Versus Personas.....163
Experience Maps.....163
Benefits of Experience Mapping.....165
Example of an Experience Map.....165
Service Blueprints.....165
Key Components of Service Blueprints.....167
Benefits of Service Blueprints.....167
Best Tools for User Experience Mapping.....168
Customer Journey Maps (CJMs).....168
Empathy Maps.....168
Experience Maps.....169
Service Blueprints.....169
Conclusion.....169
Key Terms.....170
5. Mastering Information Architecture and Sitemaps.....173
Introduction.....173
Structure.....173
Introduction to Information Architecture.....174
Understanding Information Architecture.....174
The History of IA.....176
Importance of Information Architecture.....177
Information Architecture Principles.....178
Principle of Objects.....178
Principle of Choices.....178

Principle of Disclosure ... 179

Principle of Exemplars ... 180

Principle of Front Doors ... 181

Principle of Multiple Classification ... 181

Information Architecture Systems ... 183

IA versus UX ... 185

Creating Information Architecture for Your Website ... 186

1. Understand Users and Define Goals ... 186

2. Create Categories and Label the Content ... 187

3. Create a Hierarchy, Develop Navigation and Sitemap ... 187

4. User Testing and Iterate ... 189

5. Document Everything ... 189

6. Stay Flexible ... 190

Information Architecture Tools ... 190

Introduction to Sitemaps ... 191

Importance of Sitemap ... 192

Types of Sitemaps ... 192

HTML Sitemap ... 192

XML Sitemap ... 194

Video Sitemap ... 195

Image Sitemap ... 197

News Sitemap ... 198

Mobile Sitemap ... 198

Creating a Sitemap ... 199

Creating a Sitemap Manually ... 199

Step 1: Review Your Page Structure ... 199

Step 2: Optimize Your URLs ... 201

Step 3: Ensuring Code Accuracy ... 201

Step 4: Integrating Your Sitemap with Root ... 202

Step 5: Submit Your Sitemap ... 203

Generating a Sitemap with a Sitemap Generator ... 203

Information Architecture versus Sitemap ... 204

Conclusion....205

Key Terms....205

6. The Power of Wireframes and Prototypes....208

Introduction....208

Structure....208

Introduction to Wireframes....209

Importance of Wireframing....210

Types of Wireframes....211

Low-Fidelity Wireframes....211

Mid-Fidelity Wireframes....212

High-Fidelity Wireframes....213

Desktop versus Mobile Wireframes....214

Benefits of Wireframing....215

Steps to Create a Wireframe....218

Creating an Image....218

Creating Text....218

Colors....218

Best Tools to Create Wireframes....220

Figma....220

Wireframe.cc....220

Pencil Project....220

MockFlow....221

Adobe XD....221

Balsamiq....221

Sketch....221

InVision....222

Introduction to Prototypes....222

Importance of Prototyping....224

Benefits of Prototyping....225

Types of Prototyping....226

Low-Fidelity Prototyping....226

Advantages of Low-Fidelity Prototyping....229

Disadvantages of Low-Fidelity Prototyping......230
High-Fidelity Prototyping......231
Advantages of High-Fidelity Prototyping......233
Disadvantages of High-Fidelity Prototyping......234
Best Tools to Create Prototypes......235
Comparing Wireframing and Prototyping......235
Conclusion......237
Key Terms......238
7. Visual Design and UI Patterns......240
Introduction......240
Structure......240
Visual Hierarchy: A Guide for Designers......241
Definition......241
Importance of Visual Hierarchy......243
Guides User Attention......243
Improves User Experience......244
Enhances Engagement......244
Increases Conversion Rates......244
Conveys Brand Message Effectively......244
Reduces Cognitive Load......244
Builds Trust and Credibility......245
Key Elements of Visual Hierarchy......245
Reading Patterns......245
Z-Pattern Layout......245
F-Pattern Layout......246
Size and Scale......247
Optimizing Design with Size and Scale......249
Color and Contrast......249
Optimizing Design with Color and Contrast......251
White Space......251
Optimizing Design with White Space......252
Typography......253

Optimizing Design with Typography ... 254

Consistency ... 255

Optimizing Consistency and Alignment ... 256

Layout ... 256

Style and Texture ... 257

Creating Impactful Visual Hierarchies ... 258

User Interface (UI) Design Patterns ... 259

Importance of UI Design Patterns ... 260

Commonly Used UI Design Patterns ... 262

Primary Action Buttons: Your User's Best Friend ... 262

Forgiving Format: Flexibility in Data Entry ... 262

Steps Left: Guiding You Through the Process ... 263

Breadcrumbs: Your Navigation Trail ... 263

Progressive Disclosure: Step-by-Step Presenting ... 264

Lazy Registration: Try Before You Buy ... 264

Hover Controls: Sneak Peek with a Hover ... 265

Subscription Plans: Pick the Perfect Fit ... 265

Leaderboard: See Who is on Top ... 266

Infinite Scroll: Keep Scrolling ... 266

Modal Windows: Focused Pop-Ups ... 266

Card Layouts: Organized Blocks ... 267

Search Auto Complete: Instant Suggestions ... 267

Sticky Navigation: Always in Reach ... 267

Implementing UI Design Patterns ... 267

Top UI Pattern Libraries ... 269

Material Design ... 269

Bootstrap ... 269

Ant Design ... 269

Foundation ... 270

Carbon Design System ... 270

Semantic UI ... 270

Fluent UI ... 270

UI Design Patterns for Mobile Apps....270

Navigation Patterns....272

Content Display Patterns....272

Input Patterns....273

Feedback Patterns....273

Interaction Patterns....274

Onboarding Patterns....274

Top Mobile UI Pattern Libraries....275

Material Design by Google....275

Apple's Human Interface Guidelines (HIG)....275

Ant Design Mobile....275

Ionic Framework....275

Flutter's Widget Catalog....275

Dark UI Design Patterns....275

Conclusion....278

Key Terms....278

8. The Power of Mockups....282

Introduction....282

Structure....282

Introduction to Mockups....283

Purpose of Mockups....284

Elements of a Mockup....285

Types of Mockups....287

Static Mockups....287

Interactive Mockups....288

Low-Fidelity Mockups....288

High-Fidelity Mockups....288

Responsive Mockups....289

Creating Mockups....289

Example in Practice....291

Best Tools for Creating UI Mockups....291

Figma....292

Adobe XD 293
Sketch 294
InVision Studio 295
Axure RP 296
Tips for Designing UI Mockups 297
Microcopy 299
Importance of Microcopy 300
Microcopy's Impact on User Engagement 302
Microinteractions 303
Benefits of Microinteractions 304
Techniques for Creating Seamless Interactions 304
Microinteractions that Drive Success in UI/UX 305
Spotify's Play Button 305
Instagram's Heart Animation 306
Uber's Ride Request Button 306
Pull-to-Refresh 306
The Impact of AI on UI Design 307
AI Tools for UI Design 307
Khroma 307
Uizard 308
Adobe Firefly 309
Visily 310
Other Powerful AI Tools That are Saving a Designer's Efforts 311
AI's Potential to Replace UI Designers 312
Conclusion 313
Key Terms 313
9. Responsive Web Design 316
Introduction 316
Structure 316
Responsive Web Design (RWD) 316
Understanding Responsive Web Design 317

The Rise of Responsive Design ... 317
Adaptive Web Design ... 318
Device-Specific Layouts ... 319
Faster Load Times ... 319
Optimized for Specific Features ... 320
Better for Legacy Systems ... 320
Greater Control over Content Presentation ... 321
Fixed Layouts for Predictability ... 321
Adaptive Design versus Responsive Design ... 321
When to Use the Adaptive Web Design ... 322
When to Use the Responsive Web Design ... 324
Importance of Responsive Design ... 326
Building Blocks of Responsive Web Design ... 326
CSS and HTML ... 327
HTML ... 327
CSS ... 327
Media Queries ... 328
Fluid Grid Layouts ... 329
Flexbox Layout ... 330
Responsive Images ... 332
Responsive Typography ... 332
Adaptive Layouts ... 333
Mobile-First Design ... 334
Key Aspects of Mobile-First Design ... 335
Linking Mobile-First with Responsive Design ... 336
Conclusion ... 338
Key Terms ... 338
10. Mastering in Design Handoff ... 340
Introduction ... 340
Structure ... 340
Understanding Design Handoff ... 340
The Role of Collaboration in Design Handoff ... 341

Strategies for Better Collaboration 341

Design Handoff Checklist 343

Design Files 343

Documentation 343

Interactive Prototypes 343

Assets 344

Design System or Style Guide 344

Feedback and Revisions 344

Functionality and Features 344

Technical Specifications 344

Contact Information 345

Project Timeline 345

Tips for Effective Design Handoff 345

Conclusion 347

Key Terms 347

11. Interview Preparation for UI/UX Designer 349

Introduction 349

Structure 349

Interview Preparation 349

Preparing and Polishing Your Portfolio 350

How to Craft a Standout Portfolio 350

Practicing Common Interview Questions 351

Preparing for a Series of Questions 352

Preparation Strategy 353

Mastering Design Challenges and Soft Skills 353

Mastering UI/UX Design Principles 354

Staying Up-to-Date with Industry Trends 354

Be Confident and Authentic 355

Future Trends in UI/UX Design 355

Final Thoughts 355

Index 356

CHAPTER 1
The Design Thinking Process

Introduction

Welcome to the world of User Experience (UX) and User Interface (UI) design! This chapter will take you on a journey through the history of UX and UI, helping you understand how design has evolved over the years. We will dive into what UX and UI really mean and why they are crucial for creating products that people love to use. We will explore the fascinating Design Thinking process – a powerful method that helps designers create innovative solutions. You will learn about its importance and how it can transform the way you approach problems.

Next, we will look at how big brands have used Design Thinking to achieve success. These real-world examples will show you the impact of thoughtful design and inspire you to apply these principles in your own work. To make things hands-on, we will discuss workshops and how they can help you practice Design Thinking in a collaborative environment.

At the end of chapter, we will provide a quick guide to essential Design Thinking tools. These tools will equip you with practical techniques to enhance your design projects.

Structure

In this chapter, we will discuss the following topics:

- History of UI and UX
- Understanding UX and UI Design
- The Design Thinking Process
- Significance of Design Thinking
- The Five Stages of the Design Thinking Process
    - Empathize

- Define
- Ideate/Design
- Prototype
- Test

- Iterative and Non-linear Process
- Big Brands' Design Thinking Success Stories
- Workshop
- Future of Design Thinking
- Design Thinking Tools: A Quick Guide
- Cost-Free Design Thinking Resources

History of UI and UX

User Experience (UX) and **User Interface (UI)** design have traveled an interesting journey, shaping how we use technology over many years. When computers were first introduced, interacting with them was somewhat difficult. To make them function, a great deal of technical knowledge was required. However, in the 1970s, Graphical User Interfaces (GUIs) were introduced. These greatly simplified matters. They made computers easier to use by introducing features like windows, icons, menus, and pointers (WIMP).

GUIs spread in popularity along with computers over time. When the internet began to gain popularity in the 1990s, designers had to consider how to create user-friendly websites. Websites used to be rather simple, largely consisting of text. However, they quickly improved, adding more images and ways for users to engage with them.

Then, in the 2000s, smartphones came. All of a sudden, people were touching little displays to make things happen. This meant that designers had to consider how to make things finger-friendly and function well on small screens. The 2007 release of Apple's iPhone, with its user-friendly touchscreen and plethora of entertaining apps, completely transformed the entire experience.

Apps and social media gained popularity in the latter part of the 2000s. Designers began experimenting with appearances. While some aimed for a simple, clean style, others made things look like actual items. Both looks survived and changed throughout time.

These days, the main focus of UX and UI design is making things visually appealing and simple to use. Designers ensure that websites and apps function properly for all users by considering their needs and wants. Additionally, designers are constantly coming up with new methods to make things entertaining and simple for us to use as new technologies like voice interfaces and augmented reality (AR) emerge.

Understanding UX and UI Design

User Experience Design (UX Design) is all about making products that people find easy and fun to use and making sure their feelings are considered while doing it. It is not just about making the software easy to use; it is also about creating good experiences with other parts of the product, like how it is advertised, how it is packaged, and how help is given after you buy it. The most important thing is solving problems and meeting needs because nobody wants to use something that does not help them in some way.

In simple words, UX design involves far more than just creating content for screens.

User Interface Design (UI design) is what you see and interact with when you use an app or website. It is all about how things look, how you can use them, and how they respond when you do.

If you are looking to rent a place, consider using an app on your phone. The information you enter, the buttons you press, and the content displayed on the screen are all components of the user interface.

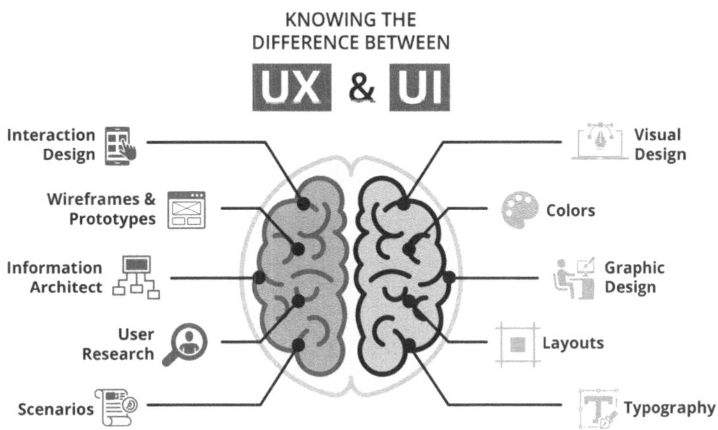

Figure 1.1: *Difference between UX and UI*

Understanding the Difference Between UX and UI

UX and UI design are often mixed up, but they have different roles. UI design makes things look good and work well, while UX design looks at how people use things.

So, *what's the difference?*

UX design involves understanding how we use something, while UI design is about making it visually appealing and functional.

In simple terms, UX makes sure a product is helpful, while UI makes sure it is easy to use. UX professionals detect problems and provide answers, as well as create blueprints and models of how users will use the product. The final appearance and feel of the product are subsequently created by UI designers using those blueprints. UI concentrates on small elements while UX considers the big picture.

But sometimes it is difficult to tell them apart. Work in UI design may be done by a UX designer, and vice versa. In the end, UI and UX are mutually dependent. The quality of the products would not be as good without their collaboration!

While UI and UX designers share some duties, they are not interchangeable. Their skills complement each other, collaborating to create products. UI designers focus on appearance and functionality, while UX designers study user interaction. Together, they contribute to the overall success of a product by integrating their expertise. The main duties of each position are as follows:

The duties of a UX designer

- Enhance user satisfaction
- Improve usability, accessibility, and pleasure in interaction
- Understand users' needs and behaviors

The duties of a UI designer

- Focus on the visual aspect of the product
- Ensure it is visually appealing
- Ensure it is intuitive to use

Now that you know about UI and UX and what designers do, let us see how they fit into the design thinking process. We will look at how they work together to create things like websites or apps, from the first idea to the finished product. By understanding their teamwork, problem-solving, and how they keep trying different things until it works, you will see how UI and UX ensure the final product is easy to use and helpful for people.

The Design Thinking Process

All the product designers, service designers, entrepreneurs, educators, healthcare professionals, social innovators, and business leaders use design thinking process to solve problems in a creative, human-centered, and collaborative way. Design thinking is a way to solve problems that puts people first and involves trying out ideas over and over again. It is about understanding what people need, coming up with lots of ideas, and testing them to see what works best.

Here is How it Works

First, we really listen to people to understand what they are going through and what they need. This helps us figure out exactly what the problem is. Once we know the problem, we brainstorm lots of different ideas, even if they seem a little crazy. We don't judge any idea at this stage.

Next, we make simple versions of our ideas called prototypes. These prototypes help us see what might work and what might not.

We show our prototypes to the people we are trying to help and ask them what they think. Their feedback helps us improve our ideas.

Then, we use the feedback to make our ideas even better. This might mean changing things or trying out new ideas altogether. Finally, we turn our best idea into something real that people can use.

Throughout this process, we stay curious, try new things, and understand that it is okay if some ideas do not work out. We see problems as chances to come up with new and better ideas.

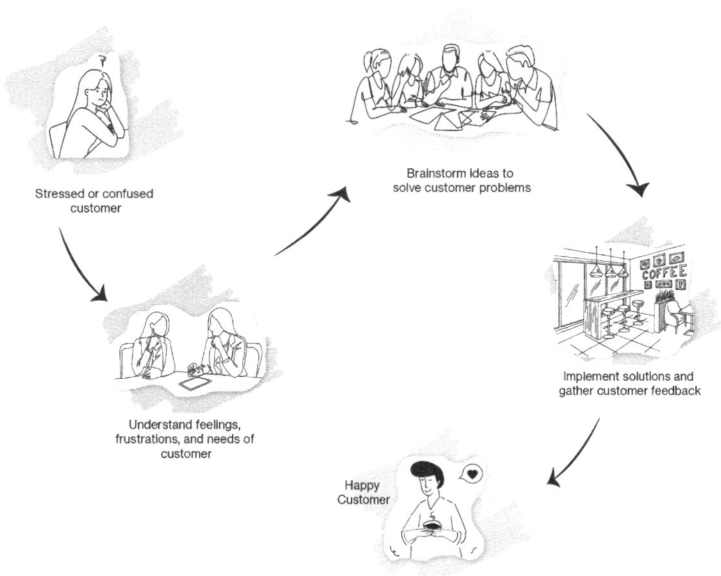

Figure 1.2: *Image showing how Design Thinking work*

Okay, let us imagine something easy to grasp this concept:

Picture your favorite coffee place or busy café in your town where there is always a line. Now your task is to improve the experience of people waiting in line at a busy coffee shop.

Here is how you can use design thinking to do it:

Begin by observing customers as they wait in line. Talk to them to understand their feelings, frustrations, and needs while waiting. Maybe they feel bored, impatient, stressed, or confused because there are too many options to choose from.

Once you have everything you need, brainstorm ideas to make their waiting time enjoyable and effective. May be try an option to offer them a digital puzzle on screen or providing information about coffee ingredients to educate and engage customers.

Next, start the main task by creating a simple prototype of these ideas. You may use a tablet with puzzle games or stick some informative and creative posters about coffee on walls or pillars. Now test it on customers. Just observe how customers react. Collect feedback from them about what they like and what could be improved.

After completing the main task, improve your ideas based on the feedback. Perhaps customers prefer learning about coffee ingredients and how their favorite flavors are made, but find puzzle games too challenging because they need to concentrate.

Finally, once everything is completed, introduce the improved prototype, making the changes customers suggested. Fantastic! You have turned the waiting experience at the coffee shop into something more interesting and enjoyable for customers, all thanks to design thinking.

Importance of Design Thinking

User testing is a critical part of the design thinking process because it helps designers understand how real users interact with their products or solutions. Here is why conducting user testing is so important:

- **Validating Assumptions**: User testing allows designers to verify whether their assumptions about user needs, preferences, and behaviors are accurate. By observing users interact with prototypes, designers can confirm or challenge their initial ideas, ensuring that the final product meets the users' actual needs.
- **Identifying Pain Points**: User testing helps uncover any usability issues or pain points that users may encounter when using the product. By observing user behavior and gathering feedback, designers can identify areas for improvement and refine the user experience accordingly.
- **Gaining Insights**: User testing provides valuable insights into how users think, feel, and behave when interacting with the product. These insights can inform design decisions, helping designers create more intuitive and user-friendly solutions.
- **Iterative Improvement**: Through iterative testing and refinement, designers can continuously improve the product based on user feedback. By incorporating

user insights into the design process, designers can create solutions that are more effective, efficient, and satisfying for users.

- **Building Empathy**: User testing fosters empathy by putting designers in direct contact with users and their experiences. By understanding users' perspectives, challenges and motivations, designers can develop a deeper appreciation for their needs and design solutions that truly resonate with them.

To summarize, design thinking is important because it helps organizations make creative solutions that really help people, promote teamwork and creativity, make failure less likely, and establish a culture of ongoing learning and development. By using design thinking, organizations can drive significant change, add value for their consumers, make them happy, and stay ahead in a fast-changing market.

The Five Stages of the Design Thinking Process

Let us first explore the origins of the design thinking process before delving into its five stages.

The fields of design and innovation are where the design thinking approach got its start. Although its precise beginnings are unknown, it rose to popularity in the twentieth century, thanks in large part to the efforts of Stanford University's D-school and design companies like IDEO. But its ideas are based on a variety of disciplines, such as business, psychology, engineering, and architecture. The demand for more innovative and human-centered methods of problem-solving, especially in complex and uncertain situations, gave rise to design thinking.

There are many versions of the Design Thinking process, but they all share fundamental principles: begin by understanding your users, concentrate on solving their issues, and continually refine solutions.

In this chapter, we guide you through the five most prevalent stages of the Design Thinking process, providing actionable steps for implementing your own design thinking approach.

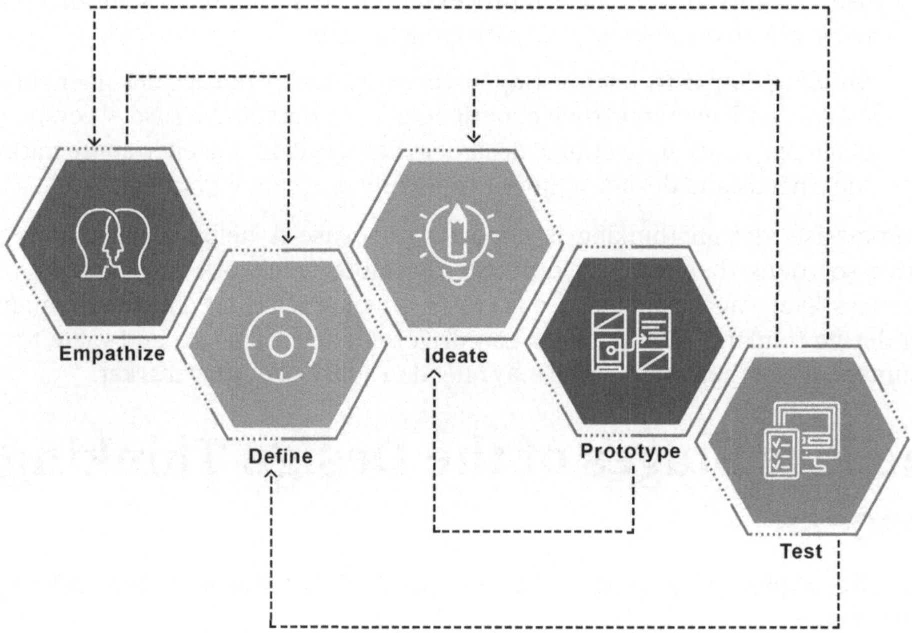

Figure 1.3: *Stages of Design Thinking process*

The five main components of the Design Thinking process are:

1. Empathize
2. Define
3. Ideate
4. Prototype
5. Test

When discussing the five steps of Design Thinking, it is crucial to understand that it is not a straight path. While we describe it in terms of sequential steps, it is actually a highly iterative cycle. Throughout each phase, you will uncover new insights that might prompt you to revisit earlier stages.

1. Empathize

Empathy is the first step in the Design Thinking process. Understanding your users and their needs is crucial to creating goods and services that people genuinely want. This includes learning about their expectations for the product you're designing as well as the difficulties they face in this situation.

Figure 1.4: *Understanding users*

You will fully immerse yourself in the reality of actual users (or representatives of your target audience) throughout the empathize phase. This could entail speaking with them in interviews, watching how they use current items, and closely monitoring their facial expressions and body language.

During this phase, designers initiate different research methods, the creation of user personas and empathy maps, analyze user journeys, and undertake similar tasks. You will learn about all these methods in the following chapters. These endeavors focus on pinpointing and illustrating the requirements of broader user groups, particularly those sharing common characteristics or challenges.

The empathize phase, which is the first step in the Design Thinking process, recommends you to let go of preconceptions. Through firsthand experience, you may create solutions that truly address consumer needs. This is what Design Thinking is all about!

2. Define

In the second step of Design Thinking, you start figuring out the specific problem that users are facing. First, you gather all the information you learned about users' needs and challenges in the first step.

Even if you found many issues in the first step, they are not clearly defined until now. Without a clear problem statement, it is hard to focus on finding solutions. So, in this step, you focus on making clear statements about the problems based on what you learned from users.

In technical terms, a problem statement is a clear and specific articulation of the challenge or opportunity that the design team aims to solve or leverage.

A **problem statement** is a concise description of the issue or challenge that needs to be addressed through the design process. In technical terms, it is the difference between how things are now (the problem) and how we want them to be (the goal) in a process.

Problem statements are occasionally referred to as point-of-view (POV) statements. In this stage, you will come across different kinds of problems, ranging from simple to complex. Instead of immediately trying to fix them, you simply describe the most common issues that need solving.

Following the idea of Design Thinking, the problem statement keeps the user in focus. The problem statement should be based on what users need, not just what the business wants.

For example, consider a problem statement:

As a business goal:
Improve online sales by making it easier for users to find and buy products.
From the user's perspective:
How can we make it simpler for customers to find and buy what they want online?

By the end of this step, you will have a clear problem statement to guide the rest of the design process. This statement helps you come up with creative ideas and find solutions that truly help users.

The question then becomes: how can we accomplish this effectively?

When you're working on a project, you might need to explain the issue or what you're thinking about in different ways. So, the problem statement can be in any format, but no matter how you say it, the main idea is to help the design team figure out a solution that will work.

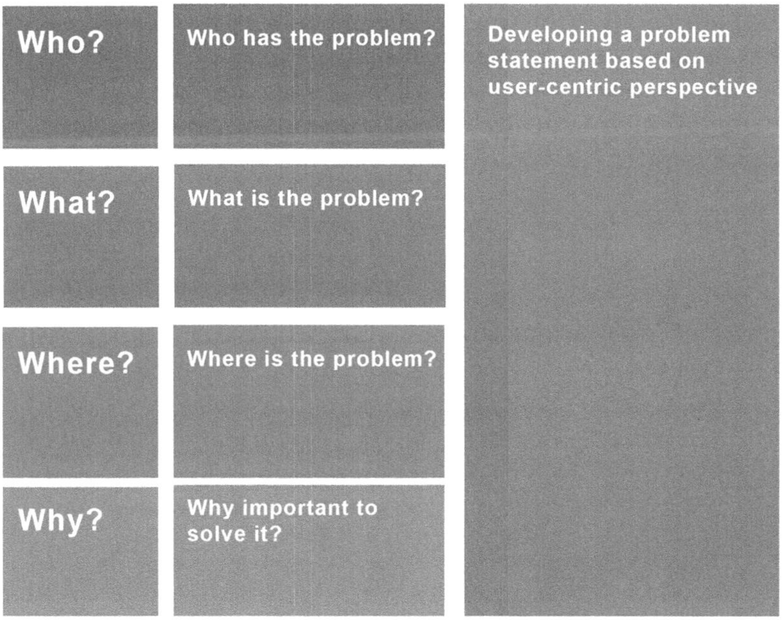

Figure 1.5: *Problem statement template*

Let us continue with the same example of your favorite coffee shop. Picture your favorite coffee place or busy cafe in your town where there's always a line.

Here are some examples of how you could explain the problem or point of view:

User's Perspective Problem Statement:

Waiting in line at the busy coffee shop is often frustrating and time-consuming for customers, leading to decreased satisfaction with their overall experience.

User Research Perspective Problem Statement:

Through user research, it's evident that customers waiting in line at the busy coffee shop express dissatisfaction due to long wait times, lack of clear communication about wait times, discomfort in the waiting area, and limited access to information about menu items or specials.

Four Ws Problem Statement:

Who: Customers at the busy coffee shop.

What: Waiting in line.

Where: At the coffee shop.

Why: To enhance the waiting experience and overall satisfaction for customers.

These statements all tackle the same problem but approach it from slightly different angles. The common thread among them is the emphasis on understanding the user, their needs, and the underlying reasons behind those needs. How you articulate and structure the problem statement ultimately depends on how you want to convey the issue and frame it within the context of the user experience.

3. Ideate

This step involves coming up with a ton of different ideas for tackling the difficulties you have identified after getting to know your people well and learning about their main concerns. There are no hard and fast rules when it comes to brainstorming ideas. The goal is to generate as many creative and outrageous ideas as you can, without considering their viability. But don't forget to remain focused on your problem statement.

Figure 1.6: *Brainstorming ideas*

It is crucial to remember that at this stage, the focus is on generating a large number of ideas, prioritizing quantity over quality. It is important not to rush into judgment, allowing everyone to feel at ease sharing their ideas. If someone questions the viability of an idea, they should be ready to provide a solid explanation for their viewpoint. This approach fosters an open and collaborative environment where diverse perspectives can contribute to the ideation process.

During ideation sessions, it is important to set a time slot of 30-40 minutes and involve the entire design team. If possible, choose a suitable environment; although it may seem insignificant, the location where you conduct your ideation session can greatly influence the outcome. Moreover, it's beneficial to consider and involve other stakeholders. Having stakeholders present can help eliminate completely impractical ideas before moving to the prototyping stage.

During this part of the Design Thinking process, your problem statement will be like your map, showing you where to go. You will keep working on it until you have a few main ideas to move forward with. These ideas will be transformed into prototypes, which you'll try out with real users to see how well they work.

Popular Ideation Methods

Now that you have set up everything for your ideation session, there is one final step: deciding which ideation techniques to employ.

Here are a few popular ideation methods frequently utilized by designers:

- **Brainstorming:** A group activity where participants freely generate ideas without criticism, aiming for quantity over quality.
- **Mind Mapping:** A visual technique where ideas are organized hierarchically around a central concept, allowing for exploration of connections and associations. In other words, drawing a diagram to show how different ideas are connected.
- **SCAMPER:** An acronym that stands for Substitute, Combine, Adapt, Modify, Put to another use, Eliminate, and Reverse, which prompts participants to explore different ways to innovate existing ideas or products. In simple terms, asking questions to think about how you can change or improve something.
- **Worst Possible Idea:** Encourages participants to deliberately generate the worst possible solutions to a problem, which can sometimes lead to unexpected and innovative ideas.
- **Six Thinking Hats:** Developed by Edward de Bono, this method involves assigning different "hats" to participants, each representing a different perspective (for example, logical thinking, creativity, emotions) to explore a problem from multiple angles.
- **Rapid Prototyping:** Quickly creating rough, low-fidelity prototypes of ideas to test and iterate upon, allowing for rapid experimentation and refinement to see what works.

These are just a few examples of ideation methods used in the Design Thinking process, each offering its own unique approach to stimulating creativity and generating innovative solutions.

4. Prototype

In the fourth step of the process, your main focus is on deciding what's most important and then creating prototypes. Prototyping means taking some of the best ideas you came up with during brainstorming and making them into something real that you can touch and see. This is important because it allows design teams to show clients and others what the product might be like in a more tangible way, which helps gather detailed and useful feedback.

Imagine you had a really productive brainstorming session in Step 3 and came up with many different ways to solve the main problem. But you can't make prototypes for every single idea, so you have to choose which ones are the most important to test out.

To help you decide, you can use a prioritization grid. This involves manually evaluating each idea by writing them down on sticky notes and then placing them on a grid based on their user value and feasibility. The best ideas will be those that are most valuable to users and also easy to put into action. This process helps you focus on the ideas that have the highest potential for success.

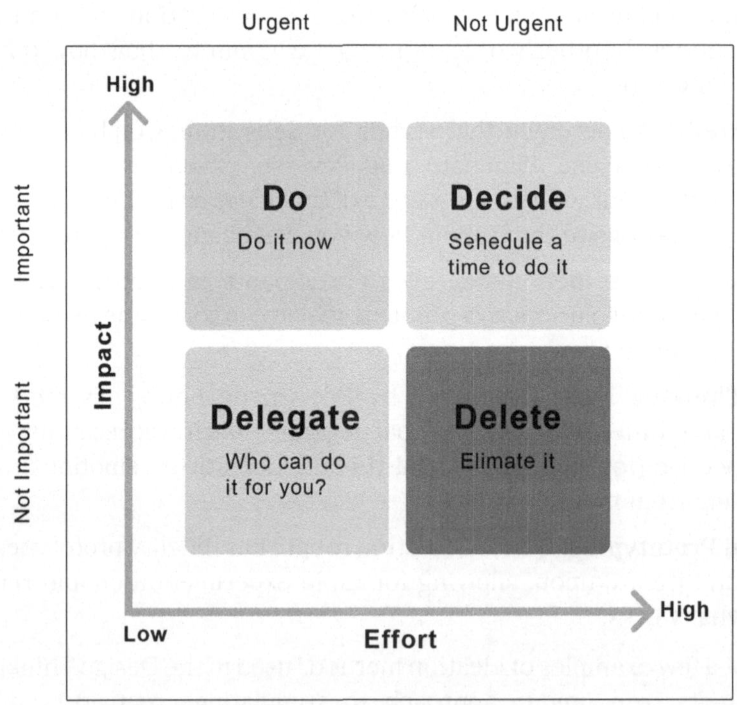

Figure 1.7: *Priority matrix*

Now it is time to decide which ways are most important for solving the problem. You will start working on these and create a prototype. Making a prototype is a really important step in the Design Thinking process. It's all about testing your ideas with real users, and prototypes help you do this without spending a lot of time or money.

Prototypes can help you in a few different ways:

- They let you see how users will use and react to your product. Watching people interact with an early version of your product depicts if it will actually work in the real world.
- They help you find any problems with how your product works or looks before it's too late. If something is not going to work, it is better to find out early. Prototypes help you spot any weak spots or problems before you've spent too much time or money.
- They help you make smart decisions about your design. If you're not sure where an icon should go in a webpage or app, or which design is best for your website, you can try out a few different versions with prototypes to see which one people like best.

Even if you've done a lot of research on what users want, it can still be hard to really understand a product until you see it in front of you. Prototypes let you keep changing and improving your product until it's ready to go out to the public.

Different Methods for Making Prototypes

Prototyping is a way to turn your ideas into something real that you can see, touch, and test. There are different methods for making prototypes, and each one has its own benefits. Let us dive into some fun and easy-to-understand prototype methods:

- **Paper Prototypes:** Picture this – you draw your app or website screens on paper, then shuffle through them like a flipbook. It's like a storyboard for your project. Want to test if your idea works? Just flip through and see!
- **Wizard of Oz:** No, we're not talking about the movie. In this method, you create a pretend version of your product. It's like putting on a play! You act out how the product would work behind the scenes while the user interacts with it, giving you valuable insights.
- **Role Playing:** Time to get into character! With role-playing, team members pretend to be users and interact with the prototype. It's like playing make-believe, but it helps you see how users might really use your product.
- **Digital Prototypes:** Think of this as a sneak peek of your final product. Using software, you create a digital version of your idea. It's like building a mini version of your app or website that people can click through and explore.
- **Prototype Apps:** Ever heard of prototyping tools like Figma or InVision? They're like virtual playrooms where you can build interactive models of your product. Just drag and drop elements to design your prototype – no coding required!

- **3D Printing**: Imagine bringing your idea to life with a magic printer! With 3D printing, you can create physical models of your product. It's like sculpting, but in the digital age.

Each of these methods is like a different tool in your creative toolbox. Whether you're sketching on paper or clicking around in a digital app, prototyping helps you turn your ideas into reality, one step at a time!

5. Test

This phase is like putting your design under a microscope. It helps designers spot any problems in the design and discover any areas where users might still be struggling. Sometimes, even if a design seems perfect to designers or clients, it can still have big issues for the people who will actually use it.

Now, you're reaching the last step of the design thinking process. It's time to put your prototype to the test with real users, gather feedback, and see how well it works. This step is similar to Step 1, where you focused on understanding your users' needs and feelings.

During testing, you'll watch your target users, or people who represent them, as they try out your prototype. You'll also ask for their thoughts and feelings about the experience. This helps you understand how users really feel about your design and where it might need improvements.

User Testing Methods

In the fifth stage of the Design Thinking process, which is all about testing your ideas with real users, there are several common methods used to gather feedback. Here are a few of them, explained in simple terms:

- **Observational Testing**: This method involves watching users as they interact with your prototype. You might observe their facial expressions, body language, and actions to understand how they are feeling and what they are thinking as they use your product.
- **Interviews**: Interviews allow you to have direct conversations with users about their experiences with your prototype. You can ask them questions to get more detailed insights into what they liked, what they didn't like, and any problems they encountered.
- **Surveys**: Surveys are a way to gather feedback from a larger group of users. You can create a questionnaire with multiple-choice or open-ended questions to collect data about users' experiences and preferences.
- **Usability Testing**: Usability testing focuses on how easy or difficult it is for

users to accomplish specific tasks with your prototype. You might ask users to complete certain actions and observe how they navigate through the product.

- **Prototype Walkthroughs**: In a prototype walkthrough, you guide users through your prototype, explaining how it works and what each feature does. This method allows you to see how users interact with different parts of the prototype and where they might get stuck.
- **A/B Testing**: A/B testing involves creating two versions of your prototype with slight variations and testing them with different groups of users. This allows you to compare which version performs better and make informed decisions about which design elements to keep or change.

These are just a few examples of user testing methods used in the Design Thinking process. Each method offers unique insights into how users interact with your prototype, helping you refine and improve your design based on real user feedback.

Iterative and Non-Linear Process

Design Thinking is indeed a non-linear process, meaning that it doesn't follow a strict step-by-step progression from start to finish. Instead, it's a flexible approach that allows for iteration, exploration, and refinement at various stages *(refer to **Figure 1.3** for a visual representation of this dynamic process).*

Let us dive into Design Thinking using a simple analogy: baking a cake.

Imagine you are baking a cake for a friend's birthday. Now, Design Thinking is like baking that cake in a really fun and creative way!

1. **Understanding Your Friend's Taste**: Before you even start baking, you want to know what flavors your friend likes. Maybe they love chocolate or prefer something fruity. So, you chat with them to get a sense of what they'd enjoy.
2. **Planning Your Cake**: Armed with this information, you start planning your cake. You think about the layers, the frosting, and any decorations. But here is where it gets interesting: instead of sticking to one plan, you jot down a few ideas. Maybe a layered chocolate cake or a fruity sponge cake.
3. **Mixing and Tasting:** Now, it's time to mix up the batter. As you are mixing, you taste it along the way. Maybe you realize it needs a bit more sweetness or a pinch of salt to balance the flavors. So, you adjust as you go, just like Design Thinking allows you to tweak and refine your ideas.
4. **Decorating and Testing:** Once your cake is baked and cooled, it is time to decorate. You try out different frosting designs and maybe add some sprinkles or fruit on top. Then, you ask your friend to taste it. They might love it as it is, or they might suggest a change, like adding more frosting or less sugar.

5. **Final Touches and Presentation:** Based on their feedback, you make some final touches. Maybe you add a birthday candle on top or write a sweet message in frosting. Then, you present the cake to your friend, who's thrilled with how delicious and beautiful it looks.

See, Design Thinking is like baking that cake. It's not a rigid step-by-step process where you follow a recipe from start to finish. Instead, it's flexible and creative, allowing you to experiment, iterate, and make adjustments along the way until you come up with something truly special and tailored to your friend's tastes.

Big Brands' Design Thinking Success Stories

At this moment, you might be feeling a bit overwhelmed and wondering with all this information about Design Thinking? No worries! Let's make it more exciting with some real-life examples to provide a clearer picture. Dive into the stories of big brands that completely transformed their business models using this awesome methodology.

UberEats

UberEats, a part of the Uber family, is a shining example of how thinking outside the box can change the game in food delivery. They have really set themselves apart by putting the customer first.

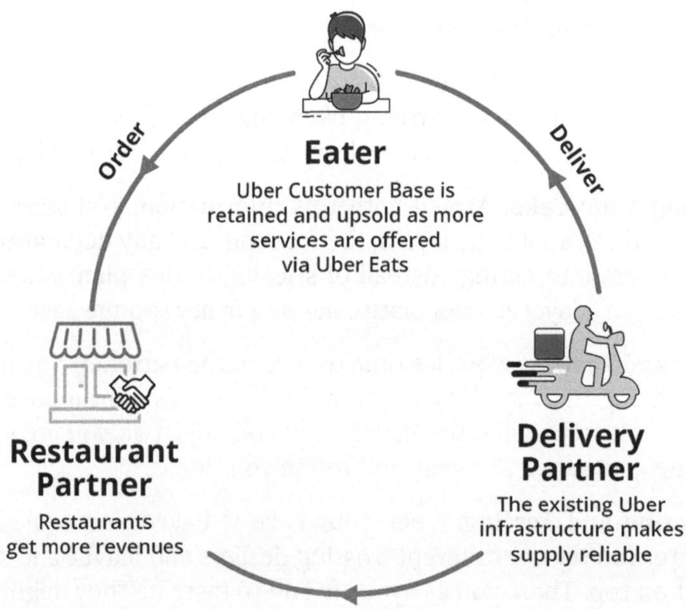

Figure 1.8: *UberEats*

Their big idea? They focus on making it easy for people to find and enjoy their favorite meals. Even though smartphones are relatively new, people have been cooking and selling food for ages. UberEats combines this old tradition with new technology to make ordering food more convenient.

Let's see how they did it and what they accomplished.

1. **Empathize**: First, they really dug deep into what both customers and the restaurants needed. They didn't just sit in their offices; they hit the streets, chatting with delivery partners, chefs, and regular customers like you who love good food. They regularly send designers to different cities where UberEats operates to really understand the local food scene. They look into how food is transported and delivered and talk to delivery partners, restaurant workers, and customers. This helps them understand the problems people face when ordering food and how restaurants struggle to reach customers effectively. They do a lot of research and watch closely to learn as much as they can.

2. **Define**: After understanding people's problems, UberEats figured out the main issue they wanted to fix: how inconvenient and inefficient traditional food delivery methods were for both customers and restaurants. Once they had a clear picture of the problem, they set out to fix it. They narrowed down their focus to their goal and decided to create a platform that would make ordering and delivering food easier for everyone.

3. **Ideate**: Then came the brainstorming phase. UberEats came up with clever ideas to fix it. They thought about making an app that's easy for customers to use. This app would let you see menus, order food quickly, and track your delivery in real-time. Plus, they wanted to make sure deliveries were speedy and hassle-free.

4. **Prototype**: Before diving into development and making the final version of the UberEats app, the team made sample versions to try out their ideas. They built models of how the app might look and tested them with people to see what worked and what didn't. They wanted to make sure everything was just right before launching. This helped them make changes and improvements before the app was finished.

5. **Test**: UberEats started trial programs in certain cities to see how well their platform worked in real life. They paid close attention to what users said and did to see if their solutions were working. This testing phase gave them helpful information about what was good and what needed to be changed.

And, did it pay off? UberEats quickly became a hit, thanks to its slick app and lightning-fast deliveries. Customers loved how easy it was to order, and restaurants saw their business boom.

Iterate - Iterate - Iterate:

They didn't stop there. They kept on listening to what people had to say and making little changes to make their design even cooler. They even brought delivery folks, chefs, and customers right into their offices to chat about their UberEATS adventures.

Since it's tricky to recreate the real deal inside their offices, they hurried to try out their ideas in the real world as soon as possible. Designers watched closely and made tweaks whenever they spotted a chance to make things even better. By always working to improve and come up with new ideas, Uber Eats didn't just shake up the food delivery market; they completely changed it.

Achievement

By following the principles of Design Thinking, Uber Eats achieved several significant outcomes:

- **Speed is Super Important:** UberEats is like a big market where lots of people need to come together fast to make it work well. Delivery partners and restaurants need lots of orders to make money, and customers want lots of options for where to eat and fast deliveries. So, UberEats needs to make things quickly so they can grow their customer base fast. By making changes quickly, they can keep things moving and ensure their design is perfect.
- **Better User Experience:** UberEats made a platform that's super easy to use. Now, you can order food from your favorite spots with just a few taps on your phone.
- **Faster Deliveries:** UberEats made their delivery system work better by using smart technology. This means you don't have to wait as long for your food, and restaurants can serve more people.
- **Changing the Game:** UberEats shook things up in the food delivery world. They challenged the old way of doing things and brought in new ideas that changed how the whole industry works.

AirBnb

Airbnb is a global online marketplace that connects travelers with unique accommodations and experiences. Founded in 2008, it offers a platform where hosts can list their homes, apartments, or even just a spare room for guests to book. Travelers can discover a diverse range of lodging options, from cozy cottages to luxurious villas, and immerse themselves in local culture. With a user-friendly website and app, Airbnb has revolutionized the way people travel, providing a more personalized and authentic alternative to traditional hotels. It fosters a sense of community by enabling hosts to share their spaces and stories, creating memorable and enriching travel experiences worldwide.

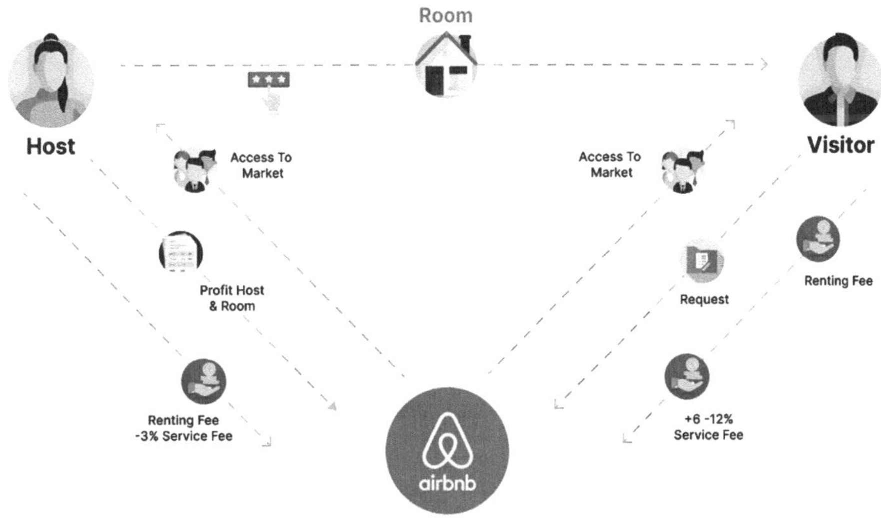

Figure 1.9: *AirBnb*

Airbnb's journey is a fantastic example of how Design Thinking can shape the success of a company. Let's delve into how they applied the process and what they achieved:

1. **Empathize:** Airbnb started by understanding the pain points and needs of both hosts and guests. They realized that travelers were looking for unique and authentic experiences, while hosts wanted a way to earn extra income. So, they immersed themselves in the travel experience, staying in homes around the world to understand what both parties valued.

2. **Define:** Based on their empathy work, Airbnb defined the core problem they aimed to solve: the lack of meaningful connections and authentic experiences in traditional accommodations. They narrowed down their focus to creating a platform that would connect travelers with unique accommodations and local hosts.

3. **Ideate:** With a clear understanding of the problem, Airbnb brainstormed innovative solutions. They generated ideas for a user-friendly website and app interface that would allow hosts to list their spaces easily and guests to discover and book accommodations seamlessly. They also explored ways to foster trust and communication between hosts and guests.

4. **Prototype:** Before fully developing the Airbnb platform, the team created prototypes to test their ideas. They built mock-ups of the website and app interface and conducted usability tests to gather feedback from potential users. This iterative process allowed them to refine their designs and identify areas for improvement early on.

5. **Test:** Airbnb launched pilot programs in select cities to test their platform

in real-world settings. They closely monitored user feedback and behavior to assess the effectiveness of their solutions. This testing phase provided valuable insights into what worked well and what needed adjustment.

6. **Iterate - Iterate - Iterate**: Based on the feedback received during testing, Airbnb iterated on their platform, making refinements and enhancements to improve the user experience further. They fine-tuned features, enhanced trust and safety measures, and expanded their offerings to meet the evolving needs of hosts and guests.

Achievement

By following the principles of Design Thinking, Airbnb achieved several significant outcomes:

- **Disruptive Innovation:** Airbnb disrupted the traditional hospitality industry by offering a unique alternative to traditional accommodations. They challenged the dominance of hotels and introduced a new way for travelers to experience destinations.
- **Community Building:** Airbnb fostered a sense of community among hosts and guests, creating meaningful connections and cultural exchanges. They empowered hosts to share their local knowledge and hospitality, while guests gained access to authentic experiences and insights into local life.
- **Global Expansion:** Airbnb's platform rapidly expanded worldwide, enabling travelers to access a diverse range of accommodations in destinations around the globe. They democratized travel by making it more accessible and affordable for people from all walks of life.

Overall, Airbnb's success story exemplifies how Design Thinking can drive innovation, foster meaningful connections, and disrupt industries by addressing the needs and desires of users in creative and impactful ways.

Workshop

Solving the Gift Dilemma for 7–12-Year-Olds

Selecting a gift for children aged 7 to 12 presents a common challenge for parents: finding a balance between usefulness, educational value, and fun. This age group is at a crucial developmental stage where they are eager to learn, explore, and have fun. Parents want to choose gifts that not only entertain but also contribute to their child's growth and development. However, with the vast array of toys and products available, it can be overwhelming to find something that ticks all the boxes.

Parents often seek gifts that stimulate curiosity, encourage creativity, and foster learning in a fun way. Educational games, science kits, art supplies, and interactive books are popular choices. The challenge lies in selecting a gift that engages the child's interests while providing educational value and entertainment.

Design Thinking can be a valuable approach when it comes to selecting a gift for children aged 7 to 12 years. This age group is diverse, with varying interests, preferences, and developmental stages.

Here is how you can apply Design Thinking to this scenario:

Empathize

- Think about what kids of this age group really love to do. Do they enjoy drawing, playing sports, or maybe exploring science?
- It's really helpful to go outside to a park and talk to kids in this age group in real life. You can ask kids in your family or friends' circle too. Write down all the details on paper, including their names, ages, and what they like to do.
- Imagine how tough it can be for parents or gift-givers to pick the perfect present. They might not know what the child is into right now or want something that's both fun and educational.
- Jot down all the information that shows different kinds of kids in this age group. Like the one who loves sports, the artist, or the science enthusiast. This helps understand what each type of kid might like as a gift!

Define

From what we learn about people in the empathy stage, we can create personas (*a persona is a fictional character that represents a group of real users with similar traits, needs, and behaviors*). We will learn about creating personas in detail in the following chapters. These personas help us understand what motivates them, what challenges they have, their goals, and what makes them who they are.

Based on your understanding, define the criteria for a successful gift. This could include:

- Educational value
- Entertainment factor
- Age-appropriateness
- Durability
- Potential for creativity and imagination

For your reference, here is details of the persona: Lily the Artistic Explorer

Name: Lily

Age: 10 years old

Interests: Art, drawing, painting

Personality Traits:

Creative: Lily is constantly doodling and experimenting with colors and shapes.

Curious: She loves exploring new art techniques and materials.

Patient: When working on her art, Lily can spend hours focused on perfecting her creations.

Favorite Activities:

Drawing in her sketchbook

Spends most afternoons playing at the local park with friends

Enjoys playing the guitar on occasion

Goals:

To improve her artistic skills and try new techniques

Dreams of becoming a professional artist one day

Challenges:

Doesn't always have enough art stuff and wants time every day to do art

Sometimes finds it hard to do homework after playing outside for a long time

Wanting feedback and encouragement for her artwork

Insights:

Lily is a 10-year-old artist who is deeply passionate about art. She enjoys experimenting with various mediums and techniques to create unique pieces. However, she faces challenges such as limited access to art supplies and occasional difficulties finding inspiration. Lily seeks encouragement and opportunities to learn and improve her skills.

From this step, you will gather all the cool stuff about children and make a little persona that tells us about what she likes, what makes her tick, her dreams, and more.

Based on this, we can create a good problem statement.

Example Problem Statement:

User Research Perspective Problem Statement:

We need a gift for a 9–12-year-old child that is engaging, educational, and aligns with their interests in exploration.

Ideate

Ideate is when we take the info and personas we made earlier and come up with lots of new ideas for our user.

Brainstorm gift ideas that meet the defined criteria. Encourage creativity and think beyond typical toys.

Consider a range of options, such as:

- Science kits for experiments
- Educational games or puzzles
- Art and craft supplies
- Building sets like LEGO or robotics kits
- Books or educational subscriptions
- Outdoor exploration kits (for example, binoculars, insect-catching kits)
- Any musical instrument

Think about how each idea meets the child's interests and provides value in terms of learning and entertainment. Every solution might just be the perfect one, even if it doesn't seem like it at first. That's why it is smart to jot down all the ideas we have before we move on.

Prototype

Select one or more of your best gift ideas and create a prototype or concept plan.

This could be a digital mock-up of an educational game, a list of supplies for a science experiment kit, or a description of a book series or ideas on paper as a drawing. Include details such as how the gift will be presented, any additional materials needed, and how it will engage the child.

Let's move on to our research:

Based on our collected information, let us plan out a gift for Lily. We can give her kit of Art and supplies or may gift a Guitar with advanced features.

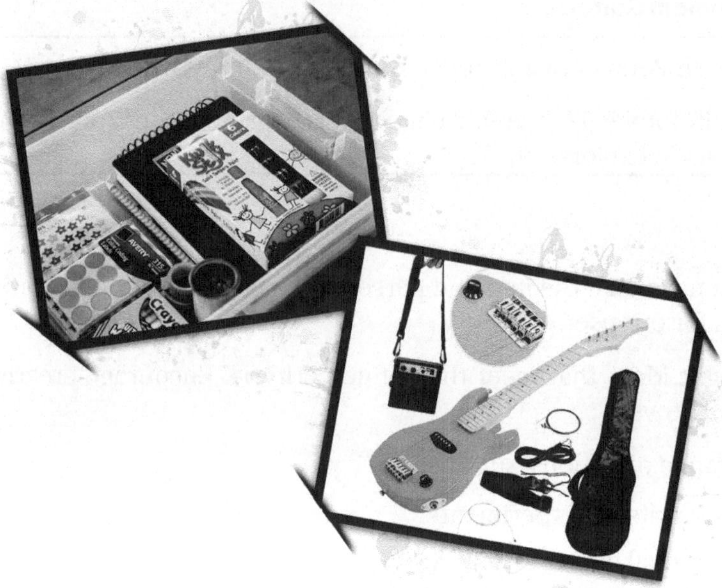

Figure 1.10: *Gift ideas*

Test

Use feedback to refine your selection and make any necessary adjustments.

We picked out the best gifts we thought Lily would love based on her interests, but it turned out differently. That's why the testing and feedback phase is crucial – it lets us hear from Lily herself about what she likes. A solution that seems perfect for one person, like something that works great in an office, might not be what someone actually wants. To bridge this gap between expectation and reality, get feedback directly from Lily or the end user.

Feedback from Lily:

Lily enjoys art supplies, but she already has many basics such as crayons, sketchbooks, and stationery. However, she really liked stickers because she can use them for her future projects and drawing ideas.

As for the guitar, she likes it but only plays it occasionally and isn't familiar with advanced features. So, both gifts are good choices, but Lily can't use them to their fullest potential.

It's like having a puzzle with missing pieces – it's almost complete, but not quite. To ensure Lily gets the most out of her gift, we need to find something that she will use and enjoy fully. This shows why it is important to get feedback directly from Lily to understand her preferences and needs better.

Iterate - Iterate - Iterate

Completing Step 5 does not mark the end of the process. Sometimes, you might find it necessary to return to Step 3 to come up with additional ideas or go back to Step 4 to prototype a different solution. It is all about staying flexible and willing to revisit previous stages as needed to find the best possible outcome.

Now, we have feedback and let's use it to refine your selection and make any necessary adjustments. We will revisit the idea stage and make quick changes to our prototypes.

In Lily's situation, giving her a musical instrument isn't the best idea. Instead, we can make her Art kit even better. We could add paints, a book to learn new art skills, or fun craft activities that she can do with her existing art supplies.

Additionally, including instructions or creative project ideas such as drawing challenges or DIY crafts can further enhance her experience. These prompts can ignite her imagination and encourage exploration of new artistic techniques.

By focusing on what Lily loves and enjoys, we can create a gift that sparks her creativity and brings her joy. This is the magic of Design Thinking – making sure our ideas fit the person we are designing for.

Here are specific gift ideas that align with the Design Thinking approach:

Art and Craft Set:

Figure 1.11: *Gift ideas after feedback*

Hooray! You've reached the finish line of the design thinking process... or have you?

Design thinking is not a one-and-done deal – it is a journey that's always evolving. It's like a never-ending adventure because the process is fluid and keeps looping back on itself.

Here's the scoop: you are designing for real people with real needs, not robots in a perfect world. Your users will always have challenges, and you'll always need to find ways to help them out. That's why we suggest you build a cycle of user research, problem-solving, idea brainstorming, picking solutions, and testing into your design routine. This way, you're always in tune with what your users need and can keep improving your designs over time.

Here are some other specific gift ideas that align with the Design Thinking approach:

- **Science Experiment Kit:**
  - Create a kit with materials and instructions for fun and educational experiments.
  - Include items such as test tubes, magnifying glass, safety goggles, and a booklet of experiments.
  - Emphasize hands-on learning and exploration of scientific concepts.
- **Educational Board Game:**
  - Choose a board game that combines fun with learning, such as a math-based game, a geography quiz, or a strategy game.
  - Look for games that encourage critical thinking, problem-solving, and teamwork.
- **Coding or Robotics Kit:**
  - Select a beginner-friendly coding kit or robotics set that introduces programming concepts in a playful way.
  - Look for kits with easy-to-follow instructions and the ability to create projects like building a simple robot or coding a game.

Additional Considerations

Some additional considerations are listed as follows:

- **Age Appropriateness:** Ensure the gift is suitable for the child's age and developmental stage.
- **Safety:** Consider safety aspects of the gift, such as non-toxic materials and age-appropriate complexity.
- **Long-Term Engagement:** Aim for gifts that provide ongoing engagement and learning opportunities.

- **Inclusivity:** Consider diverse interests and preferences to ensure the gift is inclusive for all children.

By following these steps, students or gift-givers can approach the task of selecting a gift for children aged 7 to 12 with a thoughtful and user-centered mindset, ensuring the chosen gift is not only enjoyable but also enriching and aligned with the child's interests.

Future of Design Thinking

The future of the Design Thinking process is looking bright and exciting, with its principles becoming even more essential in solving complex problems and driving innovation across various industries. Here's a look at what we can expect:

- **Human-Centered Solutions:** Design Thinking will continue to focus on people's needs, emotions, and experiences. As technology advances, it will become even more crucial to create products and services that resonate with users on a personal level. This means designing with empathy and understanding to create meaningful and impactful solutions.
- **Collaboration and Diversity:** Design Thinking thrives on collaboration and diverse perspectives. In the future, we will see more interdisciplinary teams working together, bringing a range of skills and backgrounds to the table. This diversity sparks creativity and leads to more innovative ideas.
- **AI and Digital Transformation:** AI and machine learning will greatly improve the design process by offering data insights, automating tasks, and predicting trends. Designers will use AI to better understand user needs and create personalized experiences. As digital technologies advance, design thinking will adapt to create smooth and user-friendly digital experiences, address privacy and security concerns, and enhance user interactions through AI.
- **Sustainability and Social Impact:** Design Thinking will play a crucial role in addressing global challenges such as climate change and social inequality. There will be a greater emphasis on creating sustainable solutions that minimize environmental impact and promote social equity. Businesses will integrate social responsibility into their design processes, aiming to make a positive difference in the world.
- **Agility, Iteration, and Data Utilization:** The future of design thinking will be characterized by agility and a strong reliance on data. Companies will adopt rapid prototyping and iterative testing, allowing for swift adjustments based on user feedback. This nimble approach, coupled with leveraging big data and analytics, will enable designers to make informed decisions by understanding user behavior and preferences. Continuous feedback loops will be established to gather user input throughout the design process, ensuring that designs are constantly refined and improved based on real user experiences.

- **Comprehensive Integration and Adoption:** Design Thinking will become a standard part of education across disciplines, from business and engineering to healthcare and education. More organizations will adopt Design Thinking methodologies, not just in product design but also in strategy, leadership, and organizational culture.
- **Evolution of Design Education:** As Design Thinking becomes more widespread, education will focus not just on technical skills but also on soft skills such as empathy, communication, and collaboration. Continuous learning through online courses, workshops, and professional development will be essential for designers to stay current with new tools, technologies, and methodologies.
- **Virtual and Augmented Reality:** As VR and AR technologies mature, Design Thinking will explore new possibilities in creating immersive and interactive experiences. From virtual product prototypes to augmented reality applications in healthcare and education, these technologies will open up new frontiers for innovative design.

In essence, the future of Design Thinking is about putting people at the center of innovation, embracing diversity, leveraging technology responsibly, and driving positive change in society. It's a future where creativity, empathy, and collaboration lead to solutions that truly make a difference in the world.

Design Thinking Tools: A Quick Guide

There is a wide range of tools for the design thinking process, with some being free and others requiring payment or membership. Imagine a toolbox filled with software, methods, and techniques that spark innovation and solve complex problems with a human touch. These are the design thinking tools, the magic wands of problem-solving that place the user front and center.

In this world of design thinking, it is all about empathy, creativity, and teamwork. Picture creating personas, mapping out user journeys, diving into empathy maps, and unleashing the power of brainstorming and prototyping. These tools aren't just gadgets; they are catalysts for teams to dive deep, understand users' needs, and craft solutions that truly make a difference.

Creating Personas

When you create personas, you're basically inventing characters that represent different types of users for your product or service. These personas help you understand who you're designing for, what they need, and how they might use what you're creating. It is like creating a cast of characters to guide your design decisions.

User Mapping

User mapping is like creating a roadmap of your users' journey. You are mapping out every step they take when interacting with your product or service. This helps you identify pain points, areas of delight, and opportunities for improvement. It's a bit like following your users on a treasure hunt to uncover what they really want.

Empathy Maps

Empathy maps are tools to help you step into your users' shoes. They're like a window into their minds and hearts, showing you their feelings, thoughts, and behaviors. By filling out an empathy map, you gain deep insights into what makes your users tick, allowing you to design with empathy and understanding.

Brainstorming

Brainstorming is all about letting your ideas run wild. It is a creative session where you and your team come up with as many ideas as possible, no matter how wild or impractical they might seem at first. It's like a brainstorming storm where lightning strikes of creativity can lead to groundbreaking solutions.

We will delve into these techniques extensively in the upcoming chapters.

Think of Design Thinking tools as the secret sauce for teams to crack open problems, see through the eyes of users, and create solutions that aren't just effective, but meaningful. It is the ultimate recipe for success in the world of innovation.

Benefits of Design Thinking Tools

Design Thinking tools are like a superhero's utility belt for problem-solving! They're the secret sauce that makes the creative process more exciting and effective. Imagine having a magic wand that sparks your creativity, letting ideas flow like never before. These tools also help you understand people better, like a pair of special glasses that let you see the world through their eyes. When everyone on the team uses these tools, it's like unlocking a superpower for collaboration. Ideas bounce around, get polished, and turn into something truly amazing together.

But it doesn't stop there. Design Thinking tools also let you test and improve your ideas. It's like having a crystal ball to see into the future and know if something will work before you've even made it. You can build prototypes, try them out, and make things better based on real feedback. They're not just for small projects either; these tools can tackle big, hairy problems by breaking them down into manageable pieces.

Using online Design Thinking tools can assist in organization of your ideas and charting a path towards innovative product development. So, think of design thinking tools as your trusty sidekicks on the adventure of creating something awesome!

Cost-Free Design Thinking Resources

Do free Design Thinking tool kits exist? Even though they might not offer all the features of their paid counterparts, using a no-cost design tool is ideal for smaller teams or those wanting to explore the software before making a commitment.

Here are some free tools you can use to create personas, user mapping, empathy maps, and facilitate brainstorming for the Design Thinking process:

- **Canva:** Canva offers templates for creating personas. You can customize these templates to represent different user types, their needs, and preferences.
- **Miro:** Miro is a versatile online whiteboard tool that's great for user mapping and empathy maps. You can create virtual boards, add sticky notes, and collaborate with your team in real-time.
- **Empathy Map Template:** This is a simple and free template available online that you can print out or use digitally. It guides you through the process of understanding what your users see, hear, think, and feel.
- **MindMeister:** MindMeister is a free mind mapping tool that's perfect for brainstorming sessions. You can create mind maps collaboratively, jot down ideas, and organize them into categories.

These tools can be a great starting point for your Design Thinking process, providing a foundation for understanding users and generating innovative ideas.

Conclusion

As we reach the end of this chapter, we have explored a powerful approach to creating user-centered experiences. Design Thinking isn't just a set of steps; it's a way of thinking that puts the user first. We have seen how important it is to empathize with users, generate creative ideas, prototype solutions, and test them to make improvements. This process is not just for designers – it is for anyone who wants to create products and services that truly meet users' needs.

So, what is the takeaway? Let us remember to always start by understanding our users' perspectives. By empathizing with them, we can uncover valuable insights that drive our design decisions. Then, let us embrace creativity in ideation, thinking outside of the box to come up with innovative solutions. Prototyping helps us bring these ideas to life quickly and test them with users for feedback. This iterative process ensures we are continually refining and improving our designs based on real-world insights.

Moving forward, let's stay curious, open-minded, and eager to learn from our users.

Design Thinking isn't just a process; it's a mindset that can transform the way we approach design. So, as we close this chapter, let us continue our journey with enthusiasm, empathy, and a commitment to creating user-centric designs that make a difference. The next chapter is a guide that explores the details of UX design, including different strategies, problems designers face, and new ideas.

Key Terms

- **User Experience (UX) Design:** The process of creating products that are easy and enjoyable for people to use, considering their needs and emotions throughout the design process.
- **User Interface (UI) Design:** The visual and interactive aspects of a product, focusing on how it looks, how users interact with it, and how it responds to their actions.
- **Graphical User Interface (GUI):** A visual way of interacting with computers, introduced in the 1970s, featuring elements like windows, icons, menus, and pointers (WIMP).
- **Usability:** The ease with which users can interact with a product to achieve their goals effectively and efficiently.
- **Accessibility:** The extent to which a product can be used by individuals with diverse abilities and characteristics, including those with disabilities.
- **Design Thinking:** A problem-solving approach that prioritizes human needs and involves iterative ideation, prototyping, and testing to create innovative solutions.
- **Empathy:** The ability to understand and share the feelings and experiences of others, crucial for designing solutions that truly meet user needs.
- **Prototype:** A preliminary version of a product or solution used for testing and validation purposes, ranging from low-fidelity sketches to interactive digital models.
- **User Testing:** A method of gathering feedback from real users to evaluate the usability, effectiveness, and satisfaction of a prototype or product.
- **Problem Statement:** A concise description of the challenge or opportunity that a design team aims to solve or leverage through the design process, providing focus and direction for ideation and solution development.
- **Iterative:** A process characterized by repetition and refinement, where ideas, designs, or solutions are continuously improved through cycles of testing and feedback.

- **Creative Problem-Solving:** A method of addressing challenges or opportunities by generating innovative ideas and exploring unconventional solutions, often associated with design thinking to encourage out-of-the-box thinking.
- **Collaboration:** The act of working together with others to achieve common goals, essential in design thinking to leverage diverse perspectives and expertise for problem-solving and solution development.
- **Non-Linear Process:** A problem-solving method that does not follow a strictly sequential or linear progression, allowing for flexibility, exploration, and iteration at different stages.
- **Human-Centered Design:** An approach to design thinking that prioritizes the needs, preferences, and experiences of users throughout the design process, aiming to create solutions that are intuitive, accessible, and meaningful to users.
- **Adaptability:** The capacity to adjust and modify strategies, plans, or approaches in response to changing circumstances or feedback, a critical skill in non-linear processes like design thinking.
- **Digital Transformation:** The integration of digital technologies into all aspects of business operations, leading to fundamental changes in how organizations operate and deliver value to customers.
- **Agility:** The ability to respond quickly and effectively to changing circumstances or opportunities, often associated with iterative and adaptive approaches to problem-solving.
- **Virtual Reality (VR) and Augmented Reality (AR):** Technologies that create immersive, computer-generated environments (VR) or enhance real-world environments with digital elements (AR), offering new possibilities for design and user experience.
- **Brainstorming:** A creative technique for generating a large number of ideas or solutions through open and spontaneous discussion within a group.
- **User Mapping:** The process of creating visual representations of users' interactions with a product or service, often used to identify opportunities for improvement and innovation.
- **Persona:** A fictional representation of a target user group, based on demographic, psychographic, and behavioral characteristics, used to guide design decisions and strategies.

CHAPTER 2
Fundamentals of UX Design

Introduction

Step into the world of User Experience (UX) design. This chapter will examine the ways in which human interaction and technology combine to create the digital world. Context, Content, Communication, and Community are the four key facets of UX design that we will begin examining. They function similarly to the fundamental components of outstanding digital experiences. However, it is not always simple to have everything go as planned. We will discuss the difficulties, such as how to apply the 4Cs efficiently and how to apply the Seven-Step Method to solve problems in an original way. We will also learn about the UX designers – the individuals that create UX design. To create things user-friendly, they combine their creative thinking, technological expertise, and understanding of people. By prioritizing users, they create digital content that truly resonates with users. Prepare to discover how UX design is transforming our perception of the digital world as you dive into this fascinating field!

Structure

In this chapter, we will discuss the following topics:

- User Experience (UX)
- Importance of UX Design
- The 4 C's of UX design
- Difficulties in Implementing the 4 Cs
- C-P-S Hypothesis
- The Seven-Step Method
- Creative Problem Solving (CPS) versus The Design Process
- Introduction to UX Designer
- Roles of UX Designers

- User-Centered Design
- Benefits of User Centered Design
- User-Centered Design Process
- User-Centered Design versus Design Thinking
- Factors that Influence User Experience

User Experience (UX)

User Experience – how people interact with a product or service. In other words, every little tap, click, or swipe as you use an app or a website. But it is not just how it looks; it is also about how it feels and how easy it is to use.

UX Design – the behind-the-scenes magic that makes using something smooth and enjoyable. Designers plan everything to the smallest details so that the use of a product is as seamless as can be. What is the goal for them? To give users an experience that feels natural, efficient, and relevant.

This sounds awesome, but how does one become a UX designer, and what exactly do they do? They do this by utterly effectively understanding the individuals who will use their product. They think about what the user requires, desires, and becomes irritated with. It's not only the user; they consider what the company desires to achieve as well.

Figure 2.1: *Designers working on details*

Their role is to make things seem beautiful, but they are more concerned with making things easy and enjoyable to use. They picture themselves in the user's shoes and determine the fastest method to guide them through the product. Start to finish, it feels kind of like a wind.

> *No product is an island. A product is more than the product. It is a cohesive, integrated set of experiences. Think through all of the stages of a product or service – from initial intentions through final reflections, from first usage to help, service, and maintenance. Make them all work together seamlessly.*
>
> *– Don Norman, inventor of the term User Experience*

The Story Behind UX

Just think about an app or a website that you last used. Chances are you found it a bit confusing, or perhaps it was super easy to navigate. That is where User Experience (UX) comes into play.

When technology first began to take off and we started seeing all these amazing devices and websites, people came to the realization that usability is just as important as appearance.

Consequently, specialists began researching how people use technology. They examined factors like the ideal placement of buttons, the colors that promote happiness, and even the speed at which a page should load. With that, UX was born!

Businesses today focus heavily on user experience (UX) because they want us to enjoy using their products. They want us to enjoy browsing their app or quickly locating the information we require on their website. That's the reason you'll hear about UX designers – they are responsible for ensuring that our technological interactions run well.

Importance of UX Design

Think about when everything started going digital around 2010. Back then, making things easy for users became super important. Then along came Covid, showing us just how much digital health care can do. It is not just about fancy gadgets; it is about making tech work for people. This pandemic might just be the big push we need to use computers to solve worldwide health issues.

Ever found yourself lost in a rabbit hole of websites, effortlessly clicking away for hours? Or struggled to even figure out what to click on a poorly designed site? It's all about User Experience design. So, instead of scratching your head in frustration, let us dive into how we can use UX to make our products shine by putting the user front and center and why UX design matters for the retention journey and business success.

Let us examine several key points that demonstrate the importance of UX:

- **Satisfying User Needs:** Picture using an app or visiting a website that seemed customized specifically for you each time. Effective UX accomplishes this. It is like having an online personal assistant that knows exactly what you need and makes it really simple for you to get it. Users are happier, more inclined to make purchases (conversion) and return for more when they believe that their demands are being addressed (retention).
- **Creating Positive Experiences:** Consider your preferred product or brand. Most likely, you love it for how it makes you feel as much as for what it delivers. Good user experience design is all about making people feel good. It's like taking a pleasant, smooth journey as opposed to a rough one. Great user experiences increase the likelihood that users will remain and develop into devoted supporters of the brand.
- **Building Relationships:** Do you ever feel that a business truly understands you? This is a result of the customer journey map they have created. Creating a user experience (UX) roadmap for your product or website is similar to developing one. It is about developing loyalty and trust, not just about making sales. Users are more likely to stay around when they feel appreciated and understood.
- **Cutting Costs:** It might be costly to conduct marketing campaigns, update features frequently, and fix errors. However, effective UX can reduce these expenses. You will save time and money by creating a product that is simple to use and comprehend in the future. Also, satisfied customers are more likely to recommend you to others, which will save you money on advertising.
- **Increasing ROI:** Increasing ROI is similar to getting greater value for your money. You are investing in your users' pleasure and contentment when you prioritize excellent user experience. Additionally, satisfied customers are more likely to make purchases, tell their friends about your goods, and stick around over time. Thus, you ultimately reap greater rewards from your investment.
- **Making an Impression:** Often, it is not necessary to invent the wheel. It is about improving the wheel that you already have. User-focused design can help with it. You can take an ordinary idea and turn it into something spectacular by prioritizing the user and truly knowing what they want. It is like painting an old house a new coat of paint; it may not be brand new, but it surely looks nice.
- **Offering Intuitive Experience:** Have you ever utilized an app or website that seemed to fit right away? It was made with you in mind, which explains why. Making things intuitive is the cornerstone of good user experience design, allowing people to navigate tasks with ease and without excessive thought. It is similar to operating an automobile with all the switches and buttons in their proper locations. And users are more likely to stay around when things feel comfortable and familiar.

UX is essentially about improving items' usability for users rather than just having them seem nice. And everyone benefits when it is done correctly.

The 4 Cs of UX Design

In this section, we take a deeper look at the 4 Cs as we explore the field of UX design. These functions are similar to the building elements needed to create exceptional user experiences. Think of them as the hidden components in your go-to recipe for the ideal website or app.

Our primary objective as UX designers is to produce user-friendly interfaces, captivating interactions, and eye-catching layouts that enhance users' experiences. Early on in the design process, it is critical to keep in mind some important design concepts. That is where the user experience design's four Cs are useful:

- Consistency
- Continuity
- Context
- Complementary

Let us explore the 4 Cs individually.

Consistency

Similar to the constant pulse of your favorite song or the dependable rhythm of your everyday routine, consistency is important in UI/UX design. It all comes down to ensuring that a website or application behaves, feels, and appears consistently across. It would be chaotic if a button changed its behavior each time you clicked it. Users find their experience more pleasurable and intuitive when things are consistent and familiar.

Example

Let us consider a social networking app such as Instagram as an example. The navigation bar at the bottom, the profile icon in the upper corner, and the feed in the center all have the same layout regardless of where you are in the app. Users benefit from this consistency as they explore the app's various features and areas, feeling at ease and confident.

Not only does consistency pertain to appearances, but it also affects functionality. If, for example, tapping on a photo always opens it in full screen mode, people may navigate with ease and rapidly understand what to expect. In a similar vein, users can interact with buttons without hesitation, provided their appearance and functionality are consistent throughout the application.

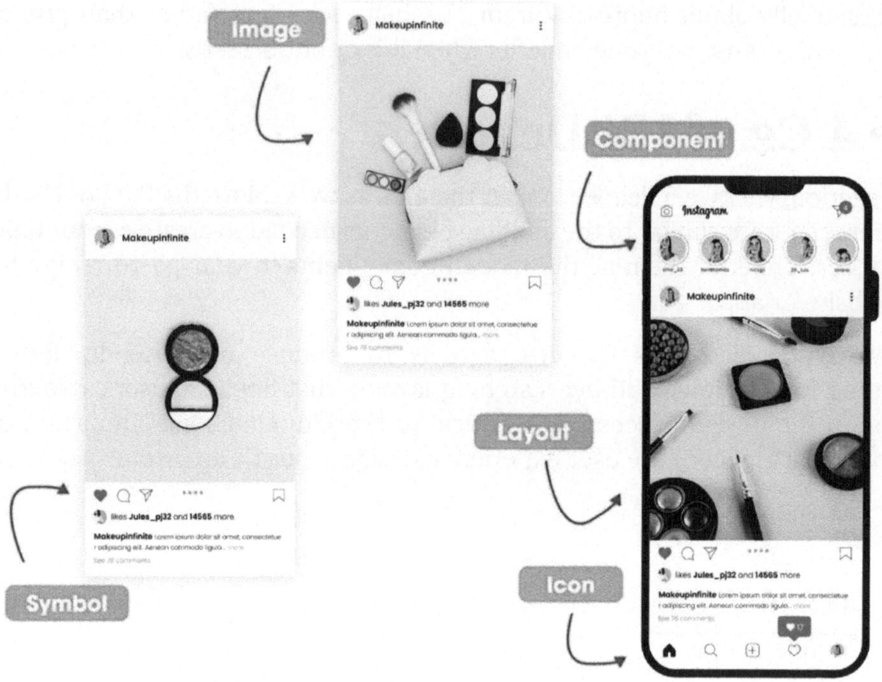

***Figure 2.2**: The consistency of the Instagram application*

Put simply, consistent UI/UX design facilitates the user experience and increases user trust in the product. It produces a seamless, dependable, and polished experience, similar to enjoying a well-performed music. Users can navigate around and enjoy utilizing the digital product more easily when there is consistency.

Power of Design Consistency

Web development companies can benefit greatly from consistent design aspects in user experiences. They facilitate user experience by establishing a dependable and comfortable atmosphere. Imagine it like entering your go-to coffee shop; you can find anything there without even having to think about it.

- Consistent design features facilitate seamless and effortless navigation by acting as a language translator for users when they repeatedly meet the same patterns and visual signals. Everything feels comfortable and natural to them, so they don't need to pause and try to figure things out. They will have less mental strain as a result, allowing them to concentrate on their intended task rather than fumbling with complex designs.
- Trust and confidence are also fostered by consistency. If your closest buddy consistently appeared with a new hairstyle, you could begin to question your ability to rely on them! The same is true with design; when elements appear and function consistently, users are reassured.

- Prominent companies such as Apple, Google, and Meta (formerly Facebook) fully understand the value of consistency. Consider how easy to use and intuitive your iPhone is, or how Google's apps all appear to use a common design language. It all comes down to creating a powerful brand identity and a welcoming environment for users. These businesses demonstrate that consistency changes the game for user comprehension and brand recognition – it's not simply a nice-to-have.

Continuity

When it comes to UI/UX design, continuity is like a smooth journey without any hiccups or obstacles. Ensuring that visitors can easily navigate between various sections of a website or application without experiencing confusion or disorientation is the key. It would be quite startling if you were reading a book and the text and images abruptly changed in color and arrangement with each page flip, don't you think? That is prevented in the digital world by continuity.

Example

Consider the case of an e-commerce app such as Amazon. Continuity makes sure that your search history, preferences, and shopping cart are all effortlessly transferred when you browse for products on your laptop and then switch to your phone to complete a transaction. So, you don't have to start over from scratch or waste time searching for items you have already found.

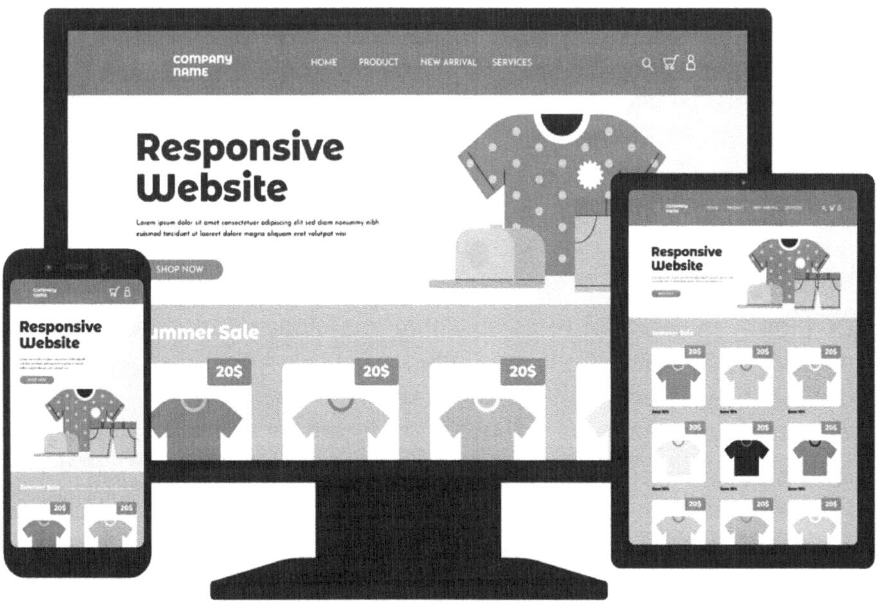

Figure 2.3: *Data seamlessly transferred between various devices*

Another example is watching a video on YouTube. Continuity guarantees that you can resume where you left off if you pause a video on your computer and then open the YouTube app on your phone. This eliminates the need to hunt for the video or scroll through to find your position.

Essentially, uniformity in UI/UX design guarantees that, regardless of the platform or device being used, the user experience remains consistent. Users are spared the trouble of having to perform tasks repeatedly or look up information on their own. Moving about the digital world is seamless and pleasurable thanks to continuity; it's like dancing to a well-orchestrated dance.

Power of Continuity

There are several advantages of using continuity in UX design, and they greatly improve the user experience. Continuity makes a website or app's transitions between sections smooth and seamless, giving consumers a consistent and easy-to-use experience. Users can interact with the product's features, move through it more easily, and accomplish their objectives with the least amount of difficulty because of its fluid flow. Because of this, there is a greater chance that users will be delighted and involved with the experience, which will increase user loyalty and retention.

- Enhancing user engagement and retention is one of continuity's main benefits. Users are more likely to stick with a product longer when they can switch between platforms, devices, or tasks with ease and without interruption. By encouraging customers to experiment with different features and functionalities, continuity helps users engage with the product more frequently and build a stronger bond with it over time.
- Enhanced user interaction efficiency is a result of continuity. Continuity simplifies the user journey and lowers needless friction by removing the need for users to repeat actions or re-enter information while switching between touchpoints. By offering a more easy and hassle-free experience, this efficiency not only saves users time and effort but also improves their overall pleasure with the product.
- Continuity is essential to establishing confidence and trust in the brand or product. Users are given confidence and are reinforced in the product's dependability when they consistently experience the same thing through various channels and interactions. Users are more likely to view a product as reliable and trustworthy when they can count on a smooth and consistent experience, which over time can strengthen brand loyalty and advocacy.

To put it simply, consistent UX design is necessary for a positive and lasting user experience. Continuity ensures coherence and consistency across many touch points and interactions, which maximizes the efficacy of UX design and contributes to the overall success of the product or service.

Context

A significant factor in the meaning of user interactions is context. Users require information that is relevant to their activities and engaging in order to have a positive experience. Content in this context refers to text, images, videos, and clickable elements. It all comes down to providing consumers with accurate information, evoking emotions in them, and assisting them in reaching their goals.

Whether or not you stay around can be greatly influenced by the stuff you view. When something is well-designed, it can attract your interest, entice you to stay on a website or app longer, and encourage you to return. However, if it's disorganized or nonsensical, it may irritate you and make you want to leave. Users' perceptions of a website or app and their level of enjoyment with it are influenced by the quality and relevance of the information.

Figure 2.4: *Tailoring context to meet user needs*

Example

To design an experience that feels relevant and personalized, it all comes down to understanding the user's environment, needs, and scenario. It wouldn't make much sense if, upon entering a library, you were met by blaring music and flickering lights rather than books. Context makes ensuring that an application or website's design blends in with the user's environment, which facilitates comprehension and interaction.

Another example is a food delivery app such as UberEats. Here, the user's location, the time of day, and their preferences are all considered part of the context. The customer wants to see nearby eateries that are operating right now and offer cuisine that fits their dietary requirements when they open the app. The software helps users identify and order food more easily by showing appropriate options based on their context.

Context, to put it simply, is knowing what people require and modifying the design to provide them with a more tailored and intuitive experience. By taking into account variables such as user preferences, time, and location, designers may produce experiences that feel unique and customized. Users become happier and more involved as a result. It's like enjoying a meal that's exactly what you wanted - a well-thought-out design makes users feel valued and understood.

Power of Context

Within the context of the UX design 4 Cs, context provides numerous advantages that greatly improve user experiences.

- Its capacity to increase user relevance and meaning of interactions is one of its main benefits. Designers can customize features and information on a website or app to suit the unique requirements and preferences of users by taking into account the context in which they are accessing it. A weather app that delivers personalized forecasts according to the user's present location, for instance, provides more pertinent information than a general forecast, enhancing and personalizing the user experience.
- Context is essential for directing users on their travels and assisting them in effectively achieving their objectives. Through an awareness of the environment in which users are interacting with a product, designers are better able to predict users' requirements and offer suggestions or pertinent information to help. Context is used, for example, by an e-commerce website that makes product recommendations based on a user's browsing history or past purchases to improve the shopping experience and raise conversion rates.
- By fostering experiences that feel unique and customized for each user, context helps to increase user loyalty and retention. Users are more inclined to stick with a product and come back later when they find features and content that align with their interests and preferences. This improves customer pleasure while fortifying the bond between the user and the platform or brand.

Context makes user interactions more efficient, meaningful, and tailored, which improves the overall efficacy of UX design. Designers may develop experiences that are more valuable, engaging, and rewarding for consumers by taking into account the context in which they are accessing the product and customizing the experience accordingly. This will ultimately lead to higher retention and loyalty.

Complementary

Complementary elements in UI/UX design are combinations of features that, when combined, result in a tasty and well-balanced meal. It all boils down to ensuring that different elements of the design work well together to enhance the user experience overall. If every piece of furniture in the room clashed with everything else when you were decorating it, it wouldn't look very friendly, do you get what it means? For a website or application to be cohesive and visually appealing, each element must work well with the others. We call this complimentary design.

Figure 2.5: *Cohesion in website*

Example

Think about an app like Spotify that streams music. Colors, fonts, and graphics are just a few of the design components that have been thoughtfully selected to work well together and produce a captivating listening experience. Users may explore and discover new music in an attractive and entertaining setting, including the use of brilliant colors, clean typography, and captivating imagery.

Another example is a recipe app like Tasty. This app's design components– text, graphics, and interactive elements – all have been thoughtfully chosen to work well together and produce a fun culinary experience. Every component of the user's cooking journey, from the delicious pictures to the interactive features and clear directions, works in unison to support and enhance the experience, making cooking more pleasurable and fulfilling.

To put it simply, complementary design in UI/UX makes sure that all components of the product operate in unison to give users a seamless, aesthetically pleasing experience. Designers may build cohesive and polished experiences that ultimately increase user pleasure and engagement by maintaining consistency and coherence across various design aspects. Just like a well-coordinated outfit or a beautifully composed piece of music, complementary design delights the senses and leaves a lasting impression on users.

Power of Complementary

Complementary design provides a number of advantages within the framework of the 4 Cs in UX design, all of which help to create a more interesting and productive user experience.

- **Improved Engagement:** Users are drawn in and encouraged to explore more when users are presented with a unified and eye-catching experience, thanks to complementary design. Longer user engagement periods are associated with harmonic interactions between various design elements.
- **Better Understanding:** Users are able to explore and comprehend the product more easily when every piece of the design works in harmony with one another. Users experience less uncertainty and annoyance when they can make sense of the interface, thanks to consistent visual signals and well-designed patterns.
- **Greater Memorability:** Users are more likely to remember a well-organized and composed design. When many components of the design function together harmoniously, customers are more likely to recall their experiences using the product and come back later.
- **Stronger Brand Identity:** By highlighting the brand's values and identity, complementary design helps set the product apart from rivals. A unified brand image that connects with consumers and gradually fosters trust and loyalty is produced by the consistent use of colors, fonts, and imagery.
- **Higher User Happiness:** Complementary design ultimately results in higher user happiness. Customers are more likely to think highly of a product and promote it to others when they have a visually pleasing and well-rounded experience. This increases customer satisfaction and encourages good word-of-mouth recommendations.

To summarize, the four Cs of UX design – complementary design, comprehension, memorability, brand identification, and user contentment – all improve engagement, understanding, and user satisfaction, which in turn increases the product or service's overall success.

Wrap-Up the 4 C's

In conclusion, user experiences are greatly influenced by the fundamental ideas of Consistency, Continuity, Context, and Complementary–often referred to as the 4 Cs of UI/UX design. Designers may produce interfaces that are engaging and user-friendly, leading to successful business outcomes by giving priority to these concepts.

Designers should keep in mind the particular requirements and preferences of their target audience while incorporating these concepts into their design approach. Maintaining excellence in creating digital experiences that successfully satisfy user demands requires keeping up with industry trends and best practices, which are constantly changing in the field of user experience design.

Essentially, designers may confidently navigate the shifting terrain of UI/UX design by adhering to industry innovations and adopting the 4 Cs. This will ultimately result in the delivery of delightful and satisfying user experiences.

Difficulties in Implementing the 4 Cs

For a variety of reasons, applying the four Cs to UI/UX design may be challenging. It might be challenging to keep all of the design's elements – like layouts, colors, and typefaces –consistent. Another challenge is making sure users know what to do at every turn in the communication and navigation process.

Moreover, providing ease to customers through smooth job transitions and rapid information access necessitates careful planning and execution.

Implementing the 4 Cs is difficult, because it requires an understanding of user requirements and preferences, creating relevant and engaging content that aligns with the overall design can be difficult. Overcoming these challenges generally requires creativity, painstaking attention to detail, and a deep understanding of both user behavior and design principles.

C-P-S Hypothesis

Have you ever encountered an obstacle when attempting to tackle a problem? This is a common source of dissatisfaction, particularly in the business sector. The standard approaches to problem-solving just aren't effective sometimes. Even when the obstacles you confront appear insurmountable, you still need to find a way to move forward. At such point, it is necessary to think creatively and unconventionally in order to address the issue head-on.

***Figure 2.6**: Exploring diverse solutions for a challenging issue*

The methodical process of approaching problems by applying creative problem solving (CPS) to x (a specific problem or challenge that is being addressed) and coming up with unique solutions. Fundamentally, CPS entails determining the issue, generating original ideas, assessing possible fixes, and putting the best ones into practice. The first step in the process is to precisely define the issue at hand, comprehend its root causes, and identify the intended results. Next, without limitations or criticism, individuals or groups produce a wide range of ideas through brainstorming sessions or other creative processes. Following the collection of a wide range of ideas, each solution is assessed according to criteria including practicality, efficacy, and viability. The most promising concepts are determined with the aid of this examination and subsequently turned into workable programs.

Finally, in order to properly solve the issue, the selected solutions are then put into practice, evaluated, and improved as needed. CPS can be used in a variety of contexts, including business, technology, and interpersonal and personal problems. It promotes creativity, innovation, and efficient problem-solving techniques.

The Seven-Step Method

While creativity has been a problem-solving technique for decades, it was formalized as creative problem-solving (CPS) by Sidney Parnes and Alex Osborn. Developed by Osborn, the man who popularized brainstorming, and Parnes, the Creative Problem-

Solving Process (CPSP) has been taught at Buffalo College's International Centre for Studies in Creativity in Buffalo, New York, since 1950s.

Notwithstanding its origins, CPS has evolved into a variety of approaches, each with its own set of techniques and tactics. However, the core of CPS often consists of seven simple yet effective processes. These steps are as follows:

1. Identify the problem
2. Research the problem
3. Formulate creative challenges
4. Explore ideas
5. Evaluate the ideas
6. Draw up an action plan
7. Take action

1. Identify the Problem

Finding the source of an issue is similar to being a detective looking for hints to unravel a mystery. It is critical to identify the true nature of the issue before attempting to resolve it. Consider yourself attempting to repair your kitchen's leaking tap. You could initially assume that the issue is just that the tap is spilling water. However, upon closer inspection, you find that the leak can be the result of a number of underlying problems, such as a loose pipe or an old washer.

You need to ask yourself, or perhaps a friend or family member, a number of questions to get to the bottom of the issue and determine its fundamental cause. Simple inquiries such as "What seems to be the problem?" or "What am I trying to achieve?" are a good place to start. Next, delve further by posing questions such as "What's causing this issue?" or "Why is this happening?" Ask "Why else?" or "What else?" repeatedly to investigate many viewpoints and aspects.

Other things to think about are, "What do I really want to accomplish?" and "What obstacles am I facing?" Consider your long-term objectives and how resolving this issue will contribute to achieving them. You might also consider the approaches and methods that other people, such as your friends or coworkers are employing to address comparable problems.

You will be able to comprehend the issue at hand more clearly if you take the time to carefully assess the circumstances and formulate pertinent inquiries. Like a detective putting together hints, you will be more adept at identifying a solution that deals with the underlying issue and produces a positive result.

2. Research the Problem

Investigating a challenge in Creative challenge Solving is similar to travelling to a foreign country in pursuit of lost riches. You start by learning as much as you can about the issue. This could be reading books or articles, speaking with others who have experienced similar problems, or even carrying out experiments to gain a better understanding of the situation. Let us imagine you are attempting to determine the reason behind the poor growth of plants in your garden. You could look into many elements that can impact plant growth, such as water content, sunlight, and soil quality.

After gathering sufficient data, you begin examining it to find trends or patterns. This aids in your understanding of the problem's underlying causes. For instance, if the soil is very dry or the plants aren't receiving enough sunlight, you may notice that they are withering.

3. Formulate Creative Challenge

It is time to formulate the issue into a question when you've gathered all the necessary information. This should be a straightforward query that gets right to the core of the matter. It should also be flexible, allowing for a broad range of recommendations and concepts without imposing any rigid standards for assessment.

As an illustration, suppose you are looking for strategies to lessen traffic in your city. You may create a more focused challenge question, such as "How can we encourage more people to use public transport during peak hours?" instead of a general one such as "How can we solve traffic problems?" This is a clear, targeted question that promotes creativity by allowing for a range of thoughts and ideas.

4. Explore Ideas

Pick a creative task, and then set aside some quiet time to come up with at least thirty ideas, regardless of whether or not they solve the challenge directly. You can either go on this adventure by yourself or ask loved ones to participate in the brainstorming session.

Whichever strategy you choose, write down your thoughts on a paper. Whether you type them out on a computer, write them down in a list, or create a mental map, the most crucial thing is to adhere to a few essential criteria rather than selecting a specific approach.

Start by jotting down any thought that occurs to you, no matter how ridiculous or outlandish. Ignore your inner critic and write down all you have to say since sometimes it prevents us from being creative. Being kind and encouraging of others' thoughts is crucial when brainstorming with others. Rejection can stifle originality, so maintain an optimistic and receptive attitude. If you're brainstorming by yourself, push yourself to generate more than thirty ideas. To keep things going in group meetings, consider imposing a time limit of twenty or thirty minutes. After that, compile all of the suggestions and inquire as to whether anyone has any more.

Recall that you don't need to be at your work to brainstorm. To get new ideas, try changing up your environment. Perhaps go for a stroll and let your thoughts wander, or find a quiet area in your house or garden, at your preferred restaurant, and more.

It's time to start thinking of answers after you receive your challenge question. Never forget that the objective is to come up with as many ideas as you can, without considering at this point if they are workable or practical. You can encourage greater creativity and ingenuity in the problem-solving process by leaving the query open-ended and devoid of evaluation criteria.

You will start to notice patterns emerge and possible solutions take shape as you experiment with various concepts and possibilities. The secret is to maintain an open mind and welcome the variety of viewpoints that you encounter. You'll be well on your way to coming up with novel solutions to even the most difficult situations by creating challenge questions and investigating inventive answers.

5. Evaluate the Ideas

It is like embarking on a mental journey when you explore concepts. The first step is brainstorming, in which you allow your creativity to run wild and write down any and all ideas that occur to you, no matter how ridiculous. This is significant because often the most brilliant ideas lurk beneath those that initially look a little strange. After you have jotted down a number of ideas, take a rest. Taking a little break from your ideas might help your brain unwind and recharge, much like stopping for a break during a strenuous walk.

After your break, it is time to sort through your ideas. You might notice that some ideas are similar or can be combined to make even better ones. It is like putting together puzzle pieces to create a bigger picture.

Next, you will want to evaluate your ideas. Depending on what you're working on and which ideas come out on top, you might be ready to start putting your ideas into action. But sometimes, ideas need more work. This is where SWOT analysis comes in handy. SWOT stands for Strengths, Weaknesses, Opportunities, and Threats. You will look at each idea and think about what it's good at, where it might need some work, what opportunities it could bring, and what challenges it might face.

After you have given your ideas some thought, you may begin implementing them. It is possible that you will decide to combine several ideas to create something even greater, or you can want to concentrate on just one. It is similar to choosing which route to take on your adventure. Remember that exploring ideas requires innovative and open-minded thinking. So, don't be afraid to take chances and use your imagination!

6. Draw Up an Action Plan

Creating an action plan for your finalized problem-solving ideas, utilizing the Creative Problem Solving (CPS) method entails taking a methodical approach to transforming concepts into doable actions. Converting the most promising concepts from your brainstorming session into a detailed action plan is the next stage.

The first step is to deconstruct each concept into distinct jobs and activities. Think about the tasks that need to be completed, the people who will be in charge of each task, and the materials needed. To make sure that every facet of the solution is covered, this stage needs to be planned out and approached with great care.

Setting specific goals and targets for your action plan is crucial after that. Define success and set quantifiable goals so that you can monitor your progress. Throughout the implementation phase, your team will remain motivated and focused if you set clear, attainable goals.

When creating your action plan, take the implementation schedule into account. Give each task a deadline and divide it up into smaller, more doable pieces. This will support you in staying on course and guarantee that you make progress towards your objectives.

Throughout the action planning stage, communication is essential. Ensure that all parties are aware of their respective roles and duties as well as the plan's overarching goals. Keeping everyone informed and on the same page throughout the implementation process will be made easier with frequent communication.

By following these steps and applying the principles of Creative Problem Solving, you can develop a robust action plan that turns your ideas into tangible solutions for the problem at hand.

7. Take Action

Putting your thoughts into practice step-by-step is what it means to execute the plan. Assign duties to team members at the outset, ensuring that everyone is aware of what has to be done when. Next, adhere to the timetable you've established, finishing assignments on time to maintain progress. Check in on your progress frequently and make any necessary adjustments. Effective communication is essential to maintaining everyone's awareness of events and fostering teamwork. Reward yourself for reaching goals to maintain your motivation. And never forget to maintain your flexibility and be prepared to modify your plan if something unexpected happens. Adaptability and flexibility are critical traits in problem-solving, and your chances of success will rise if you are prepared to modify your strategy in response to criticism and outcomes. You may make your ideas a reality and find a solution to the current issue by acting consistently and maintaining your focus on your objectives.

Purpose Behind Designers' Use of CPS

The Creative Problem Solving (CPS) method is used by designers because it offers a methodical way to solve problems in creative and efficient ways. CPS pushes us to think creatively, developing a broad range of concepts and taking into account many viewpoints. CPS assists us in finding original answers that might not have been immediately apparent by utilizing imagination. Furthermore, CPS places a strong emphasis on cooperation and teamwork, creating a welcoming atmosphere where each person's views are respected. Complicated problems can be solved more easily when we use this strategy to break them down into smaller, more manageable steps. In the end, CPS gives us the ability to face issues with resilience, creativity, and confidence, which produces better results.

Creative Problem Solving (CPS) versus the Design Thinking Process

You studied the stages of the Design Process in the previous chapter. There may be parallels between that and what you're studying about CPS at this time. There are clear parallels between the UI/UX Design Process and Creative Problem Solving (CPS) in the field.

	Creative Problem Solving (CPS)	**The Design Thinking**
Focus	In UI/UX, Creative Problem Solving (CPS) is addressing design problems with an emphasis on coming up with creative solutions. It pushes designers to overcome usability problems and satisfy user needs by encouraging them to think outside the box, investigate novel concepts, and take into account several viewpoints. Divergent thinking is emphasized by CPS in UI/UX, as designers strive to produce a broad range of concepts before settling on the most viable solutions. To encourage experimentation and creativity, this method frequently uses tools like mind mapping, rapid prototyping, and brainstorming.	In UI/UX, the Design Process usually adheres to a more formal framework with distinct phases such as ideation, research, prototyping, testing, and implementation. Although creativity is still crucial to the design process, it is integrated into these stages as opposed to serving as the main focal point. Through research, designers obtain insights into user behavior. They then set design objectives and specifications, produce design concepts, prototypes, test usability with users, and iterate in response to feedback. UI/UX design is frequently an iterative process that involves several iterations of testing and improvement to make sure the finished product successfully satisfies user wants and objectives.

Summary	In conclusion, CPS in UI/UX emphasizes creativity and innovative problem-solving techniques, while the design process of UI/UX follows a structured framework with defined stages for research, ideation, prototyping, testing, and implementation. Both approaches aim to create user-centered designs, but they differ in their emphasis on creativity and the specific methodologies used.

Table 2.1: *Differences between Creative Problem Solving (CPS) and the Design Thinking Process*

Introduction to UX Designer

A User Experience (UX) designer, often known as a digital architect, creates the user interface and functionality of websites and mobile applications. They function similarly to an app's or website's problem solution! Consider tracking your daily spending with a new personal finance or budgeting software. A user experience designer would ensure that the application is intuitive to use, with buttons strategically placed and unambiguous directions for tracking your spending. They consider how you will navigate the app, ensuring that you won't become disoriented or impatient. To assist customers in managing their finances more effectively, they often include tools like budget management, transaction categorization, financial insights, and spending monitoring.

Figure 2.7: *A UX Designer exploring diverse solutions for a challenging issue*

It is their responsibility to make your experience as seamless and pleasurable as they can. Consider the time you spend using your preferred social media app. It all seems so obvious, don't you think? It is because of UX design. It's simple to locate what you're searching for, and the buttons are where you would expect them to be. All of that is the result of a skilled UX designer. UX designers are concerned with having things function properly in addition to looking good.

To put it briefly, a UX designer's responsibility is to develop digital experiences that are both efficient and easy to use. Making your life easier and more fun is the main goal of UX design, whether you're shopping online, using an app, or visiting a website. UX designers create digital products that users enjoy using by applying design thinking and creative problem solving (CPS). It involves imagining yourself as the user and creating with their requirements and preferences in mind. And for that reason, in the modern digital environment, user experience designers are crucial. They could be employed by any number of digitally focused businesses, from small start-ups to major tech organizations.

Roles of UX designers

Depending on their particular responsibilities and areas of expertise, UX designers might hold a variety of roles or titles within the industry. Some typical UX designer types and their roles are as follows:

- **UX Designer:** This is the collective name for a person who creates a product or service's entire user experience. To guarantee a user-friendly design, they concentrate on comprehending user needs, performing research, generating wireframes and prototypes, and working with other team members.
- **UI Designer:** User Interface, or UI, designers work on creating a product or service's visual components, like buttons, menus, and images. Their tight collaboration with UX designers guarantees that the interface is intuitive to use and aesthetically pleasing.
- **Interaction Designer:** This professional focuses on creating interactive features for products and services, including micro interactions, animations, and transitions. Their main goal is to develop user interactions that are both intuitive and captivating, thereby improving the user experience.
- **Information Architect:** To facilitate users' finding of necessary information within a product or service, information architects organize and structure information. To assist users in navigating complicated information environments, they create taxonomies, site maps, and navigation tools.
- **User Researchers:** It is the duty of user researchers to carry out investigations to comprehend the requirements, habits, and preferences of users. They gather information for the design process using a range of research techniques, including surveys, usability testing, and interviews.

- **UX Writer:** UX writers are responsible for creating written content for products and services, including error warnings, user interface text, and onboarding guidelines. They guarantee that the text is understandable, succinct, and easy to use, which enhances the user experience in general.

These are only a handful of the various positions and designations that UX designers may hold. In reality, the precise roles and designations could change based on the project's nature and the organization involved.

User-Centered Design

The core idea behind User-Centered Design, or UCD, is creating digital goods with actual users in mind. It places people at the center of the process rather than attempting to infer what they want. To ensure the product fulfils their needs, this entails having direct conversations with users at important junctures. Every customer interaction with a website is like a tiny, meaningful moment. According to UCD, we should carefully examine each of these situations to make sure the user has a seamless and pleasurable experience.

There are four important things to keep in mind with UCD:

- **Visibility:** When users first arrive on your website, can they quickly figure out what it's all about and how to use it?
- **Accessibility:** Is your website easy for users to access? Can they find what they're looking for without any trouble? Important action buttons, navigation menus, and search options should be easy to find.
- **Legibility:** Can users read the text on your site easily? It is important that the words are clear and easy to understand.
- **Language:** Is the language on your site easy for users to understand? It is best to avoid using complicated words or phrases that might confuse them. Keep it simple and straightforward.

User-Centered Design Examples

Consider the well-known e-commerce site Amazon to gain a thorough understanding of user-centered design, or UCD.

- **Comprehending User Needs:** Prioritizing user needs and wants when conducting online shopping is how Amazon starts. They carry out research to discover the inclinations, purchasing patterns, and problems of people.
- **User-Friendly Interface:** Users can easily find what they're looking for on Amazon's website thanks to its simple, user-friendly interface. The search box is easily accessible at the top of the page, enabling customers to look up products with ease. Navigating between departments is made easy for users with the navigation menu's obvious category organization.

- **Personalization:** To enhance the user experience, Amazon leverages information from previous purchases and browsing habits. By offering personalized product recommendations based on each user's interests and preferences, they facilitate the process of discovering new things that they may find appealing.
- **Reviews and Ratings:** Product ratings and reviews are available on Amazon to assist customers in making well-informed selections. Before making a purchase, users can read what other people think about a product, which increases their confidence and sense of trust.
- **Convenience:** To make users' purchasing experiences as easy as possible, Amazon provides options like one-click ordering and quick shipping. They guarantee a hassle-free buying experience by offering a range of payment choices and simple returns.
- **Continuous Improvement:** Amazon regularly requests user feedback and modifies the website in response to their comments. To enhance the user experience and keep ahead of the competition, they test and refine new features frequently.

Because it gives consumers' wants and preferences first priority throughout the whole design process, Amazon is a shining example of user-centered design. Every feature of the website, from the user-friendly layout to the tailored suggestions, is intended to make shopping easy and fun for visitors.

To delve deeper into the concepts of user-centered design (UCD), let us examine an additional example using the well-known fitness software MyFitnessPal.

- **Recognizing User Objectives:** MyFitnessPal starts by determining users' fitness objectives, such as increasing muscle mass, decreasing body weight, or enhancing general health. They collect data regarding users' dietary choices, exercise routines, and present fitness levels.
- **Personalized Experience:** Depending on each user's unique tastes and goals, MyFitnessPal offers a personalized experience. Users of the app can specify particular objectives, including calorie intake or macronutrient targets, and the app offers advice and recommendations to assist them reach these objectives.
- **User-Friendly Interface:** MyFitnessPal's user-friendly interface makes it simple for users to log their food intake, exercise routine, and goal progress. With just a few touches, users can register their meals and workouts using the app's fitness tracker and food journal, which provide a summary of daily goals and progress.
- **Food Database:** MyFitnessPal's extensive food and recipe database makes it simple for users to keep track of their caloric intake and nutritional values. The app automatically computes calorie counts and macronutrient breakdowns,

and users can easily register their meals by searching for specific foods or scanning barcodes.

- **Community Support:** MyFitnessPal has a built-in community feature that allows users to connect with others who share similar goals and interests. Users can join groups, participate in challenges, and share their progress with friends for added motivation and support.
- **Feedback and Progress Tracking:** To assist users in staying on track towards their objectives, MyFitnessPal offers feedback and progress tracking features. Viewing their progress over time, tracking weight and body measurement changes, and getting insights and recommendations based on their eating and activity habits are all available to users.

MyFitnessPal prioritizes the requirements and objectives of its users throughout the design process, making it a great example of user-centered design overall. Every feature of the app, including straightforward monitoring tools, community support, and personalized goal setting, is made to make it easier and more fun for users to reach their fitness objectives.

Benefits of User Centered Design

Numerous advantages of user-centered design (UCD) make it both useful and intriguing to learn about. Here are a few explanations for why UCD is so revolutionary:

- **Improved User Experience:** UCD prioritizes the needs, preferences, and behaviors of users throughout the design process, guaranteeing that goods and services are customized to meet their demands. Users have intuitive, pleasant, and ultimately more gratifying experiences as a result.
- **Enhanced User Satisfaction:** UCD produces goods and services that connect with customers more deeply by putting their needs first. Customers are more likely to be pleased with their experience and grow devoted to a company when they believe that a product is made just for them.
- **Better Usability:** UCD focuses on lowering the learning curve for consumers and minimizing irritation by creating products that are simple to use and navigate. Higher adoption rates, more engagement, and ultimately better results for people and businesses are the results of this.
- **Improved Problem Solving:** UCD promotes a greater comprehension of users' requirements and difficulties, which results in more creative and efficient problem-solving. Through developing empathy for consumers and observing the environment from their perspective, designers might find opportunities and insights that might otherwise go unnoticed.
- **Lower danger:** UCD helps lower the danger of creating products that don't connect with the intended market by incorporating consumers into the design

process. Designers can find and fix problems before they become expensive ones by testing concepts and prototypes frequently with actual users.

- **Enhanced Efficiency:** Involving consumers in the design process can, despite its seeming paradox, ultimately result in time and resource savings. Designers may focus their efforts on what really matters and avoid wasting time and resources on features that don't fulfill user needs by evaluating ideas and concepts early on.

Essentially, the goal of user-centered design is to create experiences that genuinely engage users on a meaningful level, rather than merely producing products. Designers may unleash a world of possibilities and produce solutions that excite, empower, and delight by prioritizing the needs and wants of their users.

User-Centered Design Process

The goal of the user-centered design (UCD) process is to develop goods and services that cater to the wants and needs of users. It entails doing research to comprehend the goals, motivations, and behaviors of users and applying this knowledge to each step of the design process. Here is a quick rundown of the essential steps:

1. Research
2. Align
3. Build
4. Test
5. Iterate

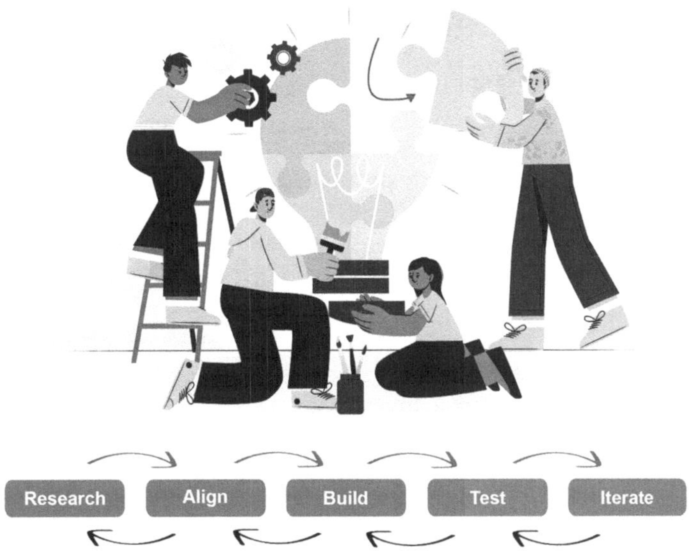

***Figure 2.8**: User-centered design steps*

1. **Research:** This first stage entails learning as much as possible about users, their needs, preferences, and behaviors. It all comes down to knowing your customers and what they need from your product or service.
2. **Align:** After conducting research, it's critical to match the results to the project's aims and objectives. By taking this step, you can make sure that the design process stays concentrated on meeting user demands and producing the intended results.
3. **Build:** Based on the research findings and goals that are in line, designers begin developing product or service prototypes or mockups. During this stage, concepts are translated into concrete representations that can be examined and assessed.
4. **Test:** In order to get input on usability, functionality, and general satisfaction, prototypes are tested with actual users. Before the design is finalized, testing helps discover any usability flaws or areas that need work.
5. **Iterate:** Designers improve and modify prototypes in response to input they get throughout testing. Utilizing user feedback during this iterative process helps to improve the design and make sure it successfully satisfies consumers' wants and expectations.

The user-centered design process guarantees that the finished product or service is based on user insights, is in line with project objectives, and goes through constant refinement to offer an ideal user experience by going through these steps: researching, aligning, building, testing, and iterating.

User-Centered Design versus Design Thinking Process

Prioritizing the requirements and experiences of users is a key component of both design thinking and user-centered design (UCD). Although they are similar, they are also very different from one another.

	User-Centered Design	**The Design Thinking**
Focus	Understanding and addressing user wants, preferences, and behaviors throughout the design process is the main goal of user-centered design (UCD). It places a strong emphasis on user happiness, functionality, and usability.	Conversely, design thinking follows a more comprehensive strategy, emphasizing the identification of issues' underlying causes and the creation of creative solutions. It promotes experimentation, empathy, and creativity.

Process	UCD usually adheres to a set procedure that includes phases including design, prototyping, testing, implementation, and research. It is frequently applied when creating digital goods and services. Design thinking emphasizes an attitude of curiosity, experimentation, and continual learning and is more adaptable and iterative. It frequently involves phases like define, empathize, brainstorm, prototype, and test; however, these phases are not always sequential and can be repeated as necessary.	
Scope	UCD is mostly focused on creating goods and services that satisfy consumer demands. It is frequently utilized in disciplines including product design, human-computer interaction (HCI), and user experience (UX) design.	Beyond product design, design thinking has a wider application and can be used to address a variety of issues, such as organizational change, social innovation, and commercial strategy.
Tools and Techniques	In order to comprehend user demands and assess design solutions, UCD commonly uses tools and techniques like personas, wireframing, usability testing, and user research.	In order to promote creativity, cooperation, and invention, design thinking employs a variety of tools and approaches, including empathy mapping, brainstorming sessions, prototyping, and storytelling.
Summary	In conclusion, while UCD and design thinking both aim to provide solutions that satisfy user demands, they take distinct approaches to problem-solving and place emphasis on various stages of the design process. UCD concentrates on comprehending and meeting user demands all along the way, whereas design thinking adopts a more comprehensive strategy, stressing experimentation, empathy, and creativity to produce novel solutions.	

***Table 2.2**: Differences between User-Centered design and the Design Thinking Process*

Factors that Influence User Experience

These days, small enterprises as well as large corporations need to prioritize excellent design and user experience. When it comes to introducing a new product or making improvements to an existing one, user experience design (UX) is crucial.

What then ought to designers bear in mind to ensure user satisfaction? Peter Morville, a well-known UX designer who has written popular books and advises big companies, has identified seven essential components of an excellent user experience. The 'User Experience Honeycomb,' which he created by arranging these seven components, has gained a lot of traction in the design community. Think of these components as the individual cells of a honeycomb; they come together to form a delightful and fulfilling whole.

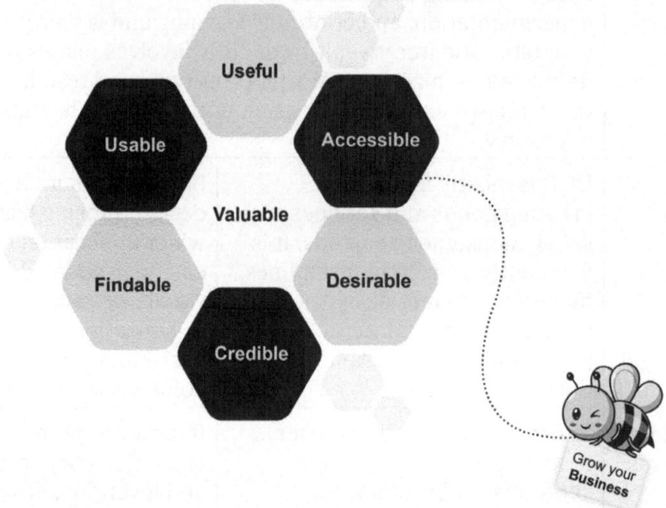

***Figure 2.9**: Peter Morville's 7 UX Honeycomb Factors*

These 7 factors help us understand what makes a good user experience and how to create products that people will like. These factors are:

- Useful
- Usable
- Findable
- Credible
- Desirable
- Accessible
- Valuable

So, the next time you are working on a project, think about the User Experience Honeycomb and make something sweet!

Useful

The most crucial factor in creating products that people enjoy using is ensuring that they are beneficial. It is hardly of much use if it doesn't meet their needs or provide the answers to their difficulties. But they will use it if it fulfils their needs. It's similar to asking yourself, "What's the point of making a toy if no one plays with it?" In order to create products that people would continue to use, they must be extremely beneficial.

There are five basic approaches to improve your product's user experience, according to Richard Koch (British author, who is an expert in business matters).

- Vary performance
- Improve quality
- Add new capabilities without affecting ease of use
- Provide a wider range of products
- Personalize

People are more likely to want to keep using something if it is genuinely helpful and makes a positive impression. Additionally, when you improve it over time – for example, by speeding up or repairing malfunctions – users will become even more accustomed to it.

If it makes people happy or makes them laugh, then something is still excellent even if it has no practical value, such as a useless toy.

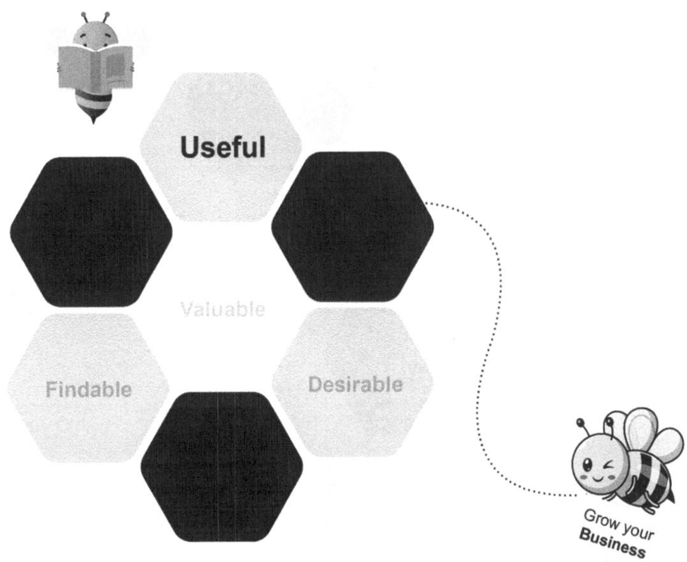

Figure 2.10: *UX Honeycomb Factor 1. Useful*

Example:

- **Glow-in-the-dark Stars:** To resemble a night sky, bedroom ceilings might be decorated with stickers shaped like stars. Even though they are useless, they may make a wonderful atmosphere and cheer people up, especially kids.

- **Desktop toys:** In an office setting, objects such as magnetic sculptures (small metal pieces that can be rearranged into various configurations) or Newton's cradle (a sequence of swinging spheres that demonstrate conservation of momentum and energy) can be entertaining and conversation starters.

Simply question yourself, "Why am I doing this?" whenever you're hesitant about a design decision. In this manner, you can ensure that your designs align with the goals you have for your product.

Usable

To put it simply, usability is the gauge of how simple a thing is to use. Usability is a fundamental UX design principle because without it, you cannot build a product that offers a satisfying user experience. Good usability products are efficient, easy to use, and don't put users through needless obstacles or complications.

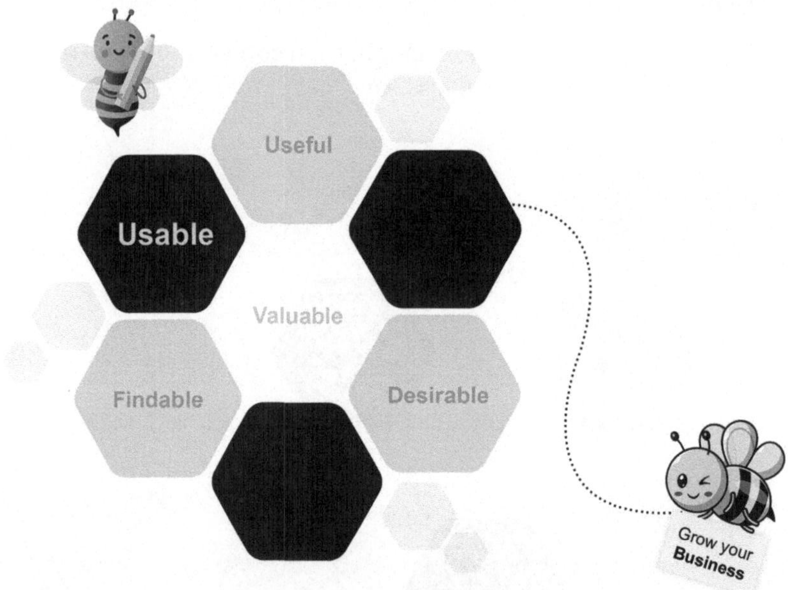

***Figure 2.11**: UX Honeycomb Factor 2. Usable*

Example:

Smartphone: A smartphone is a portable device that integrates multiple functions, including messaging, calling, web surfing, taking pictures, and installing programs. With features like touchscreens, streamlined menus, and app interfaces that let users explore and get information fast, it's made to be intuitive and simple to use. Furthermore, to ensure that they continue to be functional and relevant over time, cellphones frequently receive upgrades that enhance performance, increase security, and introduce new features

Products that are not useful are ones that, for some reason – such as inadequate functionality, unclear user interfaces, or frequent errors – are unable to accomplish their goals or offer a positive user experience.

Example:

An example of an unusable product could be a virtual assistant that regularly misinterprets user instructions and finds it difficult to carry out simple duties. Its inadequate recognition and execution make it frustrating and impracticable to utilize successfully, even when its intended aim of aid and convenience is acknowledged.

Findable

The findability principle necessitates a search system, information structure, and user-friendly navigation. A findable product is one that is simple to discover online and off. It should be easy for users to locate the product itself or the material they are looking for. Users may become frustrated and give up on a product due to poor findability.

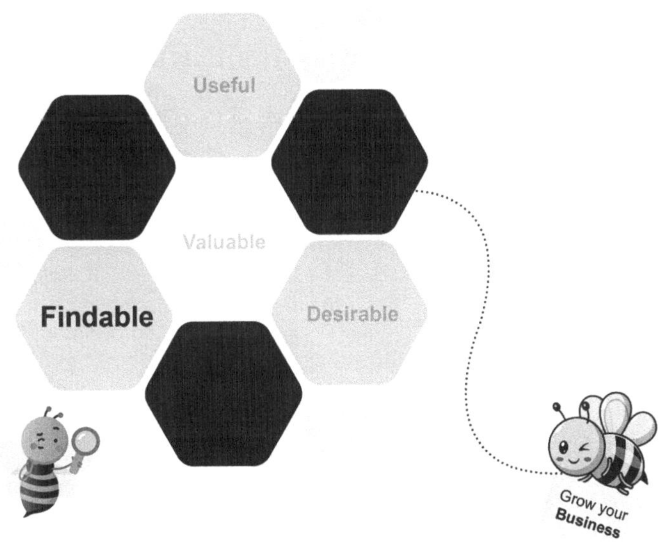

Figure 2.12: *UX Honeycomb Factor 3. Findable*

Example:

Findability is a key component that affects user experience by influencing how simple it is for users to locate desired material in digital interfaces. Picture an e-commerce platform that specializes in fashion clothing. The purpose of a user's visit to this website is to buy a white dress for an upcoming occasion. From the time a visitor arrives on the homepage, the website's strong findability features are put to work.

A clearly visible search box at the top of every page invites visitors to enter their queries. Our user initiates a search by typing "white dress" into this search window. The website instantly produces a list of pertinent results, including a variety of white gowns that are for sale. The user can easily refine their search by using the filtering tools available on the search results page. The user can efficiently reduce the number of possibilities by using parameters like size, price range, and brand. As a user chooses a dress to examine more closely, breadcrumb navigation helps them keep context and makes it simple to return to earlier search results as needed.

Autocomplete suggestions provide immediate insights into frequently searched terms while the user works with the search field, enabling the user to easily narrow down their search.

The e-commerce platform's strong findability features in this thorough example not only make it easier for the user to find a white dress, but they also greatly increase their level of satisfaction and chance of making a successful purchase.

Credible

The basis for confidence in a product is its credibility. Users have an endless number of options in today's digital age across all industries, thus firms must establish themselves as reliable suppliers. Customers frequently click away from goods or services after just a few attempts if they don't live up to their expectations. It becomes difficult to provide a great user experience when confidence is lacking. Credibility establishes an atmosphere for user interactions, much like first impressions. Users will like using a product even if it is not perfect if they believe the developer is reliable and honest.

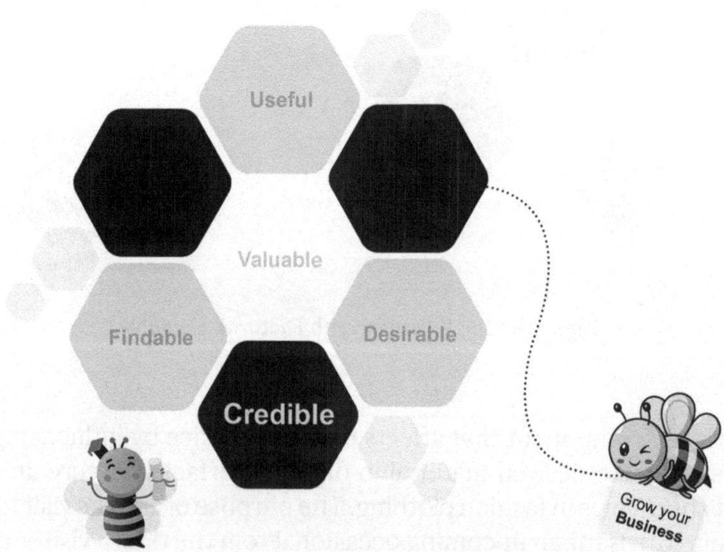

***Figure 2.13**: UX Honeycomb Factor 4. Credible*

Example:

Connect used to be a well-liked social media site where users could interact with friends, exchange pictures, and read news updates. But like Facebook, Connect has experienced a crisis of credibility in recent years.

Connect's credibility suffered as a result of allegations of improper treatment of user data. Connect is still not trusted by the public, despite CEO Mark Zuckerberg's testimony before Congress. Consumers worry about privacy and the platform's security of their personal information.

This example shows how important credibility is to preserving users' confidence and loyalty. Users may lose confidence in a platform's ability to safeguard their privacy and data if it cannot maintain its reputation, reducing user trust and usage.

Desirable

One of the main elements influencing user experience (UX) is desirability. It describes how enticing and desirable a good or service is to customers. A product or service that satisfies users' visual, emotional, and cultural needs is considered desirable. It includes elements such as user engagement, emotional resonance, brand perception, and aesthetics. Desirability is essentially concerned with eliciting a favorable emotional response and strengthening the bond between customers and the good or service, which improves the customer experience as a whole.

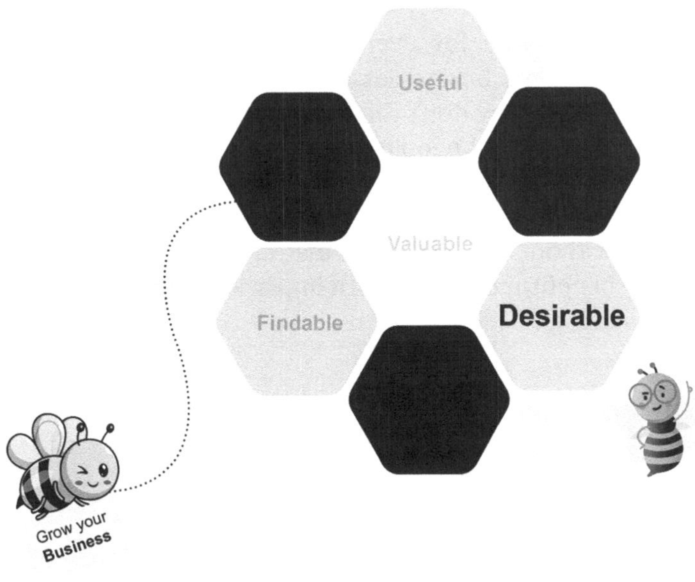

Figure 2.14: *UX Honeycomb Factor 5. Desirable*

Example:

Let's explore a good example of a desirable product. Picture a brand-new smartphone model that has an intuitive user interface, a svelte form, and brilliant colors. It boasts a strong camera, a gorgeous display, and cutting-edge capabilities like facial recognition. In addition to its usefulness, users can't wait to use this smartphone due of its sleek and sophisticated appearance. Many consider the brand to be a must-have device because of its reputation for quality and dependability, which increases its appeal.

Example:

Let's delve deeper into an example of a product that lacks desirability. Currently, picture a different smartphone model with a dated OS, a clumsy design, and a small app store. Its unappealing appearance and average performance make it difficult for consumers to get interested or imaginative. Due to its ugly design and subpar user experience, this smartphone struggles to draw in users even if it has capabilities that are comparable to those of other smartphones on the market. Even if the more visually appealing and user-friendly options cost a little bit more, users might still choose them.

In the end, desirability is about prompting a favorable emotional response and strengthening the bond between customers and the good or service, which improves the user experience as a whole and increases customer happiness.

Accessible

Making something easily usable for everyone, regardless of impairment, is the definition of accessibility. Some businesses assume that only a small percentage of people have disabilities, thus, they don't think it's worth the effort. The World Health Organization estimates that 15% of people on the planet suffer from a disability. This implies that more than a million people are impacted. Therefore, it makes sense to consider accessibility while designing things. When a product is accessible, it indicates that anyone can use it without any issues, no matter what their constraints are. Not only does accessibility benefit individuals with impairments, but it also improves and simplifies life for all users.

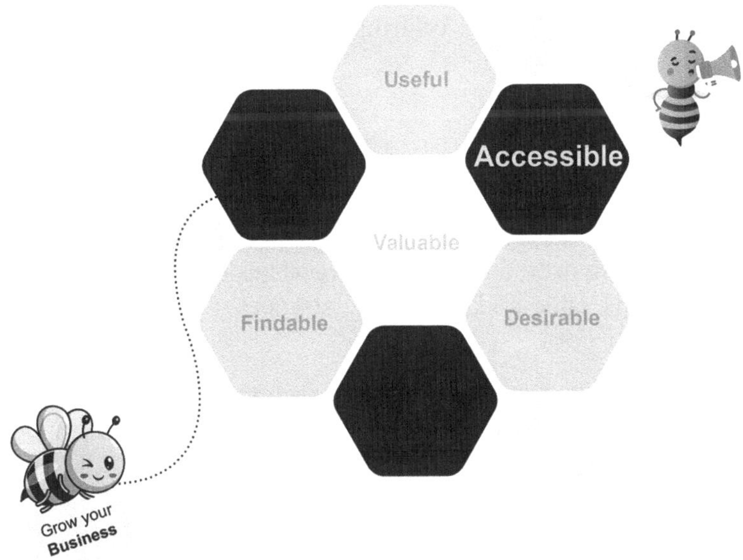

***Figure 2.15**: UX Honeycomb Factor 6. Accessible*

Example:

The World Wide Web Consortium (W3C) website is a great illustration of a platform that was created with accessibility as a first priority. W3C sets an example by making sure that its own website is accessible to all visitors, regardless of their skills or disabilities, as the organization in charge of creating worldwide web standards. Every element of the W3C website, from design to operation, has been thoughtfully considered to offer a welcoming user experience that meets a range of requirements.

The W3C website uses structured HTML markup, which gives the content a clear structure and meaning. This is one of its primary features. Users with impairments can access and understand the content with accuracy because of its semantic framework, which is made possible by assistive technology like screen readers.

Visual components are also included in the category of accessibility. Users with visual impairments or color blindness will find it easier to read and recognize content on the W3C website since it uses high contrast colors and provides enough color contrast between text and background elements. To further ensure that users with low vision or blindness can comprehend the context and purpose of visual elements, the website includes informative alt text for every image.

The W3C website has forms that are developed with accessibility features in mind, such as appropriate labeling, directions for input fields, and understandable error messages. These features guarantee that users can properly interact with and submit forms on the website, even those who rely on voice input devices or screen readers.

Additionally, the adaptable design of the website guarantees that it adjusts to various screen sizes and devices with ease, offering a uniform user experience on tablets, smartphones, and desktop computers.

Valuable

In the end, the product must have an impact. It's important to provide genuine value to the users in addition to satisfying the needs of the company that makes it. Value is determined by how well a product delivers advantages or solves issues in relation to its cost. A product gains value and attracts customers when it provides noteworthy advantages relative to its cost.

It's your responsibility as a designer to balance all the elements to give users the greatest experience possible. Users may place varying values on different features of a product; for some, the most important factor is how much they want it, while for others, accessibility is the most important factor. This implies that value isn't a single entity but rather the culmination of all the various components of the user experiences coming together.

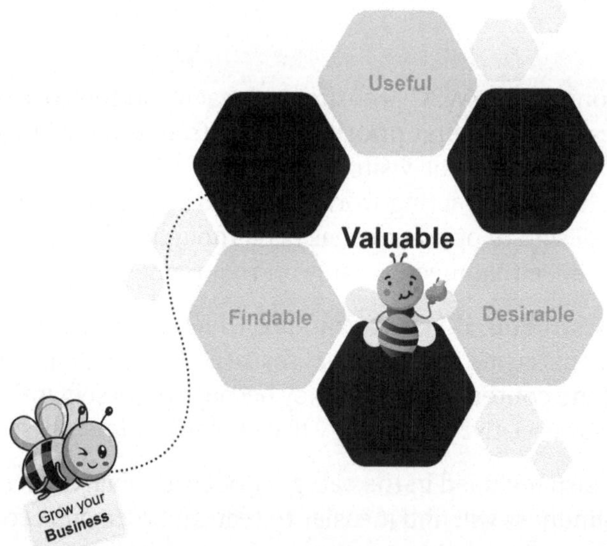

***Figure 2.16**: UX Honeycomb Factor 7. Valuable*

Example:

Take into consideration a fitness tracker that tracks multiple health parameters, including heart rate, quality of sleep, and activity levels. This reasonably priced gadget gives consumers insightful information about their overall fitness and health improvement. Users are able to pinpoint areas for improvement and make well-informed decisions to live a healthier lifestyle by monitoring their sleep and daily activity habits. The fitness tracker's worth is found in its capacity to enable users to take charge of their health and wellbeing, which eventually results in better fitness outcomes. Because of this, people who are concerned about their health are drawn to this product because of how well it works to help their fitness objectives.

In simple words, value plays a pivotal role in what we choose to buy. Suppose we have a situation where a low-cost product solves a major problem, while a high-priced product fixes a small problem. Whereas in the second scenario the product's attractiveness is weakened by the disparity between value and cost, in the earlier scenario the alignment of these two factors results in an appealing proposal.

Wrapping Up

Based on user preferences and content, each product and solution may change, but by following to the UX Honeycomb principle, you can make sure that the solution you develop will be enjoyable to all users. This idea touches on some crucial topics that designers like us need to pay attention to.

Conclusion

As we reach the end of this chapter, it is clear that User Experience (UX) design is crucial not only for digital goods and services but for any type of experience, whether digital or not. It is impossible to overestimate the importance of UX design because it has a direct bearing on user engagement, happiness, and eventually commercial results. Context, Content, Communication, and Community are the four pillars of UX design that act as a framework for developing meaningful user experiences.

Implementing the 4 Cs in UX design poses various challenges, from balancing technological limits with organizational goals to understanding user needs. Frameworks like the Seven-Step Method and the CPS hypothesis emphasize user-centric design and iterative problem-solving. UX designers play a crucial role with their skills in empathy, creativity, research, and technical expertise, driving the creation of products that deeply resonate with users. While Design Thinking and user-centered design share goals, they differ in focus and implementation but complement each other well. By addressing the seven elements, UX designers foster long-term engagement and loyalty. Thus, UX design merges human psychology, technology, and creativity to craft delightful digital experiences.

In the next chapter, we will explore UX research, its essential role in understanding user needs and behaviors, and examine popular user-centered research methods that inform effective design decisions, ensuring the creation of intuitive and engaging user experiences.

Key Terms

- **UX Design:** The process of designing digital products or services with a focus on enhancing the user experience by ensuring ease of use, efficiency, and relevance.
- **Consistency:** A fundamental principle in UX design that involves maintaining uniformity in the appearance, behavior, and functionality of elements throughout a digital product or service.
- **Continuity:** The seamless flow of user interactions across different sections or platforms within a digital product or service, ensuring a consistent and uninterrupted user experience.
- **Context:** Consideration of the surrounding circumstances, environment, and user preferences to tailor the design of a digital product or service for a more personalized and relevant experience.
- **Complementary Design:** The harmonious integration of various design elements within a digital product or service to create a cohesive and visually appealing experience that enhances user engagement and satisfaction.
- **Creative Problem Solving (CPS):** A structured process for approaching problems creatively, involving defining the problem, generating ideas, evaluating solutions, and implementing the best ones.
- **Seven-Step Method:** A problem-solving approach that includes seven key stages: problem identification, research, formulating creative challenges, exploring ideas, evaluating ideas, drawing up an action plan, and taking action.
- **Research the Problem:** The stage of problem-solving involving gathering information and analyzing data to gain insights into the problem's underlying causes.
- **Formulate Creative Challenges:** Defining the problem as a question that encourages creativity and allows for a wide range of solutions.
- **Draw Up an Action Plan:** Creating a detailed plan to implement the selected solutions, including tasks, goals, deadlines, and communication strategies.
- **SWOT Analysis:** An analysis method that examines the strengths, weaknesses, opportunities, and threats associated with a particular idea or solution.
- **User Experience (UX) Designer:** A professional responsible for creating digital experiences that are intuitive, efficient, and enjoyable for users.
- **UI Designer:** A designer who focuses on creating the visual elements of a digital product, ensuring an aesthetically pleasing and user-friendly interface.
- **Interaction Designer:** A designer specialized in creating interactive features for digital products, aiming to improve user engagement and experience.

- **Information Architect:** A designer responsible for organizing and structuring information within a digital product to facilitate user navigation and understanding.
- **User Researcher:** A professional who conducts research to understand user needs, preferences, and behaviors, providing insights for the design process.
- **UX Writer:** A writer responsible for creating clear, concise, and user-friendly text for digital products, enhancing the overall user experience.
- **User-Centered Design (UCD):** A design approach that prioritizes the needs and preferences of users throughout the product development process.
- **Visibility:** The degree to which essential elements of a website or digital product are immediately apparent and understandable to users upon arrival.
- **Accessibility:** The ease with which users can access and navigate a website or digital product, including finding necessary information and performing desired actions.
- **Legibility:** The clarity and readability of text on a website or digital product, ensuring users can easily comprehend the information presented.
- **Personalization:** Tailoring a product or service to meet the specific needs and preferences of individual users.
- **User-Friendly Interface:** An intcrfacc dcsigncd to bc intuitivc and casy for users to navigate, allowing them to interact with a system or product with minimal effort.
- **Design Thinking:** A problem-solving approach that emphasizes empathy, experimentation, and creativity to develop innovative solutions.
- **Usability:** The ease with which users can interact with a product or service to achieve their goals effectively and efficiently.
- **Findability:** The ease with which users can locate desired information or features within a product or service.
- **Credibility:** The trustworthiness and reliability of a product or service, often influenced by factors such as reputation and user feedback.
- **Desirability:** The appeal and attractiveness of a product or service, often influenced by factors such as aesthetics and emotional resonance

CHAPTER 3
Research and Analysis for UX Design

Introduction

Welcome to the world of UX research, where we will delve into understanding user behaviors, needs, and motivations through various investigative techniques. In this chapter, we will explore the essence of UX research, a crucial process that helps design products and experiences that truly resonate with users.

We will start by introducing you to the UX research process, a structured approach that guides us from identifying research goals to gathering and analyzing data, and finally to applying insights for design improvements. This process is the backbone of creating user-centered products that are both effective and enjoyable to use.

Next, we will dive into the different UX research methods, each with its unique strengths and applications. Whether it is conducting interviews for qualitative insights or leveraging analytics for quantitative data, we will show you how to implement each method effectively. You will learn when to use surveys, usability testing, A/B testing, tree testing, and five-second testing, among others, and how to gather the most valuable information from each.

Structure

In this chapter, we will discuss the following topics:

- Introduction to UX Research
- UX Research Process
- UX Research Methods
- User Interviews
- Focus Group
- Surveys

- Card Sorting (Open/Hybrid)
- Card Sorting (Close)
- Diary Studies
- Usability Studies
- Field Studies
- Tree Testing
- Eye Tracking
- A/B Testing
- Five Second Testing
- UX Research Tools
- Real-World UX Research Case Studies

Introduction to UX Research

For designers, UX research is essential. Research is the first step towards gathering knowledge before designing anything. Designing things that genuinely speak to your users is difficult if you don't know them. The UX research procedure functions similarly to a problem-solving road map. Identifying the most appropriate research methodology for your project begins with asking:

- What goals do your users wish to achieve?
- What goals do they have?
- What do they want to accomplish?

Your user research should shed light on these issues and help you develop designs that successfully satisfy the needs of users.

Goal of UX Research

Understanding your users and gaining context and viewpoints can help you make wise decisions and create user-centered products. This is the aim of UX research: to create and release products that effectively solve user needs, as these are the ones that will become popular.

Assume you are working to develop the ideal product, a superhero cape for your customers' daily activities. However, you must familiarize yourself with the opinions, abilities, and enemies of your superheroes before you begin sewing.

This is where UX research becomes useful! It all comes down to getting very involved in your consumers' lives and learning about their aspirations, difficulties, and desires.

Talking with them, watching them work, and getting a glimpse into their world allows you to gain invaluable knowledge that informs every step of your design process.

UX research is a continuous process, like a loyal friend who supports you well beyond launch. The cyclical flow in the graphic illustrates how testing can happen at any stage, ensuring your product remains a user favorite by adapting to changing needs and providing fresh insights throughout its lifecycle.

***Figure 3.1**: UX research is a continuous cycle of testing, learning, and improving*

UX research is, in short, the magic ingredient that elevates your design above the standard. Producing experiences that genuinely connect with your consumers and help them feel like the superheroes are more important than just producing for yourself!

Importance of UX Research

Imagine if everyone who used your product loved it instantly, told their friends about it, and could not wait to use it again. Though it may seem like a dream, it is achievable! To make a product users will adore, you need their input throughout the process. It is like baking a cake – you need everyone's help to get it just right. By engaging with users and listening to their needs, you can create something they truly enjoy. Success is not just about meeting targets; it's about making people happy. Just as you would ask kids what they want in a playground, UX research helps ensure your product meets user expectations.

Some key reasons highlighting the importance of UX research are as follows:

1. **Understanding People:** UX research aids in our comprehension of the target market for our good or service. UX research helps us understand the preferences, wants, and behaviors of the people who will use our websites, apps, or any other product, in the same way that interviewing the kids helps you figure out what they like to do on the playground.
2. **Improving Design:** You may create better designs when you are aware of what appeals to and bothers individuals. Assume that a majority of children prefer climbing walls than swings. If your research has shown you this, you should build more climbing walls in your playground. In a similar vein, UX research directs us toward creating goods, apps, and websites that users find simple and fun to use.
3. **Solving Problems:** Occasionally, users may experience difficulties with particular features of a product. Perhaps an app's buttons are too small, or the slide is too steep. UX research helps in the early detection of these issues so that they can be resolved before they become major problems. Finding an issue with the swing beforehand prevents injuries to others!
4. **Saving Time and Money:** Just picture spending a lot of money on a massive playground only to discover afterwards that the neighborhood kids don't enjoy it. Both money and time are wasted on that. These kinds of errors are prevented by UX research. By knowing what consumers want up front, we can save money on expensive redesigns down the road.
5. **Creating Happy Users:** The ultimate objective of every good or service is to bring happiness to its users. UX research makes sure that the things we produce are in line with people's needs and desires. Users are more inclined to stick with and recommend our creations to their friends when they find pleasure in utilizing them. It is similar to having children who eagerly anticipate returning to your playground each day!

Thus, UX research is similar to possessing a magic ingredient that enhances, enriches, and increases the utility of whatever we do for its users, addressing their needs, desires, and requirements. The main goal is to ensure everyone enjoys themselves on the technological playground!

Benefits of UX Research

In the fast-paced digital landscape of today, UX research acts as a guiding light, illuminating the desires and needs of consumers. By shedding light on these insights, it not only empowers the product and the company behind it but also enhances the experience for the end-users.

- **Product Benefits:** UX research uncovers how, when, and why people use a product, helping identify key issues and effective solutions.
- **Business Benefits:** UX research speeds up development, reduces costly redesigns, and boosts customer satisfaction by integrating user needs early.
- **User Benefits:** UX research provides direct feedback from users, ensuring their opinions are recognized and considered by the business.

UX Research Process

In this chapter, we have created a guide for anyone, from experienced UX researchers to newcomers. Research is crucial for great UX design and development. A systematic approach ensures each design version improves with valuable data, but flexibility is key. There's no one-size-fits-all method–effective UX research adapts to your team's, users', and business's needs. This guide outlines how to build a strong UX research process in seven steps, based on lean UX principles of user feedback, testing, and continuous improvement. Remember, UX research is an ongoing cycle, with insights and feedback shaping the design and development process continuously.

1. Setting Clear Research Goals

Establishing clear goals and objectives marks the initial and most crucial step in any user research endeavor. Without them, you are essentially navigating blindly through the process, which is not conducive to effective user research.

To pinpoint your research goals, consider the following questions:

What information do I aim to uncover?	This fundamental query serves as the cornerstone, eventually evolving into specific, actionable, and practical research questions.
What knowledge gaps exist?	Identifying these gaps and limitations early on enables you to address them proactively.
How does this align with company objectives?	Familiarizing yourself with your organization's business model and key performance indicators helps ensure that your research efforts are in sync with broader company goals.
At what stage of product development am I?	Your research objectives will vary depending on whether you are in the discovery phase, validation and testing phase, launching a product, or engaging in ongoing feedback collection.
What decisions will this research inform?	Understanding how stakeholders will utilize the insights gleaned from your research is essential in shaping your approach.

What outcomes do I anticipate from this research?	Envisioning the desired results provides clarity on what success entails for your research endeavors.

***Table 3.1**: Questions to consider when defining your research goals*

Conducting Stakeholder Interviews

Conducting stakeholder interviews is essential for any research project. Stakeholders, including team members, managers, and clients, offer valuable insights that shape the project and ensure alignment. Start by identifying your stakeholders, scheduling interviews, preparing questions, and setting clear objectives.

Use a mix of open-ended and closed-ended questions to gather comprehensive data. Here is a concise interview guide:

1. **Introductions:** Introduce yourself and explain the interview's purpose.
2. **Project Importance:** Ask about the project's importance and desired outcomes.
3. **Success Criteria:** Define success and its fit within the broader business context.
4. **Roles and Responsibilities:** Discuss the stakeholder's role and contribution.
5. **Impact Assessment:** Evaluate the project's impact on their work.
6. **Challenges and Concerns:** Identify potential challenges and solutions.
7. **Feedback and Questions:** Invite questions and additional insights.
8. **Conclusion:** Thank them for their time and insights.

Creating targeted research questions involves identifying goals, addressing information gaps, and ensuring questions are clear and relevant. Test questions beforehand to refine them for clarity and effectiveness.

Good research questions are:

- **Specific:** Clearly defined to know when they are answered.
- **Practical:** Realistically answerable within the project scope.
- **Actionable:** Provide results that can guide team actions.

Finally, communicate your approach and objectives to stakeholders to gain their support and enhance the research impact.

2. Selecting Your Research Methods

Think of UX research as planning a journey. Just as you would pack for a trip, you need to choose the right tools and methods for gathering information, such as surveys, interviews, or user observations. Proper planning keeps you organized and focused.

Using a combination of methods ensures comprehensive coverage and addresses potential gaps. Your choices depend on users, business needs, and resources. Different stages of product development require specific approaches, guided by your research questions, data needs (qualitative or quantitative, attitudinal or behavioral), and decisions you aim to support.

Behavioral research tools like heat maps, A/B testing, user recordings, and eye tracking observe user actions. Attitudinal research methods like focus groups, interviews, card sorting, and surveys explore users' thoughts and feelings. Combining both provides a complete view of user behavior, bridging the gap between what people say and do, and mixing qualitative and quantitative data offers a deeper understanding of user preferences and trends.

3. Preparing a Strategic User Research Plan

After establishing your research questions and UX analysis methods, develop your research plan to engage with customers and understand their needs. The Interaction Design Foundation suggests starting with a concise, one-page plan, which can be adjusted to suit your needs.

Here is a one-page research plan template:

- **Title:** Clearly name your project for easy reference.
- **Author:** List the responsible person and their contact details, along with others who can receive feedback.
- **Stakeholders:** Include details and contact information of all involved in the study and those receiving the findings.
- **Date:** Note the start date and any revision dates for updates.
- **Project Background:** Provide a brief summary of the research motivation and relevant background.
- **Main Goal:** State the primary objective of your research in one clear sentence.
- **Research Questions:** Outline the key questions to be answered, guiding your methods and focus during analysis.
- **Research Methods:** Describe the qualitative and quantitative methods, specifying whether the research will be moderated or unmoderated, and the estimated duration.
- **Participant Information:** Define your target audience, including demographics and the number of participants needed.
- **Schedule:** Create a timeline with study dates and milestones to track progress.

- **Budget:** Outline the financial resources and allocation for different aspects of the research.
- **Supporting Information:** Include any additional data that could influence the research project or outcomes.

Example

User Research Plan: Enhancing Mobile Banking Experience	
Title	Enhancing Mobile Banking Experience
Author	Sharanpreet Kaur, UX Researcher
Stakeholders Information	Project Manager: Sarah Johnson Design Lead: Sharanpreet Kaur Development Team: UI/UX Developers, Mobile App Developers Marketing Team: Jane Williams Customer Support: Emily Clark
Date	May 1, 2024
Project's Background	With the increasing shift towards digital banking, our mobile banking app has become a crucial touch point for customers. However, recent feedback suggests that users are experiencing challenges with certain features and navigation elements. This research aims to identify pain points, preferences, and opportunities for improvement to enhance the overall mobile banking experience.
Main Goal	To identify key areas for improvement and optimize the mobile banking app to meet the evolving needs and expectations of users.
Research Questions	What are the primary challenges users encounter while navigating the mobile banking app? What features do users find most valuable, and which ones do they find cumbersome or unnecessary? How do users perceive the security and reliability of the mobile banking app? What improvements can be made to streamline the account management and transaction processes? What additional functionalities or services would users like to see added to the mobile banking app?
Research Methods	User Interviews 2. Usability Testing 3. Surveys 4. Competitor Analysis

Information About Participants	**Demographics:** Varied age groups (18-65+), diverse socioeconomic backgrounds **Banking Experience:** Novice to experienced users **Mobile Device:** Android and iOS users **Geographic Location:** Nationwide representation
Schedule	**Week 1-2:** Prepare interview scripts and usability testing scenarios **Week 3-4:** Conduct user interviews and usability testing sessions **Week 5:** Distribute surveys to a sample of users **Week 6:** Analyze research findings and conduct competitor analysis **Week 7:** Compile research report and prepare presentation **Week 8:** Present findings to stakeholders and discuss actionable steps
Supporting Information	Access to mobile banking app analytics Budget for participant incentives and research tools/software
Budget	Participant Incentives: $2000 Research Tools/Software: $1000 Total Budget: $3000

***Table 3.2**: Example of user research plan*

4. Recruiting Participants

Consider this step as a way to invite others along on a thrilling journey. The individuals who will be using your product are the ones that best represent your target market. You can reach out to your present users or recruit them using social media, internet platforms, or other means.

Ask focused questions about certain product pages or features as well as open-ended inquiries about the experiences and desires of your customers to engage them.

Clearly define the people you wish to hire. Imagine the perfect individual who can offer the precise, useful, and practical insights you require. To make sure you locate the ideal volunteers for your study, create a list of requirements.

Designing a Screening Survey

Picture a screener survey as a sort of gatekeeper for your study – it helps you decide who gets in and who does not. Let us say you are on the hunt for folks who have splurged on Soy sauce in the past 4 months. Now, you cannot just ask, "Hey, bought any Soy sauce lately?" That would be too easy, right?

Instead, you need to get a little more cunning. Offer up a bunch of pantry items and ask folks to pick which ones they have snagged in the past 4 months. Sneaky, right? Here is how it could look:

Which of these goodies have you nabbed in the past 4 months?

- Balsamic vinegar - Nope.
- Soy sauce - Ding ding! You are in!
- Fish sauce - Not quite.
- Olive oil - Uh-uh, not this time.
- Canola oil - Nope.
- None of the above - Swing and a miss!

See? By being a bit crafty with your questions, you can filter out the Soy sauce aficionados without giving away the answer.

Finding the Ideal Rewards for Your Audience

Now that you have identified your target participants, consider what type of reward would be fair compensation for their participation. Participants often prefer incentives like cash or gift cards. The suitable incentive varies based on your study's requirements, the characteristics of your participants, and your available budget. However, attracting participants can be challenging.

5. Exploring Research Opportunities

It's time to embark on your research journey! Whether you are conducting surveys, interviews, or observing user interactions, this phase is crucial for collecting valuable data. You might ask about the user-friendliness of your website or the most beneficial features.

Here are essential tips for conducting moderated user research:

- **Foster Genuine Connections:** Show empathy and treat participants with warmth and respect.
- **Embrace Silence:** Allow participants to reflect and provide insights at their own pace. Observe their behaviors and non-verbal cues.
- **Provide Context:** Manage expectations about research outcomes but avoid sharing your assumptions to prevent bias.

- **Take Thorough Notes:** Have a colleague take notes or use transcription tools to capture key insights, allowing you to stay fully engaged.

Remember to start your research early and conduct it frequently to ensure your solutions meet actual user needs.

6. Analyzing and Integrating Results

Once you are back from your research adventure, it is time to unpack and sift through all the info you have gathered. Look for common themes and important insights that help you understand your users better. This is where you find the real gems hidden in your data.

How you analyze your data depends on how you collected it. Quantitative data analysis means looking at numbers to find trends. Qualitative data analysis is more about understanding what users are saying. Organize your data neatly, focusing on what users find frustrating. Spot any recurring problems and ask more questions if needed. Once you have figured out what users need and what issues they're facing, it is time to use those insights to make your product better.

Create easy-to-understand reports and stories about user experiences. And do not forget to share important findings with everyone in the organization. This way, everyone can use the research to make better decisions.

7. Sharing Your Research Findings

Sharing your research findings with your team or company is just like telling stories about your trip. It helps everyone see things from the user's perspective and decide what to do next with your product. But you might be wondering: How do you do it? What's the best way to tell stakeholders about your user research results?

Well, there isn't just one way to do it. Unlike academic researchers who write formal reports, UX researchers have lots of options. You can share your findings through:

- Written reports or summaries (we've got a UX research summary template we use at User Interviews)
- Slideshows (we've got another template for you!) that you can present in meetings or as a video recording or slide deck
- Interactive workshops
- Emails or messages on Slack
- Articles on the company wiki
- Quick research updates
- Case studies

Iterate and Improve

Integrate the methodology of UX research into your design philosophy. UX research is a continuous process that should not be abandoned once designing and development are underway. Keep in mind that UX research is an ongoing endeavor. After you go back home, organize another trip and continue to get feedback and develop your product. Great user experiences are mostly a result of this cycle of learning, making improvements, and then learning some more. Setting high priority for excellent UX research will enhance your design culture, increase conversions, and maintain happy, involved users.

Here you have it: a basic overview of the UX research methodology!

UX Research Methods

Now that your goals and research framework have been established, it's time for the exciting part: selecting the research methodology that will best advance your project's aims and yield the necessary insights. This section will walk you through the most often used research methodologies and assist you in selecting the most appropriate one for your purposes.

Every research technique falls into one of these groups, each with specific aims and objectives:

- Qualitative versus Quantitative
- Behavioral versus Attitudinal
- Generative versus Evaluative

Qualitative versus Quantitative	**Behavioral versus Attitudinal**	**Generative versus Evaluative**
Information that can be measured quantitatively and provides statistical and numerical insights is referred to as quantitative data. On the other hand, non-numerical insights and descriptive data make up qualitative data, which provides a deeper comprehension of underlying patterns, behaviors, and motivations.	The activities consumers take when interacting with products, finishing tasks, or solving problems are tracked by behavioral data. On the other hand, attitudinal data records users' ideas, viewpoints, and convictions and offers a window into their motives and beliefs.	The goal of generative research is to generate fresh concepts and remedies that benefit users. Evaluative research, on the other hand, aims to determine how consumers react to and perceive an existing solution in order to evaluate its effectiveness and pinpoint areas in need of development.

***Table 3.3**: Categories of UX research methods*

Qualitative versus Quantitative

Qualitative approaches delve further into comprehending user demands and behaviors, highlighting the reasons behind their actions. Teams can learn why users act in certain ways by using this method. Qualitative research provides answers to queries such as:

- Why?
- How?
- How can this be fixed?

Conversely, **quantitative** approaches concentrate on gathering and examining numerical data in order to identify trends and patterns. They provide statistical insights and conclusions by quantifying user behaviors, preferences, and attitudes.

Quantitative research provides solutions to queries like:

- How much?
- In what number?
- How frequently?

Combining these techniques gives teams a thorough understanding of their users, resulting in more efficient and user-focused solutions.

Behavioral versus Attitudinal

Instead of focusing on what people say, they would or do **behavioral** research to examine what users really do. In order to better understand user behavior, this type of research frequently relies on observational techniques like heat maps, eye tracking, and usability testing.

Behavioral research can assist you in addressing inquiries such as:

- What is the user interface for this new feature?
- What is the average time taken by users to finish a workflow?
- What is the greater conversion rate CTA?
- Is the user interface navigable?

The goal of **attitude** research is to comprehend the attitudes, perceptions, and beliefs of users. It explores the 'why' of user choices and behavior. It frequently entails asking consumers questions about their opinions, preferences, and sentiments regarding a good or service through surveys or interviews. It is subjective in nature and seeks to convey the feelings and viewpoints of the viewer.

You can get answers to queries like:

- What do people think of this feature? What is the use of attitude research?
- What do individuals claim to desire?
- What kind of difficulty do people currently have?
- What mental models do they have?

Generative versus Evaluative

The main goal of **generative** research is to produce fresh thoughts, ideas, and insights to support the design process. To stimulate creativity and direct the creation of user-centered solutions, you can conduct co-design workshops, card sorting, and brainstorming sessions with user groups.

With the use of discovery methods, you can get the answers to queries like:

- Who are our users?
- What issues do they have?
- How do they reason?
- Is this solution truly necessary?
- What should we construct?

Assessing the usability, efficacy, and general quality of current designs or prototypes is the main goal of **evaluative** research. After you have created a prototype for your idea, it is time to assess its advantages and disadvantages. Through A/B testing, you may compare many iterations of a feature or product design to make sure your UX design fulfils customer expectations.

Evaluative techniques assist you in addressing issues such as:

- Which design is preferred by users?
- Is it easy to use this interface?
- Is this functionality functioning as planned?
- Are we constructing the appropriate thing?
- Is there anything better?

All research methods are either quantitative or qualitative. Here is a quick overview:

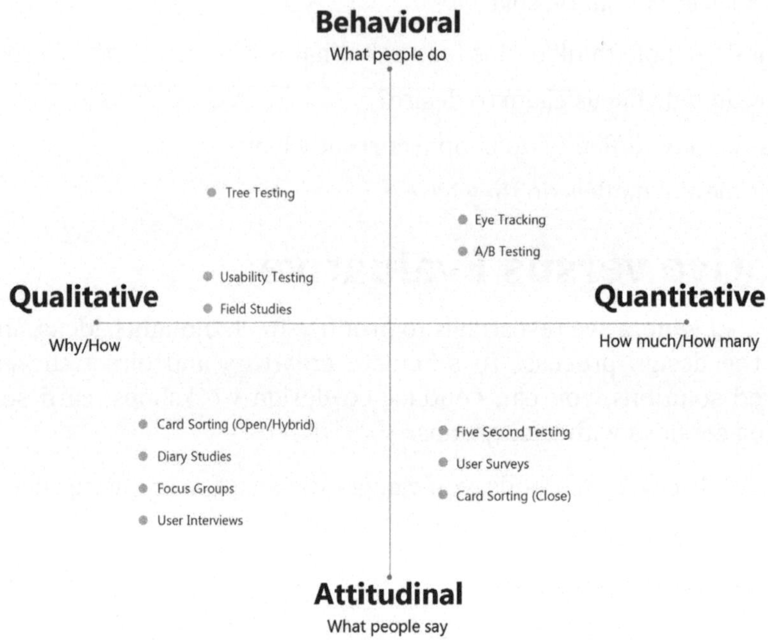

***Figure 3.2**: Categorized Graph of UX Research Methods*

The following are the objectives of user research methods:

- Identify key difficulties, barriers, and problems
- Identify user behavior and attitudes
- Look for opportunities to apply innovative solutions
- Test what functions work and what does not

Selecting the right approach is crucial for UX research. By choosing the most effective ways to respond to specific questions about your customers, you may enhance your offerings and go above and beyond what they would expect. The right techniques will depend on your goals, but often the optimum approach is a combination of both quantitative and qualitative data. This combination helps you understand not only the motivations behind user activity but also itself.

With this strategy in place, let us look at some of the best approaches for conducting user research.

User Interviews

One interviewer would usually speak with one person at a time for 30 to 60 minutes during an interview. Interviews can be conducted in person, over the phone, or through live video streaming. In-person interviews give you the chance to record both spoken and nonverbal indicators, such as feelings and body language that could indicate a candidate's excitement for the offering or discomfort with the inquiries.

Effective Timing for User Interview Sessions

Usually, you will apply this technique at the beginning and finish of your project. You can gain a thorough grasp of your target consumers' viewpoints and the environment in which they will engage with your product at the outset of a project.

By the project's end, fresh user interviews – typically with a new group of people – provide an indicator for the usability and appeal of your product by offering firsthand recollections of experiences, perceived strengths, and possible areas for improvement.

***Figure 3.3**: Conducting User Interviews for UX Research*

Effective Techniques for User Interview

Getting in-depth knowledge about the needs, habits, and motivations of your users can be achieved through conducting user interviews. This is an in-depth guide to assist you in conducting user interviews successfully:

1. Establish your goals
2. Make a list of the subjects and issues you wish to address
3. Choose the correct participants
4. Prepare the interview space

5. Choose a recording technique such as written notes, video, tape recorder, and more.
6. Perform at least one interview trial run.
7. Carry out the Interview
8. Examine the information
9. Recap the main conclusions drawn from your interviews.

Successful user interviews rely on a few key practices: remain neutral to avoid bias, and show genuine interest and empathy to build trust. Emphasize that there are no right or wrong answers to create a comfortable environment for honest feedback. Aim for a natural, conversational flow instead of a rigid Q&A format, which helps participants relax and provide richer, more detailed insights. By following these practices, you will collect valuable information about user experiences, allowing you to create products that better meet their needs and expectations.

Downsides of User Interviews

User interviews are a treasure trove of insights, but they come with a few challenges. They are often time-consuming and expensive, demanding meticulous planning and experienced interviewers. The data gathered can be subjective, potentially swayed by the interviewer's biases or leading questions. Participants might also give answers they think are expected rather than their genuine opinions. Moreover, the small sample sizes in interviews make it hard to generalize findings to a larger audience. Analyzing qualitative data is no easy feat – it's complex, labor-intensive, and can be tricky to extract clear, actionable insights from the varied individual responses. Despite these hurdles, when done right, user interviews can provide invaluable, in-depth understanding of user behaviors and needs.

Focus Groups

Focus groups are a type of qualitative research technique where a small group of people–typically fewer than ten–are studied to get insight into their attitudes and views. This method tends to be informal and offers a lot of information rapidly. Focus groups are useful for learning about users' preferences, pain points, and potential uses for a product.

Effective Timing for Holding Focus Groups

It is preferable to employ focus groups while you are still refining your idea for a product or service. They assist in generating ideas, getting preliminary responses, and investigating consumer preferences. Focus groups in their early stages are beneficial because they allow for big improvements to be made at a low cost.

Figure 3.4: *Utilizing Focus Groups in UX Research*

Effective Technique to Conduct Focus Groups

To conduct user experience research using focus groups, follow these steps:

1. Plan a schedule that allows time for recruiting, testing, analyzing, and incorporating results.
2. Gather your team and assign roles: moderator, note-taker, and discussion leader.
3. Determine the scope of your research: What questions will you ask? How deeply do you want to explore answers? This guides the number of participants and groups.
4. Develop a discussion guide with 3-5 topics.
5. Recruit potential or current users who can offer valuable feedback.
6. Run the focus group sessions and take notes.
7. Analyze the data and prepare a report.

Following these guidelines will make it easy to maximize the efficacy of your user groups. To start, formulate precise, open-ended questions that are relevant to your study subjects in order to get thorough and attentive responses. Second, to guarantee a full examination of every issue, limit the number of topics discussed to three to five in a ninety-minute session. Finally, include three to six people to create a lively and stimulating environment while balancing different points of view and active involvement.

Downsides of Focus Groups

Though they have advantages, focus groups can have disadvantages. More peaceful voices may be overshadowed by strong-willed people, which can distort debates and produce biased conclusions. People may feel under pressure from the group dynamic to voice their true ideas rather than to comply to common opinions. Additionally, setting up focus groups can be expensive and time-consuming. The moderator's presence may unintentionally affect replies, and the controlled environment could not exactly reflect real-world behaviors. Finally, because focus groups are qualitative in nature, results may not be statistically represented, which would restrict how broadly applicable they can be.

Surveys

A flexible and necessary instrument for exploring both qualitative and quantitative user research is the survey. They provide an insight into the demands and needs of people about different items. Surveys are a wide concept that includes a variety of question types. In essence, surveys are made up of a set of questions that fall into one of two categories:

- **Closed-ended Questions:** These questions either offer a list of predetermined multiple-choice options or conclude with simply answering "yes" or "no." They work well for gathering pertinent information and seeing trends among users. Closed-ended questions yield readily quantifiable, graphical, and analytical data.
- **Open-ended Questions:** These inquiries permit participants to provide free-form, in-your-own-word answers. Open-ended questions yield qualitative data that provides in-depth, extensive insights into the thoughts and experiences of users.

For effective surveys, keep these recommendations in mind:

- **Clarity:** Ensure questions are clear and simple, avoiding complex terms.
- **Neutrality:** Avoid leading questions to get impartial, honest answers.
- **Variety:** Use both closed-ended and open-ended questions for comprehensive insights.
- **Respect:** Treat participants with respect, avoid invasive questions, and assure them their information is private.

Additionally, select a broad and diverse group of participants to ensure the results accurately reflect your user base and are statistically relevant.

Effective Timing to Conduct Surveys

Surveys can be used at different times and for varied purposes depending on your research objectives, which makes them a flexible tool for various phases of the product development process. Surveys are a great way to collect early data and find patterns, trends, or potential user segments during the conceptualization stage. Surveys can be used after a product launch or during iterative design cycles to gather input on how features are used, how satisfied users are, and what could be improved.

Large-scale user sentiment can be effectively measured with surveys. Because of their adaptability, you can position them on particular pages, which makes it simple to pose inquiries when appropriate. For example, you may place a survey on your "thank you" page to get feedback from customers who have recently made a purchase. This will give you quick and useful data.

***Figure 3.5**: Implementing Surveys in UX Research*

Effective Technique to Conduct Surveys

Surveys today are typically performed online, with data automatically collected and analyzed by survey tools. This information helps inform future UX studies and improve your product. To optimize online surveys, keep them concise by focusing on essential questions, especially when participants are not incentivized. This respects their time and enhances completion rates and data accuracy. Ensure clarity by using straightforward language to prevent confusion and guarantee reliable responses. Maintain participant engagement by incorporating a mix of multiple-choice and open-ended questions, striking a balance that keeps interest high and yields both quantitative and qualitative data. These practices collectively contribute to the effectiveness and success of online surveys.

Conducting an online survey involves several key steps:

1. **Identify goals and objectives**: Define what you aim to achieve with the survey.
2. **Create survey questions**: Develop questions that align with your objectives.
3. **Select a survey tool**: Choose an online survey platform like SurveyMonkey or Qualtrics.
4. **Recruit participants**: Find and invite people to take part in your survey.
5. **Conduct the survey**: Distribute the survey and collect responses.
6. **Analyze and report**: Examine the data collected and report the findings.

By following these steps and best practices, you can create effective and engaging online surveys that provide valuable insights.

Downsides of Surveys

Unfortunately, there are issues with this approach as well. Users tend to say one thing and do another, which might lead to incorrect conclusions. Furthermore, users' responses may be adversely affected by questions that are poorly formulated. Length might also be a problem, since many individuals find lengthy surveys to be annoying. Because of this, it is critical to design brief surveys in order to increase user completion rates and participation in ongoing research projects.

Card Sorting

Card sorting is like a creative puzzle that helps designers build user-friendly structures in digital worlds. It is not just about organizing information; it's also a brainstorming tool where users contribute ideas and naming styles. Participants receive a deck of cards representing various categories or concepts. Their task? Sort them into groups based on their own logic and understanding, revealing unique insights into user perspectives.

There are three main types of card sorting:

- **Open card sorting**: In this type, participants group topics into logical categories and name these groups for themselves. In addition to encouraging innovation, this approach can reveal fresh perspectives on how people perceive information architecture.

- **Hybrid card sorting:** In this type, participants can develop new categories in addition to using pre-established ones. This method accommodates both pre-established organizational frameworks and user-generated concepts, providing a balance between structure and flexibility.
- **Closed card sorting:** In this type, participants are given predetermined categories and given the responsibility of organizing things into these groups. By measuring how effectively users can match items to established categories, this method assesses how well the predefined structure fits into users' mental models.

Based on what you want to achieve, you can pick different ways to do card sorting:

- **Moderated or unmoderated**: A researcher can lead the session (moderated), or users can do it by themselves (unmoderated).
- **Paper or digital:** You can write topics on paper cards or type them into a computer program.

Making information architecture on a website or app user-friendly and relevant can be greatly helped by this research method.

Effective Timing to Conduct Card Sorting

If you want to learn more about how users organize and understand information, card sorting is the technique of choice. Imagine yourself coming up with name ideas or deciphering the naming conventions. Or maybe you are negotiating the expectations of users over how to navigate a website. Maybe you're thinking about the best way to arrange material on a brand-new website or improving the layout of an existing one. Card sorting turns out to be a trustworthy partner in each of these scenarios.

***Figure 3.6**: Card Sorting Method in Action for UX Research*

Effective Technique to Conduct Card Sorting

Let us quickly review the steps involved in doing card sorting:

1. First, list the elements on cards that you want users to organize, such as sections of your website or app. For in-person sessions, these can be physical cards, or they can be digital cards for online card sorting.
2. After that, ask participants to arrange the cards into groups according to how they feel. In the event of an open card sort, the players will name the groups themselves. They will arrange the cards into pre-made categories of your selection if it is closed.
3. In order to gain insight into participants' mental models, watch how they arrange the cards you've provided. These findings can then be used to create information architecture that people would find intuitive right away.

Whether you're building a new website or revamping an existing one, adhering to these best practices will help you maximize the effectiveness of your card sorting session and obtain dependable, actionable insights:

1. Keep the number of cards manageable.
2. Select and arrange card names thoughtfully.
3. Avoid mixing child and parent categories.
4. Carefully choose your card sorting method.
5. Randomize the card order.
6. Recruit suitable participants.

That's how you conduct card sorts, but there are a lot of other things to consider, such choosing the best card sorting technique, recruiting the correct participants, and properly analyzing the findings.

Downsides of Card Sorting

Like any research technique, card sorting has its benefits and drawbacks. A few of the drawbacks of card sorting include:

Unmoderated card sorting might not yield thoroughly insightful results. It can take a long time to analyze the findings of a card sort, especially one that is done on paper.

Card sorting does not take into consideration the tasks at hand or the larger context. For instance, we might classify tomatoes as "fruits" in the context of a store, but they might actually belong in the "vegetable aisle."

Diary Studies

Through consistent journaling of their thoughts, feelings, and behaviors throughout time, participants in diary studies become storytellers of their own lives—a fascinating research tool. With this method, researchers can get a glimpse of long-term experiences and behaviors in a natural environment. Participants may provide light on their routines and contacts with goods and services by making daily notes or noting specifics when certain events occur. The resulting data is a treasure trove for identifying trends, revealing problems, and identifying areas that should be improved.

Effective Timing to Conduct Diary Studies

Diary studies are invaluable for gaining insights into long-term behaviors and experiences. They empower participants to chronicle their actions, thoughts, and feelings over extended periods, offering a comprehensive view of user interactions and capturing variations that short-term methods might overlook. Perfect for examining real-world settings, diary studies offer real-time documentation of experiences in everyday environments, providing genuine insights into how users interact with products or services.

These studies work especially well when looking at uncommon or intermittent occurrences, such as certain health concerns or infrequent product use. Diary studies avoid depending on participant recollection by recording in-depth, real-time accounts as these events happen. Through in-depth accounts and individual insights, the approach produces rich, qualitative data that reveals underlying motives and feelings. This abundance of data is essential for developing user personas, directing design choices, and pinpointing areas where goods and services need to be improved.

Figure 3.7: *Participants document their daily interactions and experiences*

Effective Technique to Conduct Diary Studies

Follow these steps to conduct user experience research using diary studies:

1. **Define Objectives:** Clearly outline the goals of the study. Understand what specific behaviors, experiences, or events you want to investigate.
2. **Recruit Participants:** Select participants who represent your target audience. Ensure they are willing and able to commit to the study duration.
3. **Design the Diary:** Create a structured format for participants to follow, including prompts and questions that align with your research objectives. Ensure it is user-friendly and accessible, whether digital or paper-based.
4. **Provide Instructions:** Clearly explain how and when participants should make entries. Offer guidelines on the level of detail needed and the types of events or experiences they should document.
5. **Pilot Test:** Conduct a pilot study with a small group to identify any issues with the diary format or instructions. Make necessary adjustments based on feedback.
6. **Monitor Progress:** Stay in regular contact with participants to ensure they are consistently completing entries. Offer support and answer any questions they might have.
7. **Collect and Analyze Data:** Gather the diaries at the end of the study period. Analyze the entries for patterns, themes, and insights that align with your research objectives.
8. **Report Findings:** Summarize the key insights, supported by quotes and examples from the diaries. Use this data to inform design decisions or improvements.

Depending on the objectives and nature of the study, diary studies as a UX research tool can have varying lengths. Diary studies often last anything from a few days to several months. They usually last one to four weeks in order to give enough time to record significant patterns and insights into the actions and experiences of users.

Downsides of Diary Studies

Researchers should be aware of the various challenges associated with diary studies. One major issue is the participant burden, as long-term diary keeping can lead to fatigue and rushed or incomplete entries, compromising data accuracy.

Subjectivity and bias are also concerns, as entries are based on participants' opinions and interpretations, which can skew insights. Recall bias may occur when participants fill in entries later instead of in real-time, further affecting accuracy.

Over time, participant engagement may decline, reducing the quantity and quality of data collected. Analyzing diary entries is complex and time-consuming, requiring skilled researchers to identify significant patterns. Privacy concerns may arise, particularly with sensitive topics, leading to less detailed data. Additionally, technical issues with digital diaries can disrupt data collection and participant cooperation.

Usability Testing

Usability testing is a key part of UX research, involving real users from the target audience to assess a website or app's readiness for launch. It measures how easily users can complete common tasks, providing a clear picture of the overall user experience. This approach helps identify usability issues and areas for improvement before the product's formal release.

Usability tests typically involve **three components: the facilitator** (a UX researcher who conducts the test and records data), **participants** (who perform tasks designed to mimic real-life use), and the **tasks** themselves.

The benefits of usability testing include reducing assumptions by gathering real user data, which reveals whether the product will be effective.

There are several forms of usability testing, including:

1. **Moderated Usability Testing:** Conducted by a researcher who guides and observes participants in real-time, either in person or via video conference.

2. **Unmoderated Usability Testing:** Participants complete tasks independently while interactions are recorded by software, usually done remotely.

3. **Remote Usability Testing:** Participants test the product in their own environment, with options for moderated or unmoderated sessions.

4. **In-Person Usability Testing:** Conducted in a lab setting with the researcher present to observe and record.

5. **Explorative Usability Testing:** Early-stage testing to gather feedback on user needs and behaviors.

6. **Assessment Usability Testing:** Evaluates the product's effectiveness and efficiency later in the development process.

7. **Comparative Usability Testing:** Compares multiple designs to determine which design offers a better user experience.

These methods provide valuable insights into user interactions, helping to improve product usability and user satisfaction.

Effective Timing to Conduct Usability Tests

Usability testing is beneficial for a product at every step of its life cycle. As previously indicated, this technique reduces assumptions and can be applied to live websites or early website designs, even with basic website prototypes. You should undertake usability testing early and regularly in the process to help guide your design selections. You can use the following guidelines to determine when usability testing is appropriate:

- Prior to beginning any design work
- As soon as you have a prototype or wireframe ready
- Before the product's release
- After launch, at frequent periods

***Figure 3.8**: A user engages in a usability test, providing real-time feedback to improve app functionality and user experience*

Effective Technique to Conduct Usability Tests

It is critical to comprehend user behavior with your product before doing any usability testing. You can improve the user experience overall and pinpoint areas for improvement by watching how they behave and getting feedback. This is a short manual for carrying out usability testing:

1. **Define Goals**: Clearly state what you want to learn about your product's usability.
2. **Recruit Participants**: Find people who represent your target users.
3. **Create Tasks**: Develop realistic scenarios for participants to complete.
4. **Prepare Materials**: Set up prototypes or websites for testing.
5. **Facilitate Sessions**: Guide participants through tasks while observing their actions.
6. **Collect Data**: Take notes on what participants do and say.
7. **Analyze Results**: Look for patterns and problems in participants' behavior.
8. **Report Findings**: Summarize key insights and suggest improvements.
9. **Implement Changes**: Use feedback to make your product more user-friendly.
10. **Repeat if Necessary**: Conduct additional tests to confirm improvements.

Gaining proficiency in usability testing methods guarantees that your product meets user needs exactly, providing a seamless and enjoyable experience. You can improve your design by revealing important insights and making wise decisions by choosing the right kind of usability test.

Downsides of Usability Tests

Although it's a great tool for finding user experience (UX) problems, usability testing is not without its limitations. The possibility of bias brought about by the testing environment or facilitator is one restriction. Because of the artificial environment, participants could alter their behavior, producing unreliable results. Furthermore, conducting usability tests can be a laborious and resource-intensive process that involves meticulous preparation, participant selection, and evaluation. Additionally, there is a chance that specific user groups or circumstances will be missed, leaving us with just partial understandings of the usability of the product. Moreover, usability testing usually concentrates on observable behaviors, which could not accurately represent users' subjective motivations or feelings. Lastly, it takes experience to evaluate the results from usability studies, and not all insights can be immediately applied to improve designs.

Field Studies

In contrast to lab or office settings, field studies in UX research involve watching users in their natural environments. This approach reveals genuine customer demands and behaviors and gives design teams insights into how products are used in real-world situations. Through immersion in the user's environment, researchers can find problems (such as sudden disruptions or connectivity issues) that might not show up in controlled circumstances. By capturing the context and subtleties of regular product use, field studies assist designers in developing solutions that better meet consumers' actual demands and enhance the user experience as a whole.

Field studies reveal:

- How people actually use their products.
- The context in which products are used in real-world scenarios.
- Problems include multitasking, unplanned interruptions, and a lack of Wi-Fi that might not occur in a lab setting.

Ultimately, field studies involve diving into the real world to see how products perform in the everyday lives of users.

Effective Timing to Conduct Field Studies

Field studies in UX research are important at different stages of a project. They are especially useful during the discovery phase to help set direction and understand how users interact with products. Additionally, field studies are crucial during usability testing when prototypes are available, as they help evaluate the effectiveness of solutions and validate design assumptions in real-world situations. Therefore, field studies are used both at the beginning of a project to guide initial decisions and later to ensure the solutions meet user needs and behaviors in practical contexts.

In simple terms, we can say the best times to conduct field studies are at the start of a project and during usability testing. At the beginning, they help understand user needs and context, guiding the initial direction of the project. Later, during usability testing, field studies evaluate prototypes and validate designs, ensuring they meet user needs and work effectively in real-world situations.

***Figure 3.9**: Gathering authentic user insights through field studies for UX research*

Effective Technique to Conduct Field Studies

It is necessary to recognize the significance of field studies in UX research before talking about practical methods. These studies provide priceless insights into user behavior and product interactions because they were carried out at various project stages.

1. **Identify your learning objectives**: Clearly state what you hope to discover about user interactions and experiences in authentic environments.

2. **Select locations**: Decide on suitable field sites where customers will inevitably interact with your offering.

3. **Select participants**: Look for users who are willing to be watched in their natural habitat and who represent your target audience.

4. **Plan observations**: Select the facets of user behavior you wish to watch and create a methodical plan for your observations.

5. **Observe and take notes**: Go to the field sites and watch how participants use your good or service. Make thorough notes about their acts, mannerisms, and any difficulties they have.

6. **Ask follow-up questions**: Conduct quick conversations with participants to learn more about their backgrounds and driving forces.
7. **Analyze findings**: Look over your notes and interview transcripts to find trends, themes, and areas that may use better.
8. **Report insights**: Provide a summary of the main conclusions and revelations from the field research, along with suggestions for improving the design in light of user input.
9. **Iterate and implement**: Make adjustments to your product or service design based on the field study's observations. Based on customer input, make the required adjustments and enhancements.
10. **Repeat as needed**: As your project develops, carry out more field research to confirm design choices and guarantee that they remain consistent with user requirements and behaviors.

Downsides of Field Studies

In UX research, field studies have different drawbacks. Initially, objectivity may be compromised by researchers when they unintentionally affect participant behavior or interpret observations in a biased way. Furthermore, completing these studies requires a significant investment of time, energy, and resources. Another challenge is finding subjects who are open to being seen in their natural environments. Furthermore, because people's behavior can alter while they are being observed, field studies could not always obtain a sample that is entirely representative of the intended user base. Unpredictability is also introduced in field settings by external factors. It is difficult to analyze qualitative data from these researches; in order to get useful insights, a thorough review of large amounts of data is necessary. Finally, some user demographics or research objectives may make field investigations impossible or immoral. However, when carried out carefully, they continue to be vital for studying user behaviors and improving.

Tree Testing

Tree testing is a method to determine how findable your website menu items are. In tree testing, participants are presented with a simplified text version of the website's or app's hierarchy (often represented as a tree diagram) and are asked to find specific items or complete tasks by navigating through the structure. This method helps identify navigation issues such as confusing labeling, unclear hierarchy, or dead ends.

Effective Timing to Conduct Tree Testing

Tree testing is a crucial UX research method used during the design and development process to refine navigation and verify information architecture. It helps ensure that the structure of your site meets user needs and prevents navigation problems.

Another important component of website content organization is card sorting. Although these techniques are comparable to tree testing, they take distinct approaches to the issue and are applied at different phases of the investigation. Together, they work best: tree testing assesses how well users can navigate the suggested structure, while card sorting defines and tests new website architecture.

Tree testing is very useful when evaluating various information architecture models. You can decide which version of the structure to employ based on data, by determining which one facilitates better job completion and user navigation.

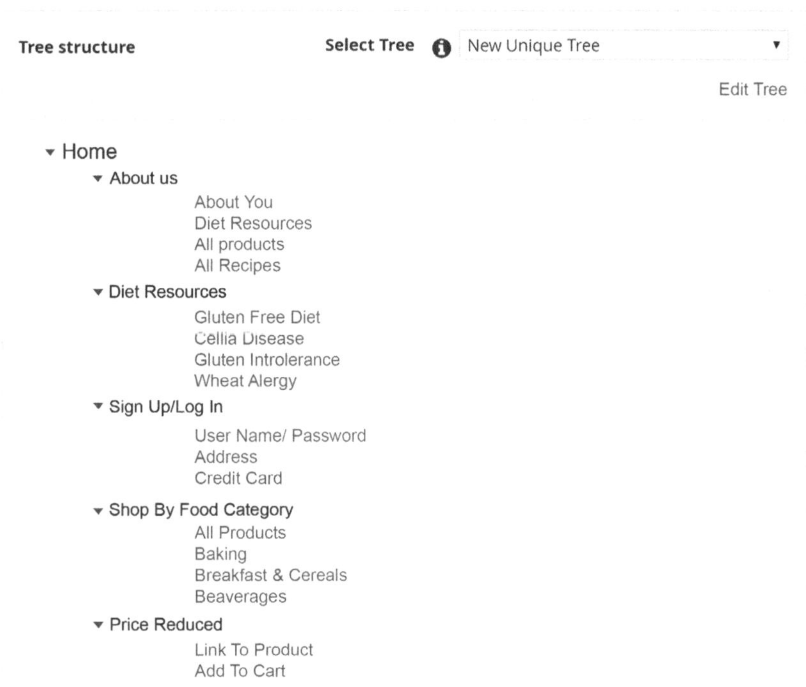

Figure 3.10: *Conducting tree testing to improve site navigation and user experience*

Effective Technique to Conduct Tree Testing

Tree testing is a simple yet effective way to assess how well your information architecture is working. To efficiently conduct a tree test, adhere to these brief steps:

1. **Define Objectives**: Determine what you hope to discover from the tree test (for example, user preferences, navigational problems).
2. **Build a Tree Structure**: Without using any visual design components, describe the application's or website's hierarchical structure.

3. **Develop activities**: Using the tree structure, create realistic activities that users must accomplish, such as "Find the contact information."
4. **Select Participants**: To take part in the test, select a representative sample of users from your intended audience.
5. **Select a Tree Testing Tool:** To set up and carry out your tree testing, use a tool like Treejack from Optimal Workshop or a comparable platform.
6. **Conduct the Test**: Using the tree structure, have participants complete the activities to conduct the test. Assure them that there are no visual clues and that the structure is the only thing to pay attention to.
7. **Analyze Results**: Examine participant pathways, success rates, and any areas of ambiguity or challenge.
8. **Make Adjustments**: Modify the information architecture to solve any issues found in light of the findings.
9. **Retest if Necessary**: After making modifications, run additional tests to make sure the original problems have been fixed.

Downsides of Tree Testing

Despite its value, tree testing has a number of disadvantages. The absence of visual context is one of its main drawbacks. Tree testing does not take into consideration the way that visual design components, such as navigation menus and icons, affect user behavior because it assesses the organization of information in a text-only format. This may result in differences between the output of tree testing and real-world user interactions on a website or application.

Tree testing has another disadvantage in that it ignores other important UX elements like content quality, layout, and general usability in favor of concentrating only on navigation and information architecture. Furthermore, it might not adequately convey the complex nature of user journeys, particularly in the case of dynamic or irregular navigation on websites or applications.

Finally, it can be difficult to comprehend the results of tree testing. Even if the data shows where customers run into problems, it might not necessarily explain why these problems arise. To obtain a thorough grasp of user behavior, this frequently calls for the use of additional research techniques like usability testing or user interviews.

Eye Tracking

A qualitative research technique called eye tracking tracks a user's gaze to determine and log where they glance on a page. It makes use of cameras and sensors. These devices track the location and motion of the eyes. The eyes are exposed to infrared light via the device. The pupil and cornea both reflect this light.

These reflections are recorded using eye tracking sensors. Algorithms then examine this information. They determine the person's point of view. Where a person focuses on a screen or in their surroundings is indicated by their point of sight. This technology aids in our understanding of how individuals perceive and interpret data.

It produces data in the form of heat maps and saccade pathways.

- **Heat Maps:** Heat maps are graphical tools that display the areas of a webpage where users are more attentive. Red areas represent longer times of focus, whereas blue regions reflect the duration of viewing. To improve the user experience, this helps identify which parts of the site are frequently visited and which are ignored, guiding layout and design changes.
- **Saccade pathways:** Saccade pathways visually show how the eyes move between points of interest on a webpage. Red circles mark focus areas, and lines trace the eye's journey. This data helps designers understand how users navigate content, revealing focus patterns and guiding design changes to improve user experience and content layout.

Effective Timing to Conduct Eye Tracking

Since eye tracking is a specialized research instrument, not all projects are a good fit for it. Nonetheless, it's helpful to recognize three essential elements when optimizing vital pages, listed as follows:

- **Blind spots:** It provides information about the areas of the website that people ignore and can be used to improve the visual hierarchy.
- **Stumbling points:** It indicates confusing spots when people keep reading the same passages.
- **Reading patterns:** This helps with readability optimization by showing how users interact with various items. Eye tracking, for example, reveals that users frequently go back to the top of tables to read the heads again, indicating that tables have to be sufficiently tiny for convenient viewing.

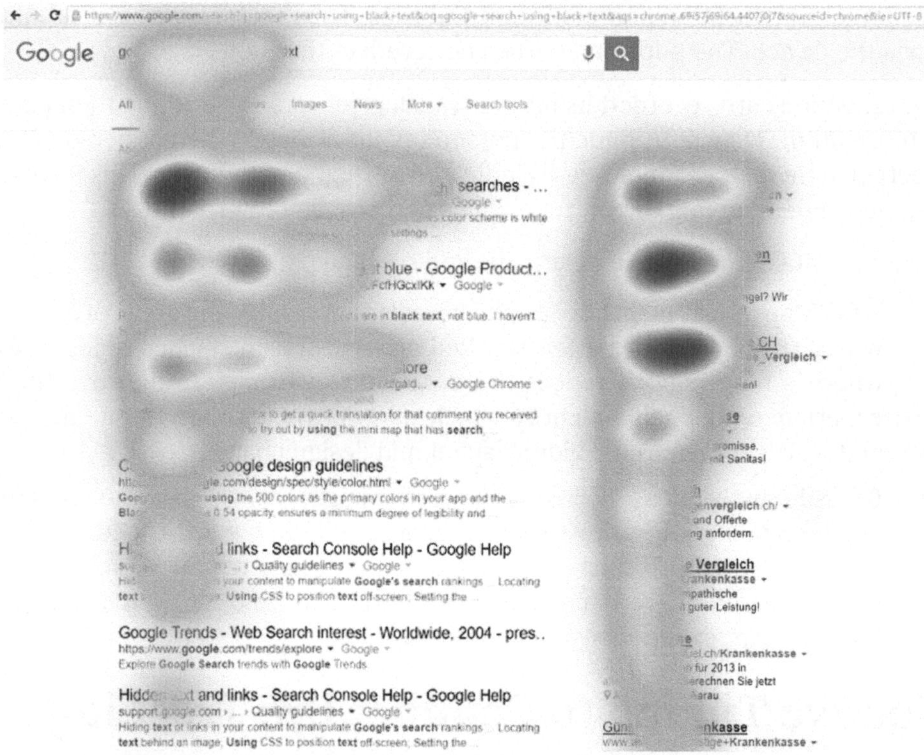

Figure 3.11: *Eye-tracking test in progress, revealing user focus areas*

Effective Technique to Conduct Eye Tracking

The following quick steps are involved in conducting an eye tracking test:

1. **Define objectives:** Determine what you hope to discover from the eye tracking test (for example, navigational problems and user attentiveness).
2. **Select participants:** To guarantee pertinent outcomes, pick a sample that is representative of your intended audience.
3. **Set up equipment:** Make sure the eye tracking software and hardware are accurately configured.
4. **Build the test:** Assign activities that replicate common user interactions with your product or page to participants.
5. **Perform the test:** As participants finish the tasks, the eye tracking system collects their gaze patterns and eye movements.
6. **Analyze data:** Examine gaze plots, saccade paths, and heat maps to find reading patterns, blind spots, and stumbling locations.

7. **Report findings:** Summarize the insights and recommend changes to improve the user experience based on the collected data.

Downsides of Eye Tracking

Though insightful, eye tracking is not without its limitations. To begin with, it isn't always able to tell if users are actually noticing everything they look at. It is possible for users to quickly scan a section of the screen without realizing its significance. This implies that user awareness of particular features cannot be ensured by eye tracking alone.

Furthermore, eye tracking does not reveal the motivations underlying users' gaze habits. It doesn't explain why users glance at particular elements, even though it displays where and how long they do so. Surveys and other supplemental tools are required to comprehend user motives and thinking.

Not every user finds eye tracking to be beneficial. Accurate tracking can be hampered by things like small pupils, contact lenses, glasses, and fast eye movements. As such, it could not be appropriate for some people, which restrict its use to a variety of user groups.

A/B Testing

Selecting between two design aspects that could impact user interaction or the overall experience presents challenges for UX designers frequently. This is where A/B testing is useful. This method allows UX designers to test user reactions to various design aspects without depending just on theoretical knowledge or intuition. The idea behind A/B testing, sometimes referred to as split testing, is rather simple: you make two or more versions of something, allow users to interact with them, and track how they are used in real-world situations. In order to allow you to compare the performance of A and B, each version is shown to a different segment of the intended audience.

Here is an example of A/B testing:

A company that runs an online news platform wants to increase the number of newsletter sign-ups. They create two different sign-up forms to test which one attracts more subscribers. Version A, the current form, has a simple layout with a single field for the user's email address. Version B, the new form, has a more visually appealing design with a headline that highlights the benefits of subscribing and includes fields for the user's name and email address.

The platform's visitors are randomly divided into two groups: half see Version A and the other half see Version B. The test runs for a month, during which the company tracks the number of sign-ups each version generates.

At the end of the month, the results show that Version B has a 20% higher sign-up rate than Version A. The enhanced design and added fields seem to have convinced more users of the newsletter's value. Based on these findings, the company decides to adopt Version B as their standard sign-up form, successfully increasing their newsletter subscriptions through this A/B testing process.

Effective Timing to Conduct A/B Testing

When you need to make data-driven judgments about modifications to your website, app, or marketing efforts, A/B testing works best. It is employed when comparing two iterations of an element to ascertain which one works better at reaching a particular objective, such as raising user engagement, conversions, or click-through rates. This approach is especially useful when the modifications you are thinking about have the potential to have a big influence on user behavior or business results. To test variants in call-to-action buttons, headlines, page layouts, or email subject lines, for instance, A/B testing is perfect. You may reduce risks, find the best design or content options, and improve the user experience based on actual user interactions by conducting controlled experiments and evaluating the outcomes.

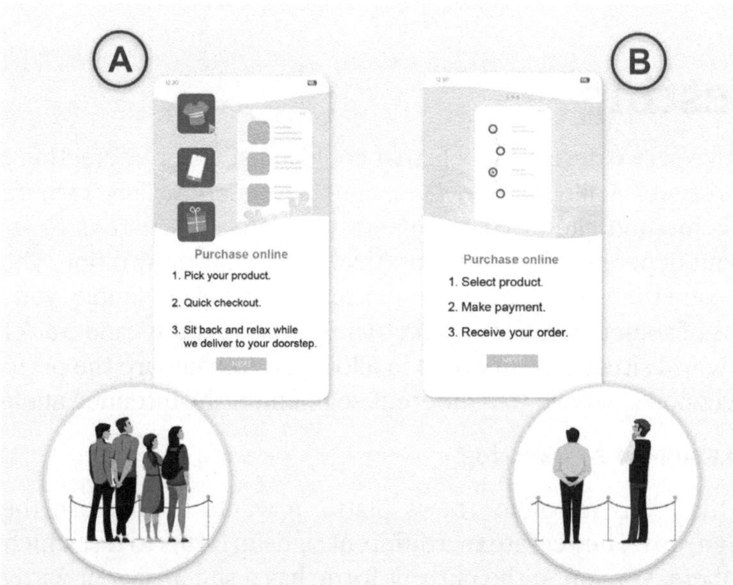

***Figure 3.12**: Comparing designs with A/B testing for better user insights*

Effective Technique to Conduct A/B Testing

The efficacy of A/B testing is derived from both its conception and its implementation. The conclusions you get from an A/B test can be significantly influenced by the way it is set up, run, and analyzed.

So, let us learn how to conduct A/B Testing:

1. **Set objectives:** Determine the aspects of your website that you would like to enhance, including user engagement, click-through rates, or conversion rates.
2. **Create variations:** Create two iterations of the element (Version A and Version B) that you wish to test.
3. **Divide your audience:** Assign your audience to two groups at random, and show one version to each group.
4. **Hit the test:** Show the variations to the appropriate groups at the same time and record the interactions between them.
5. **Analyze results:** Examine how well the two versions performed in relation to your predetermined objectives.
6. **Implement the Best Version:** Make use of the version that exhibits superior performance based on the information gathered.

Tools for A/B Testing:

- **Google Optimize:** Free tool for A/B testing and personalizing website experiences.
- **Optimizely:** Comprehensive platform for experimentation, including A/B and multivariate testing.
- **VWO (Visual Website Optimizer):** Tool for A/B and split URL testing to optimize user experiences.
- **Unbounce:** Landing page builder with A/B testing features to boost conversion rates.
- **Adobe Target:** Adobe Experience Cloud tool offering advanced A/B testing and personalization.

Downsides of A/B Testing

Although A/B testing is popular for improving user experience, it has its own downsides and challenges that need to be taken into account.

- **Limited Scope:** Because A/B testing normally only assesses one variable at a time, user behavior may be understood more narrowly. This implies that it might overlook significant information by failing to take into consideration the interactions between various items on a page or the overall user experience.
- **Time and Traffic Requirements:** To get statistically significant results, effective A/B testing needs a substantial amount of time and traffic. The optimization process can be slowed significantly for smaller websites or those with minimal traffic because it can take a while to collect enough data to make informed conclusions.

Five-Second Tests

In the field, five-second testing is a popular technique for conducting usability studies. With people's attention spans getting shorter in our fast-paced society, every second counts when it comes to holding their interest. If your goal is to provide outstanding user experiences, you've probably heard about five-second testing. The procedure is giving a member of your target audience a five-second preview of your design, whether it is a website or an app. After that, you ask the participant a few questions while hiding the image. Finding out if their initial impression matches your expectations is the goal. Did they understand the key point? Can they recall the name of the brand? Without doing a lot of usability testing, you may quickly assess the impact of your product using this method.

The five-second rule is not unqualified, though. The complexity of your design and your research goals may require you to modify this time frame. The main goal of five-second assessment is to evaluate initial impressions throughout a limited window of time while viewing.

Effective Timing to Conduct Five-second Testing

A UX research technique that works well at different phases of design and development is five-second testing. It works particularly well for perfecting your homepage's hero section or any other important page. This method assists you in determining whether your headline and introduction are obvious; if they aren't, it may be time to reconsider your design.

Five-second tests are wonderful for rapidly evaluating the effectiveness of landing pages for particular campaigns and your marketing messages. They are also useful for planning a comprehensive redesign of an already-existing product because they let you identify places that require big modifications by comparing the new and old versions of the product.

Figure 3.13: *Evaluating initial user impact with five-second testing*

Effective Technique to Conduct Five-second Testing

To get the most out of five-second testing, it's important to follow a structured approach. Here are some effective techniques to ensure your tests yield valuable insights:

1. **Define Goals and Prepare Materials:** Set objectives and gather designs.
2. **Upload Designs and Set Up Test**: Use a tool to upload designs and configure the test.
3. **Create Questions**: Develop clear questions for participants.
4. **Recruit and Test**: Find participants, show designs for 5 seconds, and ask questions.
5. **Analyze Results**: Review feedback to draw conclusions.

Key Questions to Consider During a Five-second Test

The purpose of your five-second test questions should be to gather details about the specific objectives you have in mind for evaluation. There are various types of them depending on what your study aims for.

Tests of recognition questions

- What specific components, phrases, or visuals do you recall seeing?
- Do you remember any particular text or headline?
- Which components come to mind?

Comprehension-testing questions

- What do you believe this page's primary goal is?
- Based on the design, could you explain the work that this company does?
- What is the main point being made, in your opinion?

Reorganization test questions

- Which details, phrases, or visuals do you still recall seeing?
- Can you think of a particular passage or headline?
- Which parts are you able to remember?

Test-of-completion questions

- In your opinion, what is the primary goal of this page?
- Can you explain the work that this company accomplishes using the design?
- What is, in your opinion, the main point being made?

Test questions for branding

- Was the name of the company or a brand visible? If so, do you remember it?
- Were any logos or brand symbols identifiable to you?
- Based on the design, what would you think is the main message of the brand?
- Which product do you believe this company sells?

Test-of-engagement questions

- Did the design intend for you to click, join up, or make a buy, for example?
- Did anything in particular grab your interest or compel you to read on?
- Were there any incentives, bargains, or offers made? Do you remember them?

Downsides of Five-second Testing

The five-second test has its limits, despite being a quick and efficient approach to determining users' initial thoughts. Due to its simplicity, it might not provide an in-depth analysis of the user experience as a whole. It could miss more in-depth engagement and subtle interactions that develop over time because it concentrates on short exposures to designs. Furthermore, given the short length of time, the test may not fully capture every aspect of user responses, particularly for intricate designs or jobs requiring longer user engagement. The five-second test is a great way to determine initial impressions, but it might not be enough to capture each aspect of user behavior and preferences. It's best to combine the five-second test with additional research techniques that enable deeper investigation in order to obtain a greater understanding of user experience.

Quick Guide - Categories of Methods

Understanding the categories of various research methods is essential for selecting the right approach to gather user insights. The following table categorizes common UX research methods based on whether they are qualitative, quantitative, generative, evaluative, behavioral, or attitudinal. This helps in identifying the most suitable method for specific research goals.

Method	Qualitative	Quantitative	Generative	Evaluative	Behavioral	Attitudinal
User interviews	Yes		Yes			Yes
Focus group	Yes		Yes			Yes
Surveys		Yes		Yes		Yes
Card sorting (Open/Hybrid)	Yes		Yes			Yes
Card sorting (Close)		Yes		Yes		Yes
Diary studies	Yes		Yes	Yes	Yes	Yes
Usability studies	Yes			Yes	Yes	
Field studies	Yes		Yes		Yes	
Tree testing	Yes	Yes		Yes		
Eye tracking		Yes		Yes	Yes	
A/B testing		Yes		Yes	Yes	

Five-second testing	Yes	Yes		Yes		

Table 3.4: *Research methods and their categories*

UX Research Tools

Choosing the appropriate instruments for each research approach is essential in the field of UX research in order to get relevant data and enhance user experiences. Certain tools are needed for different research approaches in order to collect and process data efficiently. Communication tools are essential for conducting in-depth interviews and focus groups with people. Structured questionnaires used in surveys yield quantitative data, and card sorting aids in information architecture organization. While usability testing assesses a design's functionalities, diary studies document long-term user interactions and experiences. While usability of website navigation is evaluated by tree testing, field studies monitor user behavior in natural environments. Eye tracking reveals where users look, A/B testing compares two versions of a design to determine the better performer, and five-second testing measures initial user impressions. The following table outlines various research methods and the tools best suited for each, aiding researchers in choosing the appropriate resources for their UX studies. These tools provide various functionalities to conduct each type of research effectively, whether it's gathering qualitative insights through interviews or quantifying user behavior through A/B testing.

Research Method	**Tools**
Interviews	Zoom, Skype, Google Meet, Microsoft Teams
Focus Groups	Zoom, Microsoft Teams, Webex, Qualtrics
Surveys	SurveyMonkey, Google Forms, Typeform, Qualtrics
Card Sorting	Optimal Workshop, UsabilityHub, Trello
Diary Studies	DScout, ExperienceFellow, Ethnio
Usability Testing	UserTesting, UsabilityHub, Optimal Workshop, Lookback
Field Studies	DScout, Ethnio, ExperienceFellow
Tree Testing	Optimal Workshop, Treejack
Eye Tracking	Tobii Pro, EyeQuant, LookTracker
A/B Testing	Google Optimize, Optimizely, VWO (Visual Website Optimizer)
Five Second Testing	UsabilityHub, Lookback, Optimal Workshop

Table 3.5: *Overview of research methods and corresponding tools*

This table provides a clear overview of the research methods and the corresponding tools commonly used for each method.

Real-World UX Research Case Studies

Real-world UX research case studies show how companies solve practical problems to improve user experiences. These examples highlight diverse research methods, how understanding user behavior and needs can lead to better product designs and higher customer satisfaction.

Google Search's Mobile Optimization

The challenge was to improve search usability on mobile devices.

Google wanted to ensure that users' web searches on mobile devices were speedy and seamless, given the increasing number of people using these devices for this purpose. They had to figure out any problems and comprehend how people used Google Search on their phones.

Goals:

- Make Google Search easy to use on mobile devices.
- Guarantee that users may locate relevant search results fast.
- Boost mobile user engagement and happiness.

UX Research Methods Used

Eye-Tracking Studies:

- **Description**: This approach made use of eye-tracking technology to track users' movements and interactions with the mobile search results.
- **Outcome:** Gave insights into the visual hierarchy of search results and user focus regions. Highlighted the components that received the greatest attention as well as the areas where users ran into problems or were confused.

Remote Usability Testing:

- **Description**: In-person usability testing was carried out with participants utilizing their personal mobile devices. Using screen-sharing software, researchers observed and gathered comments.
- **Outcome:** Highlighted real-world problems that consumers encountered, including navigational difficulty, sluggish load times, and reading concerns on smaller screens.

Contextual Inquiry:

- **Description:** While people conducted mobile device searches in their natural settings, researchers watched them. This gave background information about the typical search environments used by users.

- **Outcome**: Environmental elements like lighting, distractions and the necessity for fast information retrieval in situations involving on-the-go usage were identified as having an impact on mobile search utilization.

A/B Testing:

- **Description**: Users tested many iterations of the mobile search experience to see which design components improved usability and engagement.
- **Outcome**: Assisting in the selection of the best interactive components, font sizes, and layout. This allowed Google to adjust the user interface according to actual user preferences and interactions.

Surveys and Feedback:

- **Description**: Deployed surveys to mobile users to gather qualitative feedback on their search experiences, preferences, and pain points.
- **Outcome**: Provided direct input from users about what they liked, disliked, and wished to see improvement. Identified common themes and issues that guided design decisions.

Key Changes Implemented

1. **Design that is Simple and Responsive:**
    a. Developed a simpler, more intuitive user interface that dynamically adjusted to various screen sizes.
    b. Made sure that visible and easily available primary navigation buttons and the search bar were among the vital aspects.
2. **Optimal Times for Loading:**
    a. Enhanced the user experience overall by speeding up the loading of pages and search results on mobile devices.
    b. Reduced load times by utilizing strategies like optimized picture sizes and lazy loading.
3. **Improved Interaction and Readability:**
    a. Modified button widths, spacing, and text sizes to make them easier to read and use on smaller screens.
    b. Improved touch targets to improve user pleasure and error-free interaction.
4. **Better Presentation and Relevance of Results:**
    a. Enhanced the algorithm to give preference to mobile-friendly material and deliver more relevant results catered to mobile users.

   b. Improved the way that featured and search snippets are presented to provide succinct, understandable information.

4. **Integration of Voice Search:**

   a. Improved voice search features to accommodate mobile users who favored hands-free communication.

   b. Made certain that the voice search results were presented on mobile devices in a manner that was designed for speedy consumption.

5. **Maintaining Visual and Functional Consistency:**

   a. Ensured that various mobile platforms and devices used the same visual language and functionality.

   b. Made certain that consumers transferring between devices experienced a smooth transition from mobile to desktop experiences.

Outcome

The optimization efforts led to a significantly improved mobile search experience. Users reported faster load times, easier navigation, and more relevant search results. The enhanced readability and interaction design contributed to higher user satisfaction and longer engagement times. Google's mobile search saw increased usage and better overall performance metrics, affirming the success of the UX research and design improvements.

Amazon's Checkout Process Improvement

Challenge was to reduce cart abandonment rates during checkout.

One of the biggest online retailers in the world, Amazon, had a serious problem with cart abandonment. When customers add products to their shopping basket but depart the website before making the transaction, this happens. Elevated rates of cart abandonment may lead to significant loss of revenue and suggest areas of friction in the checkout process.

Goals:

- Identifying and removing obstacles that lead customers to abandon their carts is the first goal.
- Simplifying the checkout process to make it more user-friendly is the second.
- Increase conversion rates and overall user satisfaction.

UX Research Methods Used

Usability Testing:

- **Description**: Real users were asked to go through the checkout process, and interactions were watched and recorded by researchers.
- **Outcome**: Highlighted particular areas of difficulty or frustration for consumers, such as trouble entering shipping information, unclear payment alternatives, and unforeseen shipping expenses.

User Surveys:

- **Description**: The purpose of the surveys was to obtain firsthand feedback from users who left their carts empty regarding their reasons for not completing the purchase.
- **Outcome**: The information gathered indicated recurring problems such as the absence of guest checkout choices, security concerns, and a lack of preferred payment methods.

A/B Testing:

- **Description**: To compare which checkout process version resulted in higher completion rates, various iterations were evaluated with user segments.
- **Outcome**: Made it possible for Amazon to determine which modifications, including a simplified design and more lucid progress markers, would be most beneficial.

Analytics Review:

- **Description**: Tracked customer behavior through the checkout funnel by analyzing web analytics and identifying specific drop-off points.
- **Outcome**: Indicated particular phases during which customers were most prone to give up on their carts, directing focused enhancements.

Key Changes Implemented

1. **Simplified Navigation:**

    a. Converted the checkout procedure from numerous pages to a single page, saving the number of steps.

    b. Added clear progress indicators to let users know how many steps are left.

2. **Improved Methods of Payment:**

    a. Included more payment choices, such as installment plans and digital wallets.

   b. Enhanced the payment process's security and clarity to foster user confidence.

3. **Exact Shipping Details:**

   a. Presented shipping charges and estimated arrival timeframes up front before users could make a payment.

   b. Provided a variety of shipping choices, such as regular and expedited shipment.

4. **Guest Checkout Option:**

   a. To lower the barrier to making a transaction, a guest checkout option was introduced for those who did not wish to register an account.

5. **Enhanced Mobile Experience:**

   a. Made sure the checkout procedure was completely mobile-friendly, giving users on the go a smooth experience.

Outcome

The enhancements resulted in a notable decrease in cart abandonment rates and a rise in successfully completed transactions. Customers said that the checkout process was easier to understand and more seamless, which improved their level of happiness and platform loyalty. By removing obstacles that had prevented transactions, the expedited checkout procedure enhanced both the customer experience and Amazon's revenue growth.

Conclusion

In this chapter, we explored various UX research methods and their applications. We looked at a variety of UX research techniques and their uses in this chapter. We discovered that in order to better understand user behavior and enhance the user experience, various projects and scenarios call for various methodologies. When we apply the appropriate methodology to the correct project, we can obtain important information that informs our design choices.

Usability testing, for example, reveals areas in which customers find a product difficult to use, while surveys and interviews offer firsthand user feedback, and A/B testing allows us to compare multiple design iterations and determine which one works best. Selecting the right method for a given work is essential because each offers advantages and is appropriate in different circumstances.

We also explored a number of UX research areas and techniques. We can get the most of these tools if we know how to use them and comprehend their different categories, such as quantitative versus qualitative tools. As we wrap up this chapter, it is clear that mastering UX research methods and tools is key to creating user-friendly products. We may create experiences that genuinely satisfy user requirements and expectations by carefully implementing these techniques.

In the upcoming chapter, we shall get into User Mapping in UX. We will get knowledge on how to map the customer journey, construct user personas, and deal with user stories. These methods will support our efforts to better comprehend and represent the user experience.

Key Terms

- **Attitudinal Research**: Research methods that explore users' feelings, thoughts, and perceptions about a product or service, often involving surveys and interviews.
- **Behavioral Research**: Research methods that observe and analyze users' actions and interactions with a product, often using tools like heat maps and user recordings.
- **Competitor Analysis**: Evaluating the strengths and weaknesses of competitors' products to gain insights for improving one's own product.
- **Lean UX Design**: A design methodology focusing on user feedback, testing, and iterative improvement to create user-centered products efficiently.
- **Quantitative Data**: Numerical data that can be measured and analyzed statistically, often used to identify patterns and trends in user behavior.
- **Qualitative Data**: Descriptive data that provides insights into users' experiences, feelings, and motivations, often gathered through interviews and observations.
- **Screening Survey**: A preliminary survey used to filter and select suitable participants for a research study based on specific criteria.
- **Stakeholder Interviews**: Conversations with individuals who have a vested interest in the research outcomes to gather insights and align project goals.
- **User Research Plan**: A document outlining the objectives, methods, and logistics of a user research project, ensuring a structured and efficient approach.
- **UX Research**: The process of understanding user behaviors, needs, and motivations through various research methods to inform the design of user-centered products.
- **UX Research Methodologies**: Different approaches and techniques used in UX research to gather and analyze user data, including both qualitative and quantitative methods.

- **Key Performance Indicators (KPIs)**: Metrics used to evaluate the success of a product or project in achieving specific business objectives.
- **Moderated Research**: Research conducted with the active involvement of a facilitator or moderator to guide participants and ensure data collection aligns with research goals.
- **Unmoderated Research**: Research conducted without a facilitator, allowing participants to complete tasks independently, often used for gathering large-scale data.
- **Attitudinal Data**: Data that records users' ideas, viewpoints, and beliefs, offering insights into their motivations and attitudes.
- **Behavioral Data**: Data that tracks the actions users take when interacting with products, completing tasks, or solving problems, providing insights into actual user behavior.
- **Card Sorting**: A UX research technique used to understand how users categorize information, helping to design intuitive navigation structures.
- **Hybrid Card Sorting**: A type of card sorting where participants can develop new categories in addition to using pre-established ones.
- **Open Card Sorting**: A type of card sorting where participants group topics into logical categories and name these groups themselves, revealing unique perspectives on information architecture.
- **Focus Groups**: A qualitative research technique where a small group discusses their attitudes, views, and experiences, providing rapid and detailed insights into user preferences and potential uses for a product.
- **Surveys**: Structured questionnaires to collect both qualitative and quantitative data, adaptable to various stages of the product development process.
- **Diary Studies**: A research method where participants consistently document their thoughts, feelings, and behaviors over time, providing insights into long-term user experiences and behaviors.
- **A/B Testing**: A method to compare two versions of a design to determine which performs better in terms of user interaction or achieving specific goals. It involves showing different versions to different user groups and analyzing their interactions to make data-driven decisions.
- **Eye Tracking**: A qualitative research technique that uses cameras and sensors to track and record where users look on a page, producing data in the form of heat maps and saccade pathways to understand user attention and navigation.
- **Field Studies**: Research method involving observing users in their natural environments to understand genuine behaviors and demands, revealing real-world usage scenarios and contextual challenges.

- **Five-Second Testing**: A quick usability testing technique where users view a design for five seconds and then answer questions to evaluate their initial impressions, helping assess the effectiveness of key messages and visual appeal.
- **Usability Testing**: An essential component of UX research that involves testing a website or app with actual users to measure the ease of completing common tasks, identifying usability issues and areas for improvement.
- **In-Person Usability Testing**: A usability testing method where a researcher observes and records participants completing tasks in a controlled, lab-like environment, allowing for direct interaction and observation.
- **Moderated Usability Testing**: A usability testing method where a researcher guides the participant through tasks, observes their actions, and asks questions in real-time, conducted either in-person or via remote video conferencing.
- **Remote Usability Testing**: A usability testing method where participants perform tasks in their normal environment, which can be moderated (with a facilitator) or unmoderated (without a facilitator), using software to capture interactions and feedback.
- **Tree Testing**: A method to evaluate the findability of website menu items by having participants navigate a simplified text version of the site's hierarchy to complete tasks, identifying navigation issues such as unclear labeling or dead ends.
- **Heat Maps**: Visual representations used in eye tracking that show areas of a webpage where users focus their attention, with colors indicating the duration of focus (red for longer times, blue for shorter times).
- **Saccade Pathways**: Visual representations used in eye tracking to show the movement of the eyes between points of interest on a webpage, with red circles marking focus areas and lines tracing the eye's journey.
- **Facilitator**: In usability testing, a UX researcher who runs the test sessions, records data, and provides instructions to participants.

Chapter 4
The Art of UX Mapping

Introduction

Explore the dynamic landscape of User Experience (UX) Mapping! We will go over the fundamentals of UX mapping in this chapter, which is an important tool for comprehending and enhancing user interactions with products and services. To establish a strong foundation for comprehension, we start with the basics of UX mapping. After that, we will delve into the idea of user personas, which enable us to recognize and relate to our target market.

We will also look at other kinds of UX maps, such as empathy maps and customer journey maps, each of which has a special function in illustrating user experiences and feelings. We will also go over the effective tools that can be used to make these maps, which will make the process more effective and informative.

Structure

In this chapter, we will discuss the following topics:

- Introduction to UX Mapping
- Importance of UX Mapping
- Create a User Experience Map
- User Persona
- Key Components of a User Persona
- Types of User Experience Mapping
- Customer Journey Maps
- Empathy Maps
- Experience Maps
- Service Blueprints
- Best Tools for User Experience Mapping

Introduction to UX Mapping

An excellent technique to learn about your consumers' needs, wants, and concerns is through User Experience mapping. Even though a lot of businesses are adept at gathering consumer information, it doesn't fully capture their complaints and experiences. One of the best tools for corporate storytelling is a user experience map, which tells a story effectively.

To put it simply, UX mapping is among the greatest methods for informing your team and stakeholders about your discoveries and insights. It assists in bridging the gap between your created product and what users or customers require. Obtaining the whole picture is essential before beginning any construction or even design work.

Maps are excellent resources to:

- Keep things in perspective and focus on the core idea
- Transition from problem identification to solution discovery
- Identify gaps and problems
- Provide all of our discoveries and insights in one spot. Assemble the team and interested parties around the issue at hand.

An experience map shows the path a consumer takes when using a good or service. It also emphasizes the connection between a company's experience and that of its customers. Businesses can identify strategic opportunities, comprehend customer pain areas, and develop innovative solutions by looking at the experience from the customer's point of view.

Importance of UX Mapping

The primary objective of user experience mapping is to acquire a practical comprehension of the experiences that consumers have while utilizing your product. Encouraging customers to use your product more effectively and having a seamless overall experience is the ultimate goal.

Customer experience maps provide a broad overview of human behavior at several stages. These stages include the many design processes, the actions that users must perform, the reasoning behind each action, and the feelings that are connected to the outcome. This usually results in a thorough comprehension of the user's perspective on the product experience.

In the following ways, experience mapping might be beneficial:

- Offers a panorama perspective of the complete client journey.
- Assemble teams to address certain consumer obstacles in order to identify key customer journey patterns and areas where further development will have the most influence.

- Reduce unfavorable customer experiences by identifying critical processes and decision points, and increase customer conversion rates more quickly.
- Increased client retention by knowing how customers go through, for instance, every phase of a procurement cycle and ensuring that all relevant information is provided to and accessible by all parties.
- Gives a company the ability to focus on a single customer journey through a particular channel.
- Knowing the right metrics helps us see where customers succeed or drop off, so we can find ways to bring them back.
- Enables companies to rank the steps in their customer experience plan in order of importance.
- Highlights the gaps between different departments and channels.

Fundamentals of UX Mapping

Fundamentals of UX mapping involve creating a visual story of a user's experience with a product or service. It starts by understanding who the users are and what they need. Next, it tracks their journey step-by-step, highlighting key actions, feelings, and pain points. This map helps teams see where users face problems and find opportunities for improvement. It is a powerful way to align everyone on the same goals and make better design and business decisions. In essence, UX mapping turns user experiences into clear, actionable insights.

UX maps come in various forms, but each should incorporate a point of view, scope, and focus.

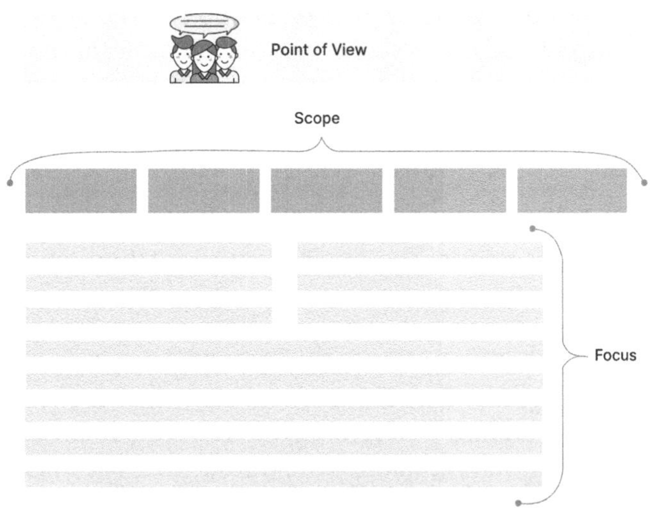

***Figure 4.1**: Essential Elements of a UX Map*

Point of View

The term "point of view" in UX design refers to viewing the product or service from the viewpoint of the user. This method helps designers gain a thorough understanding of the needs of customers, objectives, and potential frustrations. Designers may produce more efficient and user-focused solutions that directly address user pain points by putting themselves in the user's shoes. As an example, the designer would take into account the user's feelings–such as excitement, confusion, or frustration – while they browsed, picked out, and purchased the products. User experiences that are more intuitive and fulfilling are produced by using an empathy-driven design approach.

In order to acquire clarity on the business goals and plans, it is imperative that you involve the stakeholders in the process of building a point of view.

Think on these important queries:

- What is the organization's mission and direction?
- Which markets and subsets are we focusing on?
- What are the strategic and business goals?
- What knowledge gaps need filling?

Scope

The parameters of the UX mapping procedure are specified in the scope. It describes the elements of the user experience that will be present and those that won't. This makes the mapping exercise more doable and focused. The beginning and ending points of the trip, the amount of detail needed, and the channels involved must all be identified in order to establish the scope. For example, if the objective is to enhance the online buying experience, the scope may encompass the entire process from website visitation to successful purchase completion, with a concentration on desktop interactions and an exclusion of mobile app experiences.

Focus

UX mapping centers on pinpointing the crucial elements of the user journey that require attention. It entails identifying particular tasks, interactions, or pain spots that are essential to the user's experience as a whole. Designers may dig deeper into the most crucial areas and create tailored solutions by focusing their attention. For instance, if customer feedback suggests that there are issues with the checkout process, the emphasis should be on outlining and refining the procedures for choosing products, providing payment details, and completing the transaction. The most important issues are taken care of first thanks to this focused strategy.

Structure

Once you have chosen your perspective and focus, selecting the right structure for your experience map is crucial. Two common structures are chronological and hierarchical, each effective in different real-world scenarios.

- **Chronological**: This structure highlights each step of the user journey in a time-based sequence, from start to finish. It works best when the user experience involves a clear progression, such as an online shopping process from homepage to purchase. By visualizing key interactions, emotional highs, and pain points at every stage, designers can identify areas for improvement. This method is especially useful when tracking time-sensitive or step-by-step processes.
- **Hierarchical**: This structure organizes tasks and interactions by importance and dependency levels, breaking down complex processes into manageable parts. It is ideal for scenarios where multiple tasks contribute to a larger objective, such as categorizing tasks like "View Product Details," "Browse Categories," and "Checkout" under the main goal of "Purchase Product." Hierarchical structures help clarify task priority and workflow, making them effective for multi-step processes where understanding task dependencies is essential for improving the user experience.

Selecting the Format

The person or entity that will be using the information in the diagram as their primary source should be taken into account while selecting a format. Organize the work by defining the objectives of the map-making process, the issues we hope to resolve, and the knowledge gaps. Finally, decide how the map will be used and what result we hope to attain. Should our focus be on a particular issue or an overview of the system as a whole? Do we need more than one map to depict an experience's past, present, and future states?

Create a User Experience Map

Creating a UX map is essential for understanding and improving the user experience with your product or service. A UX map visually outlines the steps users take, their interactions, and their emotions throughout their journey. By mapping this experience, you can identify pain points, understand user needs, and uncover opportunities for enhancement. This process aligns your team and stakeholders, ensuring everyone is on the same page and working towards a better user experience.

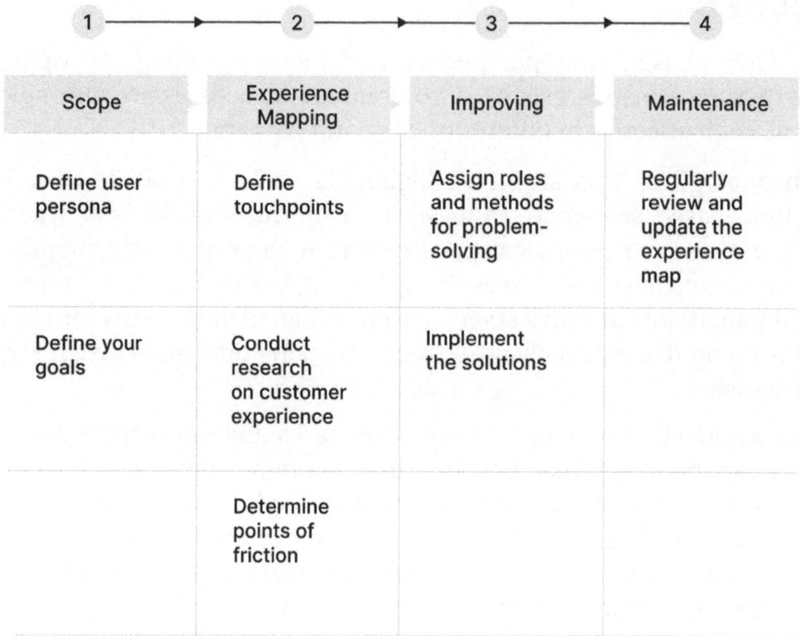

***Figure 4.2**: The process of creating an experience map*

This overview highlights the key steps needed to create an effective user experience map:

1. Develop a persona
2. Perform user research
3. Define the journey stages
4. Define customer interactions
5. Pinpoint friction points
6. Resolve issues

Step 1: Developing a Persona

Personas are made-up characters that are based on research and are meant to represent various user types that could utilize your site, product, or service in a similar way. They support your understanding of user objectives, experiences, behaviors, and needs. In order to understand your target users' needs and develop empathy for them, UX designers begin by performing user research. Based on this research, personas are created that represent the needs, objectives, and behavioral patterns of the target audience.

By clarifying issues and demonstrating how they affect people's lives, personas assist companies in connecting with clients in a more strategic manner, which is advantageous to all parties involved. Personas are frequently developed in the Define phase of design thinking when designers combine the findings from the Empathize phase. This facilitates transitioning to the ideation stage.

Step 2: Performing User Research

The next step involves directly engaging with users to gather insights. An accurate user experience map cannot rely on guesses and assumptions; it must be founded on real-time data collected through surveys, interviews, and observations from actual users. This approach allows for the development of solutions tailored to users' needs.

In the previous chapter, you already learned about different research methods. Choose the research method that suits your requirements – methods such as interviews, surveys, focus groups, and usability testing are essential for obtaining precise and relevant data on user interactions with a product or service. While you might need to incentivize participation, many users are willing to contribute if they see their feedback will lead to improvements for others.

Try to determine the following for each stage of the journey:

- What were their objectives, and what did they hope to accomplish?
- What kind of approach did they expect?
- The account of the customer's encounter with your product or service from start to finish (in their own words).
- The individual's emotional state and any pain points they felt when interacting with the various stages or touchpoints, along with the reason behind them.
- Additional ideas they had at the time.
- The amount of time needed to complete each stage of interacting with the product.

Step 3: Define the Journey Stages

User experience maps are organized into stages or phases and have a structured format. Every stage of the journey has a specific objective the user wishes to accomplish. These stages demonstrate how, when, and where customers find your product, become aware of its advantages and features, decide to buy it over opponents, and finish the buying process. This facilitates targeted enhancements to improve the entire experience by helping designers and stakeholders understand the users' interactions and decisions at each level.

Once your persona has been developed, determine the customer journey phases. Find out the steps involved in selecting and purchasing your goods or services. List the steps your consumer goes through in a nutshell, based on their persona. Specify how, when, and where customers will learn about your business, investigate your goods or services, pick you over competitors, make a purchase, and keep in touch. With a comprehensive image of the user experience provided by this thorough mapping, you can identify areas for optimization and ensure your consumers have a positive and seamless experience.

Step 4: Define Customer Interactions

Customer interactions refer to all points where a customer engages with your product or service during their journey. These interactions include every instance of contact, whether through digital platforms, physical touchpoints, or human interactions.

***Figure 4.3**: Customer purchasing lifecycle*

In an e-commerce setting, customer interactions might include:

- Browsing products on the website or mobile app.
- Checking out product descriptions, reviews, and ratings.
- Adding products to the shopping cart.
- Going through the checkout process.
- Getting order confirmation emails or SMS notifications.
- Monitoring the delivery status of the order.
- Leaving feedback or reviews once the product is received.

While this list may seem extensive, it represents just a few of the touchpoints! Each interaction offers a chance for customers to engage with the product and make decisions affecting their overall experience. Understanding and optimizing these touchpoints is vital for businesses to ensure a seamless and satisfying customer journey.

Step 5: Pinpoint Friction Points

Finding friction points comes next, after you have defined your character and comprehended their objectives. The best way to accomplish this is by working together and utilizing data from earlier studies. Enhancing the user journey requires identifying friction points in a user experience map. This entails identifying places where consumers encounter difficulties, annoyances, or inefficiencies. Begin with obtaining user input via questionnaires, interviews, usability assessments, and correspondence with customer service. Gaining insight into consumers' problems from their personal experiences is essential for making improvements.

Studying how users behave is also essential. It is possible to identify usability problems by observing how users browse and interact with the product, how often they complete tasks, and where errors occur. Session lengths, bounce rates, and conversion rates are examples of metrics that can be reviewed to provide quantitative information about user challenges.

Visualizing the user journey by mapping each step from initial awareness to post-purchase interactions helps identify where users might encounter friction. Engaging in collaborative efforts with stakeholders from diverse areas, including marketing, sales, and customer support, enhances comprehension of potential issues. By ranking these friction points according to their importance and seriousness, companies may optimize the customer experience by addressing the most pressing problems first. This proactive strategy promotes long-term loyalty and retention while raising consumer satisfaction.

Step 6: Resolve Issues

In the resolve issues stage of creating a user experience map, the primary goal is to address the challenges and friction points identified throughout the mapping process. This phase is crucial for ensuring that the final user experience is optimized and aligns with both user needs and business objectives.

It's essential to prioritize the issues based on their impact on the overall user experience and the business goals. By focusing on the most critical issues, teams can allocate resources effectively and address the most pressing concerns promptly. This involves generating ideas and considering various approaches to resolve the identified problems. Once potential solutions are identified, teams develop prototypes to visualize how the proposed changes will address the issues.

By thoroughly addressing the identified issues, teams can create a user experience that delights users and drives long-term success for the product or service.

User Persona

In this section, you will find an in-depth look into user personas.

A user persona is like creating a character in a story, but instead of a book, it is for designing products or services. It's like painting a picture of your typical customer - you give them a name, age, hobbies, and goals. This makes them feel real, helping designers understand what they need and want. Creating personas helps teams make products that people will love because they are tailored to fit their wants and needs, just like a perfect outfit made just for you!

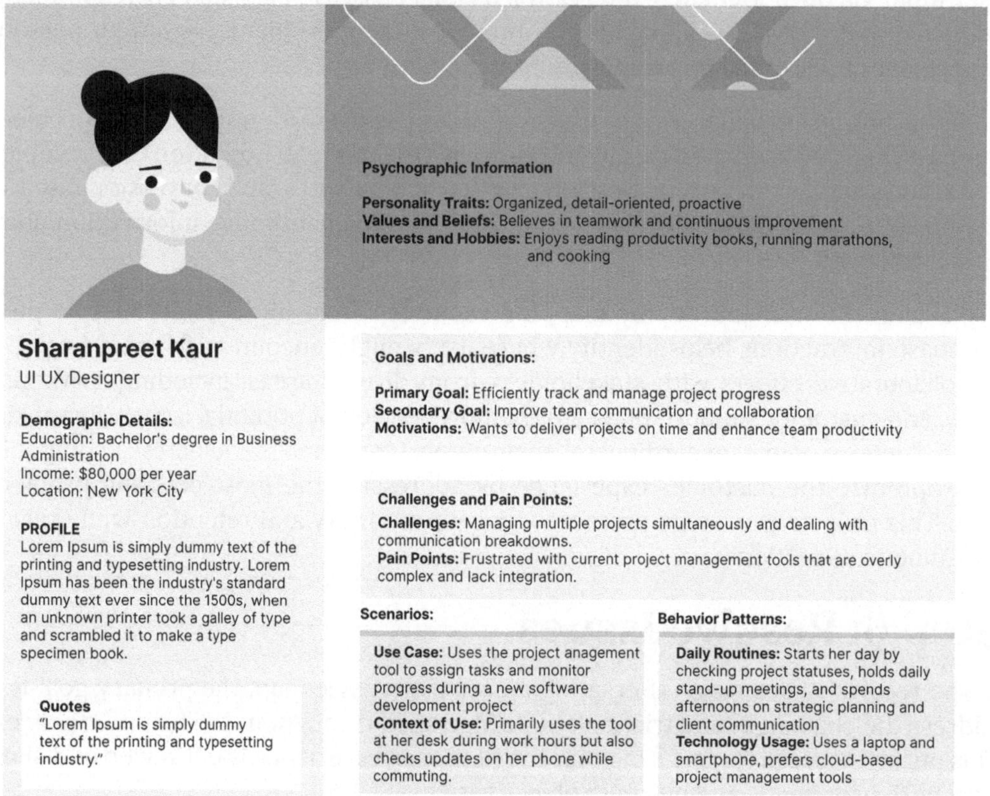

Figure 4.4: *Example of Persona*

Benefits of Creating a Persona

Whether you are creating a smartphone app or a mobile-responsive website, it is imperative that you understand your users. You need a clear and specific problem statement in order to address real user challenges in an effective manner. Here's when creating personas enters the picture.

A persona helps you pinpoint your target market by offering essential responses to questions such as:

- Who is my ideal client?
- What behavioral patterns do my users currently show?
- What goals and requirements do my users have?
- What issues and discomforts do persons in this circumstance have?

By developing a detailed character, you may discover a lot about your users and what they want from your product. With this knowledge, you may adjust your design and functionality to meet their specific needs and preferences. It is important to create personas since they help you understand your users better. Here is why it is so powerful:

- **Empathy Boost**: Personas help you and your team step into the shoes of your users, understanding their struggles and desires. This empathy leads to more user-friendly designs.
- **Clear Direction**: With personas, your design decisions are guided by real user data, not guesswork. This clarity helps avoid costly mistakes and keeps your project on track.
- **Enhanced Communication**: Personas act as a common language for your team, ensuring everyone – from designers to marketers – understands who the target audience is and what they need.
- **Better User Engagement**: When your product resonates with users on a personal level, they're more likely to engage with it, leading to higher satisfaction and loyalty.

In short, creating personas turns abstract user data into relatable, actionable insights, driving better design and stronger connections with your audience.

Tools to Create Persona

- **Xtensio:** Create personas
- **HubSpot:** Make My Persona
- **Canva:** Persona templates

You can also download a persona template from **Miro** to use offline. These tools and templates make it easy to create detailed and visually engaging personas for your design projects.

Types of User Persona

Lene Nielsen, a Ph.D. and specialist in personas, outlines four key perspectives to maximize the value of personas in a design project. These perspectives help create more effective and realistic personas. These categories focus on different aspects of user needs and behaviors.

Goal-Directed Personas

Goal-directed personas center on the objectives that customers have in mind when using a good or service. The goal of these systems is to comprehend and rank the user's objectives, driving forces, and essential tasks. This strategy guarantees that the product is customized to help consumers in successfully achieving their goals.

Key Elements:

The key elements of goal-directed personas are user goals. These comprise life goals, which are more general, individual aspirations that may have an impact on how users use the product, secondary goals, which encourage or supplement primary goals, and primary goals, which are the major objectives users want to accomplish with the product. Detailed task breakdowns and usage scenarios that illustrate how consumers engage with the product are also important aspects of behavior patterns.

Goal-directed personas heavily rely on motivations. Extrinsic motivations are outside forces that affect user behavior, such as rewards or recognition, whereas intrinsic motivations are internal wants that push users towards their objectives, such as skill improvement or satisfaction. Comprehending these incentives facilitates the creation of features that effectively appeal to users. Additionally, designers can successfully address these concerns by identifying pain spots, which are the difficulties and frustrations users face.

Creating Goal-Directed Personas:

The process of developing goal-directed personas starts with extensive user research, which includes questionnaires, interviews, and in-person observations to learn in-depth details about the objectives and habits of users. Common themes and patterns are found through the analysis of both quantitative and qualitative data. Following the synthesis of this data, significant insights are extracted by categorizing individuals into unique personas based on shared goals and behaviors. To make each persona more relatable, they are given names and backstories along with concise descriptions of their motives, behavior patterns, primary, secondary, and life goals.

Benefits:

Goal-directed personas have a number of advantages. As a result, goods better satisfy the requirements and expectations of users, as it promotes a user-centered design approach. By creating intuitive and effective interfaces, this comprehension of activities and challenges enhances usability. Goal-directed personas assist in minimizing needless complexity by prioritizing elements that directly help users achieve their objectives. In the end, goal-directed persona goods are more likely to satisfy users, increasing user engagement and loyalty.

Example:

Consider creating a tool for project management. An example of a goal-oriented persona would be "Sharan, a project manager." Her main objective is to effectively monitor the status of projects. Life goals could comprise advancing one's profession through project completion success, while secondary goals might involve managing deadlines and team communication effectively. With an understanding of Sharan's aims, the solution may be created with functionalities like an all-inclusive dashboard, smooth communications, and automated deadline reminders, all of which will assist her effectively accomplish her major and secondary goals.

In conclusion, goal-directed personas are an effective tool for user-centered design because they support the development of products that are in line with user goals, improving usability and user happiness.

Role-Based Personas

Role-based personas concentrate on the distinct roles that users assume in their personal and professional life and how these roles affect how they engage with a service or product. These personas are designed to help ensure that the product meets the specific requirements and workflows of various user types by helping to comprehend the duties, responsibilities, and context associated with each job.

Key Elements:

The first step involves defining a user's role, including their responsibilities and objectives shaped by their environment. Understanding behavior patterns, interactions, and routines helps design interfaces that align with user habits, improving product efficiency and intuitiveness. Additionally, considering collaboration dynamics offers insights into communication needs with colleagues, clients, or family members, enhancing essential coordination elements.

Creating Role-Based Personas:

Creating role-based personas begins with in-depth research into users' various roles through methods like interviews, task shadowing, and analysis. Synthesizing this data highlights similarities and differences among users in similar positions. Each persona is then crafted with a name, backstory, and detailed job descriptions, incorporating common tasks and responsibilities. Including specific scenarios helps identify pain points and areas for improvement, ensuring the product aligns with users' professional or personal goals, such as achieving productivity targets or maintaining work-life balance. This approach enhances empathy and tailors solutions that meet users' specific needs and challenges.

Benefits:

Role-based personas significantly enhance the design process by ensuring products meet the unique needs of different user types, resulting in more relevant and effective solutions. Focusing on specific roles allows designers to create features and interfaces that support users' actual workflows, improving productivity and satisfaction. Prioritizing development based on each role's critical features also streamlines the process. Additionally, role-based personas improve team communication and collaboration, providing decision-makers with a shared understanding of user needs and identities. This user-centered approach enhances adoption rates and fosters positive user experiences by ensuring the product aligns closely with its intended audience.

Example:

Think about creating an application for customer relationship management (CRM). Someone who is role-based could be "John, a sales manager." John's responsibilities include overseeing a sales team, monitoring sales goals, and upholding client relations. He coordinates with his staff, reviews sales reports, and plans strategies to reach goals on a daily basis. With an understanding of John's function, the CRM platform may be created with features that will assist his tasks and increase his productivity, such as team collaboration tools, automatic client communication templates, and customizable dashboards for tracking sales.

To put it briefly, role-based personas offer a thorough comprehension of users' distinct tasks and responsibilities, resulting in more focused and efficient design solutions. Through an emphasis on the distinct requirements and work processes of many user types, this strategy improves overall user satisfaction, productivity, and usability.

Fictional Personas

Rather of being based on actual user data, fictional personas are built on made-up circumstances and people. These personas are designed to investigate a broad spectrum of user behaviors, demands, and settings that conventional research might not instantly reveal. In the design process, fictional characters are especially helpful for fostering imagination and creativity.

Key Elements:

Creating fictional personas starts with inventing unique user traits that contrast with data-driven personas. These personas are crafted from imaginary scenarios and include details such as their name, age, profession, and lifestyle to aid in ideation and brainstorming. It is crucial to develop a detailed backstory that includes personal experiences, daily routines, and specific habits shaping how the persona interacts with the product. These fictional personas help designers understand potential users from diverse perspectives often overlooked, fostering creativity through engaging narratives. Behavior patterns are key, outlining hypothetical users' interactions, tasks, interests, and motivations, enabling designers to anticipate various user experiences and identify areas for innovation.

Creating Fictional Personas:

Creating fictional characters involves blending imagination and creativity. It begins by brainstorming different user types who could engage with the product, crafting detailed personas with unique traits and backgrounds. Balancing realism with inventiveness ensures personas are both authentic and imaginative. Each persona should include specific scenarios depicting how they might interact with the product, addressing challenges and achieving goals. This approach encourages designers to explore innovations and solutions by focusing on hypothetical motivations and pain points. Collaboration among team members is crucial, fostering a comprehensive design approach and diverse perspectives through workshops and brainstorming sessions.

Benefits:

Using fictional characters in the design process sparks creativity by encouraging designers to think outside of the box and consider unconventional customer needs and behaviors. This approach can lead to innovative design solutions that traditional, data-driven personas may overlook.

Fictional personas ensure product robustness and adaptability by exploring a wide range of hypothetical scenarios, identifying potential use cases and edge situations. By enabling designers to empathize with diverse consumer perspectives, these personas promote inclusive and user-centered designs.

Moreover, fictional personas are particularly useful when real user data is limited in early product development stages. They provide a flexible framework for exploring ideas and testing concepts before committing extensive resources to in-depth research and development.

Example:

Consider creating a fresh social media application. An example of a fictional character would be "Emma, a 35-year-old freelance graphic designer." Emma uses social media to interact with other artists and possible clients. She loves to visit art events and lives in a busy city. The background highlights the desire for a platform that facilitates professional networking and creative collaboration. It also details her transition from a corporate employment to freelancing.

Designers can experiment with features like event notifications, collaborative project tools, and portfolio sharing by imagining Emma's interactions with the app. Key areas for innovation and improvement might be identified by imagining her pain points, such as managing client communications or locating trustworthy colleagues.

To sum up, fictitious characters are effective instruments for fostering originality and creativity during the design phase. They assist designers in exploring a variety of viewpoints, anticipating a wide range of user experiences, and creating more inventive and inclusive products by creating intricate and imaginative user scenarios.

Engaging Personas

Rich tales and personal stories are frequently included into the creation of relatable, incredibly developed characters. The purpose of these personas is to promote empathy and a more profound emotional bond between the users and the design team. Engaging personas contribute to keeping the product development process user-centered and grounded in actual human experiences by improving the target audience.

Key Elements:

Creating an engaging persona starts with crafting a compelling story that breathes life into their character. This involves developing details like a fictitious name, age, profession, and backstory that resonate with their personality and lifestyle. Beyond demographics, the narrative delves into their goals, fears, interests, and personal experiences, making the persona vivid and memorable.

Contextualizing the persona's surroundings is crucial. This includes their physical environment, social relationships, and technological setup. Understanding these elements helps designers anticipate how external factors influence the persona's behaviors and needs.

Central to a persona's engagement are their motivations and goals, which should be clear and representative of their personal and professional aspirations. This understanding enables designers to create features and functionalities that align closely with the persona's fundamental needs and desires.

Creating Engaging Personas:

Creating compelling characters requires extensive research and creative storytelling. It begins by gathering data from user interviews, surveys, and ethnographic research to understand real user experiences. From this synthesis of data, recurring themes and insights are identified to craft the persona's story.

To ensure relatability, each persona should be detailed with rich information. This involves creating a narrative that explores their past experiences, current situation, and future goals. Incorporating quotations and direct customer comments adds depth and authenticity, enhancing the persona's credibility and appeal.

Visual elements play a crucial role in bringing personas to life. Including images, mood boards, and other visual aids makes the character more recognizable and approachable. Visual storytelling helps the team better understand the persona's world and experiences, enriching the overall narrative.

Benefits:

Engaging personas offer several benefits for the design process. They foster a strong emotional connection between users and the design team, promoting empathy and a deeper understanding of user needs based on real experiences rather than abstract data. This emotional engagement ensures that design decisions are grounded in human insights.

Additionally, engaging personas unify the team around a shared understanding of the target audience. This alignment ensures that designers, engineers, and marketers collaborate effectively to create products that truly meet customer needs.

Furthermore, these personas improve teamwork and communication by providing a common reference point for discussing user requirements, generating ideas, and making informed design choices. This shared understanding leads to more cohesive and user-centered design solutions.

Example:

Consider developing an exercise and health app. Imagine "Jake, a 28-year-old marketing professional" as your avatar. Jake balances his passion for fitness with a demanding job and is an enthusiastic runner. His journey from a sedentary college student to a marathon enthusiast highlights his motivations and challenges.

Jake's routine includes early morning runs, tracking progress, and sharing achievements on social media. His goals are discovering new running routes, preventing injuries, and improving marathon times. Understanding Jake's motivations – like staying healthy and achieving personal goals – can guide features such as personalized training plans, injury prevention tips, and community support.

By identifying Jake's pain points, such as accessing reliable training resources or staying motivated during busy workdays, designers can focus on enhancing the app's usability and effectiveness. Including Jake's quotes and visuals, like photos of him running marathons, makes his persona relatable and engaging.

In conclusion, compelling personas are effective instruments that establish a deep emotional bond between the users and the design team. They guarantee that the product development process stays user-centered and focused on actual human experiences by creating elaborative and relevant tales, which results in more successful and fulfilling design solutions.

Other Types of User Persona

There are four types of user personas based on business focus. These personas represent different stages of interaction with a business.

- **Buyer Persona**
- **Customer Persona**
- **User Persona**
- **Proto-Persona**

Comparing Key Persona Types

Understanding the different types of personas – **buyer, customer, user, and proto-persona** – can help businesses and design teams create more effective strategies and products. Each type has its unique focus and applications, but they also share some commonalities. Here is a comparison to highlight their similarities and differences.

Similarities:

- **Purpose**
  - All personas aim to represent a segment of the target audience to guide marketing, product development, and user experience design.
  - They help teams understand and empathize with their audience, ensuring strategies and solutions are user-centric.
- **Elements**
  - All personas typically include demographic information (age, gender, occupation, and so on), psychographics (goals, values, interests), and behavioral traits (buying habits, usage patterns).
  - They address pain points and challenges faced by the target audience to help improve satisfaction and engagement.
- **Benefits**
  - Enhancing targeted marketing and communication efforts.
  - Informing product development to better meet user needs.
  - Improving customer service by understanding preferences and expectations.
  - Allocating resources efficiently by focusing on high-impact strategies.

Differences:

- **Buyer Persona**
  - **Focus**: Represents the ideal customer for marketing and sales purposes.

    - **Key Elements**: Demographics, psychographics, buying behavior, spending habits, brand loyalty, pain points, and preferred communication channels.
    - **Example**: "*Tech-Savvy Tim*" who values innovation and efficiency, prefers online shopping, and is loyal to high-tech brands.
- **Customer Persona**
    - **Focus**: Represents existing customers to enhance ongoing customer relationships and satisfaction.
    - **Key Elements**: Similar to buyer personas but with a focus on existing customers' experiences, challenges, and interactions with the brand.
    - **Example**: "*Eco-Conscious Emma*" who values sustainability, prefers eco-friendly products, and faces challenges in finding genuinely green products.
- **User Persona**
    - **Focus**: Represents end-users to guide product and service design for a better user experience.
    - **Key Elements**: Demographics, psychographics, behavioral traits, pain points, technology use.
    - **Example**: "Freelancer Fiona" who values creativity and efficiency, uses graphic design software, and seeks tools to streamline her workflow.
- **Proto-Persona**
    - **Focus**: An initial, assumption-based persona used early in the design process to align team understanding and guide preliminary decisions.
    - **Key Elements**: Assumed demographics, psychographics, behavioral traits, pain points, technology use based on internal team insights.
    - **Example**: "Startup Sam" who is assumed to be a software developer valuing innovation and efficiency, facing challenges in managing time and staying updated with technologies.

While all four personas aim to represent and understand different segments of an audience, they serve distinct purposes within marketing, product development, and user experience design. Buyer and customer personas focus on marketing and existing customers respectively. User personas emphasize end-user needs for better design, and proto-personas provide a quick, assumption-based starting point for early-stage projects. By leveraging these personas, businesses can create more effective strategies, products, and services that resonate with their target audience.

Note:

These categories serve different strategic purposes: the first set (Goal-Directed, Role-Based, Fictional, Engaging) is about the approach to understanding personas, while the second set (Buyer, Customer, User and Proto) specifies the type of user being represented.

Key Components of a User Persona

The process of creating a user persona is compiling and arranging specific data about your intended audience. Here is a summary of the fundamental components that any user persona ought to have:

Personal Information

- **Name**

  Instead of using terms such as "apprentice," "builder," or "single mom," give your persona a genuine name such as Emily, James, Jessica, or Daniel, which helps your staff relate to the persona more easily and discuss them in conversations. Avoid using celebrity names to keep focus on the persona's traits.

- **Profile Photo**

  The photo is the heart of every persona. Avoid using generic stock images like "woman typing on a laptop" or "man shaking hands" – these don't evoke any real connection. The photo should feel authentic and relatable. Choose a portrait that offers insight into the persona's character, possibly from your research trips.

- **Demographics**

  Include details such as age, gender, occupation, education, income, and location. For example, a fitness app might need information on exercise habits and dietary preferences, while a budgeting app might focus on income sources and spending patterns.

Background

A user persona's "Background" section offers a thorough overview of the persona's background and situations. It contains important information like:

- **Personal History:** A summary of educational background and professional progress.
- **Current Situation:** Details about their living arrangements, family situation, and employment role.
- **Daily Routine:** Regular daily tasks that illustrate when and how they might use your product.

Goals and Needs

A user persona's "Goals and Needs" section focuses on the persona's objectives and the resources they need to reach these objectives. The primary and secondary goals in this section help to clearly comprehend the user's priorities and motivations.

- **Primary Goals:** These are the main objectives driving their interactions with your product. For example, Sharan, a project manager, might aim to effectively monitor and oversee projects.
- **Secondary Goals:** These are additional objectives that support the primary goals. For Sharan, improving teamwork and communication can be secondary goals.
- **Needs:** These are the specific features, functions, or resources required to achieve their goals. Sharan may need dashboard customization or a user-friendly interface.

Knowing these objectives and requirements guarantees that the product is made to satisfy the user's wants and provide a worthwhile, user-centered experience. Through concentrating on the goals and necessities of users, designers are able to order features and produce solutions that successfully tackle actual user issues.

Behavior Patterns

Designing user-centric experiences and increasing overall engagement require an understanding of behavior patterns. Some key patterns are as follows:

- **Tech Savviness:** Indicates the persona's comfort level and expertise with technology.
- **Usage Patterns:** Covers device preferences, frequency, duration, and contexts in which the product is used.

Designers can improve the user experience by developing goods that match the persona's daily routines and technological prowess by comprehending usage patterns and tech savviness.

Pain Points and Challenges

The term "Pain Points and Challenges" describes the particular issues and barriers that a persona faces on a regular basis or when utilizing a product.

Finding Pain Points:

- **Present Dissatisfactions:** Issues that cause frustration, such as complicated tools that slow down Sharan, a project manager.
- **Unmet Needs:** Problems not fully addressed by current solutions, like Sharan needing better tool integration.
- **Inefficiencies:** Time-consuming procedures, such as the lack of a central dashboard making it hard for Sharan to track team progress.

Understanding Challenges:

- **External Obstacles:** Factors beyond the persona's control, like budget constraints limiting Sharan's access to necessary software.
- **Internal Barriers:** Personal limitations or skill gaps, such as Sharan feeling overwhelmed by new technologies.
- **Contextual Issues:** Situational challenges, like communication barriers for Sharan when working remotely.

Motivations

Motivation drives user interaction with a product or service, and understanding these motivations helps create designs that resonate with users.

Intrinsic Motivations:

- **Personal Goals:** Ambitions like improving skills or achieving goals, such as Sharan aiming to manage her team effectively and see her projects succeed.
- **Emotional Drivers:** Feelings like wanting to feel accomplished or reduce stress, motivating Sharan to use project management tools to feel more in control and less overwhelmed by her tasks.

Extrinsic Motivations:

- **External Rewards:** Tangible benefits like promotions or recognition, driving Sharan to excel in project management.
- **Social Influences:** Peer pressure or fitting in, prompting Sharan to adopt new tools used by her colleagues.

Understanding these motivations helps designers create products that meet user needs and enhance the user experience.

Quotes

Including direct quotes in your persona adds depth and authenticity by capturing their emotions and thoughts. This section, straightforwardly, should feature one or two quotes that offer insight into the persona's feelings and personality.

Scenarios

Scenarios are detailed stories that bring personas to life, showing how they use products in real situations. By immersing yourself in these stories, you understand users better and can create products that meet their needs and goals. Each scenario gives new insights, helping you design solutions that improve how users interact with your product.

Scenarios typically cover:

- **Context of Use:** Where and when the persona uses the product, like Sharan checking updates on her phone while commuting.
- **Tasks:** Specific actions the persona takes, such as delegating tasks and tracking projects.
- **Objectives:** What the persona aims to achieve, such as ensuring projects are completed on time.
- **Challenges:** Issues like difficult interfaces that slow down workflow.
- **Results:** Successful outcomes that meet the persona's goals, like efficient teamwork.

Using scenarios helps anticipate user needs, solve real problems, and create products that fit seamlessly into users' everyday lives.

A well-developed user persona empowers your team to understand target users' needs and behaviors, deliver solutions that exceed expectations, and foster empathy. This ensures your product development remains user-focused, enhancing overall satisfaction and experiences.

Example of Persona

Name: Sharanpreet

Basic Information:

Age: 35

Gender: Female

Occupation: Project Manager at a mid-sized tech company

Demographic Details:

Education Level: Bachelor's degree in Business Administration

Income: $80,000 per year

Location: New York City

Psychographic Information:

Personality Traits: Organized, detail-oriented, proactive.

Values and Beliefs: Believes in teamwork and continuous improvement.

Interests and Hobbies: Enjoys reading productivity books, running marathons, and cooking.

Goals and Motivations:

Primary Goal: Efficiently track and manage project progress.

Secondary Goal: Improve team communication and collaboration.

Motivations: Wants to deliver projects on time and enhance team productivity.

Challenges and Pain Points:

Challenges: Managing multiple projects simultaneously and dealing with communication breakdowns.

Pain Points: Frustrated with current project management tools that are overly complex and lack integration.

Behavior Patterns:

Daily Routines: Starts her day by checking project statuses, holds daily stand-up meetings, and spends afternoons on strategic planning and client communication.

Technology Usage: Uses a laptop and smartphone, prefers cloud-based project management tools.

Quotes and Anecdotes:

Direct Quote: "I need a tool that's simple to use but powerful enough to handle complex projects."

Anecdote: Once missed a critical project deadline due to miscommunication within her team, highlighting the need for better collaboration tools.

Scenarios:

Use Case: Uses the project management tool to assign tasks and monitor progress during a new software development project.

Context of Use: Primarily uses the tool at her desk during work hours but also checks updates on her phone while commuting.

In summary, user personas are comprehensive profiles that encapsulate who the users are, what they want to achieve, and the challenges they face. By understanding these main components, designers can create products that are more aligned with user needs and preferences.

Types of User Experience Mapping

Design relies heavily on User Experience (UX) mapping, which visually represents the user's path and interactions with a good or service. Teams may better understand users' demands, issues, and motivations with the help of this method, which promotes the creation of user-centric solutions. UX mapping improves stakeholder collaboration and decision-making by distilling complex data into an understandable manner. Diverse UX mapping methodologies tackle distinct aspects of the user experience, providing valuable insights that propel design advancements and modifications.

Types of UX Mapping:

- Customer journey maps
- Empathy Maps
- Experience Maps
- Service Blueprints

Let us explore each type in detail:

Customer Journey Maps

"User journey mapping" and "UX journey mapping" are often used interchangeably with "customer journey mapping," as they all typically involve the experiences of your website users, who are often your customers. A customer journey map, also known as a user journey map, visually represents your customers' interactions with your business over time, from initial awareness to repeat purchases. It helps visualize the customer's journey at each touchpoint and identifies areas for enhancement to improve the overall experience.

Imagine that a customer might first notice an ad for an online toy store, beginning their journey of product discovery. They move through stages like considering product options, reading reviews, making purchases, and receiving deliveries. This journey highlights their desires, feelings, and interactions, revealing opportunities to improve, such as enhancing website speed for smoother transactions and greater satisfaction.

Importance of Customer Journey Mapping

Using a user journey map, designers can view the product through the customer's lens and it offers several benefits, such as:

- Increases empathy by focusing on the goals, feelings, thoughts, and obstacles of users.
- Serves as a point of reference for stakeholders and team members, guaranteeing that everyone is in agreement as the project is being developed.
- Maps user interactions and emotions to find design possibilities or weaknesses, resulting in better design decisions.

- Aids in the early detection of issues, provides information for wiser decisions, and boosts customer retention.
- Directs enhancements by identifying the areas that consumers find easy and difficult to utilize.
- Promotes the development of uniform protocols, employee training, and team cohesion, all of which improve the end product and user experience.

Customer Journey Stages

Every customer embarks on a five-stage journey when engaging with a brand or product:

Awareness, Consideration, Decision, Retention, and Loyalty.

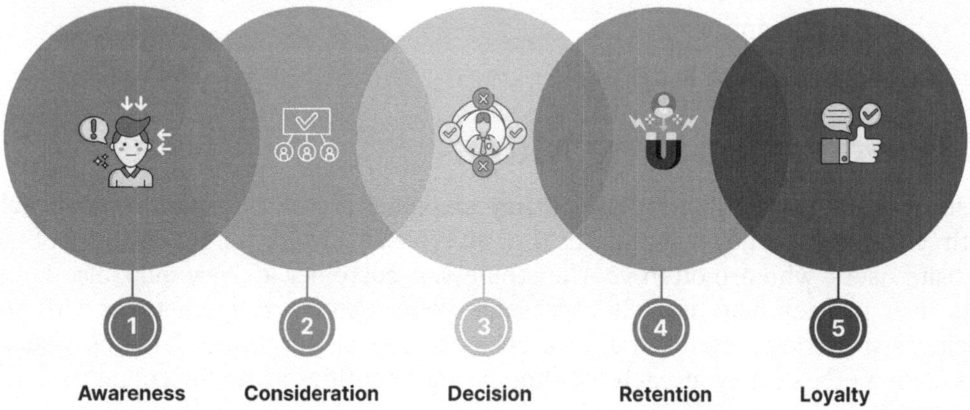

***Figure* 4.5**: *Customer Journey Map stages*

1. **Awareness Stage**

The first stage in the customer journey is when they realize they have a problem but are not sure what they need – be it a product or a service. They begin their search for answers. During this stage, brands can be incredibly helpful by providing informative content that helps customers identify their problem and offers potential solutions. The goal here is to understand the customer's problem, not to push for a sale.

In the awareness stage, you can use page views and click data to discover which web pages and blog posts attract customers as they start to recognize their need for a solution. By analyzing this data, brands can better tailor their content to address the specific problems customers are looking to solve, guiding them gently toward the next stage of their journey.

2. **Consideration**

Customers who are in the consideration stage have done their homework and are well-aware of the issues they face. When they realize they need a good or service, they start evaluating various brands and deals. Now is the time for brands to shine by offering persuasive marketing material that assists consumers in weighing their options and, in the end, selecting a good or service.

Here, assisting clients in navigating the overcrowded market will enable them to make more informed purchasing decisions. Businesses can assist consumers in understanding why their product is the greatest option by emphasizing special features, advantages, and client testimonials. The main goals of this stage are to support inquiry and increase trust in the decision-making process.

3. **Decision Stage**

In the decision stage, customers are ready to buy – they have found the solution to their problem. For brands, this is the critical moment to provide a seamless purchase experience. The shopping process should be straightforward and hassle-free, ensuring customers can complete their purchase with ease.

At this stage, the key is to remove any hurdles. Do not overwhelm customers with more information or product details. Focus on a smooth, user-friendly checkout process to ensure a flawless purchase experience. This is where simplicity and efficiency can make all the difference, helping customers confidently complete their transactions.

4. **Retention Stage**

In the retention stage, customers have made their purchase and are now deciding whether to stick with the brand or switch to another provider. This is a crucial phase where brands can solidify loyalty by delivering an outstanding onboarding experience and exceptional ongoing customer service.

To keep customers from churning, it is essential to make them feel valued and supported. During this stage, gathering feedback through customer surveys and questionnaires is vital. This solicited data helps refine and improve the overall customer experience and the customer journey map, ensuring customers remain satisfied and loyal to your brand.

5. **Loyalty Stage**

In the loyalty stage, customers not only remain with a company but also actively promote it to their family, friends, and colleagues. Also known as the advocacy stage, this is where customers become true brand champions.

During this phase, brands should focus on delivering an outstanding end-to-end customer experience. This includes everything from your website content and sales representatives to your social media presence and product's user experience.

The key to cultivating loyalty is ensuring customers succeed with your product. When they see great results, they are more likely to recommend your brand to others. Additionally, loyal customers are often willing to provide valuable feedback and insights, enriching your customer journey mapping strategy and helping you refine the overall experience.

Key Elements of Customer Journey Map

To properly describe how customers interact with your brand, a strong customer journey map must include a number of crucial elements. The following are the main elements that are usually present in a customer journey map.

Point of View:

In a customer journey map, selecting the Main Character or Hero, known as the persona, is crucial. This persona, whether an athlete or coach in a sports product, shapes the map's narrative and insights. Maintaining a single perspective per map ensures clarity and a deeper understanding of the persona's needs and experiences.

Scenario:

A scenario in a customer journey map depicts a customer's interaction with a brand or product. For example, Emma discovers an online clothing store ad, browses items, faces checkout frustrations, completes her purchase, and receives her order. This scenario highlights Emma's needs, challenges, and emotions, providing insights to enhance her overall experience and inform future product developments.

Actions, Mindsets, and Emotions:

Customer **actions** such as browsing or purchasing are key in a customer journey map. **Mindsets** reveal their thoughts and motivations, like deciding to buy or seek information. **Emotions** capture feelings – whether happy, frustrated, or excited – throughout the journey. Together, these elements provide a comprehensive view of the customer's experience, emphasizing their actions, thoughts, and feelings. Qualitative research supports these insights, helping brands identify issues and opportunities to improve the overall customer experience.

Touchpoints and Channels:

Touchpoints in a customer journey map are interactions like visiting a website, contacting customer service, or receiving a product. **Channels** are the platforms such as email, social media, stores, or phone calls, that enable these interactions. Recognizing these touchpoints and channels helps brands understand customer engagement patterns, ensuring consistent communication and enhancing overall satisfaction.

Insights and Ownership:

Insights in a customer journey map are key findings from studying customer interactions, behaviors, and feedback, guiding improvements in the customer experience. **Ownership** assigns responsibility for managing each touchpoint, fostering accountability and teamwork to ensure a smooth customer journey. Without clear ownership, there is no authority to drive change or accountability for outcomes.

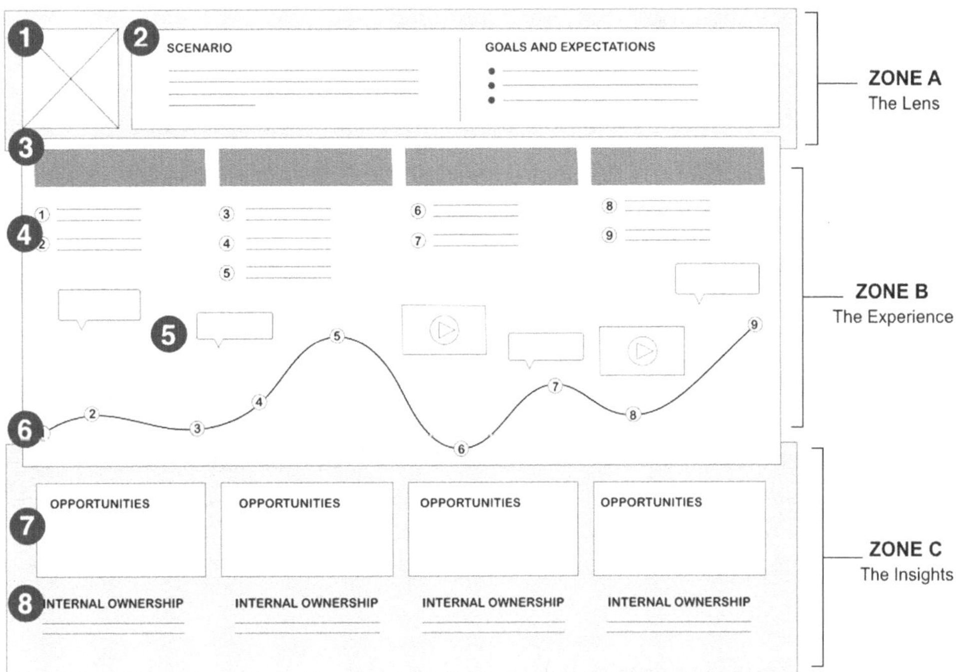

***Figure 4.6**: Three zones of Customer Journey Map by nngroup.com*

Zone A: By designating **(1)** a persona "who" and **(2)** the scenario to be investigated "what", the lens places limitations on the map. The heart of the map is the visualized experience, usually aligned across **(3)** chunkable phases of the journey.

Zone B: Research-based statements or films can be used to enhance the user's **(4)** actions, **(5)** ideas, and **(6)** emotional experience during the journey.

Zone C: Depending on the company objective the map supports, the output should differ, but it may include a description of the insights and pain areas found, the **(7)** opportunities to focus on going forward, as well as **(8)** internal ownership.

Creating a Customer Journey Map

To ensure a seamless and fulfilling customer experience, the customer journey map helps identify touchpoints, pain points, and improvement opportunities. Here are the seven essential steps to create an effective customer journey map:

1. **Clearly define the map's goals.**
2. **Describe your personalities and set their objectives.**
3. **Highlight your target customer personas.**
4. **List every touchpoint.**
5. **Assess the resources you now have and those you will require.**
6. **Go on the customer journey by yourself.**
7. **Examine your findings.**

Before following the first step, take advantage of customer journey map templates.

Using Customer Journey Map Templates

Free online templates for customer journey maps offer ready-made structures that save time and effort. Choose from editable PDFs or document formats, some with step-by-step instructions, to quickly create maps that suit your business goals. These templates streamline the process, allowing teams in design, sales, marketing, and customer support to focus more on analyzing customer experiences and implementing improvements.

1. Clearly Define the Map's Goals

Key questions to consider: before diving into creating a customer journey map, ask yourself: Why am I doing this? This essential question helps clarify your purpose. Determine your goals for the map and identify who your persona will be. Decide which scenarios you want to include in the journey. Ensure your questions and objectives align with your company's overall goals and vision.

Creating a buyer persona is an excellent place to start. There will be a ton of material and many different possibilities to look at. Based on this research, create detailed profiles of your target customers to guide your mapping process effectively.

2. Describe Your Personalities and Set Their Objectives

Next, gather customer journey analytics through thorough research. The Analytical

Strategist collects and analyzes data to identify touchpoints and pain points, ensuring the map aligns with business goals. The Empathetic Designer focuses on customer emotions and experiences, creating a user-friendly map. The visionary leader defines the overall vision, ensuring the map reflects company values and motivates the team.

The more you know about your customers and their needs, the better your journey maps will be. The Collaborative Facilitator brings together teams from different areas to get a variety of insights and a complete view, helping to identify where customers might drop off. Collect feedback from both existing and potential customers who have interacted with your company to make the journey map more effective.

3. Highlight Your Target Customer Personas

Highlighting your target customer personas means choosing a detailed profile of individuals most likely to engage with your brand. Identify a common customer and follow their journey as they interact with your business for the first time. Do not overlook any data, even if it seems irrelevant to your goal. It is best to jot down all insights in a secure place, so you can revisit and utilize them later. This thorough approach ensures you understand your customers' experiences and can improve your strategies based on real interactions.

4. List Every Touchpoint

Touchpoints are customer interactions with your brand, crucial for mapping their journey and identifying areas for improvement. List all current and potential touchpoints to gain insights into customer actions, both online (website, social media, email) and offline (store visits, customer service calls). This step is essential to comprehensively mapping the customer journey, encompassing all brand interactions beyond just digital platforms and marketing materials.

Example:

Imagine you run an online clothing store. Through your research, you identify several touchpoints.

- **Ad Interaction:** Customers see an ad on social media.
- **Website Visit:** They click the ad and visit your website.
- **Product Browsing:** They browse different products.
- **Customer Reviews:** They read customer reviews.
- **Adding to Cart:** They add items to their cart.
- **Checkout:** They go through the checkout process.
- **Order Confirmation:** They receive an order confirmation email.
- **Shipping Updates:** They receive shipping updates.

- **Delivery:** They receive their order.
- **Post-Purchase:** They leave a review or contact customer support if there's an issue.

Analyzing touchpoints reveals improvement opportunities. For example, high cart abandonment rates suggest a complex checkout process – simplification can help. If post-delivery support inquiries are common, it may indicate product or delivery issues that need addressing for a better customer experience.

Customer Actions:

A journey map tracks customer actions at every interaction with your organization, from research and customer service contact to purchases and feedback. Use tools like transactional data, web analytics, surveys, and interviews to monitor these behaviors, understanding preferences and pain points. Tools such as CRM software, consumer feedback platforms, and Google Analytics are essential for this insight. Simplifying processes, despite seeming risky, often boosts conversion rates by reducing unnecessary steps, making transactions easier for customers to complete. This data is crucial for enhancing the overall customer experience.

Customer Emotions and Motivations:

When mapping a customer's journey, emotions and motivations guide you through their experiences – excitement over products, satisfaction with smooth transactions, or frustration with checkout issues reveal what works and what needs improvement. Understanding motivations like seeking value, reliable service, or ease explains their decisions. Gather insights through interviews, surveys, and feedback to create a journey that resonates with both positive and challenging experiences. By emphasizing emotions and motivations, you transform a basic map into a compelling story, designing memorable experiences that enhance customer loyalty and satisfaction.

Customer Obstacles and Pain Points

Think of a customer journey map as a treasure map, but instead of gold, you are hunting for insights to improve your customer's experience. Along this path, obstacles and pain points are the tricky traps and hidden pitfalls your customers encounter.

- **Obstacles** are the bumps that slow them down, like confusing websites or long waits for help.
- **Pain points** are where they get frustrated, like mixed-up orders or unclear instructions.

Find these issues through surveys and feedback to understand what customers go through. By fixing these problems, you turn a tough journey into a great experience, making sure customers enjoy every step with your brand.

Example:

Let us map out the journey of Emma, an online shopper, and identify her obstacles and pain points.

Stage: Product Research

Obstacle: Emma struggles to find detailed product information on the website.

Pain Point: Frustration from vague descriptions and lack of customer reviews.

Stage: Adding to Cart

Obstacle: The website's slow loading times cause delays.

Pain Point: Annoyance from repeated page reloads, leading to second thoughts about continuing.

Stage: Checkout Process

Obstacle: The checkout process requires creating an account, adding extra steps.

Pain Point: Irritation from filling out lengthy forms and potential abandonment due to the hassle.

Stage: Payment

Obstacle: Limited payment options that don't include her preferred method.

Pain Point: Disappointment and potential drop-off if she can't use her favorite payment method.

Stage: Post-Purchase

Obstacle: Lack of clear communication on shipping status.

Pain Point: Anxiety from not knowing when her order will arrive.

Stage: Customer Support

Obstacle: Long wait times when contacting customer service.

Pain Point: Frustration from not getting timely help with an issue.

The business may concentrate on increasing website speed, giving more thorough product information, streamlining the checkout process, providing a variety of payment alternatives, improving shipment communication, and expediting customer care answers by addressing these challenges and pain areas. By taking care of these problems, Emma's journey becomes smoother and more joyful.

5. Assess the Resources You Now Have and Those You will Require

Assessing your present resources is required for creating an effective customer journey map. List the information, resources, and personnel on the team that can help with this project. Web analytics and client feedback are required. Determine how well your team does design, consumer research, and data analysis. Determine the gaps where more resources or knowledge are needed, and take appropriate action, such as purchasing new software or employing a UX professional. By estimating your resource requirements, you can ensure the help required to develop a precise and informative customer journey map that will improve the customer experience.

6. Go on the Customer Journey by Yourself

Take the customer journey on yourself to have a true understanding of their experience. Consider yourself a consumer and use your website to browse, buy, and get help. Any annoyances, confusion, or delays should be noted. By putting the user experience front and center, this practical method reveals areas that require improvement. You will have a greater understanding of your clients' problems and expectations if you put yourself in their position. The ability to directly identify possibilities and pain points through this experience is priceless in ensuring that your customer journey map represents true insights and results in more useful improvements.

7. Examine Your Findings

Finishing your customer journey map is only the first step. You now have to evaluate the outcomes. Finding important phases and touchpoints where clients engage with your brand is part of this. Examine consumer behavior for trends, patterns, and pain areas. Prioritize and validate your findings using data-driven changes. Finding methods to improve the customer experience can increase advocacy, loyalty, and satisfaction. This analysis helps with that. Make sure you adhere to your original schedule to avoid upsetting clients who might decide not to come back to view all the planned upgrades.

8. Update Your Map Over Time

Regularly updating your map is a great improvement. It helps you find gaps and opportunities to make your customer journey smoother. It also lets you address less urgent issues and tackle points you noted for future work.

Example of Customer Journey Map

A customer journey map illustrates the steps and interactions a customer experiences with a product or service. It provides valuable insights into customer needs and behaviors, helping businesses improve touchpoints and enhance overall satisfaction. Here is an example:

Phases	Awareness	Website Search	Ordering	Order Receiving and Consuming	Sharing and Reviews
Actions What is the customer's action? What they do?	[Your info here]	[Your info here]	[Your info here]	[Your info here]	[Your info here]
Thoughts What is the customer thinking or feeling?	[Your info here]	[Your info here]	[Your info here]	[Your info here]	[Your info here]
Channels What is the customer's touchpoint with the business?	[Your info here]	[Your info here]	[Your info here]	[Your info here]	[Your info here]
Feelings What do they want to change about this step?	[Your info here]	[Your info here]	[Your info here]	[Your info here]	[Your info here]
Opportunities How and/or why will we make this change?	[Your info here]	[Your info here]	[Your info here]	[Your info here]	[Your info here]

Figure 4.7*: Example of Customer Journey Map template*

Empathy Maps

It is not enough to individualize the design process via empathy mapping. Rather, it seeks to reflect a larger group of consumers with similar needs and interests. Putting oneself in the position of someone you don't often interact with can be challenging at times. You can learn more about these people's true thoughts and feelings regarding your issue, service, or product by using empathy mapping.

Consider that you are going to work with a corporation or brand to create an app called a "veterinary locator" or "pet clinic finder." The first step is to determine who your target market is. Consider working-class individuals, recent immigrants, or recent arrivals to cities of various ages. Imagine 56-year-old Olivia looking for local and internet pet services while living alone with her cat, Milli. Your team imagines Olivia's everyday activities, the technological obstacles she encounters to create an app for her. Although Olivia is a persona, many others can relate to her needs. Your team can grasp the common wants and preferences of Olivia and many other users by putting themselves in her position through empathy mapping.

To create an empathy map, you will need some drawing tools like sticky notes and pens, or you can use software with empathy map templates. Choose the persona you will be mapping before you start, and make sure everyone in your team is aware of it. Choose a persona based on real data from your research and give them a name.

Structure of Empathy Maps

The empathy map was originally created by **Dave Gray** (XPLANE's founder) and has gained much popularity within the agile community. The original Empathy Map is divided into four quadrants: Thoughts, Feelings, Actions, and Observations. Each quadrant captures a different aspect of the customer experience:

- **Thoughts:** What the customer says
- **Feelings:** What the customer thinks
- **Actions:** What the customer does
- **Observations:** What the customer feels

This structure helps you gain a comprehensive understanding of your customer's experience.

The revised version includes seven sections – the user is positioned in the middle.

Empathy Map Canvas

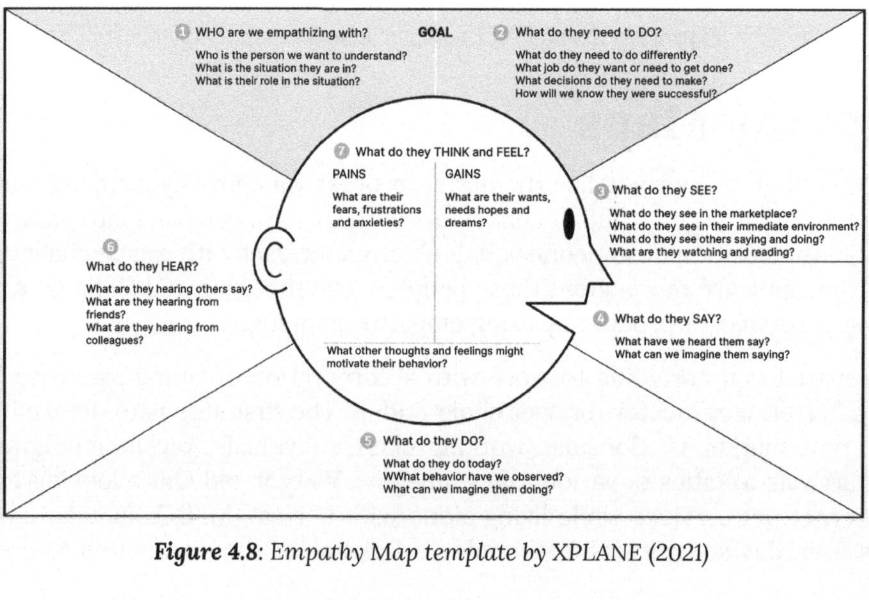

***Figure 4.8**: Empathy Map template by XPLANE (2021)*

GOAL: It is great if we write our goal at top as it will be always accessible, what do you aim to achieve with this Empathy Map?

1. **Who are we empathizing with?** As we mentioned earlier, first step will be to select persona. In this section, you might be mapping a group of customers who needs a new app designed.
2. **What do they need to do?** In this section, mention the type of change that they need or want.
3. **What do they see?** This section covers, what is available to them in the marketplace, in their surroundings, or in their daily life.
4. **What do they say?** This section contains what major points and quotes are being made by the user?
5. **What do they do?** It should reflect what actions and behavior did you notice? How customers actually use the product?
6. **What do they hear?** This could come from websites, news, coworkers, friends, and more.
7. **What do they think and feel?** This section mostly covers what feelings could the user experience? And what do they think? What are their beliefs? What are they worried or happy about?

In order to make a clear separation between observable and inferred phenomena, "thoughts" and "feelings" were combined into the core portion of Empathy Maps after they were updated from four to seven sections. Add a list of "gains" and "pains" to better understand your user or character.

Importance of Empathy Maps

In order to better understand users, empathy maps can be utilized both at the beginning of the design process and throughout the prototype-validation phase, when users are seen utilizing the proposed service.

Empathy maps has its own benefits, including:

- It lets you pay attention to specific details while watching people
- Information from practical insights that can be obtained is rapidly visualized.
- It can be applied at various stages of the design process, such as the outset or prototyping.

Creating Empathy Maps

Now you have a template or you can use a whiteboard to draw these 7 sections. It is easy and convenient to add sticky notes for your points. But how do we fill in all the sections? What data is relevant to each section?

Here is a simple approach: When exploring our audience, asking some thought-provoking questions really helps.

When thinking about what people **hear**, we might ask:

- What do leaders want to tell this person?
- Who is trying to influence this person? (Maybe publications, forums, and so on.)
- What messages is this person hearing from said influences?

When reflecting on what people **do**, we might ask:

- What is the biggest priority on this person's agenda?
- What do they spend most of their time doing?
- What do they WANT to spend their time doing?

When considering what others **see**, we might ask:

- How is their world changing?
- What market trends affect this person's role?
- What do the optics within the company tell them?

When considering what others **say**, we may ask:

- What types of things do they tell people?
- What is the essential message they convey to their peers/teams?
- What do they convey as aspirations or optimism?

When we think about what our audience is **thinking** and **feeling**, we aim to understand how they make decisions and what their **pains** or **gains** might be. We want to know their fears and hopes. What concerns them? What makes them feel optimistic? At this stage, we review what we've noted in other sections of the map. Do any insights help us understand their pains or gains better?

At this point, we might inquire about the following:

- Why do they not sleep at night?
- What are they looking forward to?
- What would be the one thing they could change about their work if they could?
- What would they be doing most of the time in an ideal world?

By following this structure, empathy maps allow you to gain an understanding of your people. They also share this understanding with your team and stakeholders, ensuring that everyone understands what users want and need. This allows you to focus on the proper things. They encourage open-mindedness and avoid judgement, which makes it simpler to develop empathy and make user-centered decisions.

Empathy Maps Versus Personas

Despite their apparent similarity at first appearance, the two are very different from one another. Following are few points to consider:

- Personas provide a more comprehensive, in-depth view of user segments, whereas Empathy Maps concentrate on the user's current thoughts and feelings.
- Personas are used to represent different user groups and provide guidance for particular design decisions; Empathy Maps are more concerned with understanding emotions and viewpoints.
- Personas necessitate more thorough investigation and data collecting, whereas Empathy Maps can be created more quickly and with greater flexibility.

In summary, personas and empathy maps cannot take the place of one another when it comes to understanding consumers' requirements and developing an empathy for them.

Experience Maps

An effective technique for visualizing the whole path a normal person takes to accomplish a certain objective is experience mapping. While a customer journey map is customized for a single company and its clients, experience mapping is more broadly focused, attempting to comprehend human behavior in general rather than concentrating on any one target market or product. In situations where the audience is not well defined, this method is especially helpful.

Experience mapping, in short, is a process flow chart that shows the actions a typical user takes from beginning to end. What is important to note is that this user does not belong to any particular category or have a preference for any specific good or service. Rather, the map depicts a common path that a multitude of individuals could travel in similar situations.

Example:

Consider the process of booking a vacation. An experience map would show the general processes that need to be taken, like looking for destinations, comparing costs, booking flight and hotel reservations, organizing activities, and ultimately departing on the trip. This map emphasizes the typical decisions and experiences that anyone may have when organizing a vacation rather than focusing on a certain airline or travel agency.

Experience mapping is very useful when attempting to comprehend a process from a broad viewpoint. It aids in locating common problems and areas for development that work in a variety of settings. This means that it can be used to learn about human behavior in a variety of contexts, independent of particular company or industrial needs.

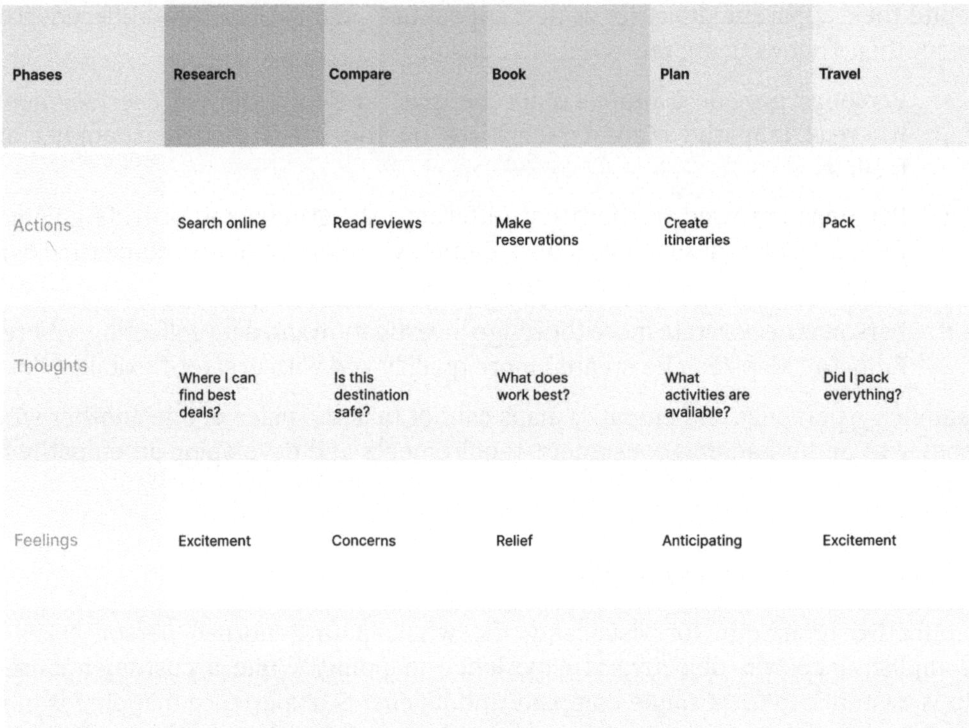

***Figure 4.9**: Experience Map example of booking a vacation*

An experience map, much like a customer journey map, is divided into four essential components:

- Phases
- Actions
- Thoughts
- Feelings/Mindset

However, the key difference is that an experience map is not limited to any specific type of user, service, or product. It is a tool for capturing the broad strokes of general user behavior, making it extremely useful when there is not a defined target audience.

Benefits of Experience Mapping

- **Understanding General Human Behavior**

  Regardless of any specific service or product, experience mapping helps in the identification of common patterns and behaviors that apply to an extensive range of users.

- **Baseline Understanding**

  It is adaptable for a range of applications since it offers a fundamental knowledge of an event that is not bound to any particular setting.

Example of an Experience Map

Imagine you are looking to understand the general process of booking a vacation. An experience map would outline the broad phases such as:

- **Phase:** Researching destinations, comparing prices, booking, planning activities, and going on the trip.
- **Actions:** Searching online, reading reviews, making reservations, creating itineraries, and packing.
- **Thoughts:** "Where can I find the best deals?" "Is this destination safe?" "What activities are available?"
- **Feelings and Mindset:** Excitement about potential destinations, stress about budgeting, anticipation of the trip.

An experience map, which captures the typical journey of holiday planning and divides the process into four categories, helps in identifying common roadblocks and opportunities for improvement. As a result, it is a helpful tool for assessing user behavior generally and enhancing user experiences.

Service Blueprints

There are situations when a single kind of UX map cannot adequately depict every interaction customers experience with a service. Different kinds of UX maps can be combined to achieve a complete view. A customer journey map, for example, is excellent in illustrating the user's viewpoint but is limited in its ability to disclose business-related information. A service blueprint map becomes useful in this situation.

A service blueprint map offers a comprehensive view of a company's behind-the-scenes activities. These diagrams visualize and analyze interactions between customers and service providers, along with the internal processes that support these interactions. They illustrate how different departments, employees, and processes contribute to the overall user experience. This type of map is particularly useful for large organizations with complex service offerings.

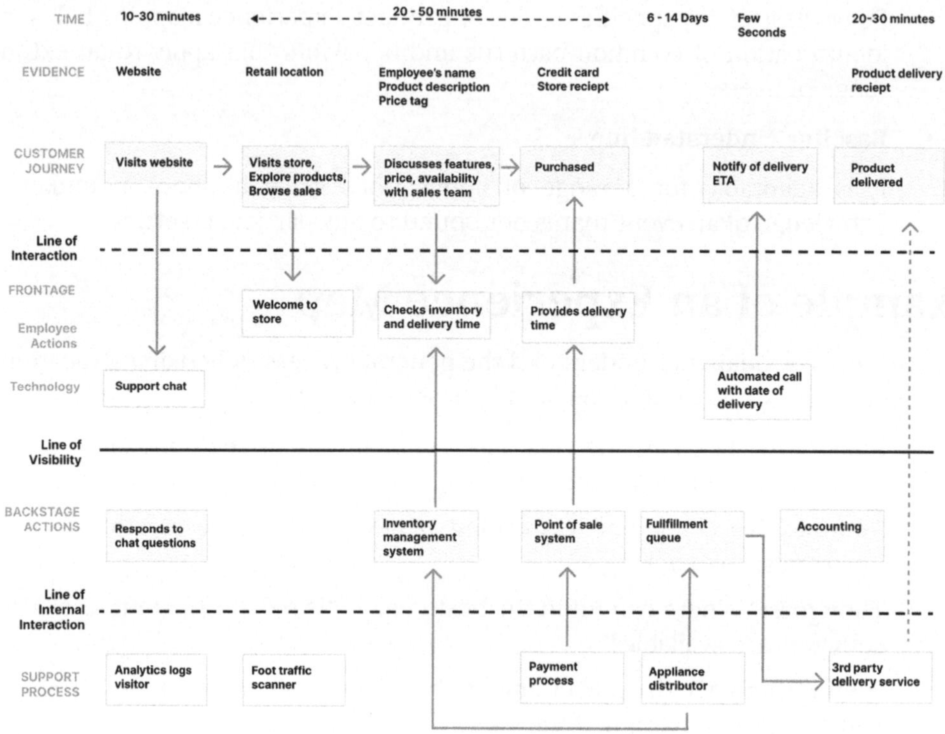

***Figure 4.10**: Service blueprint example of Appliance Retailer by nngroup.com*

Example:

A customer journey map outlines how a shopper finds and buys a product online or in-store, focusing on their experience. It doesn't cover internal operations like inventory management or customer service handling.

For these internal processes, a service blueprint map is used. It details how orders are processed, inventory is updated, and staff are informed. This dual approach helps identify inefficiencies and areas for improvement, ensuring a smoother experience for both customers and staff.

In short, using UX maps like customer journey maps and service blueprint maps gives a complete picture of internal processes and user experiences, enabling better service delivery improvements.

Key Components of Service Blueprints

Service blueprints are essential tools for highlighting the customer experience, detailing service processes, and identifying areas for improvement. They provide a comprehensive overview of both customer-facing and behind-the-scenes operations in service delivery.

Key components include:

- **Customer Actions:** Steps customers take when using a service, like booking a table or placing an order.
- **Frontstage (Visible) Interactions:** Direct interactions between customers and staff, such as servers taking orders in a restaurant.
- **Backstage (Invisible) Interactions:** Operations unseen by customers, like chefs preparing meals.
- **Support Processes:** Internal procedures necessary for service delivery, such as employee scheduling and inventory management.
- **Physical Evidence:** Tangible elements customers interact with, such as restaurant layout, menus, and receipts.

Benefits of Service Blueprints

Here are some benefits of service blueprints:

- **Comprehensive View:** Offers a complete overview of the entire service process, highlighting both internal operations and customer interactions.
- **Improvement Opportunities:** Identifies areas for process enhancement to boost service quality and operational efficiency.
- **Staff Training:** Essential for educating employees and ensuring clarity on their roles in delivering services effectively.
- **Customer Insights:** Provides valuable information on customer interactions, aiding in better understanding and meeting customer needs.

Example

Consider a hotel check-in process as an example of a service blueprint:

1. **Customer Actions:** Arriving at the hotel, providing identification, receiving the room key.
2. **Frontstage Interactions:** The receptionist greeting the guest, checking the reservation, and handing over the room key.

3. **Backstage Interactions:** The receptionist accessing the reservation system, communicating with housekeeping to ensure the room is ready.
4. **Support Processes:** The housekeeping staff prepares the room, and the maintenance team ensures the room's facilities are functioning properly.
5. **Physical Evidence:** The reservation confirmation email, the hotel lobby, the room key card, the welcome booklet in the room.

In conclusion, service blueprints are effective instruments for assessing and improving the provision of services. They assist firms in increasing productivity, improving client experiences, and making sure all internal processes are in line with service objectives by outlining each step and interaction.

Best Tools for User Experience Mapping

Software programs called user experience mapping tools are made to assist in visualizing and analyzing all aspects of a user's interactions with a good or service. These tools help with the creation of various maps, including experience maps, empathy maps, service blueprints, and customer journey maps (CJMs). Here are a few frequently used tools for every kind of UX map:

Customer Journey Maps (CJMs)

Customer journey maps show the steps a customer takes, emphasizing their requirements, problems, and feelings when interacting with a product or service.

Tools:

- **Smaply:** Specializes in journey mapping and persona creation, making it easy to visualize customer journeys.
- **UXPressia:** Offers templates for creating detailed customer journey maps, personas, and impact maps.
- **Canvanizer:** Provides various canvas templates, including customer journey maps, for collaborative brainstorming.

Empathy Maps

Teams can gain insights into the motivations and challenges of users by using Empathy Maps to better understand their feelings, ideas, and behaviors.

Tools:

- **Mural:** A digital workspace for visual collaboration that includes empathy map templates.

- **Stormboard:** Offers templates for empathy mapping, allowing teams to brainstorm and collaborate in real-time.
- **Canvanizer:** Also supports empathy mapping with pre-designed templates for easy use.

Experience Maps

Experience Maps offer an expanded perspective on user encounters, frequently spanning many contexts and periods, to comprehend user behavior in general.

Tools:

- **Miro:** A versatile online collaborative whiteboard that supports experience mapping with its variety of templates and tools.
- **Lucidchart:** A diagramming tool that helps create detailed experience maps with ease.
- **Adobe XD:** A design tool that can be used to create interactive and visually appealing experience maps.

Service Blueprints

Service blueprints highlight both front- and back-end operations and provide specifics about the internal procedures and exchanges that enable customer experiences.

Tools:

- **ServiceDesignTools:** Offers templates and resources specifically for creating service blueprints.
- **Smaply:** Also useful for service blueprints, providing a structured way to map out both customer-facing and internal processes.
- **Touchpoint Dashboard:** Helps visualize service design processes and interactions, making it easier to identify pain points and improvements.

Many of the mentioned tools provide free versions or trials, but most come with paid plans that unlock advanced features. While free versions often have limited capabilities, these tools are invaluable for saving time and effort, sparing designers from starting from scratch. However, it is entirely possible to create your own maps using Word, Excel, or even a whiteboard as a starting point. As you gain experience and recognize the benefits, you might decide to invest in the paid versions for enhanced functionality.

Conclusion

We explored the fascinating field of User Experience (UX) Mapping in this chapter. We began by going over the foundations of UX mapping and emphasized how crucial it is to comprehend user interactions. Next, we looked at user personas – crucial instruments for identifying the characteristics and requirements of our intended audience.

We talked about a variety of UX map types, such as empathy maps that help us comprehend consumers' feelings and ideas and customer journey maps that show the stages a user takes when interacting with a product or service. We also looked at a number of technologies that help to make these maps more insightful and efficient, freeing up designers to concentrate on improving user experience.

You now own a strong toolkit for evaluating and enhancing user experiences after grasping these ideas. This information is essential for creating goods and services that effectively satisfy customers' demands and have a genuine impact on them.

We shall go into information architecture and sitemaps in the next chapter. We will look at how information can be arranged and structured so that consumers can readily access and comprehend it. Prepare to discover how to develop navigation systems that are easy to use and increase the user experience in general.

Key Terms

- **UX Mapping:** A visual representation of the user's experience and interaction with a product or service, used to identify pain points and opportunities for improvement.
- **Point of View:** The perspective from which a user or a designer approaches a problem, considering their needs, goals, and challenges.
- **Scope:** The extent and boundaries of a project, defining what will be included and what will be excluded in the user experience design.
- **Chronological Structure:** An organizational method that arranges information or events in the order they occur over time.
- **Hierarchical Structure:** An organizational method that arranges information in a ranked or leveled manner, from most to least important.
- **User Research:** The process of understanding user behaviors, needs, and motivations through observation techniques, task analysis, and other feedback methodologies.
- **Customer Interactions:** The various ways in which customers engage with a brand, product, or service, including in-person, online, and through customer service.
- **User Persona:** A semi-fictional character representing a segment of users, based on user research and data, used to guide design decisions.
- **Goal-Directed Personas:** Personas focused on what the user wants to accomplish, emphasizing their goals and tasks.

- **Role-Based Personas:** Personas based on the user's role in an organization or in their daily life, highlighting their responsibilities and workflows.
- **Behavior Patterns:** Recurring actions or tendencies exhibited by users when interacting with a product or service.
- **Fictional Personas:** Imaginary characters created to represent user types, based on assumptions rather than real data.
- **Hypothetical Users:** Assumed users created based on potential scenarios and imagined needs, used when real data is not available.
- **Engaging Persona:** A detailed and relatable persona that effectively captures the user's story, motivations, and behaviors to foster empathy and engagement from the design team.
- **Buyer Persona:** A semi-fictional character representing the ideal customer based on market research, used primarily in marketing to target and engage potential buyers.
- **Customer Persona:** A representation of a customer segment, focusing on their needs, preferences, and behaviors, often used in both marketing and UX design.
- **Proto-Persona:** A preliminary persona based on assumptions and anecdotal evidence, used early in the design process before extensive user research is conducted.
- **Behavior Patterns:** Repeated actions or tendencies that users exhibit, which can inform design decisions by highlighting common user behaviors.
- **Motivations:** The reasons or driving forces behind users' actions and decisions, crucial for understanding user behavior and designing engaging experiences.
- **Intrinsic Motivations:** Internal factors that drive user behavior, such as personal satisfaction, curiosity, or the desire for mastery.
- **Extrinsic Motivations:** External factors that influence user behavior, such as rewards, recognition, or avoiding negative outcomes.
- **Customer Journey Maps:** Visual representations of the customer's experiences and interactions with a product or service over time, highlighting key touchpoints and emotional states.
- **Touchpoints:** Specific moments or interactions where customers engage with a brand, product, or service, crucial for understanding the user experience.
- **Empathy Map:** A tool used to gain a deeper understanding of the user by capturing what they say, think, do, and feel, fostering empathy among the design team.

- **Experience Maps:** Detailed diagrams that outline the user's experience across different stages and touchpoints, providing insights into their journey and identifying opportunities for improvement.
- **Service Blueprints:** Detailed visual representations of a service, showing the relationships between different service components, including people, props, and processes.
- **Frontstage:** The visible part of a service where users interact directly with the service and its staff, impacting their immediate experience.
- **Backstage:** The behind-the-scenes activities and processes that support the frontstage interactions, essential for delivering the overall service experience.

CHAPTER 5
Mastering Information Architecture and Sitemaps

Introduction

This chapter will cover important topics related to sitemaps and information architecture (IA), which are essential for building user-friendly websites. Information architecture is the process of organizing and arranging content so that it is easier for users to find and navigate. We will explore the fundamental ideas behind successful IA, with a focus on organization, clarity, and user-centric design.

You will come across a number of IA systems that offer logical frameworks for classifying and labeling data. A visual representation of a website's structure is provided by sitemaps, which are crucial tools for web development that facilitate planning and communication. We will examine several sitemap formats, including as XML for search engines and graphic sitemaps for stakeholders, and practical ways to generate them.

Comprehending these ideas gives you the ability to create user-friendly websites that are easy for people to navigate and find information on. Let us embark on a journey to master the art of information architecture and sitemapping for optimal web design!

Structure

In this chapter, we will discuss the following topics:

- Introduction to Information Architecture
- The History of IA

- Importance of Information Architecture
- Information Architecture Principles
- Information Architecture Systems
- IA versus UX
- Creating Information Architecture for Your Website
- Information Architecture Tools
- Introduction to Sitemaps
- Importance of Sitemap
- Types of Sitemaps
- How to Create a Sitemap
- Information Architecture versus Sitemap

Introduction to Information Architecture

Picture yourself going to a big, unknown theme park for the first time. There are a tonne of rides, shows, restaurants, and attractions at the park, but if you didn't have any direction, you would be lost and wouldn't know where to begin or where to look for your favourite ride. This is where an effective signage and park map system come in to help you traverse the intricate surroundings.

Effective theme park maps provide answers to three key questions:

- Where am I? (In what area of the park am I currently located?)
- What's here? (What rides, attractions, or amenities are in this area?)
- Where else can I go? (What other locations, rides, or sights can I see from this point on?)

For digital environments, information architecture, or IA, is comparable to a theme park map. It makes data easier to access and understand by labeling and organizing it in an intuitive manner. The map in the theme park example shows you where you are (Adventureland, Fantasyland, Tomorrowland), what you can find here (certain rides, eateries, restrooms), and where you can go in the future (more themed sections, exits, first aid stations). In a similar vein, an intuitive interface (IA) that is well-designed for a website or application helps users navigate its content and locate the features or information they require.

Understanding Information Architecture

The process of organizing a website so that visitors can browse and understand it with ease is known as information architecture. This calls for the logical and transparent arrangement of all the relevant information. In information architecture, consistency is crucial and can be attained by standardizing labels on all pages, including those for buttons, menus, and links.

The three pillars of design–content, context, and users–are united by IA. These components need to work together for IA to be successful.

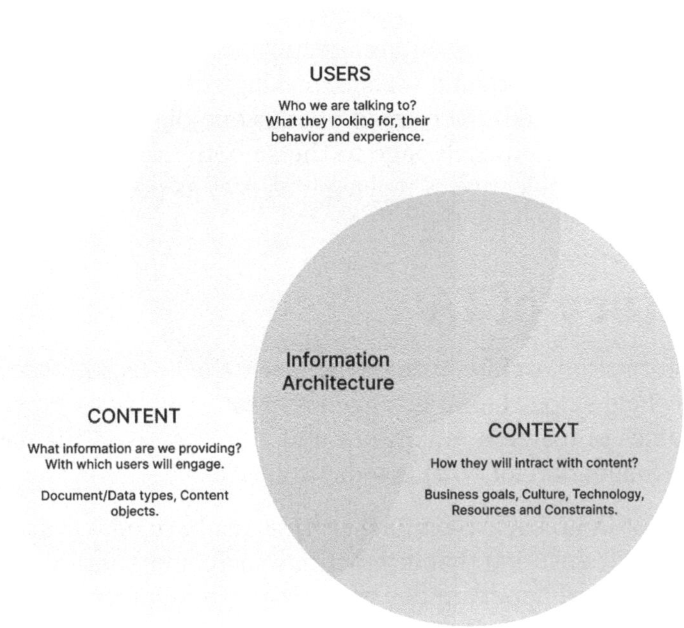

Figure 5.1: *Basics of Information Architecture*

The user's context and needs should be your two main considerations when structuring material to ensure it makes sense to users.

The setting in which people engage with your material is known as the context. To do this, arrange the content according to links, hierarchies, and classifications. To nail the context, consider the where, when, why, and how users are finding and interacting with your material.

Next, match your material to the expectations, requirements, goals, and behaviors of the user. This is called "smart labeling," where the relationships, hierarchies, and categories you have created are represented and classified using words. You must understand your users' characteristics, the benefits your content offers them, and how they utilize it in order to do this effectively.

These components work together to provide a smooth navigation system that makes it easy for users to discover what they need without getting lost or feeling overloaded with information.

Example:

Consider that you are organizing a road trip throughout a sizable and foreign nation. You meticulously plan out your itinerary to ensure that you don't get lost or miss any must-see locations. You make plans for where to dine, where to stop for petrol, and which beautiful sights you can't miss. Every choice is made with your journey in mind to make sure it goes well and you enjoy yourself.

For websites and apps, information architecture effectively performs this function. It is similar to charting the digital terrain, making sure that each piece of data and route is logically positioned. Everything about your digital environment, from the information that displays on each page to the smooth transitions between sections, is created with the one objective of making it as easy as possible for people to locate exactly what they are searching for.

The History of IA

The story of Information Architecture (IA) begins in the 1970s, long before the internet became a household staple. Librarians and archivists, who were experts in arranging enormous volumes of material in libraries and archives, ruled the day. Their efforts established the foundation for what is today known as IA.

Still, the origins of IA go back even farther. Humans have always arranged facts and information logically, ensuring that interactions and communication serve a purpose. Messaging gets lost and opportunities get missed when information is disorganized. This inherent need for structure was the seed that would grow into modern IA.

Let us go back to the 1960s. "Architecture of the IBM System/360," a seminal research paper published by IBM in 1964, defined "architecture" in computing as the conceptual organization and functional behavior of data flows and controls. This was among the first official acknowledgements of the necessity of a consistent information structure. The Xerox Palo Alto Research Centre scientists laid the conceptual groundwork for what is now known as information architecture (IA) just a few years later, in 1970, by developing technology to support the "architecture of information."

Let us start with architect and graphic designer Richard Saul Wurman, who originally used the phrase "Information Architecture" in the 1970s. Wurman observed parallels between the architecture of buildings and the requirement for digital space organization. His initial discussion of "information design" and the competencies required of designers later gave rise to the notion of "information architecture," which became the title of one of his major works.

IA became crucial with the 1990s internet explosion. The "Polar Bear Book," or "Information Architecture for the World Wide Web," was published in 1998 by Lou Rosenfeld and Peter Morville, who are frequently referred to as the godfathers of IA.

This seminal work gave IA a framework and defined values and procedures that shaped the industry for many years to come.

Information Architecture (IA) has grown significantly since the mid-1980s. It was quite unstructured and open at first, but it has since developed into a field with distinct procedures. These days, IA plays a major role in user experience (UX) design, organizing everything from mobile app interfaces to website navigation. It is constantly changing to stay up with new developments in technology and information usage patterns. When you use an app, navigate a digital library, or browse a website, IA is at work in the background to make sure you can find what you need quickly and effortlessly.

Placing Information Architecture at the center of design will benefit both the modern and future worlds. IA will always remain a part of our lives as long as technology does. It will continue to be a crucial component of our interactions with the abundance of information around us, facilitating easy and intuitive digital travel.

Importance of Information Architecture

Picture yourself in a disorganized library with all the files and books scattered around. You would think it would be time-consuming and frustrating to find the book you wanted. If there is no clear hierarchy, the same thing occurs in the digital realm. Information architecture, or IA, is useful in this situation.

- **Improving the User Interface:** Users can locate what they are looking for with ease on a well-organized website or app. Similar to how aisles are indicated by signs in a well-organized store, effective information architecture facilitates consumers' easy navigation of content. Because of their excellent experience, visitors are more inclined to visit the website again and refer others to it.
- **Enhances Availability:** IA makes sure that all users, including those with impairments, can access the content. It makes the content easier to find and comprehend for all users, regardless of ability, by employing clear labels and logical information organization.
- **Increases Productivity:** Effective IA can help firms save money and time. Workers can complete tasks more quickly and with less annoyance when they can easily locate the information they require. This effectiveness may result in increased output and a more positive work environment.
- **Encourages SEO:** Search engines can better comprehend your site's structure and content if your IA is coherent and clear. By doing this, you may raise your website's search engine rating and facilitate potential clients' discovery of you. Enhanced visibility has the potential to result in higher traffic and more business.
- **Facilitates Content Management:** Managing content can get harder as websites get bigger. A solid information architecture foundation facilitates

the addition, updating, and removal of content without causing disruption. It guarantees that, despite its evolution, the website will always be organized and user-friendly.

- **Lessens Clutter and Redundancy:** IA helps prevent clutter and duplication by efficiently organizing content. It guarantees that every item of information has a designated spot, making the website easier to navigate and cleaner overall.
- **Improves the Overall Design:** A website or app visual design is enhanced by effective IA. An aesthetically beautiful and harmonious user experience is produced by well-organized content, which lets the design take center stage. It resembles having a well-organized space where everything has a designated spot.

To put it briefly, information architecture is similar to a building's blueprint. It guarantees that everything is conveniently located, easy to find, and enjoyable to use. Good user experience (UX) design is essential for producing a satisfying, productive, and successful user experience on any digital platform, be it a website, an app, or another.

Information Architecture Principles

With over 20 years of experience under his belt, Brown crafted eight key principles to guide designers in making smart decisions when developing their build strategies. His mission was to create a set of "guidelines rooted in universal truths that define what makes any information architecture truly effective." When an information architect or designer masters these principles, they can easily tackle even the most complex IA challenges and design user-friendly websites.

Here is a detailed explanation of each principle of information architecture:

Principle of Objects

According to the Principle of Objects, content needs to be viewed as dynamic entities with distinct behaviors, lifecycles, and properties. Every book, for instance, is more than just a static item in a digital library catalogue. It contains metadata with the following: title, author, and genre; availability status (checked out or available); and user-generated content with reservations and reviews. This perspective on content helps designers build more responsive and interactive systems that better represent the complexity of the material in the actual world and facilitate users' ability to locate, comprehend, and interact with the information they require.

Principle of Choices

In order to prevent overwhelming consumers, the Principle of Choices places a strong emphasis on giving them a concise, manageable list of options. These choices have to be appropriate for the particular job at hand. A user may become frustrated and indecisive if there are too many options. Instead of providing dozens of filters, an e-commerce site might restrict its product filter options to just the most important ones, including size, color, and price range. This targeted strategy improves the entire purchasing experience by assisting people in finding what they need fast and without being overly overwhelmed by options.

The options should be related to a specific task. As illustrated in the following image, the website shows that an email subscription form popup should provide the user with only three choices: subscribe, don't subscribe, or close the popup. This simplifies the decision-making process for the user, making their experience more straightforward and pleasant.

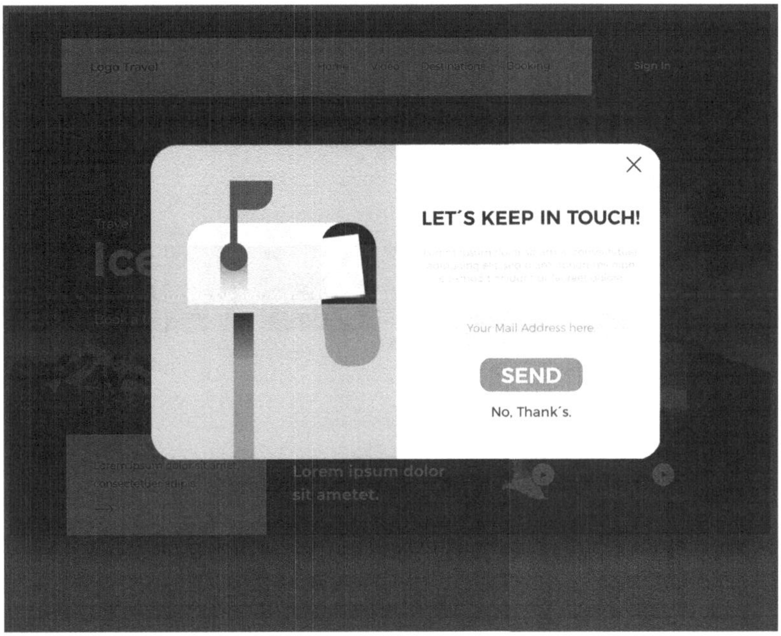

***Figure 5.2**: Example of a popup displaying a specific task with a minimal number of choices*

Principle of Disclosure

The goal of the Principle of Disclosure is to provide consumers with just enough information to help them comprehend what's coming without going overboard. As consumers delve deeper, information is gradually revealed to them, enabling them to make wise decisions.

For example, an online course platform might offer a synopsis, instructor bio, and a few salient elements for each subject. Users can select whether to investigate further by reading student reviews or studying a complete syllabus after taking a quick look.

Users are directed through the content with ease and feel less cognitive stress and better overall when information is revealed gradually.

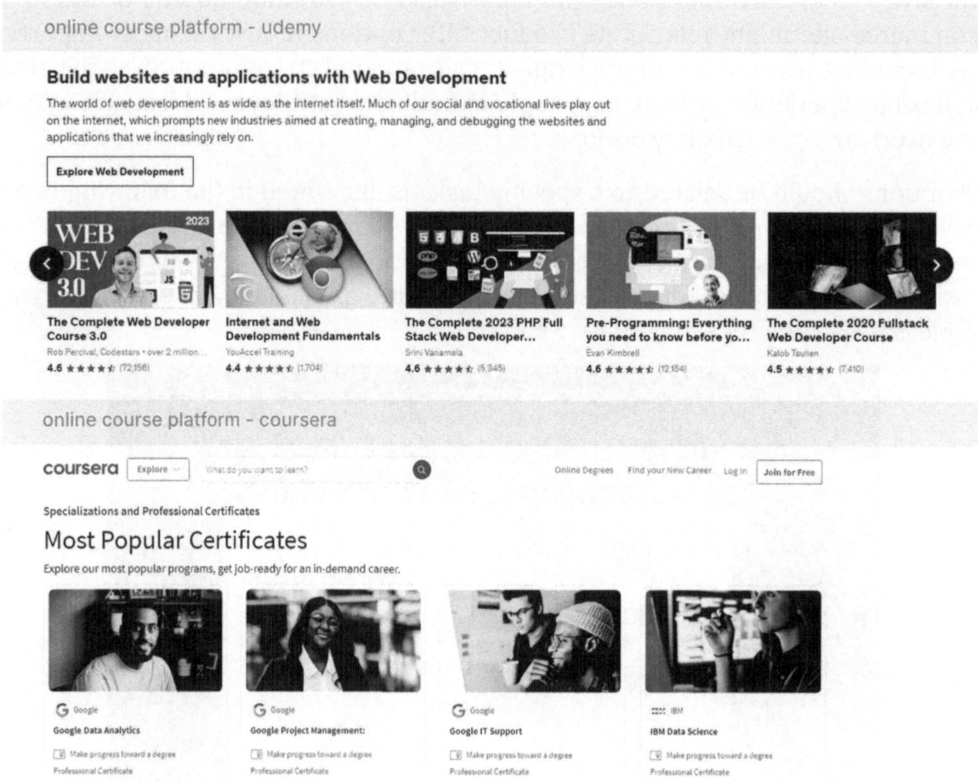

***Figure 5.3**: Example of online courses reveal content in certain amount at a time*

Principle of Exemplars

By employing examples, the Principle of Exemplars aims to make topic categories more understandable. Even if users don't fully comprehend the names for each category, they can still better understand and navigate a website or app when visual examples of various content kinds are provided. This method makes it easier and faster for users to find what they're looking for, which greatly improves the user experience.

For instance, a recipe website on the internet might group dishes together under headings like "Healthy Choices" or "Quick Meals." The website can display pictures of a simple stir-fry or a crisp salad next to these labels in addition to text. With the aid of these visual cues, users are better able to navigate to the material they are looking for by quickly understanding the sort of recipes included in each category. The website uses visual examples to simplify and lessen uncertainty, making the user's experience more pleasurable and intuitive.

Principle of Front Doors

The Principle of Front Doors emphasizes that not all users will enter your site through the homepage. Therefore, it is crucial to design your site with the understanding that users may land on any page. Ensure that every page provides context, navigation options, and essential information, so visitors always know where they are and what steps they can take next.

For instance, imagine a user searching for a specific blog post and arriving directly on that post's page. If the page includes a clear site menu, breadcrumbs, and related content links, the user can easily navigate to other parts of the site without feeling lost. By providing consistent navigation aids and key information across all pages, you make it easier for users to explore your site seamlessly, regardless of their entry point. This approach enhances user experience by making navigation intuitive and ensuring that all visitors can easily find their way around.

Principle of Multiple Classification

Providing consumers with multiple options for searching and navigating your website's content is part of the Principle of Multiple Classification. Although top-level menus and search bars are standard approaches, it is crucial to offer alternate routes for people who want to browse or investigate through hierarchical structures. This guarantees that various user needs and preferences are met by the information architecture.

For instance, to improve user experience, an instructional website could include several classification alternatives. The content could be searched for by grade level (for example, elementary or high school), subject (for example., math or science), or resource type (for example, worksheets, videos, or articles). The site is more user-friendly and accessible because of this multifaceted approach, which enables visitors to find the information they need in a way that fits their surfing habits. You may make an environment that is more adaptable and user-friendly by allowing for several navigation modes.

1. **Principle of Focused Navigation:** Consistency and relevancy in navigation menus and aids across your website are critical, as highlighted by the Principle of Focused Navigation. Make sure all of the content on your menus is consistent and relevant; do not mix in irrelevant topics that could confuse users. Don't list other services on a menu dedicated to product categories, for instance. Likewise, if the menu is meant to be navigated, take off any marketing or functional components.

   For example, a product menu on an e-commerce website should only have categories like "Electronics," "Clothing," and "Home Goods." Unrelated elements like "Customer Support" and "Special Offers" should not be on it. You may improve users' experience on your site by helping them locate what they are seeking for fast and simply with targeted navigation. Navigation is made simple and easy with consistent and relevant menus, which lowers the risk of user irritation.

Amazon is an excellent example of an e-commerce website that keeps its navigation organized. It displays all product categories in the main menu while placing customer support and other services in the footer section.

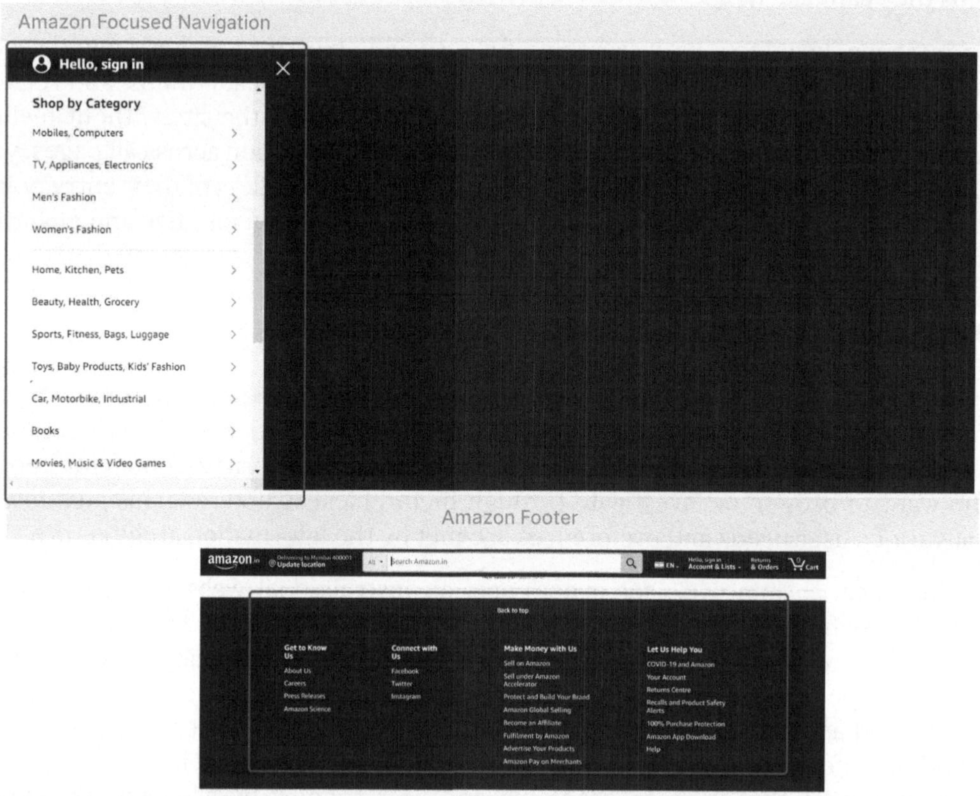

Figure 5.4: *Amazon's well-organized navigation menu*

2. **Principle of Growth:** The main goal of the Principle of Growth is to create a framework that can easily accommodate new content without needing to be completely redone. The general layout of a website, including the navigation and search functions, should be easily expandable to meet future needs. This strategy guarantees that the website may grow sustainably, irrespective of the kinds of material that are added throughout time.

   A news website, **for instance**, might begin with a few primary categories like "World," "Technology," and "Sports." The website ought to be able to expand by adding additional sections like "Health," "Entertainment," or "Environment" without having any trouble keeping the current design in place. The website can effortlessly add new content areas and change continuously if expansion is planned for from the start. Even when the website grows, consumers will always enjoy a consistent and well-organized experience, thanks to its scalability.

Following these principles allows designers to create intuitive, user-friendly information architectures that can evolve over time.

Information Architecture Systems

Understanding the user is an information architect's primary responsibility. To make information easier to use and locate, they employ information architecture systems to identify, organize, and structure the data. Architects design a system that meets the needs of users by understanding their objectives, goals, and methods of information search. **This calls for familiarity with four crucial areas: Search: How to set up search functions; organization: How to arrange material; labeling: How to label it; navigation: How to create navigation**. Every component is thoughtfully made to make it easier for users to find what they need.

- **Search Systems:** By entering keywords or phrases, users can find information via an IA's search mechanism. It is simple for users to find what they are seeking for quickly when a search system works well. In order to make search results easier to interpret, it also takes that into account. Users of advanced search engines can be able to refine their search and locate exactly what they're looking for by using choices to filter and sort results. Information architects make sure that consumers can quickly find the information they need by creating a user-friendly search system.
- **Organization Systems:**
  - **Hierarchical**: Information is grouped into broad categories that branch out into more focused subcategories, creating a structure similar to a tree. An online store may, for instance, have a primary category called "Clothing," which is further subdivided into "Men's Clothing," "Women's Clothing," and more.
  - **Sequential**: Information is presented in a particular order to lead consumers through an organized process. This is typical of multi-step forms or tutorials.
  - **Matrix**: Content can be viewed by users in a variety of ways, including popularity, date, and price.
- **Labeling Systems:** Labels give users context and point them in the direction of more information. For your website to effectively communicate with their audience, they must be comprehensible, familiar, and clear.

As an **example**, let us say a customer goes to the homepage of an online retailer to view their shipping and return policies. The information architect may choose to designate a section of the main menu as "Customer Service" rather than stuffing the homepage with this information. Users can locate necessary policies and support choices more quickly with the help of this well-known label.

- **Navigation Systems:** On a website, navigation aids users in finding specific information. It consists of various components that combine to create recognizable patterns for guests. Information architects now create the paths people will take to navigate the website and specify how the pages connect to one another.
    - **Global Navigation:** The principal navigation menu that is accessible from every page and leads to the site's key parts.
    - **Local Navigation:** Area-specific menus that direct viewers to related material within a certain section or page.
    - **Contextual Navigation:** Pointers to related information or resources that are located inside the material.

Example

Take into consideration a vacation website "`Tripadvisor`" that improves UX with IA systems. Content may be categorized by "`Travel Guides`," "`Hotel Reservations`," "`Flight Booking`," and "`Destinations`" under the organization system. The navigation system features a global menu for convenient access to different parts, and each category is clearly labeled. Furthermore, a powerful search engine enables users to rapidly locate particular locations or travel advice. This extensive IA system guarantees that customers may easily browse the website, get pertinent information, and make reservations for their travels.

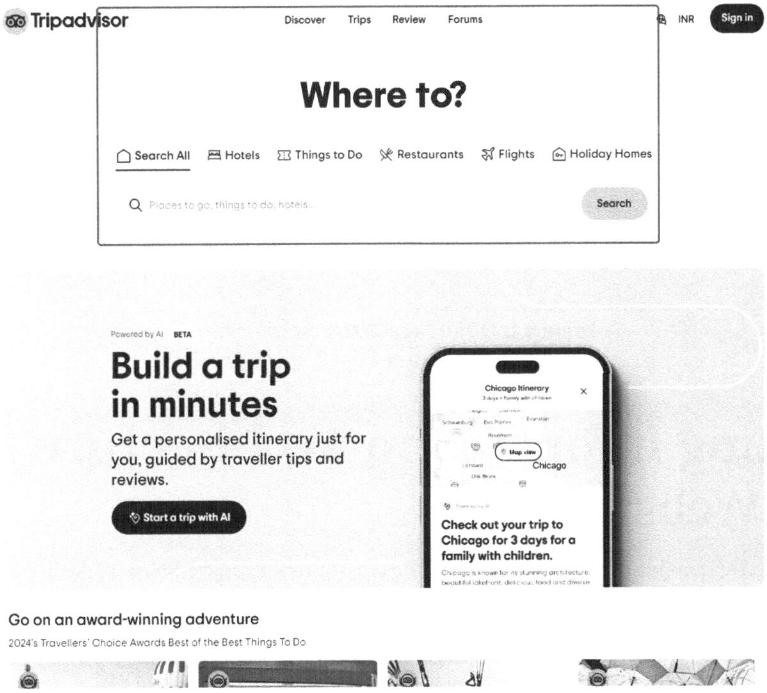

***Figure 5.5**: Tripadvisor homepage with elements of IA system*

IA versus UX

Information Architecture (IA) and User Experience (UX) are related but distinct aspects of designing digital products.

	Information Architecture (IA)	User Experience (UX)
Focus	Organizing and structuring content	Overall experience and satisfaction of the user
Goal	The main aim of IA is to help users understand where they are, what they have found, and what to expect. It ensures that the content is accessible and logical	The main aim of UX is to create products that are not only functional but also enjoyable and satisfying to use. It focuses on the overall experience a user has with the product
Components	Hierarchies, navigation systems, categorization, labeling	Usability, design, accessibility, interaction design, user research

Task	Organizing content on a website into clear categories and creating a navigation system	Ensuring that the navigation system is easy to use, visually appealing, and aligns with users' mental models
IA concentrates on information organization and structuring, whereas UX adopts a more comprehensive approach, including every facet of the user's engagement with the product. UX relies heavily on effective information architecture (IA), since a user's experience is more seamless and intuitive when information is arranged properly.		

Table 5.1: *Difference between Information Architecture (IA) and User Experience (UX)*

Creating Information Architecture for Your Website

A logical structure is necessary for each new business application or your new website. Each IA project is different, therefore there may be variations in the order of steps. Nevertheless, you can complete the required research, analysis, and organization by following these steps. This procedure will assist you in creating a framework that works and will make your digital project user-friendly and well-organized.

The process of organizing and structuring your content to make it easy for people to discover what they need on your website is known as information architecture (IA).

1. Understand Users and Define Goals

Begin by understanding user habits. Identify your audience: Who are they? What do they need? Conduct surveys, interviews, or use analytics to gain insights into their behaviors and preferences. If you are working solo, remember that your perspective may differ from that of your users. Categorizing information can be intuitive, so resist relying solely on your personal preferences. Focus on the unique needs and desires of your users.

Next, understand your users' language preferences. For instance, in banking apps, terms like "account" or "balance" are frequently used. In the US, "balance" might be more commonly understood, whereas in Australia, "available funds" could be more popular. Selecting the appropriate terms can greatly improve the user experience and clarity.

Lastly, define your goals. What is your website's purpose? Whether you aim to boost sales, share information, or provide services, having clear objectives will shape your IA decisions.

2. Create Categories and Label the Content

The first step in efficiently organizing the information on your website is to make a list of all the articles, product pages, and videos that you currently have or intend to add. A thorough list facilitates the development of a coherent framework. Sort your information into categories that are easy for your viewers to understand. A tech blog, for instance, would include sections labelled "Gadgets," "Software," "Reviews," and "Tutorials."

Sort and prioritize content using the findings from your user research. Think about the way people intuitively arrange information. If your cookery website, for instance, has a ton of recipes for breakfast, lunch, and dinner, you might group them together under the heading "Meals."

Try utilizing a few of the procedures used by information architects. To assist you in organizing the content, apply tree testing and card sorting strategies.

Card Sorting: To find out how consumers classify various products into different groups, we employ a participatory design process called card sorting. They are asked to arrange the terms, features, or concepts printed on the cards into groups.

Tree Testing: You can observe how your users react to labels and navigation with the aid of tree testing. This procedure will demonstrate to you how user-friendly your website is for finding information.

After that, divide these categories into groups. Examine the websites of rival businesses to see how they organize their material. Choose which of their tactics to use and which to adjust. You may come across content during this procedure that doesn't cleanly fit into any one category. This content occasionally falls into more than one category or doesn't belong in any existing group. To keep a coherent structure, evaluate and decide how to handle such content.

Maintaining a user-friendly and relevant website for your audience requires regular reviews and updates to your content organization.

3. Create a Hierarchy, Develop Navigation and Sitemap

Establish a distinct hierarchy before you begin organizing the material on your website. Consider this as laying the groundwork for a house. The primary categories, which are similar to the main rooms of a house, must be chosen before moving on to the subcategories, which are similar to the more specific areas inside the primary rooms. Users will find it easier to navigate your information with the support of this structure, creating a logical flow.

After establishing your hierarchy, the next step is to create a user-friendly navigation mechanism. Think of this as creating pathways and signs throughout your home to make it simple for guests to find their way around. This system has search capabilities, menus, and links that are all intended to help users navigate your website easily. The key is to keep it simple and intuitive, so users don't feel lost or overwhelmed.

The next important question is: How will users access this stuff now that your groups and content are set up? You must first define your information architecture (IA) before you can create a sitemap and navigation. IA can be compared to your home's blueprint, which provides the layout but is not always visible to guests. But because it serves as the foundation of your website, it is essential. IA can be graphically represented using spreadsheets and diagrams, which are also called sitemaps.

Sorting, labeling, and organizing your content into a diagram is the process of creating a sitemap. This is identical to mapping out the locations of all the rooms and sections in your house. The navigation elements can be developed after you have your sitemap. These resemble your home's doors, corridors, and signage. They consist of the footer as well as local navigation elements like filters and breadcrumbs as well as global navigation menus. For people to explore your website with ease, these components need to be meaningfully connected to one another.

You may make a website that is user-friendly and well-organized by following these steps. Similar to a well-designed home, visitors to your website will feel at home and be able to easily discover what they need.

Additional Details Regarding Navigation

Take into account the following ideas while creating a navigational structure for your website so that it serves your audience's needs:

Models of Navigation:

- **Single-page Models:** Ideal for information-rich websites where all content may be accessed by scrolling down a single page.
- **Flat Models:** Helps ensure that every page is just a few clicks away from the homepage, ideal for small to medium-sized websites with a handful of categories.
- **Hierarchical Models:** Content is arranged into primary categories and subcategories on these expansive, intricate websites.

Navigation Types:

- **Main Navigation:** The primary menu, often located at the top of the page, directs visitors to the most crucial areas of your website.
- **Secondary Navigation:** Extra menus, frequently found in sidebars or footers, that offer access to less important elements.

- **Hidden Navigation:** Menus like drop-downs, hamburger menus, and flyouts that are not initially visible and only show up when manipulated are referred to as hidden navigation.

4. User Testing and Iterate

Validate your IA by testing it with actual users. Perform usability tests to determine if users can effortlessly locate what they need. Collect feedback and make the necessary adjustments. It is crucial to test early and frequently.

You have a couple of options for this. You can conduct additional testing with your initial user group to evaluate your final website labels and categories. Alternatively, you can assemble a new informal group for usability testing.

Tree testing and **closed card sorting** are other options which are invaluable tools when designing a website's structure, each offering unique benefits to ensure a user-friendly experience.

Imagine you are building a library. **Tree testing** helps you see if visitors can easily find their way around. It tells you if the section names make sense, if they clearly convey what they contain, and if each title is distinct. By guiding users through a simplified version of your site, you can determine whether your content is organized in a way that makes sense to them.

Closed card sorting, on the other hand, lets users organize content into given categories. It is like asking your library visitors to sort books into labeled shelves. This process reveals if the category names accurately describe the content and if users can easily distinguish between titles. It also ensures that the organization is user-centered, reflecting how people naturally group information in their minds.

By combining tree testing and closed card sorting, you create a website structure that is intuitive and easy to navigate. Both methods ensure that category names are clear, content is correctly categorized, and information is easy to find, making your website as welcoming and accessible as a well-organized library.

5. Document Everything

Clearly documenting everything is an essential first step in developing a successful information architecture (IA). Make a wireframe or sitemap to begin with so that your IA is represented graphically. Consider this to be your website's blueprint, much to a building's architectural designs. The relationships between the various pages and components of your website are illustrated in a sitemap. For designers and developers, this visual depiction is quite helpful since it gives them a clear idea of how the website is laid out. It guarantees that all project participants are aware of the connections between various site sections and are on the same page. Wireframes go one step further by offering a basic layout for every page, including navigation, content, and call-to-action placement. This documentation guarantees a coherent structure, minimizes confusion, and speeds up the design and development process.

6. Stay Flexible

Effective IA creation is a continuous process rather than a one-time event. Prepare yourself to continually update and improve your IA as your material expands and user needs change. Continuing to be adaptable is necessary to keep your website user-friendly. Review your IA frequently to find any places that might require modification. This could be the result of usability test results, newly additional material, or modifications in user behavior. You can guarantee that your website remains user-friendly and intuitive by being flexible and making the required adjustments. This continuous improvement helps your website stay current and better meet the changing needs of your consumers.

These procedures will help you build a strong interface architecture (IA) that will improve the usability and navigation of your website. Cheers to your successful structuring!

Information Architecture Tools

Tools for information architecture (IA) are essential for developing and structuring apps and webpages. They make it easier to create logical content arrangements for users and help create intuitive navigation systems. These are a few popular free tools for information architecture:

- **Diagrams.net:** Flowcharts, sitemaps, and diagrams may all be made with Diagrams.net (previously Draw.io). It is web-based and provides a variety of templates for illustrating concepts such as IA.
- **MindMup:** A free mind mapping application that facilitates idea organization and brainstorming. It is helpful for illustrating the connections and hierarchical structures among the various IA components.
- **Pencil Project:** A free and open-source GUI prototype tool that lets you make wireframes, diagrams, and UI prototypes. It is simple to use and meets a range of IA design diagramming requirements.
- **XMind:** XMind is an additional free brainstorming and mind mapping tool that facilitates idea organization. Through the visual representation of hierarchies and linkages, it aids in information structure and IA planning.
- **FigJam:** The main purpose of FigJam is to serve as a collaborative whiteboard tool for ideation and brainstorming in teams. It can, however, facilitate

information architecture tasks by letting users generate site maps, flowcharts, and user journeys. It is a useful tool for visualizing complicated information structures because of its user-friendly interface and real-time collaborative capabilities.

- **Miro:** Another cooperative whiteboard tool for creativity and teamwork is called Miro. It assists information architecture activities in addition to its primary function of enabling brainstorming sessions. Information can be organized and visualized with the aid of mind maps, wireframes, and diagrams that users can develop. Its adaptability makes it a valuable tool for efficiently organizing information.

These tools are affordable alternatives for designers and developers since they include all the necessary features for developing and improving Information Architecture.

Introduction to Sitemaps

Imagine you have just opened a bookstore, filled with shelves upon shelves of incredible books. You want your customers to find the perfect book easily and enjoy their shopping experience, right? But if the store is unorganized, with no signs or sections, customers will leave in frustration. The same goes for your website. A website without a sitemap leaves your visitors and search engines wandering aimlessly.

You have created a website to connect with clients and drive sales. However, as websites grow larger and more complex, search engines can struggle to navigate the vast amount of content available. This means that even your most valuable content can get buried, making it hard for both search engines and visitors to find it.

Enter the sitemap, the unsung hero of your website's organization. A sitemap acts like a detailed map of your bookstore, highlighting key sections and must-read books. It ensures that search engines and visitors can quickly and easily find your most important pages, enhancing their experience and boosting your site's performance.

Creating a sitemap is the next crucial step in optimizing your website, making sure that all your fantastic content gets the attention it deserves.

The Technical Role of Sitemaps in Web Architecture

A sitemap is a list of all the URLs on a website along with metadata about each URL (such as its relative relevance and the date it was last updated). It makes sure that all significant pages are indexed and reachable by assisting search engines with their more effective crawling and understanding of the site's structure.

Importance of Sitemap

There are several situations in which a sitemap comes in quite handy.

For instance, Google usually uses links to find online pages. In order to help Google find your pages if your website is new or a site without many external backlinks, you must create a sitemap.

Furthermore, for Google to find every page on your multimillion-page e-commerce website, flawless internal linking and a substantial quantity of external links are required. A sitemap is essential in these situations since it guarantees that search engines can access all of your information.

A sitemap is crucial for optimizing your website for several reasons, such as:

- **Enhances SEO and Search Engine Crawling:** Sitemaps give search engines a road map of your website, ensuring that all crucial pages are found and indexed. By aiding search engines in comprehending the architecture and content of your website, this raises your site's search engine ranks.
- **Enhances User Experience:** A well-organized sitemap facilitates users' navigation of your website, enabling them to obtain the information they require fast.
- **Manages Large and Complex Sites:** A sitemap is necessary for websites with a lot of pages. It facilitates the efficient navigation and indexing of your information by search engines, which might be difficult with traditional crawling alone.

Types of Sitemaps

Sitemaps come in two primary varieties: HTML and XML. Web pages are coded in two languages: XML (Extensible Markup Language) and HTML (Hypertext Markup Language). Every kind has a distinct function on your website. We will go into more detail about a couple of additional kinds of sitemaps as well.

HTML Sitemap

The main purpose of an HTML sitemap is to assist users of the website. This website focuses on improving navigation for people, not search engines, by methodically listing and classifying links to every other page on the website. An HTML sitemap can be made more aesthetically pleasing and functional by using CSS to improve its appearance.

An HTML sitemap's primary goal is to make it easier for visitors to find particular pages or content they are interested in, cutting down on search time and boosting user interaction. By ensuring users can easily access the relevant data, this feature not only enhances the overall user experience but also helps your site's SEO rating. To put it simply, an HTML sitemap is a useful tool for improving user experience and making a website perform better in search engine rankings.

HTML sitemaps have a hierarchical structure that makes them resemble traditional index cards or tables of contents. They make it simpler for users to explore and find information on websites, especially those with intricate structures or a lot of content. HTML sitemaps can enhance user experience by delivering a concise summary of your site's content offers and structure by sorting links either alphabetically or in categories.

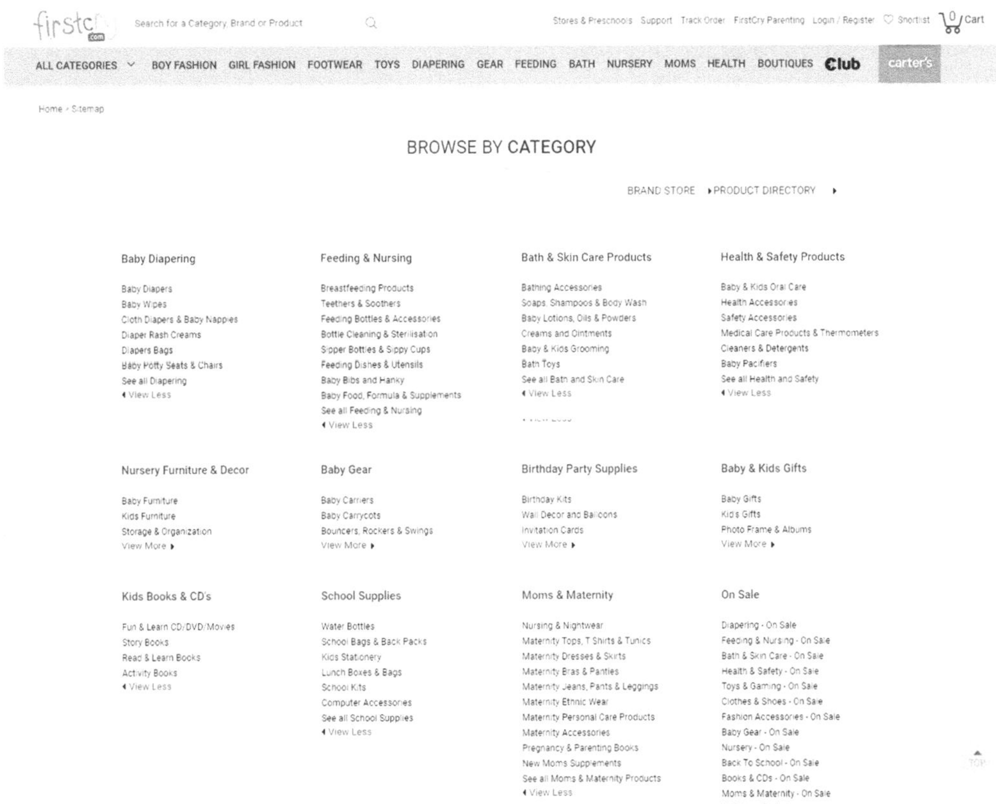

Figure 5.6: *Explore the HTML Sitemap of Firstcry Shopping Website*

Example: Envision the website Firstcry Shopping, providing an extensive selection of baby items, guidance on raising children, and practical tools. Links could be arranged into categories like "**`Baby Diapering`**," "**`Feeding and Nursing`**," "**`Baby and Kids Clothing`**," and more in an HTML sitemap. Links to pertinent pages would be included in each area to help users locate what they are looking for quickly and without having to go through several pages.

Essentially, HTML sitemaps improve usability by offering a road map of your website's content that is easy to navigate and makes users happier.

XML Sitemap

A file specifically prepared in XML (Extensible Markup Language) called an XML sitemap aids search engines in effectively crawling and indexing the content of websites. XML sitemaps are made exclusively for search engines to traverse and index a website's web pages, in contrast to HTML sitemaps, which are made for human visitors. Because they are XML files kept in the website's root directory, they are hidden from users of the website. They offer comprehensive details on the URLs on the website, including metadata about the last update, how frequently they are changed, and how important they are in relation to other URLs on the page.

Because they guarantee that search engines can identify and index all relevant sites – including those that could be challenging to find through routine crawling, including pages with little internal linking or dynamically created content – XML sitemaps are essential for search engine optimization. Webmasters can improve the visibility of their site's content by uploading an XML sitemap to search engines, such as Google.

Think of an online news website with plenty of articles, tags, and categories, for instance. Each article, category, and tag page would have its URL listed in the XML sitemap, together with information identifying the most recent change date for each item. By doing this, search engines are better able to comprehend the site's structure and give priority to indexing recently added or updated information.

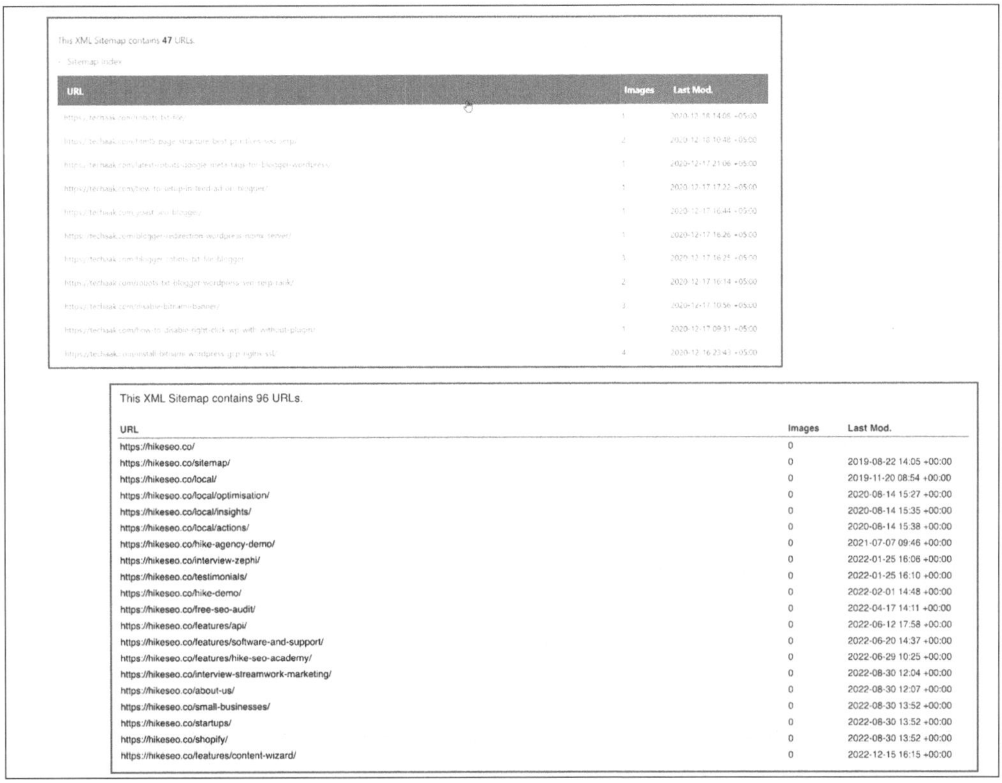

URL	Images	Last Mod.
https://hikeseo.co/	0	
https://hikeseo.co/sitemap/	0	2019-08-22 14:05 +00:00
https://hikeseo.co/local/	0	2019-11-20 08:54 +00:00
https://hikeseo.co/local/optimisation/	0	2020-08-14 15:27 +00:00
https://hikeseo.co/local/insights/	0	2020-08-14 15:35 +00:00
https://hikeseo.co/local/actions/	0	2020-08-14 15:38 +00:00
https://hikeseo.co/hike-agency-demo/	0	2021-07-07 09:46 +00:00
https://hikeseo.co/interview-zephi/	0	2022-01-25 16:06 +00:00
https://hikeseo.co/testimonials/	0	2022-01-25 16:10 +00:00
https://hikeseo.co/hike-demo/	0	2022-02-01 14:48 +00:00
https://hikeseo.co/free-seo-audit/	0	2022-04-17 14:11 +00:00
https://hikeseo.co/features/api/	0	2022-06-12 17:58 +00:00
https://hikeseo.co/features/software-and-support/	0	2022-06-20 14:37 +00:00
https://hikeseo.co/features/hike-seo-academy/	0	2022-06-29 10:25 +00:00
https://hikeseo.co/interview-streamwork-marketing/	0	2022-08-30 12:04 +00:00
https://hikeseo.co/about-us/	0	2022-08-30 12:07 +00:00
https://hikeseo.co/small-businesses/	0	2022-08-30 13:52 +00:00
https://hikeseo.co/startups/	0	2022-08-30 13:52 +00:00
https://hikeseo.co/shopify/	0	2022-08-30 13:52 +00:00
https://hikeseo.co/features/content-wizard/	0	2022-12-15 16:15 +00:00

Figure 5.7: *Example of XML Sitemap*

In conclusion, an XML sitemap serves as a thorough manual for search engines, guaranteeing that all significant pages of a website are found and appropriately indexed, increasing the visibility of the website in search results.

Video Sitemap

A specific kind of XML sitemap called a video sitemap gives search engines metadata about the videos on your website. The title, description, length, location (URL), thumbnail URL, and publishing date of the video are all included in this metadata. A video sitemap enhances your videos' discoverability and indexing by providing search engines with this comprehensive information, which helps them comprehend the content and context of your films.

For websites that primarily use video content, such media websites, educational platforms, or online courses, video sitemaps are essential. They guarantee that videos are properly indexed, increasing the likelihood that they will show up in video search results and improving the site's SEO in general. Proper indexing of video content can lead to higher visibility and increased traffic from search engines.

Example: Consider a cooking website with a vast collection of recipe videos. Every video features a new recipe and provides detailed instructions. This website would have a video sitemap that included URLs for every video as well as metadata like the title ("How to Make Chocolate Cake"), description ("A step-by-step guide to baking a delicious chocolate cake"), length (5 minutes), and thumbnail URL (link to the video's thumbnail image). By giving search engines this data, they can more fully comprehend and index the video content, which makes it simpler for viewers to locate these movies when looking for recipes that go along with them.

The following **example** demonstrates a standard sitemap with video extensions. It features two video entries nested within a single **`<url>`** tag. The first **`<video>`** entry includes all the tags that Google can utilize, while the second entry contains only the essential tags.

```
<?xml version="1.0" encoding="UTF-8"?>
<urlset xmlns="http://www.sitemaps.org/schemas/sitemap/0.9"
    xmlns:video="http://www.google.com/schemas/sitemap-video/1.1">
  <url>
    <loc>https://www.example.com/videos/some_video_landing_page.html</
loc>
    <video:video>
      <video:thumbnail_loc>https://www.example.com/thumbs/123.jpg</
video:thumbnail_loc>
      <video:title>Grilling steaks for summer</video:title>
      <video:description>
        Alkis shows you how to get perfectly done steaks every time
      </video:description>
      <video:content_loc>
        http://streamserver.example.com/video123.mp4
      </video:content_loc>
      <video:player_loc>
        https://www.example.com/videoplayer.php?video=123
      </video:player_loc>
      <video:duration>600</video:duration>
      <video:expiration_date>2021-11-05T19:20:30+08:00</video:expiration
_date>
      <video:rating>4.2</video:rating>
      <video:view_count>12345</video:view_count>
      <video:publication_date>2007-11-05T19:20:30+08:00</video:
publication_date>
      <video:family_friendly>yes</video:family_friendly>
      <video:restriction relationship="allow">IE GB US CA</video:
restriction>
      <video:price currency="EUR">1.99</video:price>
      <video:requires_subscription>yes</video:requires_subscription>
      <video:uploader
        info="https://www.example.com/users/grillymcgrillerson">
```

```
GrillyMcGrillerson
      </video:uploader>
      <video:live>no</video:live>
    </video:video>
    <video:video>
      <video:thumbnail_loc>https://www.example.com/thumbs/345.jpg</
video:thumbnail_loc>
      <video:title>Grilling steaks for winter</video:title>
      <video:description>
        In the freezing cold, Roman shows you how to get perfectly done
steaks every time.
      </video:description>
      <video:content_loc>
        http://streamserver.example.com/video345.mp4
      </video:content_loc>
      <video:player_loc>
        https://www.example.com/videoplayer.php?video=345
      </video:player_loc>
    </video:video>
  </url>
</urlset>
```

In summary, a video sitemap is a crucial tool for enhancing a website's video content discoverability and SEO since it makes sure that videos are correctly indexed and easier for viewers to access through search engine results.

Image Sitemap

A specific kind of XML sitemap called an image sitemap aids in the discovery and indexing of images on your website by search engines. Image sitemaps include more information about the images on those pages, such as the image URL, title, caption, license, and other pertinent details, in addition to the URLs of the web pages that they link to. By providing more context and information, the upgraded data increases the likelihood that the photographs will show up in image search results.

Websites that primarily rely on visual material, including e-commerce sites, blogs with rich media, and photographic portfolios, can benefit greatly from image sitemaps. Webmasters can make sure that their photographs are indexed by search engines, improving their visibility and bringing more visitors to the website, by putting all pertinent images in the sitemap.

Example: Think of an online art gallery that features a variety of artworks, for instance. There are excellent photos, descriptions, and artist details available for each piece of art. For this website, an image sitemap would include the picture URLs as well as metadata like the title ("Starry Night by Vincent van Gogh"), the caption ("A famous painting by Vincent van Gogh"), and the type of license (public domain or copyrighted).

By doing this, search engines are better able to index the photographs and increase the likelihood that users searching for similar artwork will find it in the results of their image searches.

To sum up, an image sitemap is an essential tool for enhancing a website's image discoverability and indexing. By making sure search engines can appropriately decipher and rank the visual information, it improves the overall SEO of the website and increases the amount of organic traffic that comes from picture searches.

News Sitemap

An XML sitemap created especially for websites that post news material is known as a news sitemap. It facilitates the swift and effective discovery and indexing of news stories by search engines, especially Google News. By including metadata such as the article title, publisher name, keywords, and publication date, news sitemaps guarantee that consumers looking for news material can quickly find the most recent and pertinent news pieces.

For news websites, news sitemaps are critical because they allow new items to be quickly indexed, which is necessary for timely news distribution. Webmasters can guarantee that their content appears in search results as quickly as possible and hence increase traffic and reading by providing the most recent items in the sitemap.

Example: An online news portal that covers everything from sports to politics. Each news article that has been published in the last 48 hours would have a URL on this site's news sitemap, along with metadata like the title ("Election Results 2024"), the publication date ("2024-07-15"), and keywords ("election, 2024, results"). This facilitates the speedy discovery and indexing of the new articles by search engines, giving readers looking for the most recent election updates access to them.

In conclusion, news sites need a news sitemap to make sure that fresh content is quickly indexed and available to anyone looking for up-to-date information. It raises the site's organic traffic count, increases search engine ranking, and makes news material more visible.

Mobile Sitemap

A mobile sitemap is a unique type of XML sitemap created to help search engines find and index material on a website that is tailored for mobile devices. Websites must be responsive to users across several platforms, including smartphones and tablets, as mobile internet usage surges. The visibility and ranking of mobile-optimized pages are enhanced by a mobile sitemap, which aids search engines in identifying and prioritizing information designed for mobile users.

Websites with discrete mobile-friendly pages or independent mobile versions benefit most from mobile sitemaps. The URLs of mobile-specific pages are included in these sitemaps, along with pertinent metadata like the page's priority in relation to other URLs on the website and the date of its last modification. A mobile sitemap makes sure search engines can appropriately index and present the right material to mobile consumers by giving them this information.

Example: An online retailer with a mobile-specific website. All mobile-optimized pages, including product listings, category pages, and checkout pages, would have their URLs listed in a mobile sitemap. To aid search engines in comprehending the organization and significance of these sites, metadata is included with each entry in the sitemap. By doing this, search engines can swiftly lead consumers to the mobile-friendly version of the website when they conduct product searches on their mobile devices, improving user experience and possibly raising conversion rates.

To sum up, if a website has material tailored specifically for mobile devices, a mobile sitemap is a must. It ensures that mobile users have a fluid and intuitive browsing experience by assisting search engines in effectively indexing and prioritizing mobile-optimized pages.

Creating a Sitemap

There are two primary ways to construct a sitemap: manually or using a sitemap generator. Although it can take some time, generating a sitemap manually entails detailing every page on your website in an organized manner, giving you total control over the content. As an alternative, you can automate the process by using a sitemap generator, which will automatically scan your website and create a sitemap for you. This approach guarantees correctness and saves time, especially for bigger websites. Pick the strategy that best suits your needs and available resources—both have benefits.

Creating a Sitemap Manually

You will need an intermediate to advanced understanding of HTML and XML to manually generate a sitemap. Hand-building an XML sitemap requires a lot of coding, and you have to submit it to Google Search Console so that it can be indexed.

Create a sitemap in five simple steps if you want search engines to index your website quickly.

Step 1: Review Your Page Structure

If you have a beautiful website with great content but notice it is not getting much attention from search engines, it is time to investigate why. Start by examining your website's structure. Ask yourself, "Where do all these links lead?" Begin at the homepage, just as every visitor does. From there, trace the links to other pages to understand the navigation flow. Here is a straightforward example that is easy to understand.

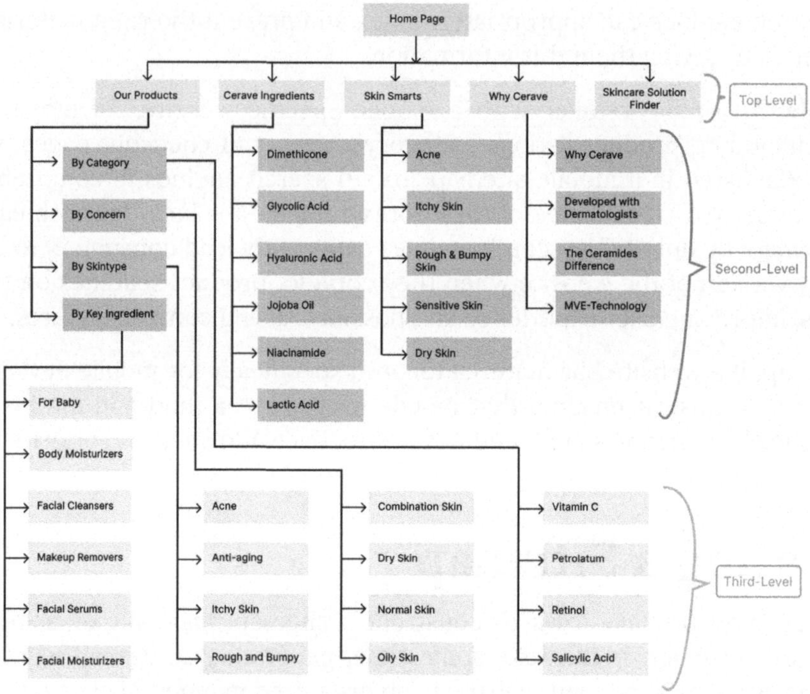

Figure 5.8: *Example of sitemap template*

You observe that certain pages are tucked away so far down that it requires five or six clicks to get there, which makes it challenging for search engines to locate and assign a ranking to such pages. In order to improve your website's performance in search engine rankings, you should make sure that any page can be accessed from the homepage with just three clicks.

Think of your website as a grand tree. The homepage is the sturdy trunk, from which you branch out to the most important pages, ensuring they are just a click away. Each of these main branches leads to smaller branches, which are just another click away. In this way, you create a clear and logical hierarchy.

By prioritizing your content into tiers and ensuring every page is easy to reach, you make your website more user-friendly and search engine-friendly. Remember to design your website so that any page can be accessed within three clicks.

Refer to *Figure* 5.8 for a better understanding:

As illustrated, the "Our Products" page is at the **top-level** and links to **second-level** categories: By Category, By Concern, By Skin Type, and By Key Ingredient. Each of these categories then links to multiple **third-level** pages, shown in yellow boxes.

The "Our Products" page is crucial, hence its position in the top-level navigation. It wouldn't be logical to prioritize the yellow-linked pages at the same level as the top-level content in blue, which is why they are categorized as third-level content.

Step 2: Optimize Your URLs

After you have determined the significance of every page and organized your website appropriately, it is time to start creating your URLs.

Imagine that you are going to use HTML or XML tags to format every URL. If you have ever experimented with HTML coding, this work should be quite simple for you. But don't worry, even if you've never done it before – it is very doable. To start, a text editor is required in order to create an XML file. You might use a program like Sublime Text or Notepad.

You open your text editor, take a seat, and begin adding the requisite code to each URL. You provide specifics like:

- The location of the page
- The date it was last changed
- How frequently it changes
- The priority of the page

As you work, the code you write for a URL may resemble this:

```
<url>
  <loc>https://www.examplesite.com/page1</loc>
  <lastmod>2019-01-10</lastmod>
  <changefreq>weekly</changefreq>
  <priority>0.8</priority>
</url>
```

You carefully look over each URL, making sure that every aspect is properly coded. Over time, the performance of your website is improved by this meticulous labor. Take your time and ensure that everything is completed correctly.

Step 3: Ensuring Code Accuracy

Human mistakes can happen to anyone coding by hand, no matter how often you do it. However, any coding errors simply won't do when it comes to your sitemap.

Fortunately, there are programs available that check your code for errors and make sure the syntax is correct. Here, internet applications can be your greatest buddy. All you have to do is type "sitemap validation" into Google and you will find a number of results.

Imagine writing a beautiful piece of code, but oh no, you forgot to include the semicolon or the beginning tag. Be at ease! That reliable validation tool takes action like a superhero, identifying the mistake right away and assisting you in fixing it with ease.

Step 4: Integrating Your Sitemap with Root

Go to your website's root folder and upload your sitemap file there to begin. It functions similarly to providing search engines with an easy-to-follow roadmap for your website.

Including your sitemap guarantees that every page is accessible and improves the organization of your website. Many websites follow this popular practice, which is to simply append "**`/sitemap/`**" to any URL, as illustrated in this example:

Check it out on the Apple website, for instance:

https://www.apple.com/sitemap/

Want to dive deeper?

Simply append "/sitemap.xml" to any website's URL to view its underlying code, just like on the HubSpot website.

Figure 5.9: *Example showing sitemap.xml code of HubSpot website*

You can also integrate it into your footer navigation under "Sitemap" as a label for quick access. Take a moment to observe the logical structure and hierarchy in each section.

Step 5: Submit Your Sitemap

Your sitemap's journey does not finish here – it is time to submit it to the search engines once it's configured and included in your website's files. What you should do is as follows:

1. Go to Google Search Console.
2. Find the "`Crawl`" section and click "`Sitemaps`."
3. Look for the "`Add/Test Sitemap`" button at the top right corner.
4. Before you submit, you can test your sitemap to make sure there are no mistakes.
5. Once it is error-free, click "`Submit`."

And that's it! Google will handle the rest. Your site will be indexed by their systems, which will improve your SEO ranking and make it simpler for users to find your pages.

Generating a Sitemap with a Sitemap Generator

Even though it's really simple to follow these five steps, some of you may be apprehensive about making manual changes to the code on your website. The good news is that you don't have to know how to code to create a sitemap because there are a tons of other options available. The process of creating a sitemap is made quick, simple, and extremely accurate with these sitemap generators.

If you use WordPress, a lot of well-known SEO plugins include built-in XML sitemap capabilities, which simplifies the procedure to a few clicks. This implies that you can concentrate less on technical details and more on guiding your website towards success.

Some alternative options are:

- **Yoast SEO:** A comprehensive SEO plugin for WordPress websites.
- **The SEO Framework:** Another SEO plugin for WordPress, focused on simplicity and performance.
- **Jetpack:** A multifunctional WordPress plugin that includes site management tools, security features, and performance enhancements.
- **All in One SEO Plugin:** A popular WordPress plugin offering robust SEO tools and optimization features.
- **Slickplan:** A tool for creating sitemaps and visual planning of website structures.

Apart from the tools listed above, there are a plethora of other options accessible on the internet for creating sitemaps, each with a unique set of capabilities to accommodate a range of requirements and tastes.

In conclusion, a sitemap is necessary for any kind of website, no matter how simple or sophisticated. Sitemaps in HTML and XML are both essential for improving your search engine rankings. XML sitemaps facilitate faster indexing by helping search engines understand the structure and content of your website. HTML sitemaps, on the other hand, improve user experience through easier navigation and longer visitor engagement.

If improving the SEO of your website is something you want to do, adding a sitemap is a great place to start.

Information Architecture versus Sitemap

Effective UX design requires an understanding of the distinctions between information architecture (IA) and sitemaps. Despite their similarities, they have varied functions and effects on the user experience. We will talk about how and why they differ from one another in this section. The following are some typical distinctions between an IA and a sitemap:

	Information Architecture (IA)	**Sitemap**
Scope and Detail	A comprehensive structure focusing on content organization, relationships, and user pathways.	A sitemap is basically a list of web pages of the website offering a bird's-eye view of the content and its flow.
Purpose and Use	Guides overall design, navigation, and content strategy to enhance usability.	Visualizes website structure for stakeholders, aiding communication and decision-making.
Adaptability	Evolves based on user research but maintains stability in key aspects like taxonomy.	Flexible and easily updated to reflect changes in website structure.
Stakeholder Communication	Complex and detailed, requiring thorough explanation for stakeholders.	Simplified and clear, facilitating efficient communication and faster decision-making.
Impact on User Experience	Directly enhances user experience by ensuring intuitive navigation and content findability.	Aids development process with limited direct impact on user interaction.

Table 5.2: *Difference between Information Architecture and Sitemap*

Conclusion

The principles of information architecture (IA) and its vital function in structuring website content for a smooth user experience were covered in this chapter. We discussed the fundamental IA systems and principles that serve as the framework for efficient information structure. We also looked at several kinds of sitemaps and went over how to make them step-by-step. With this understanding, designers may produce websites that are easier to navigate and more accessible for users. Knowing IA and sitemaps guarantees that websites are rationally organized, making it easy for users to find and interact with material and improving their surfing experience as a whole.

In the upcoming chapter, you will dive into Low-Fidelity Wireframes and Prototypes, where you'll learn about the fundamental tools and processes used to develop prototype designs for websites and applications. You will be able to verify and improve design concepts iteratively if you have a solid understanding of these tools and approaches.

Key Terms

- **Information Architecture (IA):** The practice of organizing and structuring content on websites or apps to enhance usability and user experience.
- **User Interface (UI):** The visual and interactive elements of a digital interface through which users interact with websites or apps.
- **Accessibility:** Ensuring that digital content is usable by all people, including those with disabilities, through design considerations like clear labels and logical organization.
- **Productivity:** Efficiency gains achieved by enabling quick access to information, reducing time and effort spent on tasks.
- **Search Engine Optimization (SEO):** Techniques used to improve a website's visibility on search engine results pages, often enhanced by clear IA.
- **Content Management:** The process of creating, editing, and organizing digital content, facilitated by a well-structured IA foundation.
- **Clutter and Redundancy:** Avoiding unnecessary complexity and duplication through efficient content organization.
- **Visual Design:** Enhancing the aesthetic appeal and user experience through effective IA and content organization.
- **Labeling Systems:** Consistent and clear labels that provide context and guide users to relevant information, enhancing navigation and usability.
- **Hierarchical:** Arranges information into broad categories and subcategories, resembling a tree structure.

- **Sequential:** Presents information in a step-by-step order, common in processes like forms or tutorials.
- **Search Systems:** Mechanisms that allow users to find information by entering keywords or phrases, with options for refining results to locate specific content efficiently.
- **Sitemap:** A structured list of all URLs on a website, along with metadata about each URL, such as relevance and last update date. It helps search engines crawl and index the site more effectively.
- **Metadata:** Additional information about each URL in a sitemap, including its relevance and the date it was last updated, which assists search engines in understanding the site's content.
- **Search Engine Crawling:** The process by which search engines systematically browse and index a website's content to include it in search results.
- **Internal Linking:** Links that connect different pages within the same website, aiding in navigation and indexing.
- **External Links:** Links from other websites pointing to your site, which can help improve search engine visibility and traffic.
- **Large and Complex Sites:** Websites with many pages and sections, where a sitemap is essential for efficient navigation and indexing by search engines.
- **HTML (Hypertext Markup Language):** The standard markup language used to create and structure content on the web, defining elements such as headings, paragraphs, and links.
- **CSS (Cascading Style Sheets):** A stylesheet language used to control the presentation and layout of HTML elements on a webpage, including colors, fonts, and spacing.
- **XML (eXtensible Markup Language):** A markup language designed to store and transport data, used in sitemaps to describe the structure and hierarchy of web content.
- **WordPress:** A popular content management system (CMS) that allows users to create, manage, and publish websites and blogs with a user-friendly interface and customizable features.
- **Webmasters:** Individuals responsible for managing and maintaining a website, including its content, performance, and technical aspects.
- **Search Engines:** Online tools (like Google, Bing, or Yahoo) that index and retrieve web content based on user queries, helping users find relevant information on the internet.

- **Discoverability:** The ease with which content or a website can be found by users and search engines, often enhanced through effective SEO practices and sitemaps.
- **Homepage:** The main or introductory page of a website, often serving as a central hub for navigation and access to other pages.
- **Sitemap Validation:** The process of checking a sitemap to ensure it is correctly formatted, contains valid URLs, and is free of errors to ensure proper indexing by search engines.
- **Plugins:** Software add-ons that extend the functionality of a website or content management system, such as adding features for SEO, social sharing, or enhanced security.

Chapter 6
The Power of Wireframes and Prototypes

Introduction

Welcome to the creative world of wireframes and prototypes! In this chapter, we will look at how wireframes can assist you in sketching out the structure and functionality of your digital products. You will discover the significance of wireframes in the design process and be able to see many examples that demonstrate their application. Wireframes lay the groundwork for you to precisely plan and arrange your thoughts.

Next, we will dive into prototypes, which bring your wireframes to life with interactive elements. We will cover the various types of prototypes and how using them can be beneficial for testing and improving your design concepts. In order to see how a user will interact with your design and to make the required changes prior to the final production, prototypes are crucial.

Finally, we will introduce you to the best tools and software for creating both wireframes and prototypes. By the end of this chapter, you will be equipped with the knowledge to transform your design ideas into engaging, interactive experiences efficiently and creatively.

Structure

In this chapter, we will discuss the following topics:

- Introduction to Wireframes
- Importance of Wireframing
- Types of Wireframes
- Desktop versus Mobile Wireframes

- Benefits of Wireframing
- Steps to Create a Wireframe
- Best Tools to Create Wireframes
- Introduction to Prototypes
- Importance of Prototyping
- Benefits of Prototyping
- Types of Prototyping
- Best Tools to Create Prototypes
- Comparing Wireframing and Prototyping

Introduction to Wireframes

Assume you are constructing a home. A blueprint is required prior to painting walls or placing bricks. With the help of this blueprint, homeowners, builders, and architects can all clearly see where each room, door, and window will be located. In the world of design, wireframes serve a similar purpose.

In the past, some designers saw wireframes as unnecessary, believing them to be time-consuming and unproductive. However, things have changed. With the help of modern tools, designers can quickly add interactivity to simple wireframes to create dynamic, low-fidelity prototypes. Because these prototypes make the ultimate product's functionality easier to see, wireframes are significantly more useful than static sketches.

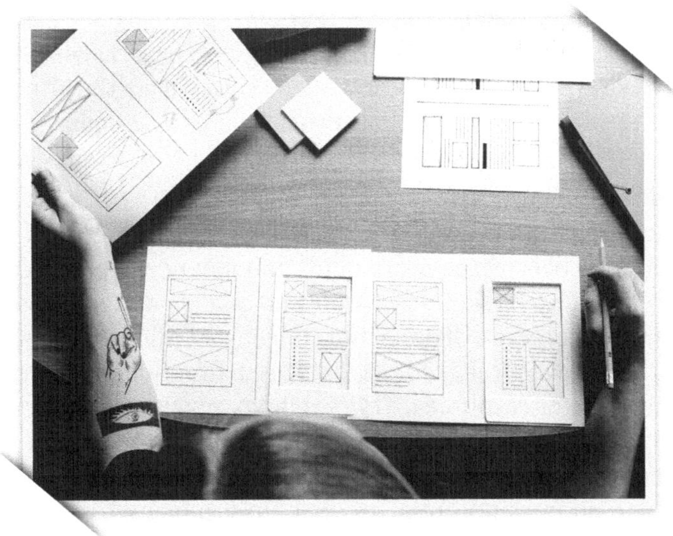

Figure 6.1: *The Basic Structure of a Wireframe Designed by Freepik*

A wireframe is like a rough draft for a webpage or app. It shows the basic layout, structure, and flow of information without any design details. Think of it as a simple block layout with lines for text and "X" marks for images. This helps everyone agree on the placement of elements before developers start building the actual product.

Wireframes are essential for UX designers, whether sketched by hand or created digitally. They ensure everyone understands the plan, setting a solid foundation for a successful project.

Importance of Wireframing

Before any design or coding is done, wireframes act as a visual reference to help stakeholders, developers, and designers understand the functionality and layout. They guarantee that all parties are in agreement, which promotes more effective project development and clearer communication.

Wireframes fulfill the following essential purposes:

- **User-Focused Screen Planning:** Wireframes are vital for planning screens with a user-centered approach. They help designers map out the layout of apps and websites, logically arranging content and features without worrying about visual design details. This clear and accessible structure allows designers to gather early feedback from users and involve stakeholders in discussions. Using placeholders, designers can ask users what they expect to see, making sure the final product is intuitive and easy to use.
- **Clarifying Features and Navigation:** Wireframes help clarify features and navigation by providing a basic outline of the app or website. They avoid going into the specifics of visual design and instead concentrate on how things are arranged and how people will interact with them. This frees up designers to focus on usefulness, making sure every element is accessible and arranged properly. Wireframes illustrate how users will navigate the interface by outlining the user flow and navigation patterns. This early emphasis on functionality guarantees that the finished product is intuitive and user-friendly while also assisting in the identification of possible problems.
- **Quick and Cost-Effective Iteration:** Wireframes are crucial for the iterative design process because they are quick and inexpensive to create. All you need is a pen and paper to sketch a wireframe quickly and for free, or you can use various tools to create a digital wireframe in just minutes. They allow designers to experiment with different layouts and functionalities without investing significant time or resources. This flexibility enables rapid iterations based on feedback from users and stakeholders, ensuring the design evolves to meet user needs effectively. By refining wireframes early and often, designers can identify and address potential issues before moving to more detailed design stages, saving time and reducing costs. This approach helps create a more user-friendly final product while maintaining efficiency in the design process.

Types of Wireframes

In the early stages of design, many designers start with sketching wireframes on paper. It's a fast and simple method that gets ideas flowing, but it has its drawbacks–sharing these sketches with a team and referring back to them frequently can be cumbersome. Additionally, paper wireframes are usually thrown away after their initial use.

To extend the life and usefulness of these paper sketches, designers can turn them into paper prototypes for usability testing. Some digital tools even allow these paper sketches to be transformed into collaborative digital formats, making them easier to share and refine.

There are three main types of wireframes: low-fidelity, mid-fidelity, and high-fidelity. Each serves a different purpose and adds unique value to the design process. Let's dive into the specifics of each type.

Low-Fidelity Wireframes

Low-fidelity wireframes are basic, rough sketches that outline the core layout and functionality of a webpage or app. They are particularly useful in the early stages of design when experimenting with different ideas and visualizing multiple concepts. These wireframes emphasize structure over visual details, using simple shapes, lines, and placeholder text to depict content and elements without precise grid or pixel accuracy. Created quickly and affordably, they are perfect for early-stage brainstorming and can even be sketched on the fly during meetings with stakeholders or clients.

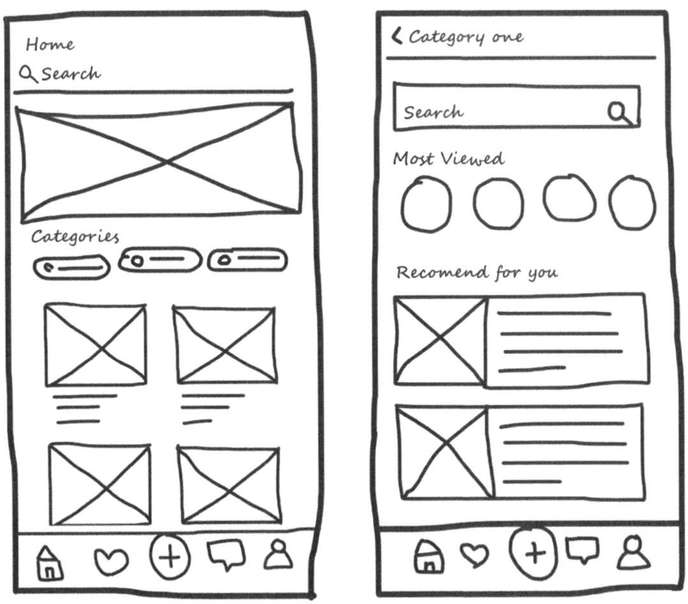

Figure 6.2: *Example of a Low-Fidelity Wireframe*

The preceding figure displays the wireframe design of the mobile application. In a low-fidelity wireframe, the header, search bar, product pictures, and descriptions may all be represented by straightforward, rough blocks and lines. This helps you see the layout and user flow and prevents you from becoming bogged down in the specifics of the design.

Mid-Fidelity Wireframes

Mid-fidelity wireframes, often referred to as grayscale wireframes as well, use different tones of gray in place of full-color or high-resolution pictures, offering a thorough overview of the structure of a website or app. These wireframes are simpler and more basic than low-fidelity versions, but they lack the intricacy of high-fidelity wireframes, which are completely polished and perfected. Mid-fidelity wireframes are used by designers to clearly illustrate the visual hierarchy and layout, which helps to communicate the significance of various elements without the visual clutter of complete design elements. These wireframes are usually made using programs like Sketch or Balsamiq, which guarantee a well-balanced and understandable depiction of the proposed design.

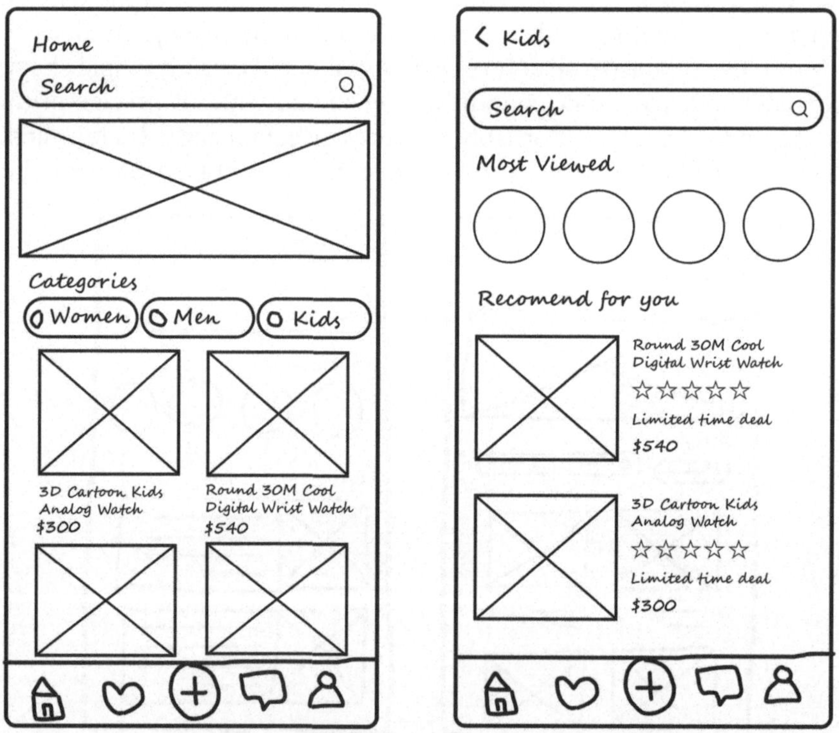

Figure 6.3: *Example of Mid-Fidelity Wireframe*

The preceding figure displays the wireframe design of the mobile application. Elements such as the header, search bar, product images, and descriptions are shown in greater depth in a mid-fidelity wireframe. Instead of just tough blocks and lines, you might see fine boxes, icons, and some real content. This method strikes a balance between complexity and simplicity, making it easier to see the layout and user flow without becoming weighed down by complex design features.

High-Fidelity Wireframes

High-fidelity wireframes are detailed and well-presented representations of a website or application's layout that closely match the final product. High-fidelity wireframes have exact space, complete color schemes, fonts, graphics, and icons, in contrast to low-fidelity and mid-fidelity versions. They give stakeholders a realistic picture of the user interface, enabling them to understand how the finished product will seem and work.

Later on in the design process, these wireframes are frequently utilized to assist the development team, collect comprehensive input, and carry out usability testing. They offer a clear depiction of visual hierarchy, interaction flow, and user experience, ensuring that all design elements are accurately communicated and aligned with project goals.

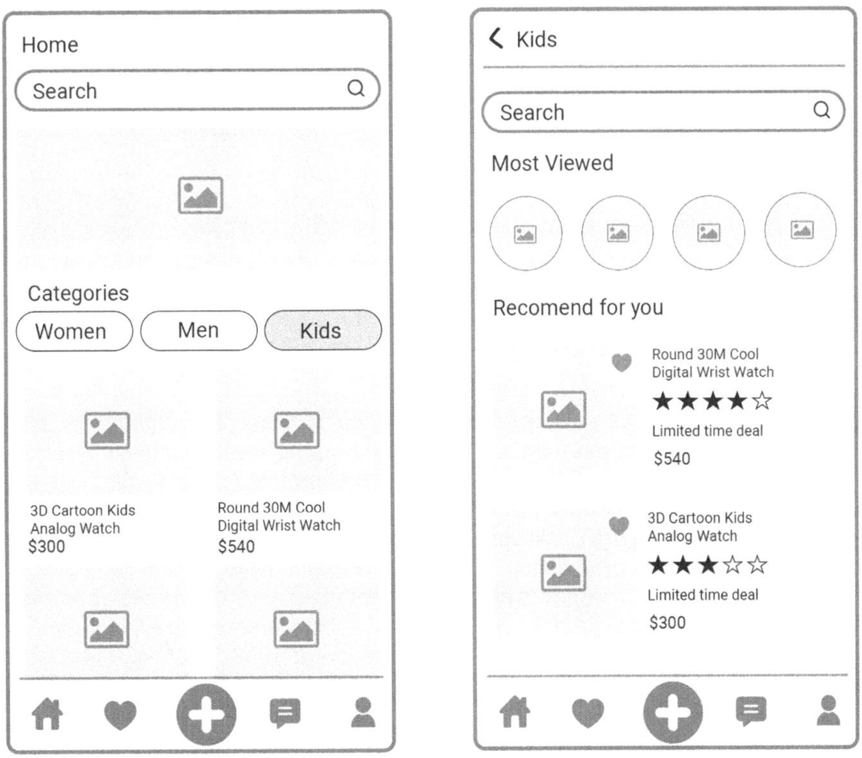

Figure 6.4: *Example of a High-Fidelity Wireframe*

The preceding figure displays the wireframe design of the mobile application. Elements such as the header, search bar, product photographs, and descriptions are depicted in a high-fidelity wireframe with correct icons, star ratings, detailed image icons, and defined margins. This method offers a nearly finished appearance that closely resembles the finished result by enabling a thorough visualization of the layout, design components, and user flow.

Desktop versus Mobile Wireframes

Users no longer visit websites just from their home computers. With mobile phones and tablets becoming incredibly popular, UX designers need to understand how, where, and why people use these devices and what works best within their limits. When designing wireframes for both desktop and mobile apps, it's important to think about size, behavior, and interaction, as these aspects greatly affect the user experience. Here are some key considerations to keep in mind when designing for desktop and mobile applications:

	Desktop	**Mobile**
Size	Larger screens help desktop wireframes by fitting more content and complex layouts. Larger graphics, complex navigation menus, and multi-column layouts are all available to designers	Simplified layouts are necessary for mobile wireframes, which must take into consideration smaller screens. To ensure readability and usefulness on small displays, content should be prioritized, stacked vertically, and have larger touch targets for buttons and simple navigation
Behavior	On a desktop, users expect more features that are visible at once and more interactions. Wide-ranging toolbars, extensive dropdown menus, and hover effects are typical. For accurate input, users usually use a mouse or trackpad	Touch interactions are the main focus of mobile behavior. Designing elements for finger taps and swipes is necessary, taking gesture-based navigation into account. Because mobile consumers are frequently on the go and demand more specialized, task-specific capabilities, designs must be quick and simple to use
Interaction	Complex operations like drag-and-drop, context menus accessible with a right-click, and multi-window multitasking are possible with desktops. Utilizing keyboard shortcuts to increase efficiency is also common	Touch motions like pinching, swiping, and tapping should be used for easy and natural mobile interactions. Designers need to prioritize key features and take into account the limits of single-screen interfaces. Furthermore, device-specific elements like GPS, cameras, and accelerometers are frequently incorporated into mobile designs

Table 6.1: *Key Factors Shaping User Experience in Desktop versus Mobile Wireframes*

By understanding these considerations, designers can create wireframes that deliver optimized and seamless user experiences across both desktop and mobile platforms.

Benefits of Wireframing

Wireframes are essential tools for designing websites or apps. They act like blueprints, helping designers and stakeholders see and agree on the layout and structure. Here are some benefits of using wireframes:

- **Visualizing Site Architecture**

  A sitemap can be huge or complex, but the visual design phase of the project begins when it transitions from a sitemap to a wireframe. The navigation, primary and subpage organization, and user flow along the conversion paths of a website are all translated into a tangible visual representation using wireframes. This phase offers a clear depiction of the finished product, emphasizing its main features and design components. Wireframes basically act as a comprehensive project road map, providing an organized framework that directs the design and development phases and ensures that all important details are prepared and conveyed efficiently.

Figure 6.5: *Wireframe Example: Visualizing the Site's Navigation Structure*

In the preceding figure, primary navigation is shown beside the logo with icons. This is the main menu at the top-left of the page, showing the most important sections.

Secondary navigation is a smaller menu that might appear on the top-right side or within specific pages, providing links to related sections or subpages.

Sometimes, a menu item labeled "More" will reveal additional options or pages when clicked.

On a sitemap, these different navigation elements can seem confusing because it's hard to see how they all fit together. However, a wireframe makes it clearer by visually organizing how the navigation will look and work on the actual website. It shows how the primary and secondary menus will be arranged and how users can access extra options under "More," making the complex navigation easier to understand and use.

- **Detailed Overview of Website Features**

  Assume you are working with a customer on a website project and they have no idea what "pop-up," "product filtering," or "Google Maps integration" mean. You begin developing the project's wireframes in order to close this gap. Your visual storytelling tool will be these wireframes, which make it evident where each feature will go on the page and how it will function.

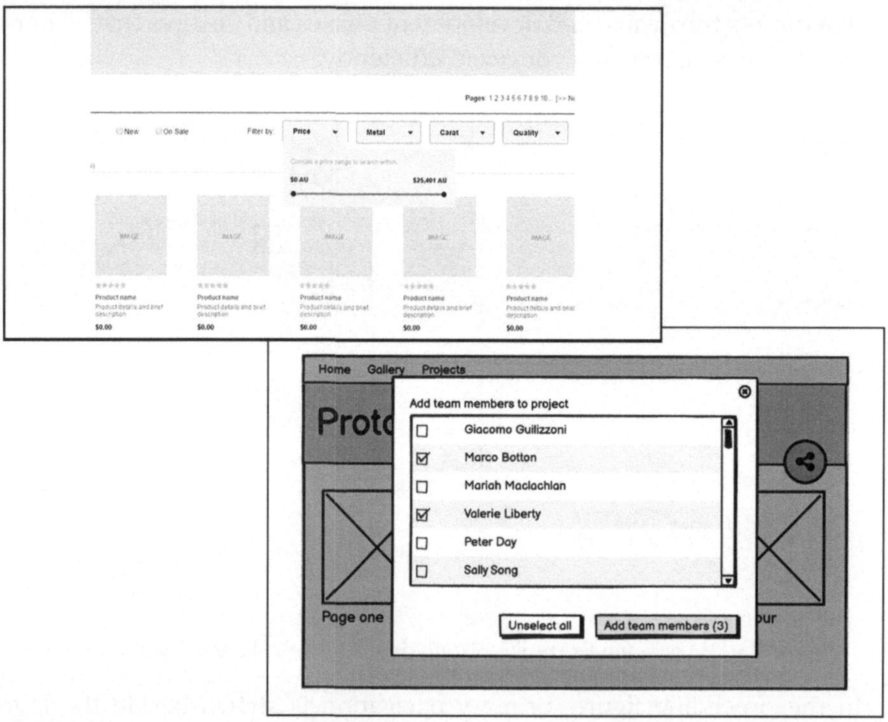

Figure 6.6: *Wireframe Example Showing Website Features as Filters and Popup*

The client can see exactly how the product filtering will facilitate better searching and how the popup will display information to catch attention as you take them through the wireframes. In addition to ensuring that the finished product will be entertaining and user-friendly, this visual method helps them grasp the design better. You may create a website that satisfies user wants and expectations by clearly defining the functionality and placement of each item.

- **Ensuring Scalability and Ease of Updates**

  Consider a client who manages a news website and plans to grow from five articles per day to fifty items per day in the upcoming year. You make a wireframe that shows how the website will handle the extra content to handle this growth. In order to maintain the website's organization and usability, the wireframe displays a scalable layout with movable parts for headlines, featured articles, and categories. A simple example would be adding a new category or creating several subcategories to organize multiple items for the future.

  The client can see how the website will easily handle the increased volume of material without sacrificing appearance or functionality as you take them through the wireframe. This strategy emphasizes the value of scalability and ease of updating, giving the client peace of mind that their website can effectively handle future growth.

- **Saves Time and Money**

  Consider a case where a retailer is creating a brand-new online store. To ensure a seamless process, the web team and client are working together. They produce thorough wireframes early in the project to show the functionality and structure of the website.

  They debate whether to create new forms at this phase or integrate the ones that already exist from third-party application forms. They also map out the user's conversion path and decide who will be in charge of each component. This common understanding guarantees that all parties are in agreement with the objectives and features of the project.

  The team saves time and resources by resolving these matters in advance and avoiding significant adjustments afterward. By streamlining the development process and enabling efficient resource allocation, this proactive strategy eventually saves time and money.

- **Efficient Development Process**

  Imagine a company developing a new app for managing personal finances. The design team produces thorough wireframes that display the features and layout of the app. The developers can follow this clear blueprint provided by these wireframes.

  These wireframes help the developers understand exactly how each screen should look and work when the development phase starts. By building the app according to the wireframes, they are able to prevent confusion and rework. Because the design was well specified from the beginning, the app was developed more quickly and correctly, and the transition from design to development was smooth.

Steps to Create a Wireframe

The method of creating a wireframe is straightforward and easy. It usually starts as a basic drawing; talent for drawing is not necessary. Begin with a basic sketch, understanding that it need not be flawless. You sketch up the general layout of the application's elements, such as the content sections and navigation bar. You can see how consumers will interact with each section of the app as you sketch. We concentrate on just one wireframe for the time being, even though this approach eventually requires multiple wireframes for the full project. This first wireframe is a great practice tool that will assist you in structuring your ideas and creating a clean layout. You realize that wireframing is more about planning and less about artistic ability. With this simple yet effective method, you gain confidence in your ability to design user-friendly interfaces.

Creating an Image

Images are displayed in wireframes as boxes or rectangles that are frequently labeled with an image icon or an 'X' to indicate their location. Designers may employ real photographs, but they keep them simple and uncluttered to minimize distractions. In order to properly communicate the placement and scale of images inside the design, this method does not include any visual content. This approach effectively conveys where images will be and their size within the design, without adding visual content.

Creating Text

When displaying text in a wireframe, it's essential to consider several factors. First, specify any character limits or expected text length for the element, helping visualize the space the text should occupy. Use placeholder text to show what the content will do, such as "introducing paragraph, 4-5 lines," or use real content examples. Avoid using "Lorem Ipsum" (dummy content) as it lacks context and doesn't accurately represent real content. Finally, any text that has links should be underlined, and titles can be a bit large in font size.

Colors

It's beneficial to stay away from colors when wireframing for a number of reasons. Maintain the gray color. It helps avoid diverting attention from crucial components like content placement and helps maintain focus on the main goal of establishing layout and functionality. Early color introduction can cause stakeholders to focus more on aesthetics than utility, which can muddy up layout discussions. By prioritizing usefulness over aesthetics, designers make sure that the wireframe effectively conveys user experience and interaction without the possibility of color misunderstanding. This method maintains efficiency and attention throughout the design process.

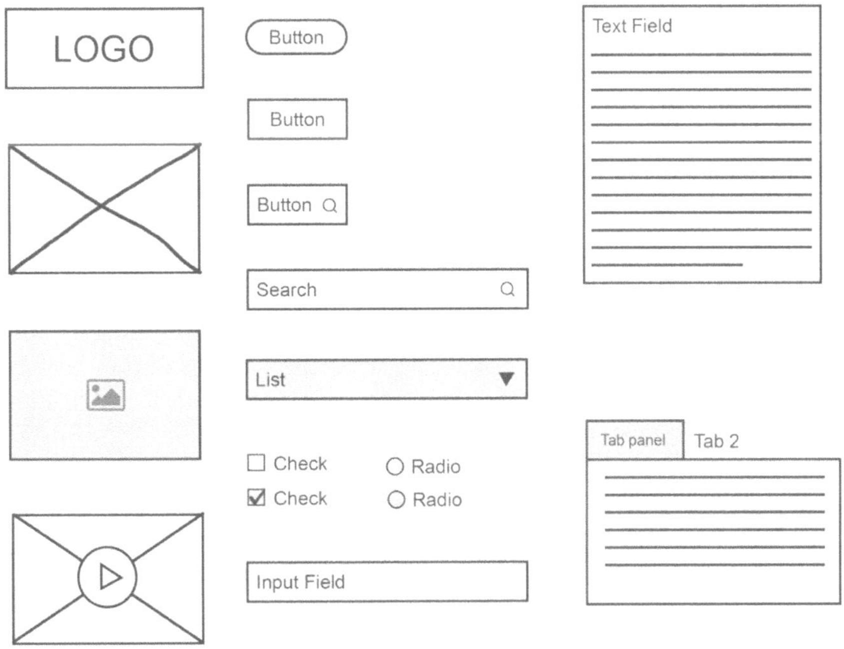

Figure 6.7: *Different Types of Input Formats for Wireframing*

The preceding figure illustrates how to present different types of content in wireframes, including images, text, icons, dropdowns, and more. With this visual guide, you now have a clear understanding of how to design each section. It's time to move on to creating the actual wireframe. To do this effectively, we need to follow a series of structured steps.

1. **Identify Elements and Draft Sketches**

   Make a list of every element that has to be on the page, including the text, headings, photos, logo, and navigation bar. Try to be as thorough as you can; extras can always be added later. Draw at least one simple low-fidelity wireframe after that. Using a pen or pencil and drawing by hand is typically faster and more flexible than using any digital software for creation. Try out numerous layouts to determine which is the best user-friendly design, and make several sketches to investigate other concepts.

2. **Refine the Wireframe**

   Choosing your finest sketch and turning it into a polished, in-depth version is the process of refining the wireframe. It should be neat and polished enough to show to stakeholders or prospective users for their input. Use mid-fidelity or high-fidelity wireframes to ensure clarity and detail. To develop this more advanced version, use design tools such as Balsamiq, Adobe Photoshop, or Figma, which enable accurate modifications and good visual depiction.

The intention is to create a wireframe that clearly conveys the design and functionality so that other people may offer insightful, helpful feedback. This feedback is essential to further refine and iterate the design, ensuring it satisfies user demands and project objectives.

3. **Gather and Iterate Feedback**

   Ask for comments from stakeholders or future users after presenting the completed wireframe. Stakeholders could be your client, business partner, supervisor, or people who will use the finished product. Make the required adjustments to your wireframe based on the input. Depending on your needs, get further input after modifications from the same group or from different participants. Continue this feedback-iteration cycle until the design is good enough and consistently gets good reviews.

Best Tools to Create Wireframes

Selecting the appropriate wireframing tool is essential to the design process. Remember, you can always use pen and paper too! Here's a detailed look at some popular free and paid options for creating wireframes:

Free Tools for Creating Wireframes:

Figma

- **Features:** For collaborative design, Figma provides a free plan with comprehensive capabilities, including wireframing, prototyping, and design systems. It is simple to share and iterate on designs when users can collaborate in real-time with other team members.
- **Pros:** Large community resources, real-time collaboration, cloud-based.
- **Cons:** Editing and file storage are restricted on the free plan.

Wireframe.cc

- **Features:** For quick and easy wireframe construction, Wireframe.cc offers a simplistic UI. It employs simple tools and focuses on creating basic wireframes.
- **Pros:** Browser-based, low learning curve, and simple to use.
- **Cons:** No sophisticated prototyping or design choices, few functionalities.

Pencil Project

- **Features:** Wireframes, mockups, and prototypes may be made with Pencil Project, an open-source application. It has several connectors and forms built right in.

- **Pros:** Free and open-source, extensive shape library.
- **Cons:** Compared to more recent tools, the interface may feel old and less user-friendly.

MockFlow

- **Features:** Users may design wireframes and mockups using a drag-and-drop interface with MockFlow's free basic plan. Sitemap and UI flow design tools are also included.
- **Pros:** Easy integrated suite for various design requirements, easy to use.
- **Cons:** There are limited features in the free plan, and collaboration features are restricted.

Paid Tools for Creating Wireframes:

Adobe XD

- **Features:** Prototyping, wireframing, high-fidelity design, and collaboration features are all included in Adobe XD, making it a complete design tool. It has good integration with other Creative Cloud products from Adobe.
- **Pros:** Lots of plugins, smooth interface with Adobe products, and strong functionality.
- **Cons:** Price depends on subscription; may be excessive for basic wireframes.

Balsamiq

- **Features:** Low-fidelity wireframes that mimic hand-drawn drawings are Balsamiq's area of expertise. It is intended to avoid becoming mired down in design elements and instead concentrate on structure and content.
- **Pros:** Focus is encouraged on functionality, easy-to-use, intuitive interface.
- **Cons:** Pricey for individual users and limited to low-fidelity designs.

Sketch

- **Features:** With its extensive feature set for wireframing, UI design, and prototyping, Sketch is a well-liked design tool among Mac users. It has a strong ecosystem of plugins and integrations.
- **Pros:** Mac-native performance, a vast plugin ecosystem, and excellent high-fidelity designs.
- **Cons:** Only available on Macs; upgrades and collaboration features require a membership.

InVision

- **Features**: InVision provides collaboration, prototyping, and wireframing tools. Interactive mockups, design handoff, and user testing capabilities are some of its features.
- **Pros**: Real-time updates, extensive design and collaboration features, and user testing.
- **Cons**: It can be expensive, and some users find basic wireframing to be less intuitive.

Each tool has its own strengths, suitable for different needs, from basic wireframes to detailed, interactive prototypes. Choose one based on what you need, your budget, and how you like to work.

Introduction to Prototypes

Designers kick off new products with prototypes, which are essential for testing and refining ideas. A prototype is an early version of a product that shows how it will look and work. Think of prototypes as early drafts or mock-ups of your product. If you are creating a new device or app, you start with a simple version that shows how it will function and look, instead of jumping straight to the final product. This could be as simple as a sketch or as complex as an interactive digital model.

A prototype helps you see how the design will work and how users will experience it. It lets you test features, find out what works, and fix what doesn't before the final version is made. By displaying these prototypes to people and receiving their feedback, you may improve your understanding of their requirements and preferences. In this manner, you can guarantee that the finished product is efficient and easy to use.

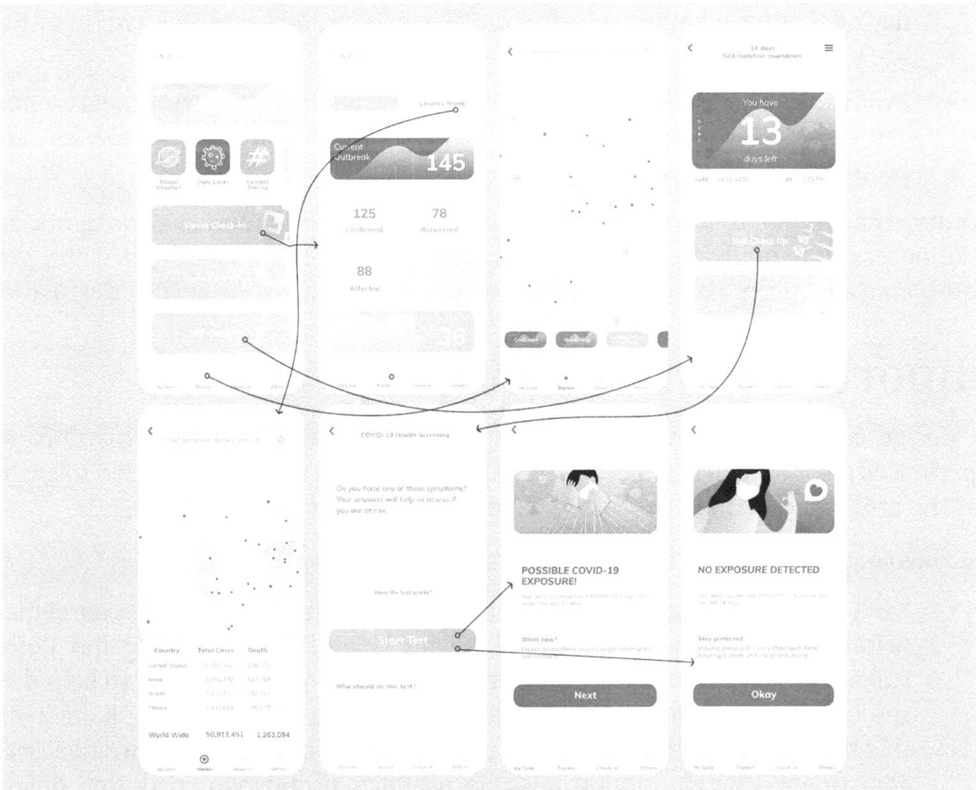

Figure 6.8: *Linking Mobile App Screens for a Smooth Prototype Experience; Designed by Freepik*

The Design Thinking approach relies heavily on prototyping, particularly in the last stages of testing. You develop a nearly functioning model, or prototype, and test it with important stakeholders and potential consumers to see if it satisfies their needs.

Prototypes are necessary because they identify issues early and save costs and time. They also ensure that everyone is aware of the project and enhance communication both among team members and with stakeholders. Prototypes, in brief, are an essential tool that helps turn concepts into tested realities during the design process.

Simple storyboards and sketches, straightforward paper models, and even role-playing situations that simulate services can all be considered prototypes.

Despite their varying forms, all prototypes shared four main qualities:

- **Representation:** This refers to the form your prototype takes, such as on paper, a mobile device, or a computer screen.
- **Precision:** This indicates the level of detail in your prototype, ranging from rough and simple (low fidelity) to very detailed and polished (high fidelity).
- **Interactivity:** This describes how users can interact with your prototype

during testing, whether they can only view it, partially interact with it, or fully use its features.

- **Evolution:** This refers to your prototype's lifecycle, where a test version can quickly be replaced with a new iteration in a process known as rapid prototyping.

Prototypes allow you to iteratively test various parts of the product, gain insights, and make necessary modifications that will help you reach your final design. Thus, your prototyping adventure continues, taking you one step closer to your final destination.

Importance of Prototyping

UX design requires prototyping in order to test and refine user interactions and experiences prior to final production. Iterative testing and feedback are used to ensure that the product meets the needs and expectations of the user.

Here are some key reasons why prototypes are important.

- **Early Problem Detection:** You must always obtain stakeholder agreement before launching a new app or making any changes to an existing app. Before stakeholders approve the design, prototypes are an excellent way to help them see the final product. Before sending the design to the development team, this is an excellent approach to collect their input and make any necessary adjustments. By identifying possible usability problems and design defects early on, prototyping enables designers to address these issues before they become more expensive and time-consuming to correct.
- **User-centered Design:** To make sure that designs are user-centered, prototyping is essential. Early user testing allows designers to learn about user preferences and demands, resulting in a more intuitive and user-friendly final product.
- **Communication Tool:** For designers, developers, and stakeholders, prototypes are a useful means of communication. Teams can use this to convey design concepts, see the final product, and offer input so that the product better meets corporate objectives.
- **Informed Decision-Making:** Prototyping offers insightful information and user input that can direct the development process and influence design choices. This guarantees that choices are not based on assumptions but rather on real user interactions and preferences.
- **Iterative Improvement:** Continuous testing, feedback, and improvement are made possible by prototyping, which facilitates an iterative design process. Final designs produced using this iterative process are more refined and functional. Before the app is constructed, UX teams can adjust their designs and find any future obstacles with the use of prototyping, an iterative process.

Prototyping is a crucial tool for UX design that aids in idea visualization, testing, and refinement, which eventually results in a better user experience and a more successful product.

Benefits of Prototyping

Prototyping brings several crucial advantages that greatly enhance the design and development process. Here are some key benefits:

- **Reduced Risks:** Projects that go through the entire prototype process are less risky than those that don't. This is so because project resources, schedules, and budgets are all directly impacted by prototyping. Prototyping lowers the possibility of expensive revisions and rework during development by seeing possible problems early on and taking action to address them. It is feasible to project the time and resources required for development through prototyping.
- **Cost-effectiveness:** A cheap way to experiment with various design concepts without devoting a lot of development resources is through prototyping. It assists in determining the best options prior to extensive development. Several prototypes should be made prior to the start of mass production in order to reduce the additional expenses associated with unsold goods and reprogramming.
- **Evaluate Technical Feasibility:** Making a prototype allows you to take a concept and determine which features are tough to implement. Thus, prototyping can reveal unexpected financial, technological, or practical constraints.
- **Improved Visualization:** Using prototypes makes it easier to communicate ideas and gain support from stakeholders and team members since they provide a tangible way of exploring and visualizing design concepts.
- **Evaluating Feasibility and Streamlining Development:** Creating a prototype helps solidify an idea and evaluate its feasibility, uncovering unexpected physical, technical, or financial challenges. Addressing design issues early during prototyping simplifies the development process. This gives developers a clearer and more accurate design, reducing misunderstandings and revisions, and ultimately saving time.
- **Planning of Feature Validation:** Prototyping provides the design team with crucial information that aids in their implementation planning. A prototype emphasizes user needs and helps in the creation of user stories. The scrum teams get a great deal from this. Using prototypes, designers can prioritize features that offer the greatest value to users by confirming the viability and effectiveness of various features.

There are several advantages to prototyping in UI/UX design, including better visualization, early user testing, cost-effectiveness, and increased teamwork. It is essential to produce user-centered designs that satisfy the requirements and expectations of users while lowering risks and shortening development times.

Types of Prototyping

Prototypes can be made in a variety of methods, and they are usually ranked according to how true to the final product they are. Depending on the specific goals and design stage, the right prototype is selected.

Let's say we have to demonstrate to a client how users will progress through the various tasks within the program. This fundamental concept can be communicated clearly with a low-fidelity prototype, similar to a set of simple drawings. However, a high-fidelity prototype, like an interactive digital mock-up, is a preferable option for gathering in-depth input when performing usability testing with a focus group.

Let's explore the most effective prototyping methods:

- Low-Fidelity Prototyping
- High-Fidelity Prototyping

Low-Fidelity Prototyping

The purpose of low-fidelity prototypes is to show user flows and the general structure of a product through simplified, basic representations. These prototypes usually make use of wireframes, which are straightforward diagrams that show how an application or website should be laid out and navigated. They support UX research teams in comprehending the information architecture of the product and in visualizing how information should be presented to users.

These prototypes are quite helpful when a project is just getting started. Teams can rapidly sketch concepts, thanks to their simplicity without becoming caught down in specifics. This facilitates the exploration of many ideas and quick iterations based on feedback. Low-fidelity prototypes can be produced quickly, easily, and affordably, which makes them useful for teams working under pressure or with limited resources.

Low-fidelity prototypes can have some disadvantages, though. Users are unable to properly experience how the finished product will work because they lack interactivity. Furthermore, they fail to convey the final product's aesthetic appeal due to its simplistic visual style. Stakeholders may find it more difficult to understand the final look and feel as a result.

Low-fidelity prototypes are a crucial tool in the early stages of design because of their benefits, even with these drawbacks. They let teams concentrate on the essential organization and flow of a product, provide the groundwork for future development, and react quickly to user feedback.

The following are some examples of low-fidelity prototypes:

- Sketches
- Paper prototypes
- Click-through prototypes

- **Sketches**

  A sketch or other low-fidelity prototype is a simple and preliminary depiction of a product design. Usually hand-drawn, it emphasizes the general idea and structure rather than specific design details. Consider it as a rough draft that facilitates fast and affordable concept visualization.

  Consider the scenario where you are creating a new website. You may include an outline for the bottom, main text area, header, and navigation menu. These quick sketches save a lot of time on details while effectively communicating your ideas to stakeholders and team members. They are ready to offer suggestions for improvement and criticism.

  Sketches and other low-fidelity prototypes are useful because they facilitate quick iterations. Before going on to more involved and time-consuming stages, you can quickly revise and improve your ideas in response to feedback.

- **Paper prototypes**

  Low-fidelity paper prototypes are simple, early versions of product designs created with basic materials like paper and pens. Despite the high-tech world of digital UX design, pen and paper remain a preferred option for quick, low-fidelity prototyping. This method is the simplest and fastest, involving hand-drawn "screens" on paper or a whiteboard to represent digital products. Paper prototyping involves sketching out concepts and user flows to visualize the design.

***Figure 6.9:** Designers Discussing Paper Prototype with Team*

Consider the scenario where you are creating a new website. You might depict various websites with sheets of paper, with drawn boxes for photos, lines for text, and arrows indicating the flow of navigation between pages. For the purpose of simulating user flows, these paper screens can be arranged on a table or a board. You can get feedback on the design and operation of the website by taking users on a tour.

Paper prototypes lack functionality, which makes them low-fidelity. Because of this, designers rarely distribute paper prototypes outside of their department. Despite this limitation, paper prototyping remains an essential step in the initial stages of UX design. It encourages teamwork and lets designers test out a lot of concepts cheaply. Information architecture mapping and user flow visualization are the main objectives of paper prototyping. These prototypes are useful for quick iteration, allowing for quick adjustments in response to input, and aiding with the design's refinement prior to proceeding to more elaborate and expensive development phases.

- **Click-through prototypes**

  A low-fidelity click-through prototype is a basic interactive model of a product that lets consumers click on various sections to move between screens or pages. Basic tools and software are used to build these prototypes, which are more concerned with the general structure and flow than with finely detailed design features. Early on in the design phase, they support designers in testing and improving the user journey.

Consider the scenario where you are creating a brand-new e-commerce website. Wireframing software can be used to produce a low-fidelity click-through prototype. Simple grayscale layouts with placeholders for text and images are used to represent each page, including the main page, product listings, and checkout. Users can click through the purchasing process by creating an interactive experience by connecting these pages with clickable hotspots.

Click-through prototypes with low fidelity are useful for evaluating user flow and navigation quickly and affordably. They offer quick insights on possible problems with usability and areas that need work. Before spending money on high-fidelity designs and extensive development, these prototypes help guarantee a seamless and simple user experience by concentrating on the essential functions and structure.

Advantages of Low-Fidelity Prototyping

Low-fidelity prototypes offer several key benefits that make them a valuable tool in the early stages of design:

- **Rapid Iteration**: Low-fidelity prototypes can be made quickly and simply. This saves a lot of time and money by enabling designers to quickly iterate on concepts and make changes and improvements in response to feedback.
- **Cost-Effective:** Few materials and tools are needed to create low-fidelity prototypes. A more basic digital wireframe, paper model, or simple sketch is less expensive than a more intricate prototype or finished product.
- **Encourages Creativity:** Low-fidelity prototyping is simple and encourages innovation. Designers are free to explore and brainstorm without being constrained by technical implementation issues or high-detail design requirements.
- **Facilitates Early User Testing:** Prototypes with low fidelity allow for early user testing and feedback. Before going on to more complicated stages, designers can find usability difficulties, comprehend user needs, and make the necessary improvements by including users in the early stages.
- **Improves Communication:** These prototypes are great means of enhancing communication. They ensure that everyone is aware of the project's main idea and direction by assisting designers in effectively communicating their concepts to clients, team members, and stakeholders.
- **Reduces Risk:** Low-fidelity prototype helps to lower risks by spotting possible

issues early in the design process. Designers have the ability to address problems before they become expensive and time-consuming to correct later on.

- **Promotes Teamwork:** Low-fidelity prototyping fosters teamwork among participants. Better overall design solutions result from allowing everyone to share ideas and offer comments in an open, iterative atmosphere.
- **Focuses on Functionality:** Low-fidelity prototypes assist teams in concentrating on the essential features and user experience because they do not include intricate design aspects. This guarantees that the foundational elements of the product are sound before incorporating aesthetic elements.

Low-fidelity prototype is an important tool in the design process that has several benefits that make it easier to produce high-quality, cost-effective products that are focused on the needs of users.

Disadvantages of Low-Fidelity Prototyping

While low-fidelity prototyping has many advantages, it also has significant drawbacks.

- **Limited Interactivity:** Because low-fidelity prototypes sometimes lack interactive features, it may be challenging for users to obtain a realistic understanding of how the finished product will work. Feedback regarding the user experience may become less precise as a result.
- **Inadequate Visualization:** Low-fidelity prototypes might not accurately capture the final product's look and feel due to its simplicity and lack of intricate design features. Because of this, it could be difficult for customers and stakeholders to completely comprehend the design goal.
- **Potential Misunderstandings:** Due to their simplicity, low-fidelity prototypes can occasionally cause team members or stakeholders to misinterpret the functionality and design of the finished product. It's possible to overlook or misunderstand important details.
- **Limited User Feedback:** Since low-fidelity prototypes may not fully represent the interaction and visual elements of the final product, users may find it difficult to provide meaningful feedback on them. When conducting user testing, this may produce less insightful results.
- **Insufficient Detail for Developers:** Low-fidelity prototypes cannot have all the information needed for developers to comprehend the project's technical specifications. This may result in omissions from the development process and the need for additional explanation down the road.
- **Short Lifecycle:** As the design process advances to higher fidelity stages, these prototypes are frequently swiftly discarded. As increasingly intricate

prototypes are made, this may lead to redundant efforts and a feeling of work being wasted.

Low-fidelity prototyping has some benefits but also some drawbacks that may affect the design process. Making educated decisions about when and how to employ low-fidelity prototypes effectively requires an understanding of these drawbacks.

High-Fidelity Prototyping

Digital prototypes with high fidelity are intricate, refined models that closely resemble the final result. By thoroughly testing and validating their designs and user flows using these prototypes, UX teams can make sure that every part of the user experience is optimized.

High-fidelity prototypes provide a far more accurate representation of the final product than low-fidelity prototypes do. They offer a more authentic user experience because they are aesthetically pleasing and frequently include advanced functionalities. UX teams proceed to develop high-fidelity prototypes after they have a firm grasp of user and stakeholder demands. This phase is essential for testing intricate user processes and making last-minute changes.

Figure 6.8 illustrates an example of a high-fidelity prototype. It features fully designed screens with all necessary elements, demonstrating how screens are linked together to create a seamless user flow.

Common types of high-fidelity prototypes include:

- Interactive prototypes
- Digital prototypes
- Coded prototypes

High-fidelity prototyping is a vital step in the design process, helping teams refine their concepts and ensure the final product meets both user expectations and business goals. Let's take a closer look at these three types:

- **Interactive Prototypes**

  An intricate and dynamic version of a product that closely mimics the final design in terms of both appearance and functionality is called a high-fidelity interactive prototype. Real photos, typography, and interactive components like buttons, menus, and animations are all included in these prototypes, which are made with sophisticated prototyping tools and software. Because they offer a realistic user experience, designers can test and improve every part of the product with their help.

  An e-commerce website is a prime example of something new. A comprehensive layout comprising photographs, product descriptions, and functional navigation would be present in the high-fidelity prototype. Customers could browse the complete selection, put products in their cart, and check out. This enables designers to find any problems and fix them before the development process starts.

Interactive prototypes with high fidelity are valuable because they provide a realistic experience. Assuring that the finished product fulfills user expectations and corporate goals, they support the validation of design decisions. These prototypes lessen the possibility of expensive revisions later in the development process by offering a comprehensive and dynamic representation.

- **Digital Prototypes**

  A refined and comprehensive version of a product that functions and appears like the final version is called a high-fidelity digital prototype. These prototypes, which are made with sophisticated design software, have correct interactions, realistic graphics, and frequently intricate animations. They are perfect for extensive testing and feedback since they provide a near-exaggerated representation of the user experience.

  An example could be a website redesign. The website's actual colors, typefaces, and layout would be displayed in the high-fidelity digital prototype. Visitors could use interactive elements like sliders and search bars in addition to navigating the website and completing forms. Before a website is fully developed, designers can evaluate its overall feel and usability with the aid of this level of detail.

  Because they offer a realistic glimpse of the finished product, high-fidelity digital prototypes are essential for designers to adjust the user experience and fix any problems before real development starts. This ensures that the final product effectively satisfies user wants and corporate objectives.

- **Coded Prototypes**

  For instance, a coded prototype for a new e-commerce website would utilize HTML to organize the pages, CSS to apply styling, including color and font choices, and JavaScript to include interactive features like picture sliders or drop-down menus. The prototype allows users to engage with the site in a manner that closely resembles the final version, including adding items to a shopping cart and completing the checkout procedure.

  Coded prototypes are useful because they offer an accurate and useful depiction of the finished product. This ensures a more seamless transition from prototype to final product by enabling designers and developers to test interactions, evaluate user flows, and make improvements based on actual performance data.

Advantages of High-Fidelity Prototyping

Several significant advantages of high-fidelity prototyping improve the process of design and development. Some of them are as follows:

- **Realistic User Experience:** In terms of functionality and design, high-fidelity prototypes closely match the final product. Users are given a genuine impression of the final product's appearance and functionality, thanks to this realism, which encourages more accurate and insightful feedback.
- **Detailed Feedback:** High-fidelity prototypes enable users to offer comprehensive input on both functioning and aesthetics since they have interactive features and realistic graphics. This aids in locating and resolving particular problems early in the design process.
- **Improved Stakeholder Communication:** High-fidelity prototypes help team members, clients, and stakeholders understand design concepts. The thorough depiction lowers misconceptions and aligns expectations by assisting all parties in grasping the product vision.
- **Refined Usability Testing:** High-fidelity prototypes allow for in-depth usability testing because of their realistic designs and interactive features. This guarantees that intricate features and interactions function as expected and aids in evaluating how consumers engage with the product.
- **Reduced Risk of Misalignment:** High-fidelity prototypes reduce the possibility of miscommunication between the design team and stakeholders by offering a near-final product approximation. This guarantees that the finished product more closely resembles the original goals and specifications.
- **Precise Technical Specifications:** Detailed specifications and interactions are frequently included in high-fidelity prototypes, which can be utilized to produce exact technical documentation. This makes the design easier for developers to comprehend and apply.
- **Enhanced Design Validation:** With greater confidence, these prototypes confirm design choices. Before proceeding with full-scale development, they aid in ensuring that user flows, interactions, and design aspects are efficient and satisfy user needs.
- **Improved User Engagement:** Because high-fidelity prototypes look polished and realistic, users are more inclined to interact with them and offer insightful comments. This interaction may yield insightful information that helps polish and enhance the finished work.

High-fidelity prototyping is a strong tool for testing and fine-tuning designs prior to full-scale development since it provides a multitude of benefits, such as realistic user experiences, thorough feedback, and enhanced communication.

Disadvantages of High-Fidelity Prototyping

High-fidelity prototypes give a thorough and accurate look at the finished product, but they also present a number of difficulties:

- **High Cost:** Producing high-fidelity prototypes requires a large financial outlay for software, design tools, and frequently specialized knowledge. When compared to less complex prototype techniques, this might be more costly, particularly if numerous iterations are required.
- **Time-Consuming:** It takes a lot of effort to create intricate prototypes with lifelike graphics and interactions. This can delay the design process, postponing comments and changes that could be made more rapidly using lower-fidelity techniques.
- **Overemphasis on Details:** High-fidelity prototypes have the ability to draw attention away from important functional flaws or user experience concerns that should be addressed sooner in the design phase by placing too much focus on visual design and little details.
- **Risk of Misleading Feedback:** Because high-fidelity prototypes are so similar to the finished product, customers may give feedback that is more focused on the design's aesthetic appeal than on its usefulness or functionality. Feedback that prioritizes aesthetics over important user experience problems may arise from this.
- **Limited Flexibility:** It might be more difficult and time-consuming to make adjustments to high-fidelity prototypes. Reworking intricate details is frequently necessary for adjustments, which can be laborious in comparison to the flexibility provided by lower-fidelity prototypes.
- **Scope Creep:** Because high-fidelity prototypes are so detailed, there is a chance that based on how realistic the prototype appears, more features or modifications will be offered. Costs may go up and schedules may take longer as a result of this.
- **Resource Intensive:** High-fidelity prototype necessitates a substantial investment of resources, such as knowledgeable developers and designers. Budgets and resources for projects may be strained as a result, particularly in smaller teams or startups.

High-fidelity prototypes have a number of drawbacks, such as high prices, time demands, and a potential overemphasis on visual aspects, even though they provide a realistic sample of the finished product. Efficient design and development necessitate striking a balance between these variables and the project requirements.

Best Tools to Create Prototypes

Depending on the kind of prototype you want to build–such as low-fidelity wireframes, high-fidelity designs, or interactive prototypes–one can require using a range of technologies. These are a few of the top tools, arranged according to their functions:

Low-Fidelity Prototyping and Wireframing

- **Balsamiq:** Great for creating quick and simple wireframes.
- **Sketch:** Widely used for wireframing, with a focus on UI/UX design.

High-Fidelity Prototyping and Design

- **Adobe XD:** Offers robust tools for designing and prototyping with interactive elements.
- **Figma:** A web-based design tool that allows for real-time collaboration and prototyping.
- **InVision:** Known for its interactive prototyping capabilities and integration with other design tools.

Interactive Prototyping

- **Axure RP:** Provides advanced prototyping features, including dynamic content and conditional logic.
- **Proto.io:** Allows you to create fully interactive prototypes without any coding.

Mobile App Prototyping

- **Marvel:** Easy to use and excellent for mobile and web prototyping.
- **Flinto:** Designed specifically for creating interactive and animated prototypes for mobile apps.

The kind of prototype you want to build, your unique demands, and your skill level all play a role in selecting the best tool. It's common for these tools to be used in combination during the prototyping phase.

Comparing Wireframing and Prototyping

When designing a product, it's essential to understand the tools used in the process. Prototyping and wireframing have different functions but are equally important. Let's compare these two methods to see how they differ and how each contributes to the design process.

	Wireframing	**Prototyping**
Description	The first stage of design, known as wireframing, aims to create a basic, low-fidelity layout for a website or application. Without incorporating specific design elements like colors or images, it just describes the overall layout and arrangement of the elements	Prototyping takes the wireframe to the next level by adding detailed design elements and interactivity. Users can engage with the design from low-fidelity (basic) to high-fidelity (detailed), testing functionality and user experience. It's similar to building a functional model of your idea to observe how it performs in actual situations
Nature	In nature, wireframes are static	In nature, prototypes are interactive
Detail Level	Low-fidelity highlights how different elements are arranged and positioned inside the design	Can be high-fidelity, which is refined, detailed, and very similar to the finished product, or low-fidelity, which is simple and basic
Visuals	Simple, monochrome designs devoid of color, imagery, and intricate stylistic features are typical of wireframes. Without focusing on the finishing details, they concentrate on the fundamental framework	A wide variety of visual elements, including colors, photos, fonts, and complex design, are used into prototypes. These components produce a more accurate depiction of the look and feel of the finished project
Focus	Places special emphasis on the overall design and the content's structural organization, making sure that everything is arranged correctly and that the information architecture makes sense	Ensures that the finished product is not only functional but also aesthetically beautiful and user-friendly by focusing on the user experience, including the visual design and interaction aspects
Costing	Wireframes are an affordable design technique that may be used to quickly and cheaply develop a basic structural layout	Depending on the degree of complexity and interaction incorporated in the design, the cost of producing a prototype can vary greatly, from modest to high
Time Investment	Since their primary goal is to swiftly outline the fundamental composition and organization of the design, wireframes can be produced in a comparatively short amount of time	Prototypes require more time to construct because of their increased degree of detail and interaction, which makes them more difficult than wireframes

Tools	Tools like Balsamiq, Sketch, and Adobe XD, which have capabilities especially made to aid in developing fundamental structural layouts and element placement, are good resources for quickly wireframing projects	In order to create more polished and functional models, prototyping calls for more sophisticated tools like InVision, Figma, and Adobe XD. These tools offer extensive options for adding detailed design aspects and interactivity
Other Key Differences	**Step in the Design Phase:** Once the fundamental layouts are finalized, prototypes are constructed later. Wireframes are created early in the design phase. **Complexity:** Prototypes take more time and effort to produce than wireframes, which can be created more quickly and easily. **User Testing:** Wireframes are mostly used for planning and preliminary layout decisions, whereas prototypes are used for usability testing and feedback.	

Table 6.2: *Key Differences between Wireframing and Prototyping*

Conclusion

To sum up, this chapter has guided you through the crucial phases of developing prototypes and wireframes, which are important stages in the design process. We looked at the various kinds of wireframes, from rough sketches to intricate designs, and comprehended how important they are for describing the organization and flow of a project. Then, we looked at prototypes in all of their forms—static, interactive, and coded—each with a specific function for user testing and obtaining feedback.

We also discussed a variety of programs and technologies designed specifically for these jobs. Every tool has a special capability to help you realize your ideas, from Adobe XD and Figma for high-fidelity prototyping to Balsamiq and Sketch for wireframing. You can effectively close the gap between concept and finished result by becoming proficient with these tools and comprehending their uses, ensuring a more seamless and intuitive user experience.

In the next chapter, we will explore the significance of visual hierarchy, which is an essential component for designers to produce interesting and user-friendly interfaces. We will examine UI patterns and learn about their significance to the user experience. By the time it's completed, you will have learnt a lot about creating visually striking designs that lead users through your digital works with ease.

Key Terms

- **Wireframes:** Basic diagrams showing the layout and navigation of a website or application.
- **Low-Fidelity:** Simple, basic prototypes used to test and explore early design concepts.
- **High-Fidelity:** Detailed, polished prototypes that closely resemble the final product.
- **Blueprint:** A detailed plan or outline of a design project.
- **Sketches:** Rough, hand-drawn representations of design concepts.
- **User-Focused:** Design approach prioritizing the needs and preferences of the end user.
- **Placeholder:** Temporary content or elements indicating where final content will go.
- **Visual Hierarchy:** Arrangement of design elements to guide viewer's attention and understanding.
- **Usability Testing:** Process where real users test a product to identify issues and provide feedback.
- **Interaction:** The ways users engage with a product, such as clicking, tapping, or swiping.
- **Interaction Flow:** Sequence of steps a user takes to complete a task within a product.
- **Scalability:** Scalability of a product to handle increased usage or growth without losing performance.
- **Prototype:** An early version of a product that provides insight into the design structure, user experience, and general concept, allowing for testing and improvement of various features.
- **Mock-up:** A prototype or early model of a product used to test and refine design concepts.
- **Design Thinking:** A design methodology that relies heavily on prototyping, particularly in the later stages of testing, to ensure the final product meets user needs.
- **Representation:** The form a prototype takes, such as on paper, a mobile device, or a computer screen.
- **Precision:** The level of detail in a prototype, ranging from rough and simple (low fidelity) to very detailed and polished (high fidelity).
- **Interactivity:** The extent to which users can interact with a prototype during

testing, whether they can only view it, partially interact with it, or fully use its features.

- **Evolution:** The lifecycle of a prototype, where test versions can quickly be replaced with new iterations through rapid prototyping.
- **Low-Fidelity Prototyping:** Simplified representations showing user flows and the general structure of a product, often using wireframes. Useful in the early stages of design for quick iteration and feedback.
- **High-Fidelity Prototyping:** Detailed, interactive digital mock-ups used for gathering in-depth feedback during usability testing.
- **Early Problem Detection:** Identifying usability problems and design defects early in the prototyping process to address them before they become more costly and time-consuming.
- **Communication Tool:** Prototypes used to convey design concepts and gather input from designers, developers, and stakeholders.
- **Informed Decision-Making:** Using insights and user feedback from prototyping to guide the development process and influence design choices.
- **Iterative Improvement:** Continuous testing, feedback, and refinement of a prototype to produce a more functional and refined final design.
- **Cost-Effectiveness:** The ability to experiment with various design concepts through prototyping without heavy investment, reducing the risk of expensive revisions and rework.
- **Evaluate Technical Feasibility:** Using prototypes to determine which features are tough to implement and to reveal unexpected financial, technological, or practical constraints.
- **Improved Visualization:** Enhancing the communication of ideas and gaining stakeholder support by providing a tangible way to explore design concepts.
- **Feature Validation:** Using prototypes to prioritize features that offer the greatest value to users by confirming their viability and effectiveness.
- **Comprehensive Version:** A detailed and complete version of a design or product that includes all features, functionalities, and design elements as intended in the final version.
- **Realistic Graphics:** Visual elements that closely mimic real-life appearances and details, providing a more lifelike and accurate representation of the final product.

Chapter 7
Visual Design and UI Patterns

Introduction

Welcome to this chapter on critical aspects of user interface (UI) design. We will start by delving into the idea of visual hierarchy, which is crucial for directing users' attention and designing user-friendly interfaces. Designers may create interesting and user-friendly experiences by knowing how to visually prioritize things. We will then examine UI design patterns, which are industry-standard approaches to typical design issues that improve usability and user happiness. We will also cover the best UI pattern libraries, which are helpful resources with pre-made elements and ideas to help you expedite the design process. Lastly, we will explore dark UI design patterns, looking at how these strategies affect user behavior and talking about how important ethical design is. By the end of this chapter, you will gain a comprehensive understanding of these fundamental UI concepts and how they impact user experience.

Structure

In this chapter, we will discuss the following topics:

- Visual Hierarchy: A Guide for Designers
- Importance of Visual Hierarchy
- Key Elements of Visual Hierarchy
- User Interface (UI) Design Patterns
- Importance of UI Design Patterns
- Commonly Used UI Design Patterns
- Implementing UI Design Patterns
- Top UI Pattern Libraries
- UI Design Patterns for Mobile Apps

- Top Mobile UI Pattern Libraries
- Dark UI Design Patterns

Visual Hierarchy: A Guide for Designers

Imagine you are an artist creating a masterpiece, but instead of paint and canvas, you are using text, images, and buttons. Your goal is to guide your audience's eyes across your creation in a way that tells a story and highlights the most important parts. This technique is called visual hierarchy, and it is like having a map that shows you how people naturally look at things.

Think about the last time you walked into a museum and saw a breathtaking painting. What caught your eye first? Maybe it was a bold color, a striking figure, or a bright light in the scene. Artists use these tricks to make sure you notice the most important parts of their work. Web designers do the same thing, but with websites.

Let us say you are building a website. You have a big, eye-catching headline at the top (that is your hero header), a bright and inviting button asking visitors to sign up or buy something (your Call to Action), and a recognizable logo that tells people they are in the right place. These elements do not stand out by accident. They are carefully placed to draw your attention just like in a museum.

This strategy is essential because it aligns with how our brains process information. We naturally look at bigger, bolder, and brighter elements first. By understanding this, you can make sure your visitors see what you want them to see, leading them through your website in the order you intend.

So, next time you are creating a webpage, think of yourself as an artist. Use visual hierarchy to highlight the key parts of your design, and you will create a beautiful, effective site that captures attention and guides your visitors exactly where you want them to go.

Definition

Visual hierarchy is a design principle that arranges elements on a page to guide the viewer's attention. By using size, color, contrast, and positioning, designers ensure the most important elements stand out first. This helps users navigate the content easily, leading them to key information and actions intuitively.

> *"Visual hierarchy controls the delivery of the experience. If you have a hard time figuring out where to look on a page, it's more than likely that its layout is missing a clear visual hierarchy."*
>
> - The Nielsen Norman Group

Let us explain visual hierarchy with an **example**. Look at the following home page:

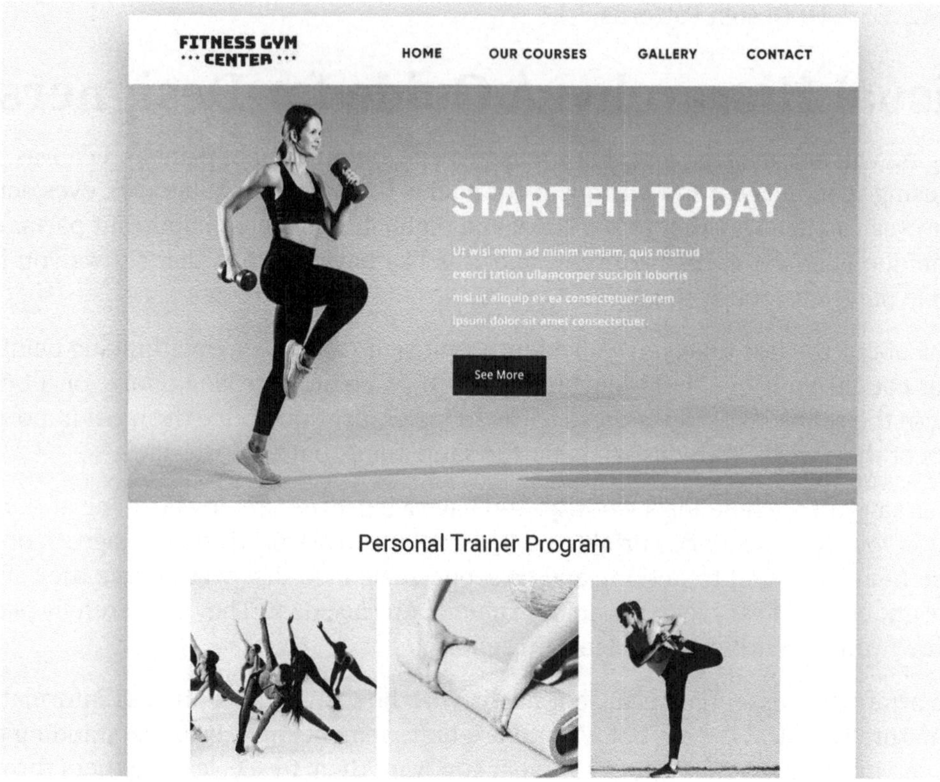

Figure 7.1: *Webpage example of visual hierarchy*

The image of dumbbells will catch your eye right away, hinting at a fitness-related subject. Your gaze will then probably go to the header on the right and the black button underneath the text. In the end, you scroll down to view further content. This flow is meant to gradually direct your attention.

Consider another **example**. This is a basic home page with just text, buttons, and headings. There are no graphics.

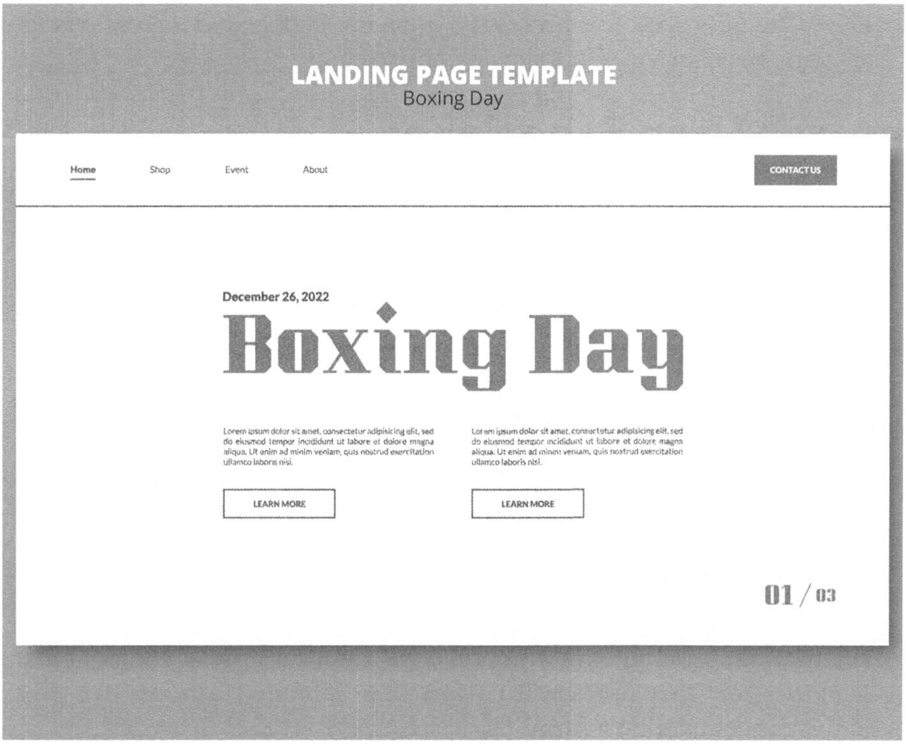

Figure 7.2: *Landing page example of visual hierarchy*

Despite its simplicity, the website uses font size and weight to create visual hierarchy, which effectively draws viewers in. The large, bold text immediately draws your eye, followed by the two button options. By applying these basic design principles, the website ensures that key elements stand out. This approach is crucial, as it quickly grabs visitors' attention and encourages them to stay on the page longer.

Importance of Visual Hierarchy

In design, visual hierarchy is essential because it directs the viewer's attention, facilitating navigation and information comprehension. There are multiple essential factors that highlight the significance of visual hierarchy in design:

Guides User Attention

- **Prioritization**: Visual hierarchy ensures that the most crucial elements stand out by drawing users' attention to them first. Emphasizing vital aspects, like headlines, call-to-action buttons, or important messaging, makes it easier for readers to quickly comprehend the most relevant information without becoming overwhelmed. This prioritization makes the content simpler to read and understand.

- **Flow**: The information is presented in an intelligible and logical arrangement, allowing the user's eye to follow its natural flow.

Improves User Experience

- **Ease of Navigation:** A well-organized website or application helps customers locate what they need fast and execute tasks with ease, which improves their overall experience.
- **Readability:** Text is easier to read and comprehend when headings, subheadings, and body text are clearly distinguished from one another.

Enhances Engagement

- **Attention-Grabbing:** Visual hierarchy facilitates rapid material scanning by arranging text and graphics in a clear, logical manner that enhances readability. In order to assist consumers understand and retain information, it draws attention to crucial components such as headlines, calls to action (CTAs), and critical messaging.
- **Interaction:** Promoting interaction with the most crucial components makes it more likely that users will perform the intended actions, like pressing a button or completing a form.

Increases Conversion Rates

- **Strategic Placement:** By strategically placing calls to action (CTAs) and critical information where users are most likely to notice them, you can increase conversion rates by encouraging users to take the required action.
- **User Journey:** Leading users through a carefully considered journey enhances the likelihood that they will accomplish particular objectives, like buying something or subscribing to a newsletter.

Conveys Brand Message Effectively

- **Consistency:** By guaranteeing that the design is in line with the company's message and values, a well-executed visual hierarchy strengthens the brand identity.
- **Clarity:** It ensures that users comprehend the purpose and objectives of the material by helping to communicate the intended message in an unambiguous and clear manner.

Reduces Cognitive Load

- **Simplification:** By organizing content in a structured manner, visual hierarchy reduces the cognitive load on users, making it easier for them to process information.

- **Focus:** By allowing users to concentrate on a single aspect at a time without becoming sidetracked by unimportant information, they can browse more effectively.

Builds Trust and Credibility

- **Professionalism:** A website or brand might appear more credible and professional when it has a well-organized design and a distinct visual hierarchy.
- **Reliability:** Because it demonstrates attention to detail and user-centric design, users are more inclined to trust and interact with a website that is simple to use and comprehend.

To sum up, visual hierarchy is a basic design principle that guarantees content is presented in an efficient and well-organized way. A design project's ability to effectively communicate messages, direct users' attention, improve user experience, increase engagement, boost conversions, lessen cognitive load, and foster trust is greatly dependent on the visual hierarchy employed.

Key Elements of Visual Hierarchy

You can use a variety of design techniques on your website to draw users in and focus their attention in the desired direction. Although you do not have to apply each of these strategies, being aware of them can enable you to make more deliberate and sensible design decisions. Let us look at the key strategies that will help you accomplish this.

Reading Patterns

When a page or screen has a strong visual hierarchy, visitors are guided to its functionality and provided with appropriate visual signals. Users react to interfaces milliseconds faster than other types of websites, making snap decisions about whether to stay or go. **Z pattern and F pattern are the two main reading layouts.** These carefully arrange material to create a coherent narrative that makes sense to visitors, thereby supporting their natural reading tendencies, which are typically left to right for most people in western countries.

Z-Pattern Layout

This well-liked design idea in visual hierarchy mimics how our eyes naturally scan information. Envision a path that is Z-shaped. It begins at the top left, travels horizontally to the right, then descends diagonally to the left, and ends with one more horizontal sweep heading to the right. People usually read from left to right and top to bottom, which is reflected in this pattern.

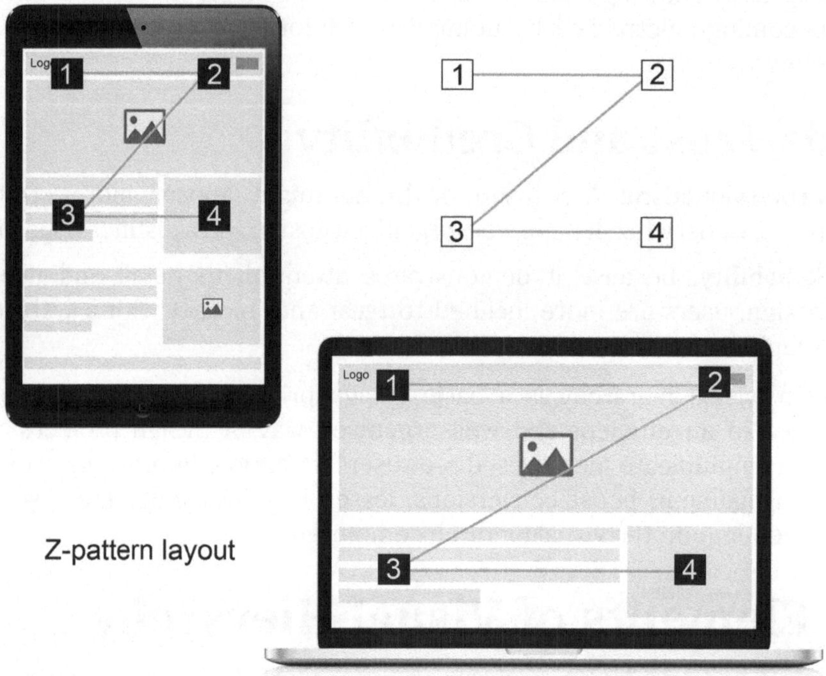

Figure 7.3: *Example of Z-pattern layout*

In actuality, the Z-pattern is frequently utilized in print and digital design to consistently direct viewers' attention. For instance, a logo or headline in the upper left corner of a website's homepage might draw visitors in at first. The eye may come across a navigation bar or the main image when it travels horizontally. An important promotional message or a call-to-action (CTA) button may be reached via the diagonal downward movement. Finally, supplemental CTAs or more information are frequently displayed in the bottom horizontal line.

This arrangement works well for producing a clean, organized design that makes it easy for people to comprehend and engage with important components. It ensures that crucial information is positioned where people are likely to look, which enhances usability and engagement.

F-Pattern Layout

Based on how people normally read and scan text-heavy content, designers created the F-pattern layout. This design mimics the letter "F," which is representative of people' innate tendency to scan from top to bottom and left to right. There are two horizontal and one vertical stroke in the F-pattern.

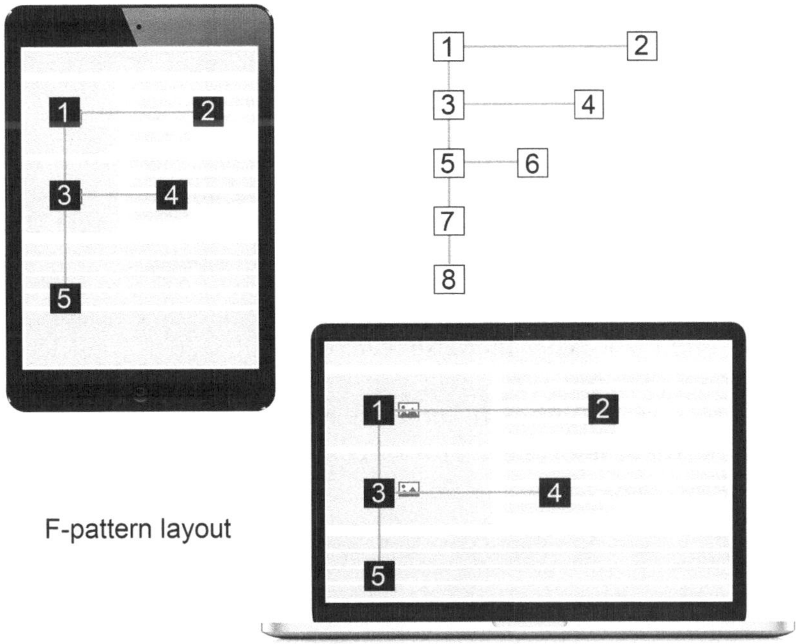

Figure 7.4: *Example of F-pattern layout*

When using the F-pattern in real life, users typically start by reading the top horizontal line, which frequently contains headlines or important information. They scan another horizontal line that is a little bit below the top as they proceed down the page; this line may contain subheadings or crucial information. Lastly, visitors usually search for further information or navigation choices by scanning vertically down the left side of the article.

The F-pattern could be used, for instance, in the following way on a news website: the top horizontal line features a big headline or important news item. Short synopses of other pieces or subheadings could appear in the second horizontal line. A sidebar with further articles or links may be included in the vertical stroke on the left. This layout works well for text-heavy pages where important information needs to be immediately accessible since it makes it easier for visitors to find and comprehend the most important content fast.

Size and Scale

Users' interactions with a design can be greatly influenced by size and scale, which are crucial components of visual hierarchy. Smaller features are frequently viewed as less significant, while larger elements typically draw more attention. Designers may direct users' attention and make sure that the most important information is prominently shown by carefully changing the size and scale of individual components.

Imagine you are walking through a lively city filled with tall skyscrapers and cozy little shops. As you walk, your eyes are naturally drawn to the tallest buildings first because of their size–they stand out and dominate the view. This is similar to how visual hierarchy works, using size to catch your attention.

Now think about the small shops tucked between the big buildings. They might not stand out as much at first, but they are still charming and have lots of interesting things to offer. In design, these smaller elements are just as important. They provide extra details and context that make the whole experience better.

Websites are subject to the same rules. For example, larger text and graphics are noticed more often and can increase click-through rates considerably. Large, attention-grabbing pictures, prominent call-to-action buttons, and bold headlines direct users' attention and promote interaction. Even though they are less visually striking, smaller text and images just provide context and depth, completing the user's journey through the material.

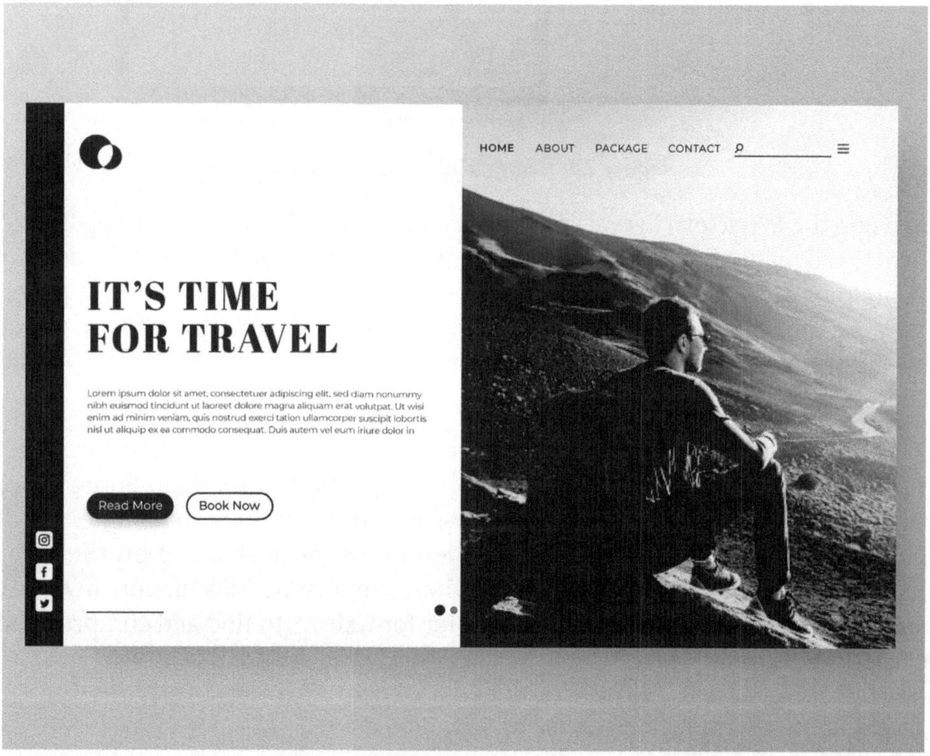

Figure 7.5: *Visual impact of large elements in design*

You have the authority to organize these components as a designer, just like an architect plans a metropolis. You may direct users' attention precisely where you want it to go by carefully varying the scale and size of different components. The most important information is seen and understood when size and scale are used intelligently, creating a visually appealing and harmonious design environment. This can be achieved with a huge headline that grabs attention immediately or a subtle detail that provides depth. Improved user engagement and increased conversion rates on your website can result from this strategic arrangement.

Optimizing Design with Size and Scale

Making use of scale and size in your design can help to establish a distinct visual hierarchy and highlight key components:

- **Prioritize Key Elements:** To guarantee that headlines, crucial photos, and call-to-action buttons get the viewer's attention first, use larger sizes for these elements.
- **Maintain Balance:** Steer clear of overburdening consumers with excessively huge elements. Larger pieces should be balanced with minor details to provide a pleasing arrangement.
- **Apply Contrast:** To make a strong contrast and highlight the most crucial components of your design, pair larger with smaller pieces.
- **Consistent Sizing:** To preserve a unified look and feel, adhere to a consistent size hierarchy among comparable elements (for example, make all headings the same size).
- **Scale Responsively:** To preserve readability and emphasis, make sure that the text and picture sizes are responsive and work well across a range of screen sizes.

Color and Contrast

For any website design, color is essential. Most of the time, you will pick a color scheme and apply it over your entire website, making sure the tones go well together and with your overall style. Even if you only use black and white, your color scheme has a big impact on how people view your website. Vibrant, high contrast colors stand out more than subdued hues, giving the impression that they are more significant. Strategic use of color can draw attention to important details and direct the viewer's gaze. But you shouldn't base your color choices just on what you believe to be attractive. Selecting colors that offer a pleasing contrast with one another can help you make the most of your palette. In this manner, you can highlight key elements on your website.

Consider yourself a painter preparing your canvas for a fresh work of art. Your selection of colors will establish the overall tone and atmosphere of the piece. Similar to this, color is a key component of web design that influences how users view a website.

Consider your website to be that unpainted wall. You choose a color scheme that goes well with the overall design of your website in addition to being visually pleasing.

These hues resemble the brushstrokes that give life to your design. User perception is greatly impacted by the way you utilize color, even if your palette is as basic as black and white.

Imagine yourself strolling through a busy market. First things that capture your attention are the stalls with the most striking difference in color. The contrast between the bright colors and the subdued background highlights the significance of these hues. You can utilize this approach on your website to draw users' attention to important places and emphasize important information.

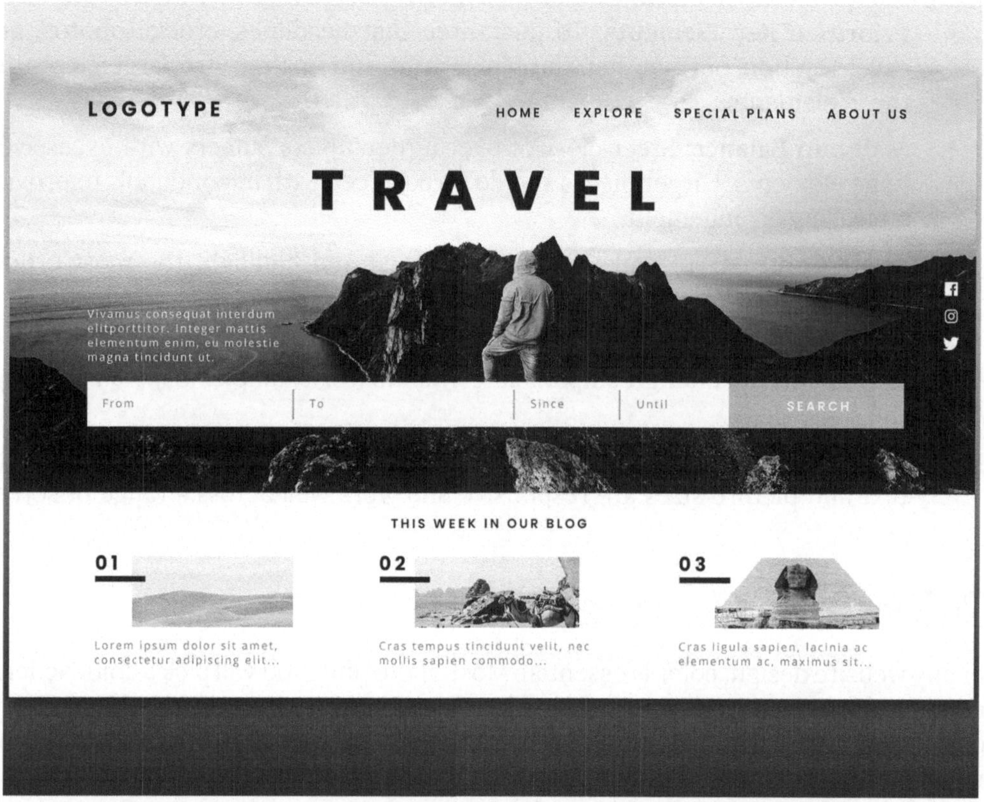

Figure 7.6: *Color contrast enhances user focus with vibrant design*

But choosing colors is about more than just what seems good. The colors you choose for your design must have good contrast with one another in order to be truly effective. This calculated decision guarantees that key components stand out like the most vibrant market stalls.

You may easily guide visitors around your website, ensuring they notice important details and grasp the main point by carefully selecting and using high contrast colors.

Optimizing Design with Color and Contrast

A visually appealing experience can be produced in your design by skillfully utilizing color and contrast to highlight important components. The following advice will help you make the most of color and contrast in your design:

- **Use Bold Colors for Important Elements:** To make call-to-action buttons and headlines stand out, use bright or contrasting colors for these elements.
- **Create Contrast for Readability:** Make sure your material is easily legible and accessible by providing enough contrast between the text and backdrop colors.
- **Keep Your Color Palette Limited:** To preserve visual harmony and prevent overpowering consumers, stick to a limited number of clashing colors in a unified color scheme.
- **Highlight with Accent Colors:** Use accent colors to direct users' attention to the most important content or interactive components.
- **Utilize Color Consistency:** To emphasize the importance of each function or category and establish a clear visual hierarchy, utilize color consistently across the site.
- **Make Use of Color Psychology:** Take into account how colors affect emotion and user behavior. For example, use warm colors to suggest urgency.

White Space

The empty space found on a webpage between and around elements is known as white space, or negative space. By eliminating clutter, it enhances legibility and visual balance, facilitating easier information absorption and helping users concentrate on important text.

Imagine walking into a beautifully arranged art gallery. Each painting is displayed with plenty of space around it, allowing you to appreciate its details without feeling overwhelmed by surrounding clutter. This open space, or "negative space," helps you focus on the artwork and absorb its essence.

White space serves the same purpose in web design. It is similar to giving each element on your website a dedicated gallery space. It is simpler for users to notice and interact with crucial items, including buttons, photos, and headlines, when there is sufficient space surrounding them.

Think of an e-commerce site crammed with too many products and ads. The cluttered layout can make it difficult for users to find what they are looking for, just as a crowded gallery can detract from the enjoyment of viewing art. By using white space effectively, you allow each element to stand out clearly, guiding visitors' attention and helping them focus on what matters most.

For example, Amazon effectively uses white space to avoid a cluttered appearance. By strategically spacing out product listings, search bars, and filters, they ensure each element stands out and is easy to focus on. By using white space effectively, users can find what they are seeking for more quickly and are kept from feeling overwhelmed. Users may browse details and compare products with ease because of the ample area surrounding each listing. This well-considered layout improves overall user experience and navigation, making the website more efficient and easier to use for buying.

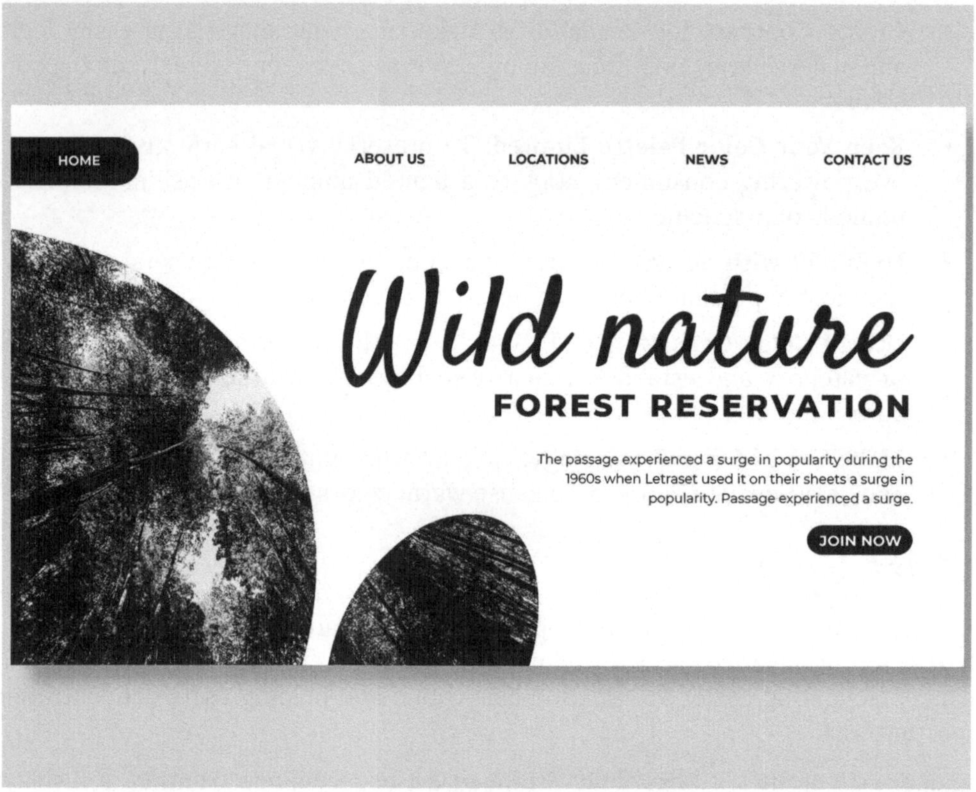

Figure 7.7: *Highlighting the main product with the power of white space*

Enough white space surrounding elements improves legibility and produces a visually pleasing, balanced design on any kind of website. This well-considered layout facilitates easier site navigation and distraction-free content absorption for users.

Optimizing Design with White Space

Adding white space to your design will greatly improve attention and clarity, making your content simpler to read and more interesting. The following are some essential pointers for utilizing white space in your layout:

- **Prioritize Key Pieces:** To make key pieces stand out and draw attention, leave plenty of white space surrounding them.

- **Divide Sections:** To make it simpler for readers to navigate and comprehend material, utilize white space to clearly identify the various sections of your website.
- **Boost Readability:** To make text blocks easier to read and less visually cluttered, add more white space surrounding them.
- **Establish Visual Balance:** To produce a unified and well-organized design, maintain a healthy amount of white space between different elements.
- **Concentrate on the Important Steps:** To grab visitors' attention and promote engagement, provide extra white space around call-to-action buttons and important information.
- **Simplify Layouts:** Make your design less cluttered by using white space to give each element a specific area. This will make your layout more aesthetically pleasing and easier to use.

Typography

The deliberate use of font styles, sizes, and weights to structure and highlight material, direct the viewer's attention, and define the relative importance of various parts on a page is referred to as typography in visual hierarchy.

Picture yourself browsing a library where the books are arranged according to style and size. Your eyes are drawn to the biggest, most elaborate volumes that are displayed prominently on the shelf. Your eyes are led through the collection by the smaller, easier books that are arranged in a systematic order as you go closer. This arrangement mimics the way typography functions in web design.

The typography on a webpage is similar to this well-organized library. Users can more quickly explore and comprehend the text thanks to the visual hierarchy created by the employment of various font styles, sizes, and weights. For example, a large, bold header draws the reader's eye right away, and the body text and subheadings are designed to accentuate rather than detract from the primary themes.

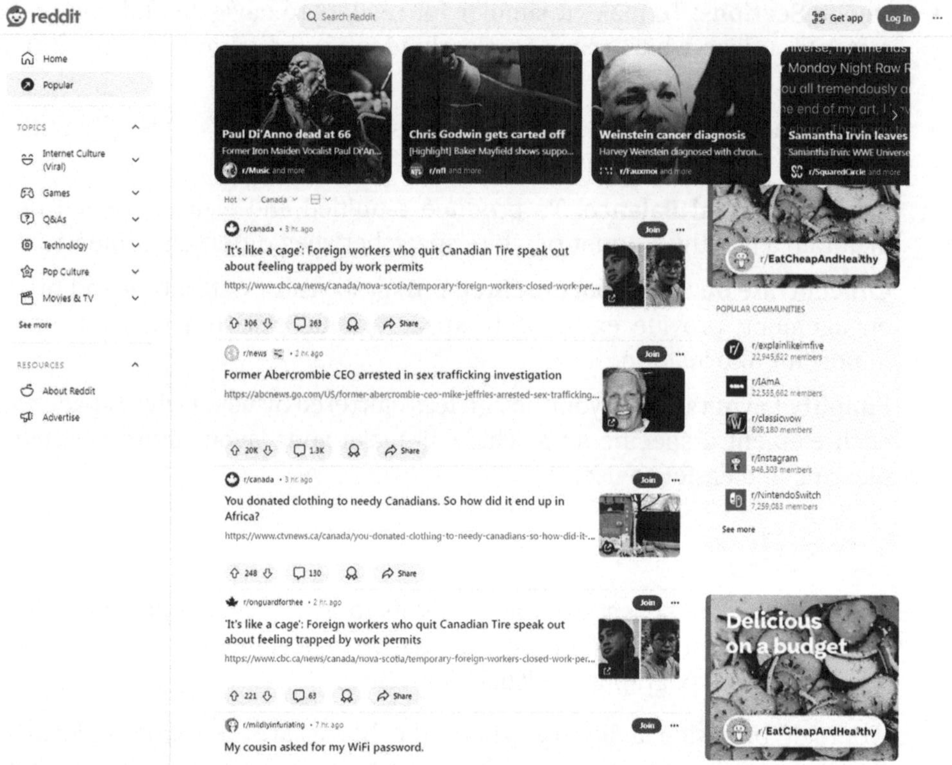

Figure 7.8: *Content-rich site with clear, engaging typography*

Selecting the correct typeface is essential. A readable typeface that is easy to read guarantees that readers can quickly take in the information, whereas decorative or extremely complicated fonts might make content challenging to understand. Like a well-stocked library improves the experience of reading, a well-designed typeface improves user experience by emphasizing important content and guaranteeing ease of reading.

Optimizing Design with Typography

Enhancing your design with effective typography is key to creating a strong visual hierarchy. Here are some tips to ensure your typography is both creative and easy to read:

- **Create a Clear Hierarchy:** Use different font sizes and weights for headings, subheadings, and body text to clearly differentiate sections, helping users quickly grasp the structure and importance of content. For example, Reddit.com (*Figure* 7.8) effectively organizes its vast information with clear, engaging typography, making navigation easy and intuitive.

- **Select Readable typefaces:** Make sure the typefaces you choose can be read easily on a range of devices. To make your work readable and accessible, put clarity above style.
- **Make Effective Use of Contrast:** Use contrasting font weights and colors for important elements to create a striking visual effect. Strong contrast draws the reader's attention and makes crucial material stand out.
- **Minimize Font Variations:** To preserve consistency, stick to a small number of font families. An excessive number of font variations might detract from the content and cause visual disorder.
- **Use Hierarchical Scaling:** Modify font sizes to establish a distinct hierarchy. Users are guided easily through the information by using larger fonts for primary headings, medium-sized fonts for subheadings, and smaller font sizes for body text.
- **Use Visual Balance:** Make sure the text blocks are aligned and spaced appropriately. In addition to improving readability, proper spacing and alignment produce a balanced, visually beautiful layout.
- **Emphasize Essential Information:** Make calls-to-action or essential facts stand out without overwhelming the reader by using inventive typographic features like bold or italicized text.

Consistency

In terms of visual hierarchy, consistency and alignment refer to the regular and systematic placement of design elements, guaranteeing a logical and user-friendly structure.

Consider creating a website to be similar to organizing a neighborhood. The streets (or layout) are precisely aligned, and every house (or webpage element) has the same style. This makes it simple for visitors to navigate their way around.

Consistency in online design is akin to making sure all houses have the same style, with consistent fonts, colors, and page space. This uniformity makes users feel more at ease and aware of what to expect when they navigate your website.

Alignment provides a clear path for guests to follow, much like maintaining all the houses in a row. The user's eye is effortlessly guided from one area of the page to another by the proper alignment of the text, photos, and buttons, which makes the website easy to navigate.

Consistency and alignment work together to make your website visually appealing and user-friendly, making it easy for people to discover what they need, much like in a well-planned neighborhood.

Optimizing Consistency and Alignment

Establishing a consistent and aligned visual hierarchy is crucial for a website to be user-friendly and well-structured. You can smoothly navigate consumers through your information by keeping design components consistent and aligned. Here are some pointers to assist you in doing this:

- **Use a Grid System:** To guarantee that all pieces are correctly aligned, use a grid system. As a result, the content is arranged in a clear, navigable manner for the user.
- **Maintain Consistency in Font and Color:** Make sure that the fonts and colors you choose are the same across your website. This makes it easier for users to traverse your website and spot patterns.
- **Align Elements Uniformly:** Make sure that buttons, text, and images are all positioned equally throughout the page. Alignment done correctly produces a visual flow that successfully focuses users' attention.
- **Establish Repeating Design Patterns:** To establish a recognizable user experience over several pages, use similar design patterns, such as button designs and header formats.
- **Space Elements Evenly:** Maintain a constant distance between items. This keeps things uncluttered and guarantees a well-balanced layout that improves readability and aesthetic appeal.

Layout

The arrangement and organization of items on a page, with the goal of directing the viewer's eye logically and purposefully and emphasizing the most important content first, is referred to as layout in visual hierarchy.

Assume you are opening a brand-new business. You want consumers to know where to find the best deals, the checkout, and any exclusive merchandise as soon as they walk in. In order to do this, you must meticulously arrange the room, putting the focal points at eye level and creating obvious routes for patrons to follow.

Layout has a similar purpose in web design. It is similar to setting out your shop so customers can quickly locate what they need. Like the featured products in your business, the most significant elements–like headlines or call-to-action buttons–are positioned prominently. The arrangement of supporting materials, such as text blocks or images, naturally guides the user's eye from one point to the next so they do not miss anything crucial.

Not only does a well-designed layout appear attractive, but it also strategically improves the user experience. It is similar to designing a flawless shopping experience where people flow from one area to another with ease, with everything in its proper position. Users that have carefully considered their layout will know where to go without being explicitly told, making online navigation as pleasurable as perusing a neatly laid out store.

Style and Texture

Using various visual effects, such as textures, patterns, or shadows, to add depth and highlight key components improves the overall design. This is known as style and texture in visual hierarchy.

Envision furnishing an area. To draw attention to particular places, use patterned pillows, a textured rug, and an eye-catching light fixture. By drawing people's attention to the areas of the room you want them to notice first, these features give the space more depth and personality.

Figure 7.9: *Website with textured background and layered styles using z-index for depth*

Style and texture have comparable functions in web design. Consider your website to be the room you are designing. You can draw the user's attention by using distinctive visual styles, such as textured backgrounds, patterned areas, or shadow effects on buttons. These visual cues indicate where the user should focus, just like a textured rug or patterned cushions do.

A call-to-action button, for instance, might stand out from the page by casting a soft shadow behind it, much as how a chic light draws attention to a space. Similar to this, you might use a patterned background to distinguish one content area from another, making it easier for people to traverse the website.

You may add layers of visual interest to your website and direct visitors' attention in the same way that you would direct a guest's gaze in a nicely decorated room by carefully altering styles and textures.

Adding Depth with Z-Index

Another important tool in creating depth is the z-index property, which controls the layering of elements on a webpage. By assigning higher z-index values to important components, such as floating buttons or banners, you can ensure they appear above other elements, drawing users' attention effectively. Just as layered textures in a room add dimension, the strategic use of z-index in web design creates a visually engaging experience by adding layers of focus.

Creating Impactful Visual Hierarchies

To ensure that readers are guided through your content and that they focus on the most important components, you must establish a strong visual hierarchy. With the help of the essential components listed above, you may create an efficient visual hierarchy by following these tips:

- **Prioritize Content:** Determine which components on your page are most crucial, then use size, color, or positioning to make them stand out.
- **Use Contrast:** To highlight important sections and provide visual differentiation, use contrasting colors, fonts, and styles.
- **Use Consistent Alignment:** Provide a clean, orderly structure that leads the user's attention naturally across the material by aligning pieces cleanly.
- **Scale Elements Appropriately:** Make sure key text or images dominate the visual field by using size and scale to highlight them.
- **Make Effective Use of White Space:** To prevent clutter and make each element stand out, leave plenty of space surrounding important components.
- **Use Visual Cues:** Direct users' attention to key places or tasks with the use of features like arrows, lines, or bold text.

- **Create a Clear Path:** Arrange content in a way that leads users from one piece of information to the next, following a logical order.

User Interface (UI) Design Patterns

UI design patterns provide tried-and-true answers to frequent design problems, much like indispensable tools in a designer's toolbox. Consider them as pre-made models or guidelines that assist designers in producing user interfaces that are clear and functional. These patterns are flexible frameworks that may be adjusted to meet the unique requirements and design preferences of a given project; they are not inflexible.

Just as a chef uses basic cooking techniques to create various dishes, designers use UI patterns to build different interfaces. The beauty of these patterns lies in their familiarity–users encounter them regularly across websites and apps. This familiarity reduces the learning curve, allowing users to quickly grasp how to interact with a new interface because the design elements are recognizable.

For **example**, consider the "hamburger menu" pattern–a simple icon with three horizontal lines. People are habituated to this icon and instinctively know that it represents a secret menu and tapping it would disclose more options. Designers can make the UI more intuitive by utilizing users' pre-existing knowledge through the use of this frequent pattern.

It is crucial to keep in mind though that there is not a single UI pattern that works for everyone. Every design must be modified to fit the particular situation in which it is applied. For example, the hamburger menu may not be the best choice for a desktop website with lots of screen space, even though it functions great for mobile apps.

Consider assembling a sandwich to get a sense of this. Whatever sandwich you choose–turkey club, BLT, or grilled cheese–it always has the same structure: something tasty between two slices of bread. Sandwiches can vary greatly in terms of fillings, toppings, and bread type, but the general structure remains the same. In a similar vein, UI patterns offer the fundamental framework of an interface. While you can alter the specifics (fonts, colors, and layout) to fit the demands of the user and the brand, the basic design stays the same, ensuring a user-friendly experience.

The utilization of UI design patterns is crucial in producing user interfaces that are efficient, consistent, and easy to use. With the use of these patterns, interface designers may create familiar functional designs that still allow for customization to satisfy particular requirements for design.

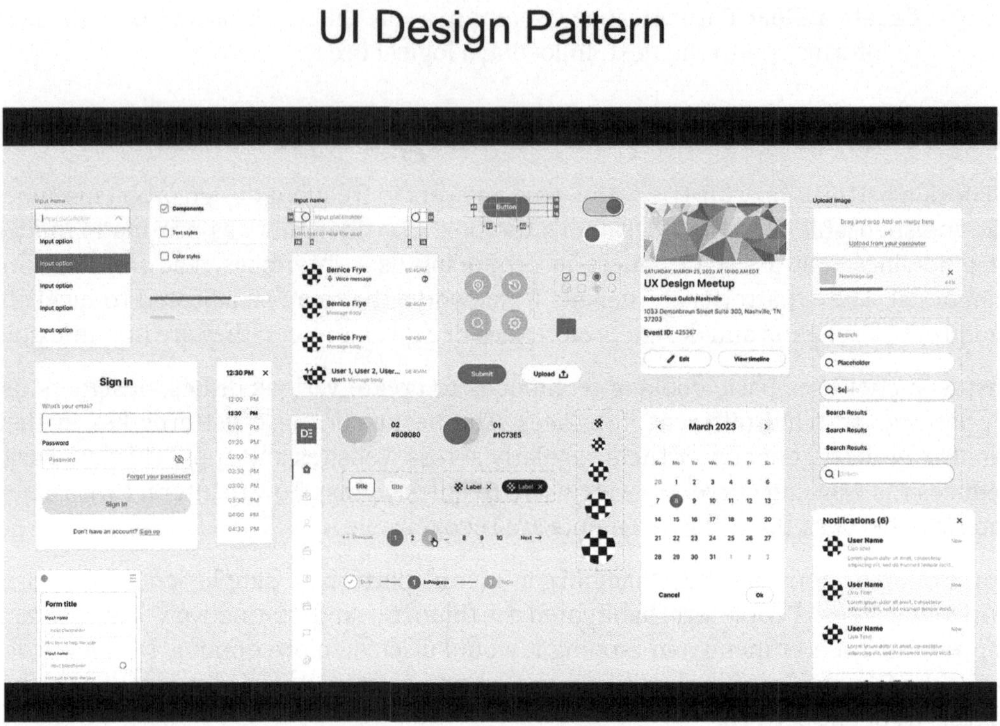

Figure 7.10: *Example of UI Design Pattern*

Importance of UI Design Patterns

UI design patterns are essential to the user experience and the design process. They give designers a common language, which lowers the possibility of misunderstandings and guarantees consistency–especially when several designers are working together on the same project. This same vocabulary makes collaboration easier and contributes to maintaining the integrity of the design concept.

Not only are these patterns helpful for designers, but they are also necessary for maintaining customer satisfaction. Because so many websites and apps adopt well-known UI design patterns, they feel natural and simple to use. Consider using a shopping site where there isn't an "Add to Cart" button on the product pages. Without this common component, consumers could become frustrated and possibly give up on the website entirely because it would be unclear how to make a transaction. When users are accustomed to seeing certain patterns, deviating from them can disrupt their experience and lead to lost conversions.

Designers reduce users' cognitive load by utilizing well-known user interface patterns, which helps the interface feel intuitive and natural. Users stay interested and continue to have faith in the product because of this familiarity.

Apart from these benefits, UI design patterns are essential for the following reasons:

- **Consistency Across Interfaces**

  Consistency between various sections of an application or website can be preserved with the use of UI design patterns. Users naturally understand how to interact with common features, such as buttons, forms, and navigation menus. Users will have a more fluid and pleasurable experience because of the consistency that prevents them from having to learn how to utilize every section of the interface again.

- **Improved Usability**

  Due to their proven capacity to solve common design issues, design patterns are useful tools for improving usability. For instance, people can easily and quickly find what they are looking for using a well-designed search bar pattern. These patterns can be used by designers to make interfaces that are simple to use and intuitive, which lowers the risk of user frustration.

- **Efficiency in Design Process**

  For designers, UI design patterns save time and effort. Designers can focus on tailoring and perfecting the design to satisfy particular demands by using pre-existing patterns as a foundation rather than beginning from scratch. Because agile development environments frequently have time constraints, this efficiency is very beneficial.

- **Reduced Learning Curve**

  Even if it is a user's first time using the product, they can pick up on how to interact with the interface fast when they come across well-known design patterns. For example, users do not require instructions to use popular patterns like pagination controls or drop-down menus because they are so commonly recognized. This lowers the learning curve and improves the overall user experience.

- **Adaptability Across Platforms**

  UI design patterns can be modified for a wide range of devices and platforms. These patterns can be modified to accommodate various screen sizes and user behavior while designing for tablets, desktop computers, or mobile devices. No matter the device they are using, this adaptability guarantees that users receive a consistent experience.

UI design patterns are essential because they promote consistency, improve usability, enhance efficiency, reduce the learning curve, and support accessibility. By leveraging these patterns, designers can create interfaces that are not only functional but also enjoyable and trustworthy for users.

Commonly Used UI Design Patterns

Here are some commonly used and highly effective UI design patterns for creating intuitive and user-friendly interfaces:

Primary Action Buttons: Your User's Best Friend

You have to complete a crucial task on a website or app, such as sending a message, logging in, or signing up for a service. Making those important actions stand out so you can locate them quickly is the main goal of the primary action pattern!

These buttons are designed to be super easy to spot. Your eyes are naturally drawn to them since they are frequently bolder, bigger, or more colorful. This eliminates the need for you to browse the screen or second-guess what to do next. You can simply click to continue, which will streamline and lessen the frustration of your experience.

The primary action buttons inside the interface function as helpful advisors, facilitating efficient and effortless task completion.

Forgiving Format: Flexibility in Data Entry

Imagine yourself completing an internet form, such as providing your phone number or date of birth. You may occasionally omit or add dashes to your phone number when typing it. Or maybe you write dates in the format "MM/DD/YY" while someone else writes "DD/MM/YYYY." One design pattern that recognizes and celebrates these variations is the Forgiving Format.

With the help of this pattern, you can enter data in different formats without the system being picky about it. It resembles a helpful form that assures you, it understands what you mean. By accepting a variety of inputs, forgiving formats simplify tasks like inputting a credit card number or providing an address for a delivery.

For **example**, an online store's checkout form may be able to differentiate between your address, "123 Main St." and "123 Main Street." It is possible that it will accept your phone number even if you type it as "123-456-7890" or "1234567890." This flexibility helps prevent annoying errors that could stop you in your tracks.

Designers ensure that users can enter information in a way that feels natural to them by using a forgiving format, which makes the user experience more seamless and pleasurable. It seems as though you are adjusting to the form, not the other way around!

Steps Left: Guiding You Through the Process

Have you ever started something online and wondered how much work remains? In order to help you understand precisely where you are in a multi-step process and how much work remains, the Steps Left pattern is useful.

This pattern represents your progress, much like a roadmap. For **example**, you may notice a progress bar at the top of the page steadily filling up as you finish each step when you are signing up for a new service. Alternatively, you might notice numbered stages, such as "Step 2 of 5," which indicates that you are almost done.

It is important to feel in control and to know what comes next, not just to finish a procedure. Consider yourself checking out from an internet shopping marathon. It feels manageable when you realize there are only two steps left to complete your order, which motivates you to complete it.

There are other methods to apply this pattern: you can use progress bars that fill up as you go, checkmarks that show up when each step is finished, or even just plain numbers that indicate how many steps remain.

The Steps Left pattern keeps you informed and motivated while completing lengthy forms, going through onboarding procedures, or making purchases, which makes it simpler to stick to your schedule and complete the task you started.

Breadcrumbs: Your Navigation Trail

Envision yourself trekking through a forest, and to aid in your return navigation, you have positioned a trail of markers. For websites and apps, breadcrumbs perform the same thing by creating a clickable trail that indicates where you have been so you can quickly go back and navigate to other sections.

For **example**, if you are looking at a particular smartphone when purchasing online, you might see a breadcrumb trail that looks something like "***Home > Electronics > Smartphones*** **> XYZ Model.**" With the help of this trail, you may easily navigate to other parts without having to start over by clicking "Electronics" or "Home" to see how you got there from the product page.

Large websites or applications, such as e-commerce sites, blogs with numerous entries, or websites with extensive categories, benefit greatly from the use of breadcrumbs. They make it easier for users to move between areas, stay on top of things, and stay afloat in a sea of information.

To put it simply, breadcrumbs act as a helpful guide that makes it easier to explore without getting lost.

Progressive Disclosure: Step-by-Step Presenting

Envision entering a library. You just get the books you need at the moment, not the entire collection. The concept of Progressive Disclosure is to avoid overwhelming you by providing information or options progressively, as needed. This pattern provides step-by-step instructions, much like a helpful handbook.

For **instance**, when you first create a new account, you could just see the required fields–your name and email address. Preferences and security settings are examples of other options that may show once those are filled in. In this manner, you avoid being overloaded all at once.

Online reading of a lengthy essay is another **example**. You may only see the first few paragraphs; if you are interested, you can click the "Read More" button to read the remaining passages. Alternatively, additional choices may be hidden inside an expanded area in a settings menu, keeping everything tidy and uncomplicated until you are ready to go deeper.

Progressive disclosure shows you only the information you require at any given time, which helps you stay focused. Whether you are filling out a long form, adjusting your settings, or trying out new features in an app, it makes difficult activities feel more doable.

To put it briefly, it's similar to gradually opening a gift–revealing just enough to keep you interested without providing too much information at once.

Lazy Registration: Try Before You Buy

Envision entering a store and not having to register for a membership in order to peruse and try on clothing. Similar to how it functions for websites, lazy registration allows you to browse and utilize features without having to register or establish an account right away for applications.

For **example**, you might visit a new app for streaming movies. Instead of being forced to register right away, you can watch a few trailers or explore the content library. This way, you get a taste of what's available before deciding to sign up for a full account.

An e-commerce website that allows you to explore things and even add them to your cart without requiring you to register for an account is another **example**. Before providing your email address and password, you can decide whether you like the website and what it has to offer.

The benefit of lazy registration is that it allows consumers to explore a platform and determine whether or not it suits their needs before providing personal information.

In terms of the platform, this keeps users interested, lowers the likelihood that they would leave without registering, and might even lead to a rise in the total number of registrations.

Lazy registration, to put it briefly, is similar to offering users a preview and an opportunity to investigate before committing.

Hover Controls: Sneak Peek with a Hover

At a party, picture yourself having to lean in to hear a friend's secret. Similar to this, hover controls function online. When you hover your mouse over an object, it exposes options or other details that aren't immediately visible.

For **instance**, you might see a number of thumbnail images in an image gallery. A larger preview or description may appear when you hover over one, providing you with additional context without taking up space in the main screen.

Another **example** is a navigation menu on a website. Sub-menus or more links may appear when you hover over a menu item, facilitating navigation without overwhelming the screen with too much information at once.

Alternatively, hovering over a data point could bring up a tooltip with more detailed information, like exact numbers or trends, without overwhelming you with data all at once. By displaying additional information only, when necessary, hover controls keep the main interface clear and concise while enhancing the usability and appeal of interactions. It functions similarly to an interactive, helpful feature that appears when needed!

Subscription Plans: Pick the Perfect Fit

Think of subscription plans like a menu at a restaurant. Just as a menu offers different dishes at various prices, subscription plans provide options for accessing services or content at different levels, prices, and features.

For **example**, imagine you are signing up for a streaming service. You might see options like:

- **Basic Plan:** \$5/month, limited shows, and no HD.
- **Standard Plan:** \$10/month, more shows, and HD quality.
- **Premium Plan:** \$15/month, all shows, movies, and 4K quality.

You can select the plan that best meets your needs and budget by selecting from a variety of advantages and features offered by each.

Another **example** could be a software tool offering:

- **Free Trial:** Limited features for a short period.

- **Pro Plan:** $20/month with advanced features.
- **Enterprise Plan:** Custom pricing with all features and premium support.

By allowing consumers to evaluate options simultaneously, this pattern makes it simpler for them to select the best plan for their needs and budget.

To put it briefly, subscription plans function as a menu of options, allowing customers to select the one that best suits their needs.

Leaderboard: See Who is on Top

Picture yourself at a sporting event with a large scoreboard displaying the best athletes or teams. For apps and games, a leaderboard accomplishes the same thing by displaying a list of top players based on particular scores or achievements.

For **instance**, you can come across a leaderboard in a mobile game where the players with the greatest scores are featured first. You can view who's in the lead and how your score compares. This configuration encourages you to raise your score by showing you how you compare to others.

Another **example** is on a social media platform where users earn badges or points. A leaderboard may display the usernames and profile images of the top contributors or most popular posts. Users are encouraged to participate more in the community and to be more active as a result.

Leaderboards can be as basic as names and scores, or they can be more complex and include pictures, badges, and more statistics. By offering consumers a target to shoot at and a competitive advantage, they increase the excitement of the encounter.

Leaderboards are essentially similar to a trophy case where you can see who is winning and become motivated to move up the ladder.

Infinite Scroll: Keep Scrolling

As you read a book, picture yourself not needing to turn pages; instead, the story is revealed to you as you go. The same concept applies to websites with infinite scroll: additional content loads automatically as you scroll down, saving you from having to click to view more.

For **instance**, new postings on social media feeds show automatically as you get to the bottom of your existing posts, allowing you to browse uninterrupted. This improves the ease and interest of browsing.

Modal Windows: Focused Pop-Ups

Modal windows might be compared to attention-grabbing pop-ups or surprise gift boxes that must be opened in order to proceed with other tasks. These are tiny windows that focus on a particular job or message and display on top of the main screen.

For **instance**, when you click "Sign Up" on a website, a modal window may appear requesting your information so you may complete the sign-up process without ever leaving the page you are on. It reduces distractions and helps maintain task focus.

Card Layouts: Organized Blocks

Think of using sticky notes to arrange your notes on a bulletin board. Every note is comparable to a short informational block. Similar blocks are used in Card layouts to convey content in a tidy and orderly manner.

For **example**, an online store might use cards to show different products, each with a picture, a price, and a short description. This makes it easy to browse through items and find what you are looking for quickly.

Search Auto Complete: Instant Suggestions

Imagine asking a buddy for advice, and they will provide you with various options right away. Similar to this, search autocomplete helps you find what you are looking for more quickly by presenting you with options as you type into a search box.

For **example**, in order to save you time and direct you to relevant results, search engines may complete your query or recommend popular searches when you start typing in a query.

Sticky Navigation: Always in Reach

Imagine that you are attending a large conference where you can always carry the event map with you. When you navigate via a website or app, sticky navigation keeps the most relevant navigation options visible on the screen.

For **instance**, a lengthy blog article may have links to various sections in a sticky menu at the side or top of the page. This makes it easy to jump to other parts of the content without having to scroll back up. These patterns make interfaces more engaging and intuitive, which contributes to a seamless, user-friendly experience.

Implementing UI Design Patterns

Effective usage of UI (User Interface) design patterns requires knowing why they are used, selecting the best pattern for your requirements, and putting them into practice in a way that improves the user experience. Here is a guide on how to use UI design patterns:

1. **Define the Issue**

   The first step in using UI design patterns effectively is to determine the precise issue or requirement that your user interface (UI) needs to solve. This entails figuring out what people need, like an easy way to locate information, which may lead you to apply a search pattern. Furthermore, examining user behavior, feedback, and data is essential to understanding the difficulties they encounter and helping you in selecting the best design pattern.

2. **Select the Correct Pattern**

   a. **Navigation Patterns**: Use menus and breadcrumbs to organize and access material.

   b. **Input Patterns:** These are used in forms and sliders to collect input from users.

   c. **Feedback Patterns:** Use feedback patterns (such as progress bars and notifications) to give consumers feedback.

   d. **Content Structuring Patterns**: Use cards and grids to meaningfully organize content.

3. **Keep Consistency and Usability in Mind**

   a. Verify that the pattern is consistent throughout your product and that it fits well with your overall design language.

   b. Take accessibility guidelines into account to make sure that the pattern functions for all users, including those with disabilities.

4. **Implement the Pattern**

   Apply the pattern to your design by incorporating it with your favorite design software, such as Adobe XD, Sketch, or Figma. Customize the pattern to align with your brand and meet user needs, but be careful not to deviate too much from the standard to avoid confusing users.

5. **Test and Iterate**

   Usability testing should be done once the pattern has been put into practice to make sure it solves the issue at hand without causing any new ones. Get user input and be prepared to make design changes in response to the knowledge gained.

6. **Stay Updated**

   Over time, UI design patterns change. Stay up-to-date on the newest trends and recommended procedures in UI/UX design.

Example Scenario

A **Form Design Pattern** could be useful when creating a login page so that users can navigate it easily. This might consist of:

- **Input Fields:** The password and username fields have clear labels.
- **Inline Validation:** Real-time feedback to indicate errors or successful input.
- **Call to Action Button:** An easily noticeable and accessible "Login" button.

These guidelines will help you leverage UI design patterns to produce an interface that is efficient, consistent, and easy to use.

Top UI Pattern Libraries

Using UI Pattern Libraries when creating user interfaces can greatly expedite the process and improve the product's consistency. These libraries provide a selection of pre-made elements, templates, and rules that cover typical design problems. They assist in making sure your interface follows best practices, is aesthetically pleasing, and is easy to use. The most well-liked and often used UI Pattern Libraries are shown below; these can be rather helpful tools for developers and designers.

Popular UI Pattern Libraries are listed as follows:

Material Design

- **Description:** Material Design is a set of standards and components created by Google that may be used to create user interfaces that are consistent and easy to use across a variety of devices.
- **Website:** https://material.io

Bootstrap

- **Description:** A popular front-end framework that provides responsive grid layouts and a set of reusable components for creating modern online interfaces.
- **Website**: https://getbootstrap.com

Ant Design

- **Description:** An extensive library of React-based components and patterns designed specifically for business applications is offered by Ant Design, a design solution for enterprise-level products.
- **Website:** https://ant.design

Foundation

- **Description:** Foundation is a responsive front-end framework with a focus on flexibility, offering UI components and patterns that are easy to customize for any project.
- **Website:** https://get.foundation

Carbon Design System

- **Description:** IBM designed the Carbon Design System, a complete design system with enterprise application-focused patterns, design rules, and a library of user interface components.
- **Website:** https://carbondesignsystem.com

Semantic UI

- **Description:** A front-end framework called Semantic UI makes use of natural language concepts to produce UI elements that are both responsive and adaptable.
- **Website:** https://semantic-ui.com

Fluent UI

- **Description:** Microsoft's Fluent UI offers a collection of React-based components and design principles to build standardized and easily navigable online experiences, especially for enterprise applications.
- **Website:** https://developer.microsoft.com/en-us/fluentui

These libraries provide a solid foundation for designing and developing user interfaces, whether you are building a small website or a large-scale enterprise application.

UI Design Patterns for Mobile Apps

People spent most of their day interacting with their smartphones, with nearly 90% of that time devoted to using apps. These apps became vital in everyday life, assisting with tasks and social connections. In this digital world, app design has become essential. An engaging and user-friendly app attracted more users, while a confusing one pushed them away.

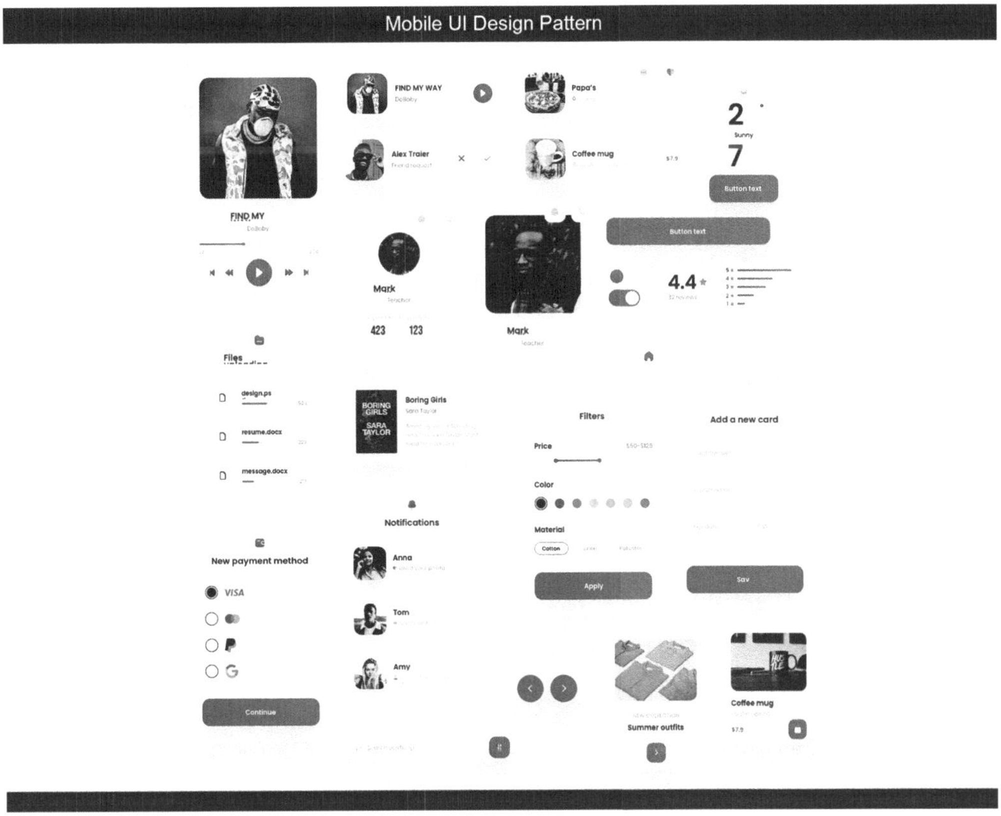

Figure 7.11: *Example of Mobile UI Design Pattern*

Making powerful mobile user interfaces (UIs) became even more crucial as technology advanced. Like expert artisans, designers understood the value of UI patterns, proven design approaches, in creating aesthetically pleasing and user-friendly applications. Additionally, they discovered that UI libraries which provide pre-made design elements were a huge help in accelerating the design process without sacrificing its quality. Designers were able to choose and alter templates to match the brand's identity thanks to these resources.

However, the designers understood that their apps needed more than just good looks. To develop a user experience that is both intuitive and pleasant, every design element, including colors, icons, typefaces, and logos, needed to work together. Mobile app design flourished and the user experience was improved due to the designers' careful selection and application of these aspects, which made navigating the app easy for users.

Here are some key aspects of UI patterns for mobile apps:

Navigation Patterns

The use of navigation patterns in mobile app design is crucial as they facilitate user access to different features and information by guiding users through the app. The hamburger menu, bottom navigation bar, and tab bar are three popular navigation designs with different functions.

- **Hamburger Menu**

  Often located in the upper corner of an application, the Hamburger Menu is a widely used navigation pattern identified by an icon consisting of three horizontal lines. This symbol can be pressed to open a hidden menu with various app sections or choices. The Hamburger Menu's primary benefit is that it conserves screen real estate, maintaining a clear and simple user interface. For example, in the Facebook mobile app, the Hamburger Menu icon opens up a side menu that includes options like profile settings, saved items, and app settings.

- **Bottom Navigation Bar**

  The Bottom Navigation Bar consists of a row of icons at the bottom of the screen, each of which stands for a distinct program part. For example, the Instagram app's bottom navigation bar makes it simple for users to switch between their profile, videos, shopping, search, and home feed. This approach makes it very user-friendly by guaranteeing that important functions are always accessible.

- **Tab Bar**

  The Tab Bar, which is typically positioned at the top of the screen, functions similarly to the Bottom Navigation Bar as it enables users to move between various perspectives or content kinds. Applications that categorize their material frequently employ this strategy. For instance, the Tab Bar in the Gmail app allows users to navigate between the Primary, Social, and Promotions email categories. Without being overly complicated, the Tab Bar offers a simple and intuitive way to switch between parts.

Content Display Patterns

In mobile UI design, content display patterns are essential for arranging content so that users can easily consume and engage with it. Lists and card layouts are two popular patterns with different functions.

- **Card Layout**

  Content is shown in separate card-like containers in the adaptable card layout pattern. Each card typically contains a piece of content, such as an image, text, or a combination of both. Information is organized in an aesthetically pleasing manner that makes it easier to digest. In the Pinterest app, for instance, every pin is shown inside its own card. This method not only makes the content properly organized, but it also makes it possible for consumers to concentrate on a single piece of information at a time, which enhances the surfing experience.

- **Lists**

  Lists are simple patterns that show things arranged vertically and allow scrolling over them. For displaying groups of related objects, like contacts, messages, or product listings, this design is perfect. For instance, chat conversations are shown in a list format in the WhatsApp app, making it simple for users to scroll through and select the conversation they wish to continue. Lists are useful for swiftly allowing visitors to browse through vast volumes of related data in an easy-to-navigate format.

Input Patterns

When it comes to mobile UI design, input patterns are crucial because they dictate how users interact with an application, particularly when inputting data or carrying out important operations. Floating Action Buttons (FAB) and Forms are two popular input patterns.

- **Forms**

  Structured input areas made especially for human interaction are called forms. Forms for mobile devices have an intuitive layout, large, tap-friendly fields, and clear labeling. They are optimized for touch inputs. This design will make it as easy as possible for users to enter data. For instance, the Google Sign-Up form's large text fields and straightforward instructions make it simple for visitors to enter their information on a small screen, including their name, email address, and password.

- **Floating Action Button (FAB)**

  A circular button known as the Floating Action Button (FAB) normally floats over content and is located in the lower right corner of the screen. It offers instant access to the main functions of the app, such as adding new items and sending messages. For example, the FAB in the Gmail app lets users rapidly begin writing a new email from anywhere in the app. The FAB is a very useful tool for highlighting the most crucial activity in an app while maintaining a clear and simple user experience.

Feedback Patterns

In mobile UI design, feedback patterns are essential since they let users know how their activities are progressing. Toast messages and progress indicators are two typical feedback styles.

- **Progress Indicators**

  Visual cues that tell users of the state of ongoing tasks, including loading or processing data, are known as progress indicators. Examples of these cues include bars, spinners, and percentage displays. As an illustration, a progress bar on Google Drive indicates the amount of the file that has been uploaded, informing the user and easing their anxiety while they wait.

- **Toast Messages**

  Short alerts called Toast messages instantly show up at the bottom of the screen. By telling users that a message was sent or verifying that a save was successful, they give them feedback on the activities they have taken.

Interaction Patterns

Interaction patterns facilitate natural motions that increase user engagement.

- **Swipe Gestures**

  It lets users swipe left or right on an item to carry out activities. For example, swiping left on an email in the iOS Mail app exposes options to archive or delete it, which streamlines user interaction.

- **Pull-to-Refresh**

  It is a gesture where users swipe down from the top of a list to refresh the content. This pattern is frequently seen in apps like Twitter, where users may swipe down to swiftly refresh their feeds and always view the most recent developments.

Onboarding Patterns

Step-by-step instructions that expose new users to the functionalities of an app are called **walkthroughs and tutorials**. To facilitate learning, they frequently incorporate tooltips, animations, and interactive demonstrations. For instance, a tutorial helps users become quickly and efficiently acquainted with the Duolingo app by guiding them through the fundamentals of choosing a language and beginning a lesson when you first launch the program.

Designing mobile apps requires the usage of UI patterns because they give consumers a recognizable experience, which lowers the learning curve and increases usability. By leveraging these patterns, designers can create intuitive, efficient, and visually appealing mobile apps that meet user expectations and business goals.

Top Mobile UI Pattern Libraries

Here are some popular mobile UI pattern libraries to help designers create user-friendly and visually appealing interfaces:

Material Design by Google

For creating apps for Android and other platforms, Google's Material Design offers thorough instructions and UI patterns. It is a go-to resource for mobile UI design since it has elements like buttons, navigation patterns, and animations.

Apple's Human Interface Guidelines (HIG)

A comprehensive collection of UI patterns and guidelines for iOS app design is provided by Apple's HIG. It covers a range of topics, such as gestures, controls, and navigation, to assist designers in producing logical and aesthetically pleasing user interfaces for Apple products.

Ant Design Mobile

A collection of UI patterns called Ant Design Mobile is dedicated to mobile web and app interfaces. It provides an extensive selection of modifiable elements and designs, which are particularly helpful when making interfaces that are easy to use and have a sleek, contemporary appearance.

Ionic Framework

Ionic offers a collection of UI elements made especially for using web technologies to create beautiful mobile applications. It comes with several ready-made UI patterns that are adaptable and cross-platform compatible.

Flutter's Widget Catalog

Google's Flutter provides an extensive widget catalog that functions as a library of UI patterns. With a large selection of customizable widgets for mobile app design, it is an effective tool for cross-platform development.

These libraries offer an abundance of resources for creating visually stunning, user-friendly mobile apps for various platforms.

Dark UI Design Patterns

Discovering the world of dark UI design patterns! Dark UI design patterns, often called **dark patterns,** are sneaky tricks used in websites and apps to push users into making choices they might not want to make. While good design aims to improve your experience and build trust, dark patterns are designed to benefit the company, often at your expense.

Here are some common examples:

- **Trick of Bait and Switch**

  Imagine you press a button, expecting it to do a certain task, but something entirely unexpected happens. For example, you may click a "Download" button in the hopes of downloading a file, but it can install undesired software or send you to a sign-up page. This design pattern misleads you by hiding the real purpose of an activity you believed to be simple.

- **Roach Motel**

  The Roach Motel design pattern refers to situations where it is easy to get into something, like subscribing to a service, but frustratingly difficult to get out. Businesses frequently make it easy to sign up with just a few clicks, but things get complicated when you want to cancel. It is possible that the unsubscribe option is hidden within a complicated set of options or that you must follow several confusing steps before being able to cancel your account. This strategy aims to keep customers using a service longer than they anticipated in order to profit the business at the expense of the customer.

- **Forced Continuity**

  Forced continuity is a design tactic where users sign up for a free trial but are automatically charged once the trial period ends without a clear reminder or an easy way to cancel.

  Let us say you decide to check out a service and sign up for a free trial. Without giving you any further notice, the service will immediately begin paying you if you forget to cancel before the trial time ends. This strategy takes advantage of users' forgetfulness, often hiding the cancellation option or making it difficult to find. The goal is that users continue to pay after the trial, even if they had no intention of doing so.

- **Hidden Costs**

  Hidden costs occur when you are ready to make a purchase, but additional fees suddenly appear at the final step of checkout, such as unexpected shipping charges or taxes. These additional expenses are not revealed until just before the transaction closes.

  For instance, after choosing a product and checking out, you can discover at the last minute that the total amount owing to additional costs is much more than what was previously displayed. This strategy deceives consumers by not disclosing the entire cost up front, which can cause disappointment and irritation because you could have thought twice about your purchase if you had known the full cost beforehand.

- **Confirmshaming**

  Confirmshaming is a strategy that makes users feel bad for saying no in order to force them into making a decision.

  When prompted to sign up for a newsletter, for instance, a pop-up window may present you with a "Yes" button for signing up and a "No" button that reads, "No, I'd rather stay uninformed." This language gives you the impression that not subscribing is a sign of irresponsibility or that you are missing out.

  Another example might be an option to join a loyalty program with the decline button labeled "No, I do not want to save money." This type of wording is used by the design to convince users into accepting something by instilling feelings of guilt or shame in them for choosing to opt-out.

- **Sneak into Basket**

  A sneaky way to add more things to your shopping cart without telling you is called "sneak into basket."

  For instance, the website may automatically add an additional fee for an extended warranty or a small donation to a charity, when you select a product to purchase online, all without notifying you. We have added these extra goods to your cart in the hopes that you won't notice them while checking out. By subtly including these extras, it is hoped that sales or donations will increase and that customers will be more willing to pay for items they had not planned to purchase.

- **Privacy Zuckering**

  The term "Privacy Zuckering," coined in honor of Mark Zuckerberg, refers to the tactic of misleading users into sharing more personal information than they planned.

  For example, the default settings on some social networking platforms may make your posts and profile publicly visible to everyone when you first create an account. Users often have to dig through complex menus or hidden privacy settings to adjust their visibility preferences. This design makes it easy for users to inadvertently expose their personal data by default, while obscuring the process of changing these settings. Users consequently disclose more information than they had planned to because the system is configured to give priority to visibility and wide access over personal privacy.

- **Misdirection**

  By directing users' attention to less significant aspects, misdirection involves diverting their attention from critical information.

  An e-commerce site might, for instance, prominently display a bright, eye-catching button that reads, "Claim Your Discount Now!" while the option to decline the offer is hidden away in small, muted writing and is labeled, "No, thanks." By directing users' attention to the more appealing option, this tactic increases the likelihood that they will click on it without giving other options a careful thought. By highlighting the enticing offer and downplaying the alternative, the design manipulates user behavior and increases the chances of converting them to take the desired action.

Dark patterns often result in irritation, regret, or financial loss by taking advantage of psychological concepts and users' innate behaviors. Although these patterns may help a corporation attain short-term objectives like boosting sales or subscriptions, over time they can harm a brand's reputation and consumer confidence.

Conclusion

We have examined the main elements of user interface (UI) design in this chapter. We began by investigating the function of visual hierarchy in directing user attention and establishing user-friendly navigation. Through the arrangement of elements that highlight important details, visual hierarchy enhances user experience.

Next, we looked at UI design patterns and learned how they improve usability and address common design problems. In order to expedite your design process, we have examined the best UI pattern libraries, which provide pre-designed elements and inspiration.

Lastly, we discussed dark UI design patterns and the significance of ethical design, as well as how they might influence user behavior. When combined, these ideas provide a strong basis in UI design that strikes a balance between functionality, user experience, and ethical standards, enabling you to develop digital interfaces that are more respectful and productive.

In the next chapter, we will delve into essential topics, including mockups, their various types, and the process of creating them. We will also review the best tools available for crafting effective mockups. Additionally, we will explore the impact of AI on UI design, assessing how AI tools are reshaping the design landscape and their influence on the creative process.

Key Terms

- **Visual Hierarchy:** The arrangement or presentation of elements in a way that suggests importance, often achieved through color contrast, size, and placement.
- **Prioritization:** The process of determining the order of importance for tasks or elements in a design, ensuring that the most critical aspects are addressed first to optimize user experience and functionality.

- **User Journey:** The path a user takes while interacting with a product or service, from initial engagement to final action, encompassing all touchpoints and experiences throughout their interaction.
- **Consistency:** The uniform application of design elements, such as fonts, colors, and layouts, across a product to create a cohesive user experience, improving usability and user trust.
- **Sidebar:** A vertical or horizontal panel on a webpage or application interface that contains navigation links, tools, or additional content, providing quick access to important features.
- **Click-Through Rates (CTR):** A metric that measures the percentage of users who click on a specific link or call-to-action compared to the total number of users who view it, indicating engagement and effectiveness.
- **Interaction:** The ways users engage with a digital interface, including clicks, swipes, and other inputs, which together define the overall user experience and how effectively the design meets user needs.
- **Color Scheme:** A selection of colors used consistently throughout a website to create a cohesive visual appearance and reflect the overall style.
- **Vibrant Colors:** Bright and intense colors that attract attention and can convey importance or urgency.
- **Subdued Hues:** More muted, less intense colors that may blend into the background or appear less dominant.
- **Palette:** The range of colors used in a design. Effective use of a color palette involves choosing colors that work well together and provide appropriate contrast.
- **Backdrop Colors:** The background colors in a design or interface that set the overall mood and provide a foundation, ensuring other elements, like text or images, stand out effectively.
- **Accent Colors:** Highlighted colors used in design to draw attention to key elements or actions, such as buttons or links, creating contrast and enhancing the visual hierarchy within an interface.
- **Typography:** The art and technique of arranging type to make written language legible, readable, and visually appealing, often involving the selection of font styles, sizes, and weights.
- **Readable Typefaces:** Fonts that are easy to read across different devices and screen sizes, ensuring clarity and accessibility of the content.
- **Font Families:** A group of related typefaces that share common design traits, often used to maintain visual consistency across a design.
- **Visual Balance:** The arrangement of text and other elements on a page in a

way that is aesthetically pleasing and easy to navigate, often achieved through proper alignment and spacing.

- **Grid System:** A framework of intersecting vertical and horizontal lines used in design to structure content, ensuring alignment, consistency, and a balanced layout.
- **Visual Cues:** Design elements like arrows, colors, or icons that guide users' attention, indicate actions, or provide feedback to improve navigation and interaction within an interface.
- **UI Design Patterns:** Predefined, reusable solutions to common design problems in user interfaces. They serve as guidelines to help designers create functional, user-friendly interfaces.
- **Hamburger Menu:** A UI design pattern represented by an icon with three horizontal lines, typically used to hide and reveal a navigation menu in mobile apps and some websites.
- **Intuitive Design:** A design approach where the interface is easy to use and understand, often because it leverages familiar patterns and user expectations.
- **Customization:** The process of modifying UI patterns to fit the specific needs, brand, or preferences of a project, ensuring that the design meets unique requirements.
- **Consistency:** The practice of maintaining uniformity in design elements across different parts of an interface, helping users navigate and understand the system more easily.
- **Framework:** A basic structure or set of guidelines that provides the foundation for building an interface, allowing designers to create variations while maintaining core usability principles.
- **Learning Curve:** The time and effort required for a user to understand how to interact with a new interface. Familiar UI patterns help to minimize this curve.
- **Functionality:** The practical use and purpose of a UI element, ensuring that the design not only looks good but also performs its intended tasks effectively.
- **Adaptability:** The ability of UI patterns to be adjusted and modified to suit different platforms, devices, or user needs, while still maintaining a coherent design.
- **Efficiency:** The ease and speed with which a user can complete tasks using the interface, often enhanced by well-designed UI patterns.
- **Content Display Patterns:** Design approaches used to arrange content in a way that is easy for users to consume and engage with.

- **Toast Messages:** Brief, non-intrusive notifications that appear temporarily on the screen, usually at the bottom, to inform users about the outcome of an action, like confirming a save or deletion.
- **Walkthroughs:** Step-by-step guides or tutorials within an app that help new users understand how to navigate and use key features effectively, often using animations or tooltips.
- **Floating Action Button (FAB):** A prominent circular button that provides quick access to the primary action of the app, usually located in the bottom right corner.
- **Multi-Step Process:** A sequence of actions or stages that must be completed in a specific order to achieve a final outcome. In UI/UX design, this often refers to tasks that require users to go through several steps, such as filling out a form or completing an online purchase.
- **Progress Bar:** A visual indicator used in interfaces to show the completion status of a task or process. It helps users understand how much of the task has been completed and how much is still pending, improving the overall user experience by setting clear expectations.
- **Modal Windows:** A type of pop-up window that appears on top of the main content to draw attention to a specific action or information. Modals often require the user to interact with them before returning to the main interface, commonly used for alerts, forms, or confirmation dialogs.
- **Pre-Made Elements:** Pre-designed components or assets that can be reused across different parts of a design or application. These elements help maintain consistency and reduce the time needed to create a user interface, often found in design systems or UI kits.

Chapter 8
The Power of Mockups

Introduction

Effective user interface (UI) design is more important than ever for capturing user attention. This chapter delves into the crucial role of mockups in UI design, exploring various types of mockups and the process of creating them. We will also highlight the best tools for crafting stunning UI mockups. Beyond the visuals, we will examine the significance of microcopy and microinteractions, small details which play a key role in enhancing user experience. Finally, we will explore the evolving impact of AI on UI design, discussing both the benefits and limitations of AI tools in the creative process. These components are fundamental to modern, user-centered design.

Structure

In this chapter, we will discuss the following topics:

- Introduction to Mockups
- Purpose of Mockups
- Elements of a Mockup
- Types of Mockups
- Creating Mockups
- Best Tools for Creating UI Mockups
- Tips for Designing UI Mockups
- Microcopy
- Microinteractions
- Techniques for Creating Seamless Interactions
- Microinteractions that Drive Success in UI/UX
- The impact of AI on UI Design
- AI Tools for UI Design

Introduction to Mockups

UI mockups are the finishing touch in UI design. We already learned about wireframes, which give you the basic outline, mockups take things a step further. They add in all the visuals–like fonts, colors, and logos–bringing the design to life. Mockups give a realistic preview of the final design, showing how it will actually look, while wireframes resemble simple sketches with arrows and boxes.

Imagine you are planning a big birthday party. Everything from the cake to the décor to the seating arrangements and even the music selection has been planned in your mind. However, you want to make sure everything is perfect before you begin, so you draft a thorough plan.

Now you choose to sketch it out rather than just writing notes. You draw the tables, indicating the precise locations of each, the design of the centerpiece, and the location of the cake display. You can also specify the kind of lights you want to hang and the colors of the balloons. This intricate layout closely resembles what is known as a mockup in design.

In the world of design–whether it is for websites, apps, products, or even interior spaces–a mockup is a visual representation of how the final product will look. This fully developed version has all the crucial features and goes beyond a basic outline or rough drawing.

Let us take the scenario where you are creating an innovative mobile application for coffee ordering. You develop a mockup of the app before you begin to build it. This mockup will depict the appearance of the app's home screen, including the buttons users will press to place orders, the menu options, the photos of coffee cups, and the logo at the top. Mockups can also be made for additional screens, such as the user profile page or the checkout procedure.

A mockup's main function is to visualize concepts in a form that is simple to comprehend. Before any real construction starts, it enables all parties involved–designers, clients, developers, and stakeholders–to see precisely what the finished result will look like. In this manner, early feedback may be obtained and adjustments can be made without wasting time or money.

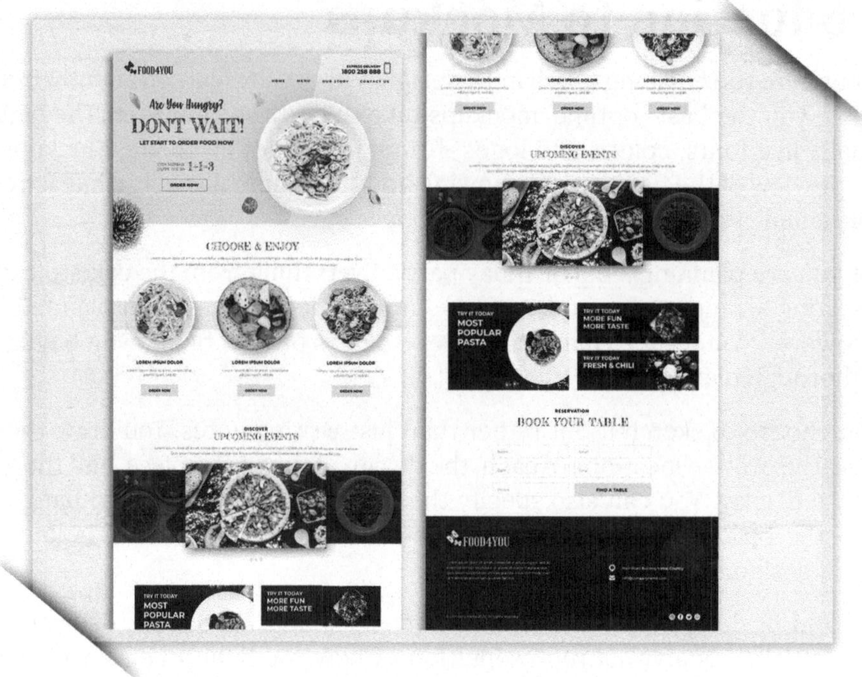

Figure 8.1: *Simple and sleek website mockup design*

The primary difference between a wireframe or prototype and a mockup is the degree of detail in the former. Similar to blueprints, wireframes concentrate on the structure and layout rather than the specifics of color, font, or imagery. Interactive prototypes mimic the functionality of the final product. In between are mockups, which are detailed but not interactive like the finished product. Though you are unable to click it or interact with it, they reflect how the product will seem.

Thus, your mockup, if you were creating that coffee ordering app, would be the beautifully rendered picture that displays the precise layout of the app's screens, down to the last visual element. It gives everyone a preview of the final product before it is actually made, like an early glimpse of what it will look like.

Mockups are essential tools in the design process, to put it briefly. They ensure that everyone is on the same page and that the finished result looks exactly as planned by helping to bridge the gap between ideas and reality.

Purpose of Mockups

Mockups are a vital part of the design process for several reasons. Some of the most common reasons include:

- **Visualizing the Final Product**

  By providing a clear and simple representation of the final product's look, mockups help stakeholders understand design concepts. Early design visualization allows all parties to coordinate on understanding and drive the project in the right direction.

- **Gathering Feedback**

  Mockups are a helpful way to get feedback from stakeholders on a product or service design. This early input allows designers to make adjustments early in the development process, leading to a more refined final product.

- **Save Time, Money and Resources**

  By seeing possible problems early in the design process, mockups help to save time and money. Through early identification and resolution of design issues, designers can reduce the need for rework down the road, maintaining projects on budget and on schedule.

- **Ensuring Consistency**

  Mockups ensure that every aspect of the design, including layouts, colors, and typefaces, is consistent throughout the finished product. Maintaining consistency is essential to creating a seamless user experience.

- **Clarity and Precision with Mockups**

  Mockups enhance communication and guide development by offering a clear, detailed representation of the final product. They help non-designers, such as clients and stakeholders, easily understand and discuss design ideas, while also providing developers with a precise blueprint to ensure the product is built according to the design specifications.

- **Exploring Design Variations**

  Mockups are a useful tool for designers to experiment with various design alternatives, including color schemes or layouts, and then compare them side by side to see which works best.

Elements of a Mockup

The essential components that give a mockup its high-fidelity, comprehensive portrayal of a final design. Knowing these elements makes it easier to create a mockup that accurately represents the appearance of the final product. Here is a breakdown of the core elements:

- **Content Layout and Structure**
  A mockup's layout and structure are essential to producing a well-balanced and useful design. Consistent alignment of pieces is guaranteed by a grid

system, which adds to the order and aesthetic attractiveness of the design. The hierarchy of content is reflected in the thoughtful arrangement of headers, footers, sidebars, and navigation menus, which also helps users navigate easily. Mockups include actual content, such as photos, UI elements, and text, in contrast to wireframes, which only employ basic boxes and lines. They frequently use patterns like the F-pattern or Z-pattern to prioritize and fit pieces within screen restrictions. Real or placeholder text is included, and a clear visual hierarchy and content organization are combined to create a realistic preview of how the content will be arranged, emphasizing the most important details and improving the user experience as a whole.

- **Typography**
  For a design to have a certain tone and be readable, typography is essential. The same fonts—along with their weights, styles, and sizes—are shown in mockups to represent how they will look in the finished project. Headlines, paragraphs, labels, and buttons are examples of text that is positioned to show how content will be presented and arranged. This meticulous attention to typography provides a realistic sneak peek into how the text will improve the whole visual experience, ensuring that the design communicates effectively and clearly.

- **Color Scheme**
  A mockup's color scheme displays the chosen palette's primary, secondary, and accent hues. To create a unified effect, these colors are used consistently in all parts of the design, from buttons to backdrops. The mockup also shows how colors interact with one another, showing how buttons change color when hovered over or how text contrasts with different background tones. This visual gives a realistic preview of how the final product will look, making sure that the color choices enhance readability and usability.

- **Images and Icons**
  Mockups include icons and pictures as they will appear in the final design, although in a less polished version. Product photographs, graphics, and background visuals are examples of high-resolution images that are meticulously cropped and arranged to blend smoothly into the layout. Despite their modest size, icons are important to the design. Their style, size, and placement are all displayed in the mockup to make sure they complement and align with the overall design. This focus on detail reflects how these components will work together to produce a polished and seamless visual experience.

- **Interactive Elements**
  Even though the mockup is not interactive, interactive components like buttons, forms, and links are visually represented in them. These components are made to stand out and point users in the direction of important tasks.

A mockup typically incorporates feedback and hover state visual signals, although it is not as interactive as a prototype. For example, it shows how a form field might glow when selected or how buttons could change color when hovered over. This enhances design clarity and helps demonstrate how interactive features will function in the final product.

- **Spacing and Margins**
  In a mockup, margins and spacing are essential to keeping the design neat and tidy. They guarantee that components are arranged appropriately, creating an airy and uncluttered style. Sufficient margins and padding increase readability and user experience. Furthermore, by providing items with adequate breathing area, the deliberate use of whitespace balances the design, improving its overall visual appeal and preventing the layout from feeling crowded.
- **Branding and User Flow**
  Branding components, such as the logo, are positioned and sized correctly in a mockup to preserve brand integrity. In order to maintain consistency throughout, the design also complies with brand guidelines for tone, color, font, and imagery. Furthermore, by displaying the screen order and the way consumers will interact with the product, mockups help to show the user flow. This provides a clear image of the entire user experience and interaction by making it easier to see how various design elements work together, such as when switching from the homepage to a product page.

Designers can produce polished mockups that function as precise blueprints for the finished product by understanding these components. Making sure that every element is taken into account to facilitate a seamless transfer from design to development is the essence of a mockup's anatomy.

Types of Mockups

Designers can produce polished mockups that function as precise blueprints for the finished product by understanding these components. Making sure that every element is taken into account to facilitate a seamless transfer from design to development is the essence of a mockup's anatomy.

Static Mockups

Detailed, static mockups are static graphic depictions of a user interface. They display every visual component–fonts, colors, photos, and arrangement–but they omit any functional features like buttons or links.

Use Case

Before developing an interactive prototype or going on to development, static mockups are a great way to get feedback on a design's visual elements. For example, a static mockup helps a client concentrate on the appearance and feel of a new website design without being distracted by interactive elements.

Interactive Mockups

Some functionality is included in interactive mockups, enabling users to press buttons, switch between displays, and observe simple transitions. These provide a more accurate representation of the real user experience than static mockups, providing a clearer idea of how the finished product will operate.

Use Case

Interactive mockups are useful for collecting in-depth client input and usability testing. An interactive mockup, for instance, lets users test out the fundamental navigation and transitions of an app before it is fully developed, which can help find any usability problems.

Low-Fidelity Mockups

Low-fidelity mockups are straightforward, rough drawings of a concept that prioritize hierarchy and structure above finely detailed imagery. Frequently, they employ simple shapes, placeholder text, and muted colors to illustrate the overall arrangement of components on the screen.

Use Case

In order to generate ideas and decide on the general layout early in the design process, low-fidelity mockups are perfect. For example, a low-fidelity mockup lets designers quickly experiment with numerous layouts when designing a new website without having to worry about the finer aspects like fonts or colors.

High-Fidelity Mockups

Finely detailed designs that closely resemble the finished product are called high-fidelity mockups. They provide a realistic preview of the final product with their accurate use of fonts, colors, graphics, and spacing.

Use Case

Later in the design process, high-fidelity mockups are usually utilized to confirm decisions and coordinate with stakeholders. For example, using a high-fidelity mockup before developing a new app design to offer it to a client helps guarantee that everyone agrees on the visual aspects.

Responsive Mockups

Mockups that are responsive show how a design changes to fit different screen sizes and devices, such as tablets, smartphones, and desktop computers. They display various designs and layouts that are adjusted for various screen sizes and orientations.

Use Case

For multi-platform designs, responsive mockups are crucial since they guarantee a unified and useful user experience across all platforms. When designing a website, for example, a responsive mockup makes it easier to see how the site will function and look on a smartphone as opposed to a desktop, enabling designers to make the required changes before development.

In the UI design process, each kind of mockup has a distinct function that aids in ideation, feedback gathering, and ensuring that the finished product fulfils the intended vision.

Creating Mockups

Mockups are a crucial part of the design process since they aid in the visualization and refinement of a product prior to development. Here is a step-by-step guide on making mockups with an example.

1. **Define the Project Requirements**

   A thorough grasp of the project's objectives, the target audience, and the technical needs are all necessary for defining project requirements. This step guarantees that all parties involved are in agreement regarding the goals of the project, user needs, and technical limitations, allowing for a focused and organized approach to the project's development.

   Example: For a new mobile app, gather requirements such as the app's purpose, user demographics, and platform specifications (iOS or Android).

2. **Research and Gather Inspiration**

   Studying UI patterns, looking at comparable goods, and compiling ideas to guide your design are all part of the research and inspiration process. This process makes sure your design is innovative and aligned with industry standards.

   Example: Look at successful mobile apps in the same category to explore and learn about popular design trends and features.

3. **Sketch Initial Ideas**

   Making rough sketches of your earliest concepts allows you to experiment with different design layouts and frameworks. In this step, you can play around with different element arrangements without getting caught down in the specifics. Before going on to more refined versions, it helps in visualizing the design's overall organization and flow.

Example: Make basic wireframes of the app's primary screens, including the product pages, navigation menu, and homepage.

4. **Create Low-Fidelity Mockups**

   Creating low-fidelity mockups involves transforming your initial sketches into basic digital designs using design tools. These mockups focus on the overall layout and structure, using simple shapes and placeholder text to represent various elements. The goal is to establish a clear visual hierarchy and design flow without delving into finer details like color, typography, or imagery. This step allows for easy adjustments and helps communicate the general concept to stakeholders before moving on to more detailed designs.

   Example: Create a basic version of the application using a tool like Figma or Sketch, indicating the positions of the buttons, graphics, and text.

5. **Review and Gather Feedback**

   Sharing your low-fidelity mockups with stakeholders or team members in order to get their views is part of the review and feedback process. Instead of concentrating on fine-tuning design details at this point, the evaluation process now focuses on the general layout, user flow, and functionality. Before going on to higher-fidelity versions, this collaboration process makes sure that the design complies with project objectives and user expectations, allowing for any necessary revisions.

   Example: Show the mockups to your team and have a discussion on where the important features should go and how users will interact with the app.

6. **Refine and Create High-Fidelity Mockups**

   Gathering feedback to improve your design and creating detailed versions that resemble the final product are key steps in refining your work and transitioning to high-fidelity mockups. In order to make sure the design is polished and prepared for further development, this step involves integrating exact UI elements, graphics, typography, and color schemes.

   Example: Create a polished version of the app that looks like the final product by using precise fonts, brand colors, and real content.

7. **Create Responsive Versions (If Needed)**

   Designing prototypes that adjust to different screen sizes is a necessary step in creating responsive versions, which guarantees the product works properly on a variety of devices. By modifying layouts and elements appropriately, this stage is essential for ensuring a consistent user experience regardless of the device being used to view the design—a smartphone, tablet, or another device.

Example: Develop sample versions of the app for both desktop and mobile screens, ensuring the design adapts smoothly to different screen sizes.

8. **Final Review and Adjustments**

   Show stakeholders the high-fidelity mockups for their final approval, and take this chance to discuss and make any necessary design decisions. Gather any more input and make the required changes to the design to make sure it meets all of the requirements.

   Example: Present the app prototypes to clients, walk them through each screen, and make necessary design revisions in response to their comments, such as adjusting the color scheme or navigation.

9. **Prepare for Development**

   Arranging and completing design files to make sure they are ready for the development team is part of preparing for development. This step entails producing comprehensive documentation, including component specifications, style guides, and annotations, to guarantee that developers comprehend the design features and the appropriate implementation methods.

   Example: Once the mockups are complete, export them in the necessary format (such as PNG, JPG, or straight from a design application) and give developers thorough notes on the design specs.

Example in Practice

This example follows the stages of the design thinking process, reflecting the detailed steps we have covered in previous chapters. The final stage involves creating high-resolution mockups using design tools, ensuring every element is polished and ready for development.

Imagine you are designing an e-commerce app. You begin by defining the app's purpose—allowing users to browse and purchase products. After researching similar apps, you sketch initial ideas and create low-fidelity mockups, focusing on essential screens like the product listing and checkout. Following a team review, you refine the design into high-fidelity mockups, incorporating real images, brand colors, and typography. You then create responsive versions for both smartphones and tablets. Finally, you present the mockups to the client, gather final feedback, make adjustments, and prepare the files for development. This process ensures that every detail is meticulously crafted and aligned with the app's goals.

Best Tools for Creating UI Mockups

In order to visualize and enhance concepts prior to development, producing high-quality user interface mockups is an essential step in the design process. Having the appropriate tools can help streamline and improve the efficiency of the user interface design process. The top resources for producing excellent UI mockups that realize your design concepts are listed as follows:

Figma

The Collaborative Design Powerhouse

Think of a design tool that not only allows you to create attractive mockups but also involves every member of your team, no matter where they are in the world. That is Figma. You and your team can collaborate on a design in real-time with its features; there is no need to exchange files via email. It resembles an online whiteboard that is constantly updated. Also, Figma is the tool of choice for designers who wish to execute their concepts with accuracy and style because of its user-friendly interface, strong vector tools, and extensive plugin library.

Figure 8.2: *UI design Tool - Figma*

Price: Basic functions are free; premium plans are available for enhanced functionality.

Advantages

- Real-Time Collaboration: No matter where they are, collaborate with your team at the same time.
- Cross-Platform Flexibility: Figma is compatible with a wide range of operating systems due to its web-based architecture.

Drawbacks

- Internet Dependency: For best results, a reliable internet connection is necessary.
- Limited Offline Capabilities: While there is some offline capability, it is not as extensive as that of other competitors.

Adobe XD

The All-in-One Design and Prototyping Tool

The Swiss Army knife of UI design tools is Adobe XD. With Adobe XD, you can create anything from a basic wireframe to an interactive prototype. Because of its smooth interaction with other Adobe Creative Cloud tools, you may quickly begin designing by importing elements from Illustrator or Photoshop. The revolutionary responsive resize function in XD lets you seamlessly adapt your design to any screen size. Additionally, you may design experiences that are just as realistic as the finished product owing to its voice prototyping and auto-animate features.

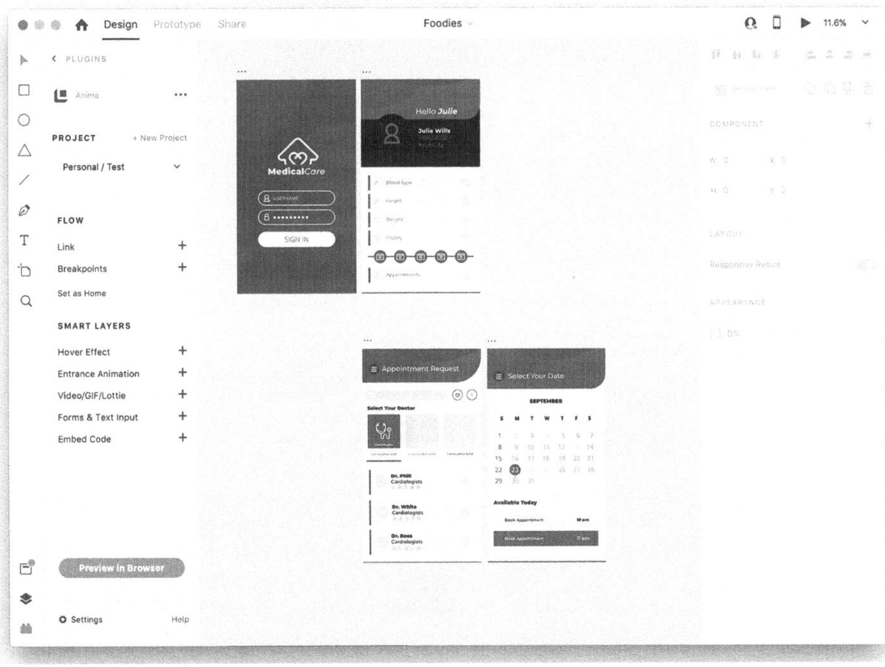

Figure 8.3: *UI design Tool – Adobe XD*

Price: Paid; however, a limited-featured starting plan is available for free.

Advantages

- Perfectly integrates with other Adobe Creative Cloud applications, such as Photoshop and Illustrator, for a seamless user experience.
- Responsive Resize: This feature saves time by automatically adjusting your design to fit various screen sizes.

Drawbacks

- Constrained Plugin Environment: The plugin library is not as large as some other programs, despite its growth.
- Windows Performance: It is frequently observed that, despite being available on Windows, performance sometimes lags behind the macOS version.

Sketch

The Industry Standard with a Creative Edge

With good reason, Sketch has been a favorite tool for UI designers for a long time. It is a tool designed primarily for interface design, providing a clear, user-friendly workspace ideal for creating intricate mockups. You can ensure uniformity across your design by creating reusable components with Sketch's robust symbols tool. Additionally, you may customize Sketch's capabilities to fit your workflow because of its extensive ecosystem of plugins. Designers at large and small businesses rely on Sketch because it is a flexible tool that works well for web, mobile, and desktop design.

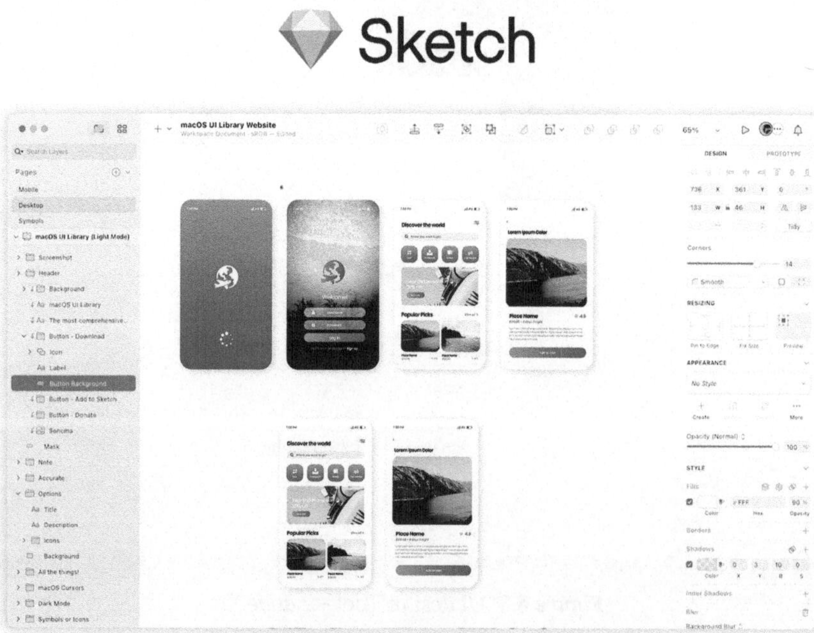

Figure 8.4: *UI design Tool - Sketch*

Price: Paid, requiring an annual subscription or a one-time purchase.

Advantages

- Strong Symbols Feature: Enables reusable components so your design remains consistent.
- Large Plugin Library: An abundance of plugins to personalize your workflow and increase its capabilities.

Drawbacks

- Exclusive to macOS: Only available on macOS, so Windows users are not included.
- Lack of Built-In Prototyping: Sketch is a great designer, but for more sophisticated prototyping, you will need to use outside tools.

InVision Studio

The Motion Design Maestro

InVision Studio could become your new best friend if you want to add some (or a lot) of motion to your mockups. With the sophisticated animation features of this tool, you can produce interactive prototypes that feel lifelike and seamless transitions, elevating UI design to a new level. Timeline-based animations in InVision Studio allow you to precisely control every movement, which makes it simple to produce intricate, well-thought-out designs. Additionally, as it is a component of the InVision package, sharing your work with stakeholders and getting feedback can be done in a smooth, integrated workflow.

Figure 8.5: *UI design Tool - InVision*

Price: Paid plans are available for more extensive options; free for limited features.

Advantages

- Advanced Animation Tools: Make sophisticated, fluid transitions to breathe life into your mockups.
- Integrated Workflow: Easily share designs and gather feedback in one location with this InVision suite feature.

Drawbacks

- Steep Learning Curve: Learning how to use the advanced animation tools can take some time due to their complexity.
- Resource-Intensive: May put a lot of strain on your system, especially when handling big tasks.

Axure RP

The Ultimate Tool for Complex Interactions

Axure RP comes into its own when your project requires more from an interface than just looks nice. With this application, you can easily create practical prototypes that go beyond simple user interface mockups. You can create dynamic content, conditional logic, and interactions with Axure that resemble the behavior of the finished product. It is like having a developer's expertise in your design toolkit. Axure's extensive documentation tools also help you communicate your design decisions to developers, ensuring your vision is fully realized.

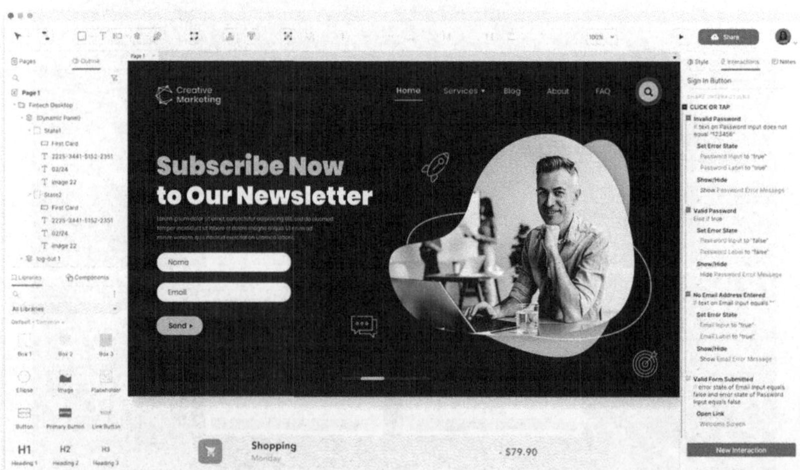

Figure 8.6: *UI design Tool – Axure RP*

Cost: Paid; a complimentary trial is offered.

Advantages

- Advanced Interactivity: Create intricate prototypes with dynamic content, conditional logic, and elaborate interactions.
- Robust Documentation: To ensure a seamless handoff, it is simple to provide comprehensive documentation for developers.

Drawbacks

- Steeper Learning Curve: Novices may find it overwhelming to use due to its sophisticated features.
- Higher Cost: As one of the priciest technologies available, smaller teams may find it more difficult to use.

Whether it is the precision of Sketch, the motion expertise of InVision Studio, the collaborative wonder of Figma, the interactive power of Axure RP, or the variety of Adobe XD, each of these top-tier tools has something special to offer. One of these tools will undoubtedly be the ideal choice for your upcoming design job, depending on your needs.

Tips for Designing UI Mockups

Creating UI mockups is an important step in turning concepts into tangible interfaces. It bridges the gap between wireframes and final designs, allowing you to see how the product will look and work. Developing good UI mockups can be difficult, even with a firm design in place. To ensure your mockups properly express your ideas, adhere to fundamental design principles that improve clarity, usability, and visual appeal.

1. **The Art of Observation**

   Before beginning a new design, practice the skill of observation by studying successful work in your industry. Rather than copying, the goal is to analyze good techniques and discover what resonates with users. By analyzing trends and successful techniques, you may learn what appeals to your target audience and avoid common traps, ensuring that your design stands out while still aligning with current user preferences.

2. **Less is More**

   When designing mockups, simplicity is essential. Avoid overloading your design with too many elements or flashy features. While intricate designs might catch the eye, focus on functionality and user accessibility. Make effective use of whitespace to highlight key components, including calls to action, and keep your layout simple and easy to read. Instead of overwhelming users with cluttered designs or distracting fonts, aim for a balanced design that improves usability.

3. **Adjusting the Visual Design**

   To provide an inclusive experience, you must make sure your visual design is accessible. To make your website or app accessible for people with disabilities, make necessary adjustments to the colors, typefaces, and element sizes. For instance, text is simpler to read when elements are scaled appropriately, and the use of high contrast colors aids individuals with visual impairments. These improvements enhance the user experience for all users, not just those with impairments, and make your design more efficient and user-friendly. Making accessibility a top priority guarantees that your design fulfils a range of needs and reaches a larger audience.

4. **Libraries of UI kits and Components**

   By providing pre-designed elements like buttons, forms, and icons, UI kits and component libraries greatly expedite the design process. These materials are particularly helpful since they offer a consistent base upon which to build for teams that test and refine their designs on a regular basis. By using well-established design frameworks, like Material Design or Bootstrap, designers can concentrate on innovation rather than having to reinvent the wheel when it comes to consistency and efficiency.

5. **Trust Common Patterns**

   Incorporating well-known design patterns is essential for user comfort and productivity, even while innovation is necessary. Because they are used to these common elements, visitors will find it easy to browse your website or app if you follow established interface patterns. Deviating from these widely accepted norms too much may cause consumers to become frustrated and confused and may even drive them away. A smooth and simple user experience can be achieved by striking a balance between novelty and familiarity.

6. **Speed Up UI Mockup Design with AI**

   Make great time and resource savings by using AI to automate your UI mockup creation process. AI solutions can boost overall productivity by automating tedious operations, suggesting design improvements, and generating layouts rapidly. This frees up your time to concentrate on strategy and creativity.

Here is a snapshot of how the design phases unfold:

- **UI Sketching:** After generating and analyzing multiple ideas, designers select the most promising ones.
- **Wireframes:** The main goals of this process are to outline important features, organize information, and lay out the structure of the system.
- **Mockups:** These are in-depth illustrations of how the design will appear.

- **Prototypes:** Prototypes give an indication of how the final product will work and add interactivity to the design.

In earlier chapters, we explored the critical skills needed in the UI/UX design process, such as wireframing, prototyping, and sketching–fundamental tools for shaping and refining design concepts. This chapter focused on the role of mockups in the design process, highlighting their importance in transitioning from wireframes to the final product by offering detailed visual representations. Understanding mockups allows designers to refine user interfaces before development, ensuring a cohesive and intuitive end result. These steps help UI designers efficiently test, iterate, and improve their designs before seeking stakeholder approval, benefiting both new designs and interface updates.

Microcopy

Imagine you are navigating a complex city without a map, and suddenly, little signposts appear to direct you in the right direction. In a digital world, **microcopy** serves that purpose. Little but powerful information that may be found on websites and apps, such as buttons, labels, and helpful suggestions, can point you in the proper direction. These words might not appear like much in relation to the overall app design at first. Surprisingly though, those insignificant text passages can have a significant effect on conversions.

Effective UX microcopy should be simple, clear, and easy to understand. It should blend seamlessly with the overall design, matching the brand's language and tone. Microcopy is crafted to address user needs, provide solutions, and create empathy. For instance, a welcoming "Forgot your password?" link not only helps users navigate but also reassures them that assistance is readily available, making the experience feel more supportive and personal.

Figure 8.7: *Example of Microcopy. Use of simple words to guide users*

The preceding figure shows an example of how Slack effectively uses microcopy to guide users toward the right action. Additionally, the blue landing page design features a subtle line beneath the action button, which creates a simple and inviting starting point for users.

With so many factors to take into account when designing a great user experience–such as flows, content, and color schemes–it can occasionally feel overwhelming. But frequently, the smallest elements–like microcopy–can have a significant impact on the entire experience.

Importance of Microcopy

In user experience design, microcopy is essential because it directs users, improves interactions, and fosters a relationship with the brand. But just because microcopy is small, it does not mean it is easy to design. When creating excellent microcopy, a number of things come into play.

Here is why it is important, along with some examples:

- **Guides User Actions**

  Microcopy offers concise instructions or prompts to assist users in completing a variety of tasks.

  For example, a website's "Sign Up Free" button makes it clear to consumers what to expect right away, which makes it easier for them to take action without being confused. A form field that says "Enter your email address" is another example, helping users understand exactly what information is needed.

- **Reduces Friction and Confusion**

  Good microcopy reduces user frustration by making all confusing points clear.

  For example, a notification indicating an error, such as "*Oops! We were unable to complete your payment*". A more helpful message than a *general "Error" is "Please check your card details and try again."* By educating users on what went wrong and how to fix, it reduces the likelihood that they will be abandoned.

- **Builds Trust and Empathy**

  Microcopy can build empathy and trust between users and the brand.

  For example, a nice confirmation message such as "*You're all set!*" The message "*Your order will be shipped shortly*" ensures users that their action was accomplished. This type of encouraging language makes consumers feel at ease and valued.

- **Enhances Brand Voice**

  Microcopy enhances the brand's personality and voice.

  For example, an enjoyable message such as "*You're almost there!*" or "*Just one more step to complete your profile*" on a social networking platform conveys a casual, welcoming tone that is consistent with the brand's identity, making conversations more personal.

- **Encourages User Engagement**

  Well-crafted microcopy can increase engagement by making interactions more appealing.

  For example, on a cooking app, a call-to-action button that reads "*Discover Your New Favorite Recipe*" encourage users to explore content rather than a generic "Click Here".

- **Provides Reassurance**

  Microcopy is frequently used to calm users in delicate situations.

  For example, messages like "*We have received your feedback and appreciate your input*" following a survey submission tells users that their thoughts are valued and will be taken into account.

Microcopy is important because it guides people, minimizes uncertainty, fosters trust, expresses the brand's personality, promotes engagement, and provides comfort. Its smart implementation improves the overall user experience and encourages more positive interactions with the interface.

Microcopy's Impact on User Engagement

Microcopy plays an important role in increasing user engagement by changing interactions into more intuitive and engaging experiences. Here are some interesting examples:

- **Makes Actions Clear and Inviting**

  Microcopy transforms unclear buttons and prompts into direct, compelling calls to action. Instead of a standard "Submit" button, adding "Send Your Feedback" makes it more visible and appealing, encouraging people to submit their ideas. This clarity and attractiveness can dramatically boost the likelihood of user interaction.

- **Adds a Personal Touch**

  Personalized microcopy can help users feel more connected. For example, a message like "Welcome back, [User Name]!" "Are you ready to continue where you left off?" gives a personal touch that helps consumers feel cherished and engaged, as opposed to just another face in the crowd.

- **Creates a Sense of Progress**

  Microcopy allows consumers to track their progress, making them more likely to stay interested. For example, progress indicators with friendly messaging such as "You're halfway there!" can keep users engaged when navigating long processes or forms, encouraging them to finish the activity.

- **Encourages Exploration and Discovery**

  Microcopy may spark consumers' interest and encourage them to investigate further. For example, a cheerful prompt like "See What's New!" or "Explore Our Latest Features" encourages users to delve further into content or functionality they might not have noticed otherwise.

- **Provides Instant Feedback and Reassurance**

  Microcopy provides immediate feedback, which can reassure people and keep them interested. For example, following a successful action, send a message like "Great job!" "Your changes have been saved" immediately reassures users that their activity was effective, lowering worry and keeping them engaged with the platform.

- **Fosters a Conversational Tone**

  Using genuine, conversational microcopy can make interactions more engaging. For instance, a warm "Need assistance?" followed by "Click here, and we'll help you right away" creates a friendly tone that encourages users to ask for help without feeling frustrated or overwhelmed.

- **Encourages Positive Behavior**

  Microcopy can subtly direct users towards desirable behaviors. For example, a subtle reminder like "Don't miss out–subscribe now for exclusive updates" can encourage users to do a positive action, such as subscribing to a newsletter, by emphasizing the advantages.

Microcopy improves user engagement by making interactions more explicit, personalized, and entertaining. It helps customers navigate their journey, keeps them engaged, and builds a stronger relationship with the brand, resulting in a more engaging and fulfilling experience.

Microinteractions

Let us explore this concept through an example of how someone uses it in their daily routine.

In a bustling digital city, Mia, a busy professional, navigated her day with the usual stream of tasks and notifications. Her phone buzzed gently, a subtle vibration that didn't jar her focus but quietly nudged her attention. She glanced at the screen–an important message from her team. With a swift tap, the notification expanded, revealing the full text, while a smooth animation guided her eyes.

Later that afternoon, Mia found herself adjusting the volume on her tablet as she prepared for a virtual meeting. As she slid her finger along the volume bar, a soft sound echoed, confirming each adjustment. The device responded instantly, and the process felt natural, almost effortless.

In between meetings, Mia took a brief break, scrolling through her social media feed. She double-tapped a post she liked, and a small heart appeared, pulsing softly before settling in place. The moment was brief, but it brought a smile to her face.

Throughout her day, these interactions unfolded seamlessly, almost unnoticed. Yet, each tiny motion, each swift response, added to her experience. The slide of a menu as she explored an app, the smooth glide of a card off the screen as she dismissed a notification–these were the invisible threads weaving through her digital life, making every interaction feel fluid and intuitive.

Mia never paused to think about these details, yet they played a crucial role in her day. They were the **microinteractions**–small but powerful moments that turned her digital routine into something more than just a series of tasks. They made her feel connected, in control, and, most importantly, delighted with every interaction.

Benefits of Microinteractions

Microinteractions are small yet effective components that improve the user experience in digital products. These minor elements, such as a button that changes color when clicked or a notification that comes in gradually, make interactions feel more immediate and natural. They play an important role in navigating users through an app, verifying their actions, and minimizing errors. Beyond utility, microinteractions offer a layer of refinement and personality, making the interface not just usable but also enjoyable. By concentrating on these minute details, designers may create experiences that are both engaging and emotionally resonant.

Following are some benefits of Microinteractions:

- Creates a smoother, more enjoyable user experience.
- Provides quick feedback to confirm user actions.
- Improves usability through easy and fluid app navigation.
- Encourages users to interact with the app by responding to notifications and sharing content.
- Reduces the possibility of user errors.
- Adds entertaining and interactive aspects to stimulate user attention.
- Ensures interface elements serve a clear purpose.
- Demonstrates the brand's identity with unique animations and sounds.
- Provides consumers with clear visual clues and smooth transitions.
- Provides a sleek, professional interface.
- Enhances engagement and emotional connection.

Techniques for Creating Seamless Interactions

Here are some effective techniques for creating seamless interactions:

- **Clear and Concise Feedback**

  Clear and concise feedback ensures that consumers understand the results of their activities. For example, when a user clicks the "Submit" button, a temporary color shift or a loading spinner communicates that the action is being processed. This rapid visual answer ensures the user that the system is processing their request, eliminating uncertainty and improving the overall experience.

- **Progressive Disclosure**

  Breaking down complex processes into smaller, more manageable steps improves the user's knowledge while reducing cognitive stress. This technique guides consumers through the interaction one step at a time, making the entire process more straightforward.

- **Contextual Cues**

  Designers can improve the user experience by providing relevant information through contextual signals at the appropriate time.

  For example, when a user hovers over an unknown icon, a tooltip or microcopy may emerge, describing its purpose. This timely assistance enables users to traverse the interface more confidently and comprehend the meaning of various items without confusion.

- **Seamless Transitions**

  Transitions between screens or states should be fluid and natural.

  For example, while moving from a homepage to a product page, a smooth animation offers a sense of continuity, assisting consumers in maintaining their mental flow. This smooth transition strengthens the connection between the various sections of the interface, making the whole experience more intuitive and unified.

Effective microinteractions rely on a strong grasp of user behavior and preferences. By focusing on clarity, context, and smooth transitions, designers can enhance the user experience, turning simple interactions into memorable and engaging moments that stick with users even after they leave the interface.

Microinteractions that Drive Success in UI/UX

Well-executed microinteractions have an evident impact on UI/UX design. Exploring real-life examples and case studies enables us to understand the strategies that underpin their successful implementation, providing practical lessons on how these little but powerful interactions can dramatically improve the entire user experience.

Spotify's Play Button

Spotify, the popular music streaming site, has successfully incorporated microinteractions into its UI/UX design with the Play Button function. Users can begin playing music immediately by clicking the Play Button on external websites or social media posts. This simple yet effective microinteraction increases user engagement and provides a smooth, uncomplicated music experience, allowing users to get right into listening without any additional steps. This seamless connection demonstrates how well-designed microinteractions may simplify actions while improving the overall user experience.

Instagram's Heart Animation

Instagram, a popular social media network, effectively employs microinteractions to increase user happiness and elicit positive feelings. When users double-tap a post, a heart animation displays, providing immediate feedback and creating a sense of connection. This simple yet impactful interaction has been a defining feature of Instagram's user engagement, contributing significantly to the platform's popularity as a visually appealing social network. The heart motion not only improves the user experience, but it also highlights the platform's emphasis on establishing meaningful, visual interactions.

Uber's Ride Request Button

Uber, a popular ride-sharing service, employs microinteractions to improve user experience and streamline the ride-request process. When users hit the "Request a Ride" button, a loading animation shows that their request is being handled. This short but significant microinteraction reduces user anxiety by providing comfort and increasing faith in the platform's stability, making the overall experience smoother and more confident. By focusing on these minor things, Uber improves the user experience, making consumers feel safe and informed throughout the transaction.

Pull-to-Refresh

Consider using a news app on your phone. When the content becomes outdated, you can refresh it by pulling down on the screen. As you do so, a little animation displays, such as a spinning icon or a bouncing refresh indicator, indicating that new content is loaded. This microinteraction not only visually shows that the refresh is in progress, but it also keeps you updated on the status of your request. It transforms a simple task into an interesting experience by displaying the app's current content update.

These examples–Spotify's Play Button, Instagram's heart animation, and Uber's trip request button–show how important microinteractions are in creating excellent UI/UX design. These small, thoughtfully designed interactions enhance usability while crafting memorable user experiences that resonate emotionally. By honing in on these details, designers can elevate both the functionality and attractiveness of their products, ensuring every interaction is intuitive and satisfying. Ultimately, these microinteractions are not just minor touches; they play a vital role in building user trust, engagement, and long-term loyalty in today's competitive digital landscape.

The Impact of AI on UI Design

UI design is being completely transformed by artificial intelligence (AI), which provides fresh approaches to producing more efficient, intuitive, and customized user experiences. AI has made it possible for designers to customize user interfaces for specific users, changing components according to context, user behavior, and preferences. AI, for example, might examine a user's previous interactions to recommend features or content that are best appropriate for them, increasing user satisfaction and engagement.

Smart, responsive interfaces that anticipate user needs can also be created with AI. AI-driven chatbots, for instance, that are incorporated into apps and websites, offer users immediate support and task guidance without the need for difficult navigation. By continuously refining their responses based on user interactions, these chatbots provide a more seamless and effective experience.

AI can automate time-consuming design tasks like layout adjustments and A/B testing, allowing designers to focus more on creativity and innovation. Tools powered by AI, such as Adobe Sensei, analyze user preferences and design trends to help designers make data-driven decisions that improve both usability and visual appeal.

To put it simply, artificial intelligence (AI) is a game-changer that makes it possible to create dynamic, user-centric experiences that alter in real-time, improving interfaces by making them more responsive, engaging, and customized to each user's needs.

AI Tools for UI Design

Many AI tools are available to help UI designers streamline their daily tasks. Here are a few popular ones in use today:

Khroma

Khroma is an AI-powered application made to assist designers in swiftly and effectively determining the ideal color combinations. Khroma is exceptional in that it can adapt to your preferred color scheme. Khroma allows you to choose your 50 favorite colors from a list of alternatives when you first use it. After that, the AI creates an infinite number of color schemes based on your preferences.

Khroma is especially helpful for designers who seek inspiration or have trouble selecting colors. With its range of display choices, which include gradients, custom text, and image previews, you can see how the colors blend together in a variety of situations. This makes it simple to picture how the color scheme you've chosen will seem in an actual project.

Khroma's great accessibility and user-friendliness make it an invaluable tool for new and experienced designers alike, which is another interesting aspect of the software. Khroma makes the process of selecting harmonious color schemes easier, saving you time and effort when designing websites, apps, or branding projects.

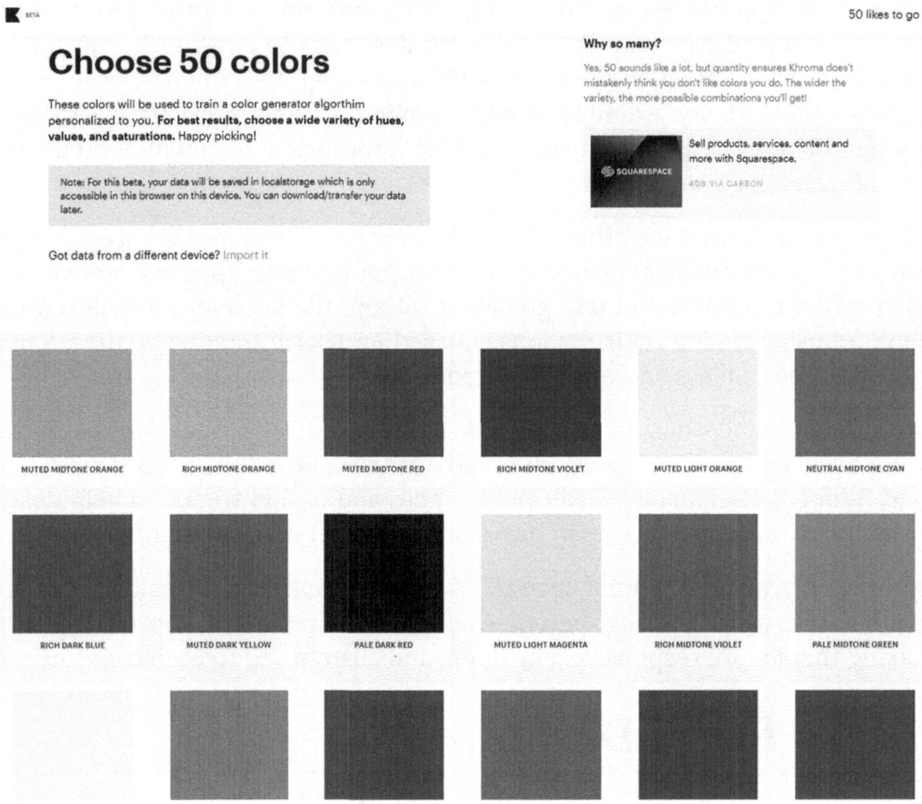

***Figure 8.8**: Khroma is an AI-powered color palette generation tool created with designers in mind*

Uizard

Even those without design knowledge can quickly and easily create digital products like websites and applications with Uizard, an AI-powered design tool. The capability of Uizard to transform sketches into digital designs is one of its best advantages. Your ideas can be written down, photographed, and uploaded to Uizard. Your crude drawings are subsequently turned into refined wireframes or even completely working prototypes by the AI.

The user-friendly drag-and-drop interface of Uizard is another important feature that lets users alter designs without any prior coding experience. A large selection of templates and components are available from Uizard, which makes it easy to create designs that look good. Startups, small businesses, and teams who need to quickly produce and refine designs may find this tool very useful.

Teams can collaborate in real-time on the same project with Uizard's support for teamwork. This facilitates the rapid creation of changes, feedback, and idea sharing. With Uizard, teams can realize their ideas more quickly and effectively by simplifying the design process. Uizard provides an easy-to-use solution for designers, developers, and entrepreneurs to bring their ideas to life.

Figure 8.9: *AI-powered UI Design Tool*

Adobe Firefly

One AI tool that facilitates design and creativity is Adobe Firefly. Type anything into it to generate photos, text effects, and even 3D models. It is a feature of Adobe's Creative Cloud. This makes it ideal for quickly converting concepts into visual material, even in the absence of design knowledge.

Firefly is an excellent tool to generate original and superior images for a variety of purposes, including art projects and marketing material. Additionally, it provides many customization choices so you can tweak the results to fit your style. Firefly is a useful tool for both novice and seasoned designers, since it expedites the process of ideation and concept development while stimulating fresh ideas.

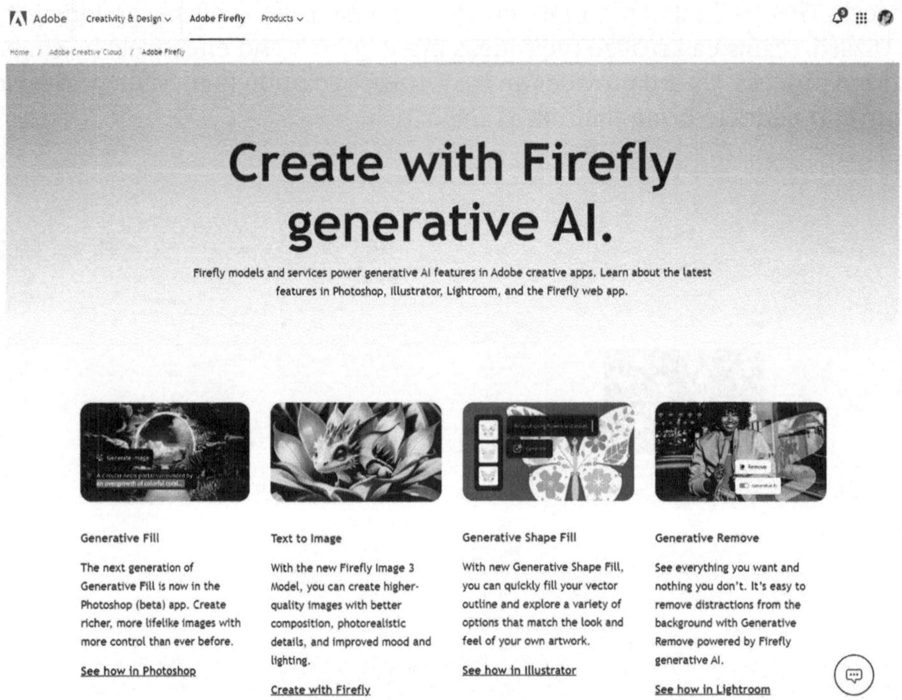

Figure 8.10: *Firefly creates images, text effects, and content from text prompts using AI*

Visily

Visily is an AI-powered design tool that simplifies creating wireframes and prototypes for websites and apps. For teams and non-designers that wish to swiftly visualize their ideas, it's ideal. You don't need any design knowledge to generate detailed mockups thanks to its user-friendly drag-and-drop interface.

Visily's capacity to convert hand-drawn concepts into digital graphics is one of its best qualities. Visily converts sketches into professional wireframes using just a few clicks of the mouse. It also makes design customization simple by providing pre-designed components and templates. Visily is a great tool for small teams and startups since it streamlines the design process.

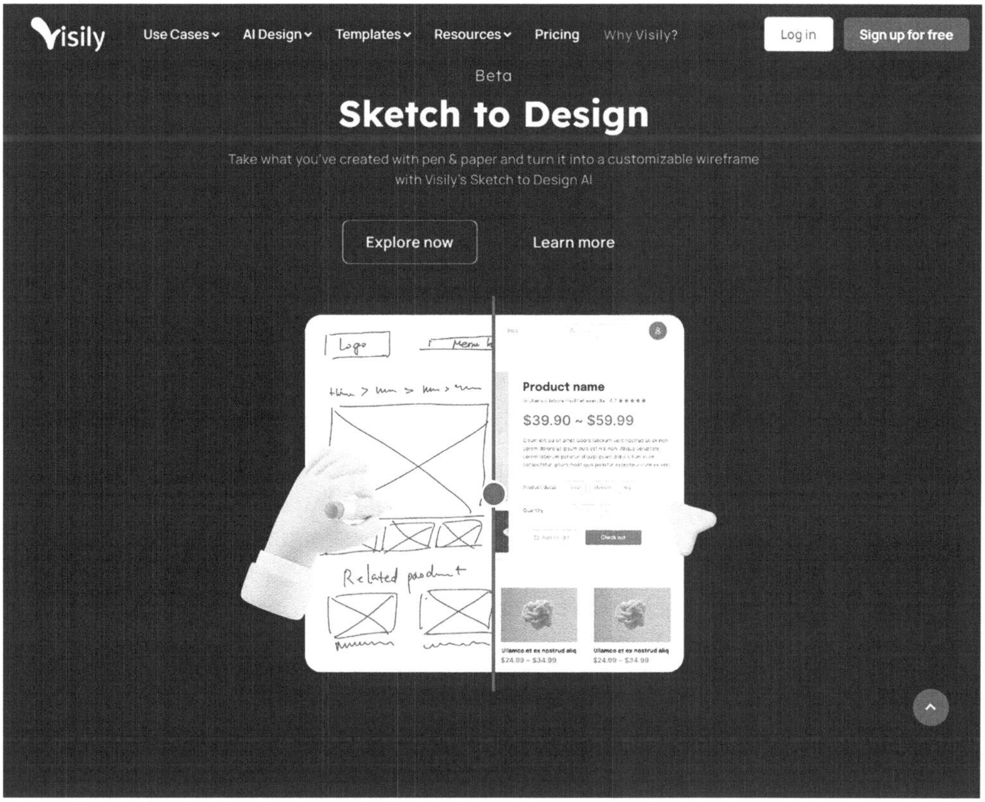

Figure 8.11: *A web-based AI-powered wireframing and design tool*

Other Powerful AI Tools That are Saving a Designer's Efforts

AI tools have revolutionized UI design, offering innovative solutions that streamline workflows and enhance creativity. Here is a list of other available tools that can elevate your design process.

- **Canva's AI-powered Magic Resize tool:** This feature saves designers time and ensures consistency across many formats by allowing them to automatically resize designs for various platforms.
- **Remove.bg:** This tool leverages artificial intelligence (AI) to swiftly eliminate backgrounds from photos, saving designers time when creating polished visuals rather than laboriously removing backgrounds by hand.
- **Microsoft's Sketch2Code:** This AI tool translates hand-drawn sketches into HTML code so that designers can rapidly iterate and see their ideas without having to start from the beginning with manual coding.

- **Coolors.co:** Coolors.co is an AI-powered color scheme generator that facilitates the rapid creation of aesthetically pleasing color schemes by designers. It ensures that the design's color choices are aesthetically pleasing and consistent while saving time by offering many color variations with a single click.

With the help of these technologies, designers may concentrate on the most creative aspects of their job while streamlining workflows and lowering manual labor.

AI's Potential to Replace UI Designers

Can AI fully replace UI designers, or does it lack the creativity and empathy needed for innovative design? This is a question that comes to everyone's mind.

UX is all about thoughtful creativity, while AI is grounded in logic. Designing an exceptional user experience (UX) requires imagination, empathy, and a deep understanding of human needs. In contrast, Artificial Intelligence (AI) functions by processing data, following rules, and applying logic. Essentially, UX is about crafting solutions that resonate with people on an emotional level, focusing on their needs and feelings. AI, however, sticks to its programmed instructions, lacking the ability to think, feel, or innovate like a human.

Example

In a busy design studio, you're deeply focused on creating a user journey for a new app. Your goal is to design an experience that resonates emotionally with users, considering every detail like color choices and button placement. This process requires creativity, empathy, and an understanding of human behavior, which are crucial for creating a great user experience (UX).

Meanwhile, an AI algorithm in the same studio is efficiently handling tasks that involve processing large amounts of data and following logical rules. AI excels at repetitive tasks, like answering common customer queries, saving time and streamlining processes. However, AI struggles with more complex, human-centered problems. It can't empathize, innovate, or think creatively.

You recognize this distinction. While AI is excellent for routine tasks, it lacks the ability to generate original ideas or create emotionally engaging experiences. As a UX designer, your role goes beyond following rules; it is about imagining new possibilities and crafting experiences that are both functional and delightful. You appreciate how AI can assist with logical tasks, but you know that it is your creativity and empathy that make a design truly extraordinary.

AI can assist UI designers but can't completely replace them. AI tools can automate repetitive tasks, suggest design elements, and streamline workflows, making the design process faster and more efficient. However, UI design involves creativity, empathy, and understanding human behavior, skills that AI lacks. Designers use these abilities to craft intuitive and visually appealing interfaces tailored to specific user needs. While AI can enhance a designer's work, the creative and human-centric aspects of UI design are irreplaceable. Therefore, AI is a powerful tool for designers, but it can't fully replace the human touch in design.

Conclusion

To sum up, mockups are an essential part of UI design since they provide a physical depiction of digital interfaces. Knowing the many kinds of mockups, from high-fidelity prototypes to low-fidelity sketches, helps designers choose the best strategy for each phase of the project. Using the best tools and becoming proficient in the creation of mockups can greatly improve the effectiveness and quality of design work. As we have seen, AI has a significant impact on UI design, with new AI tools revolutionizing the way designers develop and implement their concepts. Adopting these innovations can result in more creative and user-focused design solutions.

The following chapter will examine Responsive Web Design (RWD), an essential method for developing flexible websites that provide a consistent user experience on a range of screens and devices. We will go over the fundamentals of RWD, including flexible images, fluid grids, and media queries, which let webpages adapt dynamically to various viewing situations. We will also go over typical problems faced by designers and how to solve them, as well as best practices for creating responsive design. Understanding RWD is essential for ensuring your website remains user-friendly and visually appealing, regardless of how it is accessed.

Key Terms

- **Blueprints:** Detailed plans or designs used as a guide for constructing or developing a project.
- **Mockup:** A visual representation of a design, often used to showcase the layout, structure, and appearance before final development.
- **Resolution:** The clarity and detail of an image or display, measured in pixels.
- **UI Elements:** The individual components that make up a user interface, such as buttons, menus, and icons.
- **Visual Hierarchy:** The arrangement or presentation of elements in a way that suggests importance, often achieved through color contrast, size, and placement.
- **Typography:** The art and technique of arranging type, including font selection, size, spacing, and alignment.
- **Interactive Components:** UI elements that respond to user actions, such as buttons, sliders, and forms.

- **Anatomy:** The structure and components that make up a design or system.
- **Static Mockups:** Non-interactive visual representations of a design, used to demonstrate layout and style.
- **Interactive Mockups:** Mockups that simulate user interactions, allowing for a closer approximation of the final product's behavior.
- **Usability:** The ease with which a user can navigate and interact with a system or interface.
- **Responsive Mockups:** Designs that adapt to different screen sizes and orientations, ensuring usability across devices.
- **Orientations:** The direction in which a screen or design is viewed, such as portrait or landscape.
- **iOS:** Apple's mobile operating system, used on devices like iPhones and iPads.
- **Android:** Google's mobile operating system, used on a wide range of smartphones and tablets.
- **Style Guides:** Documents that outline the design standards, including color schemes, typography, and UI elements, to ensure consistency.
- **Annotations:** Notes or comments added to a design, providing explanations or instructions for developers and stakeholders.
- **Vector:** A type of graphic that uses mathematical equations to create images, allowing for scalability without loss of quality.
- **Plugin Library:** A collection of software add-ons that extend the functionality of a main program or application.
- **Dynamic Content:** Content that changes or updates automatically based on user interaction or other variables.
- **Interactivity:** The degree to which a user can interact with a design, often involving real-time feedback or actions.
- **Handoff:** The process of transferring design files and specifications from designers to developers for implementation.
- **Frameworks:** Pre-built structures or systems that provide a foundation for developing applications or websites.
- **Microcopy:** Brief, targeted text that guides users through an interface, such as button labels, error messages, or tooltips.
- **Slack:** A communication platform often used by teams for collaboration and project management.
- **Empathy:** The ability to understand and share the feelings of users, crucial in designing user-centered experiences.

- **Microinteractions:** Small, subtle animations or feedback in a design that enhance the user experience.
- **Progressive:** A design approach that emphasizes gradual enhancement and improvement, particularly in terms of user experience.
- **Artificial Intelligence (AI):** The simulation of human intelligence by machines, enabling them to perform tasks that typically require human intelligence.
- **Data-Driven Decisions:** Decision-making processes that are guided by data analysis and interpretation.
- **3D Models:** Digital representations of objects in three dimensions, used in design, gaming, and simulations.
- **Templates:** Pre-designed layouts or structures that serve as a starting point for creating new designs or documents.
- **Algorithm:** A set of rules or steps used to solve problems or perform tasks, often implemented in software.

CHAPTER 9
Responsive Web Design

Introduction

The use of responsive web design, or RWD, has become a standard procedure in web development to guarantee that websites offer the best possible viewing experience on a range of screens and devices. This chapter delves into the fundamental ideas of RWD, examining its essential components, including media queries, responsive images, and flexible grids. We will also look at responsive and adaptive web design, learning how they differ and when to use each. The chapter will also emphasize the significance of Mobile-First Design, an approach that takes user behavior patterns into account and puts mobile experiences first before scaling to larger devices.

Structure

In this chapter, we will discuss the following topics:

- Responsive Web Design (RWD)
- The Rise of Responsive Design
- Adaptive Web Design
- Adaptive Design versus Responsive Design
- Importance of Responsive Design
- Building Blocks of Responsive Web Design
- Mobile-First Design
- Linking Mobile-First with Responsive Design

Responsive Web Design (RWD)

Developing websites that automatically adapt to various screen sizes—whether viewed on a desktop, laptop, tablet, or smartphone—is known as responsive web design. A website has to do more than just look good on a computer these days since more and more people are accessing the internet through mobile devices. Today, most customers demand that websites be responsive to mobile devices. Designers must also take into account various tablet sizes and the variety of smartphone models on the market nowadays.

Your website will function flawlessly and look fantastic on all devices with a responsive design. As a result, users have a better overall experience, which can boost conversions and engagement. Consequently, companies can witness expansion via enhanced website functionality. In today's digital world, responsive web design is a must-have for anyone looking to succeed online.

Understanding Responsive Web Design

The goal of responsive web design is to create websites that change their layout automatically to fit different screen sizes, be it computers, tablets, or phones. Rather than creating distinct versions for every device, the layout adapts according to the platform, orientation, and screen size. CSS media queries, fluid layouts, and flexible grids are used to accomplish this.

Think about how water behaves in responsive design–it can adapt to fill every inch of space. On a laptop, a website opens with everything in its ideal order. The website seems exactly the same on your phone, but it has been shrunk to accommodate the smaller screen.

For example, websites like Amazon or Airbnb use responsive design. The website seamlessly adapts to fit the screen on both desktop and smartphone platforms, providing a consistent user experience.

The Rise of Responsive Design

Let's go back to the 1990s, a time when websites were limited to computer screens and the internet was still in its infancy. Back then, people didn't even think about using their mobile phones for web browsing–they were only used for making calls. Naturally, for many years, web designers concentrated on creating websites that functioned effectively and looked well on big desktop screens.

Then something really changed. By 2016, 50% of all web traffic worldwide was attributed to mobile devices. Individuals were using smartphones, tablets, and other mobile devices instead of only PCs to browse the internet. This meant that you could now browse websites while on the bus, waiting in line, or having lunch. Mobile devices began to replace computers for everyday browsing.

The conventional approach to web design, which was limited to desktop screens, became obsolete as a result of this change. Many companies lost out on potential clients and mobile users as a result of their slow adaptation and desktop-focused websites.

It was at this point that websites could automatically adapt to any screen size thanks to responsive web design. However, there is another option: adaptive web design, which approaches meeting the requirements of different devices in a different way.

Adaptive Web Design

Unlike responsive design, adaptive web design (AWD) creates many versions of a website, each optimized for a particular screen size or device. AWD uses pre-designed layouts that are delivered depending on the device being used, as opposed to a single layout that adjusts dynamically. A highly optimized, device-specific experience is made possible by this.

The website for Apple is a prime example. You see a layout that is ideal for mobile viewing when you visit on an iPhone, and another layout optimized for larger displays when you come on a PC. For a smoother, more customized surfing experience, the website detects your device and sends the version that fits your screen size the best.

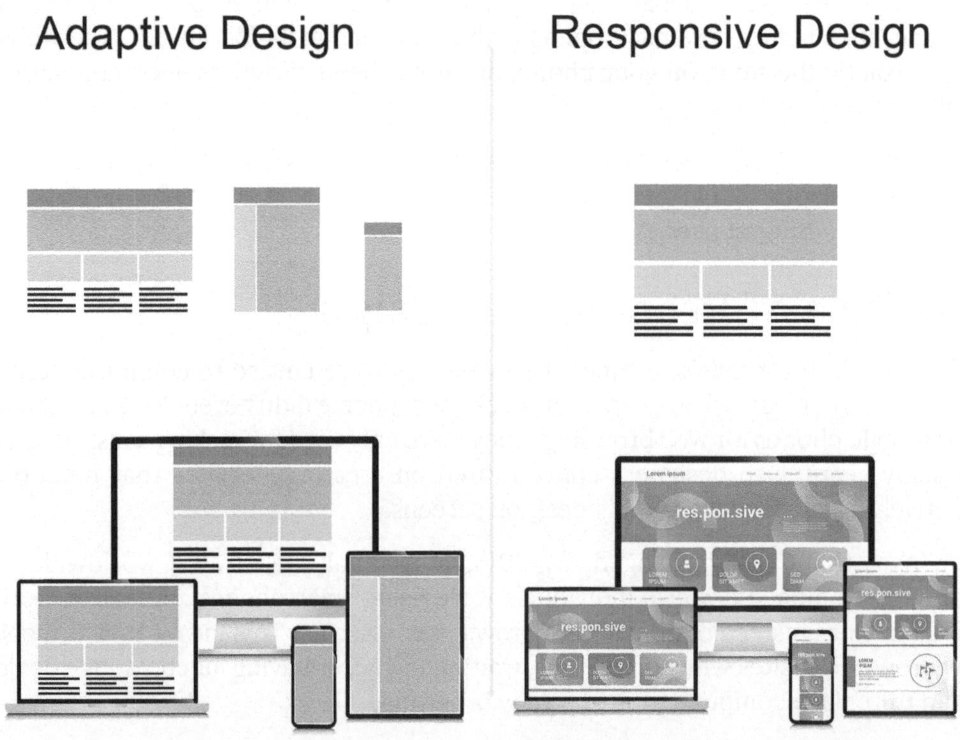

Figure 9.1: *Adaptive and Responsive Design*

Here is a thorough description of adaptive web design along with several examples:

Device-Specific Layouts

The first step in adaptive design is to develop many unique layouts for various screen sizes. Designers usually produce six main layouts for:

- Compact smartphones (width of 320 pixels)
- Big smartphones (width of 480 pixels)
- Tablets with a 600 pixel width
- Big tablets (width: 768 pixels)
- Computers (1024 px wide).
- Desktops with a width of at least 1200 pixels

The server recognizes the sort of device a user is using when they visit the website and offers the relevant layout. Adaptive design has a predetermined layout for every device, in contrast to responsive design, which fluidly adjusts to any screen size.

Example:

Websites such as Amazon provide an example of Adaptive Web Design (AWD). Whether you visit Amazon on a desktop, tablet, or smartphone, the website offers many layouts according to the device.

- **On a smartphone**, the website will appear more condensed, with bigger buttons, easier-to-navigate, and less material overall to accommodate the smaller screen.
- **On a tablet**, the design is modified to fit a medium-sized screen, providing greater room for content while maintaining touch sensitivity.
- **On a desktop** users will see the entire layout, making use of the wider screen and offering more intricate navigation and in-depth product listings.

By pre-designing these versions with AWD, Amazon ensures seamless operation and simpler browsing by providing a user experience that is optimized for each device.

Faster Load Times

Faster loading times are achieved using adaptive web design (AWD), which provides a layout that is tailored to each device. Based on device identification, AWD loads the pre-designed layout rather than dynamically scaling items to match the screen. With this method, customers see a website that is optimized for their device without having to deal with an additional load of pointless content.

Example:

Take a look at Apple's website as an illustration of flexible design. The website runs quickly on a mobile device by using features and pictures that are optimized for smaller screens. On the other hand, high-definition visuals, movies, and animations meant for bigger screens are displayed to consumers on a desktop. Apple makes sure that everyone has a faster load time and a more seamless surfing experience by providing distinct layouts for every device.

Optimized for Specific Features

Adaptive design enables developers to meet the specific needs of each device type. Mobile phones, for example, have touchscreens and smaller displays, often used in portrait mode, while desktops feature larger screens and greater processing power. AWD tailors the user experience to these differences, optimizing performance based on the device's capabilities.

Example:

Netflix demonstrates adaptive design effectively across its platform. On desktops, Netflix presents a wide view of movie categories with hover effects, large thumbnails, and keyboard navigation. Conversely, on mobile devices, the design adapts to offer larger, touch-friendly controls and a more straightforward interface, making it easy to swipe through content. The mobile version also conserves data by loading lower-resolution images and smaller videos for quicker performance.

Better for Legacy Systems

Websites that need to work with outdated browsers or devices benefit greatly from adaptive design. With AWD, developers can create layouts specifically for out-of-date computers that might not be able to support more recent web technologies, such as HTML5 or CSS3. This method guarantees that websites maintain their functionality and accessibility on multiple devices without compromising the user experience.

Example:

NASA's website and other government websites adopt adaptive designs to accommodate people with outdated technology. For users with outdated browsers, NASA may provide a condensed version of their website that removes interactive components and new design aspects. This strategy guarantees that all users have access to critical information while providing those with more recent devices with a rich, modern experience.

Greater Control over Content Presentation

With adaptive web design, content display on various devices may be more precisely controlled by designers. This is especially beneficial for companies that want to give their customers a personalized experience. Desktop users could gain from more in-depth and engaging material, but mobile users might only require simple navigation and contact information.

Example:

With its information tailored for different devices, the BBC is a prime example of adaptive design. The BBC website may offer a scrollable feed of the most recent news with larger text and convenient access to video material on mobile devices. Users are greeted with longer articles, improved navigation, and deeper news sections on desktop computers. With this strategy, all user types are guaranteed to receive the most interesting and pertinent material for their device.

Fixed Layouts for Predictability

Developers can work with a predictable framework thanks to adaptive design. Because every layout is pre-defined, designers can predict with accuracy how content will look across various platforms. This consistency makes testing easier and guarantees a well-optimized experience on all platforms.

Example:

The website for Target is a great illustration of flexible design in action. Users see intricate product grids with filters and crisp, high-definition photos on computers. The design shifts to a simpler grid with bigger buttons and a quicker checkout procedure when viewed on a mobile device. Every version of the website is meticulously designed to provide a reliable and consistent purchasing experience, independent of the device being used.

Adaptive Design versus Responsive Design

When designing a website, it's crucial to choose the right approach to ensure a seamless user experience across different devices. Two popular methods are Adaptive Design and Responsive Design, each with its own advantages and use cases. Here's how adaptive and responsive design compare.

Adaptive Design delivers distinct, fixed layouts based on specific screen sizes. It offers more control and can be optimized for performance and user experience on each device. However, it requires more work to create and maintain multiple layouts.

Responsive Design uses a flexible layout that adjusts automatically to any screen size. It's simpler to maintain since there's only one design, but it may not always be as precisely tailored for each device.

Depending on the particular requirements of the project, either approach can improve the user experience. The reactive design provides a seamless, one-stop shop that can manage a range of screen sizes with less effort, while the adaptive design is fantastic for fine control over various devices.

When to Use the Adaptive Web Design

Adaptive online Design (AWD) is a potent technique for some kinds of online projects because it works especially well in certain circumstances. Here's when to consider using AWD:

- **Redesigning an Existing Website**

  If your website is currently not mobile-friendly or has not been optimized for various screen widths, adaptive design is a great option. With AWD, you can add new layouts for mobile, tablet, and other devices while keeping the fundamental framework of your current website, saving you the trouble of starting from scratch every time. Comparing this to a whole overhaul, the move is easier and more economical.

  For example, adaptable design allows you to develop mobile-specific versions of your website without altering the desktop layout, even if your present website functions OK on desktops but appears strange on smartphones. For businesses who want to change their online presence without starting from scratch, this method works well.

- **Creating Multiple Viewports for Different Devices**

  The capacity of adaptive design to support various layouts based on the size of the device's screen is one of its advantages. You can now select how many viewports (layouts) to support thanks to this flexibility. Although it's customary to design for the six standard screen sizes (600px for small tablets, 768px for large tablets, 1024px for laptops, and 1200px for desktops), you can use as many viewports as your brand and financial constraints will allow.

  For companies that require exact control over how their content looks on various platforms, this flexibility is perfect. For example, in order to enhance user experience and conversions, an e-commerce site may prioritize alternative product presentations or checkout routines on mobile compared to desktop.

- **Focusing on Specific Devices**

  Adaptive design allows you to concentrate on making the experience as good as possible for those people if the majority of your audience utilizes a particular device or platform. For instance, rather than building a completely flexible responsive site, you can design for a few key screen sizes that will cater to the mobile traffic segment that makes up the majority of your site's visitors, based on your data. With this approach, you can provide your audience with a highly personalized experience on the most significant devices.

For example, a social networking app may concentrate more on mobile displays, whereas a website catering to business professionals may prioritize tablet and desktop designs because they are the platforms their audience uses most often.

- **Gradual Design Upgrades**

  Creating lower-resolution viewports (such as mobile phones) first and working your way up to larger screens is the ideal strategy for adaptive design. As a result, the design is freed from content constraints and prioritized for users of smaller devices, which is crucial given the prevalence of mobile usage in today's world.

  You can create an experience that functions well on mobile devices and then improve it for larger screens by designing with mobile devices in mind first. Because mobile is the most limited environment, this strategy also makes testing and development easier.

- **Better Performance Optimization**

  When performance needs to be optimized according to a device's unique capabilities, adaptive design comes in handy. Better control over load times, usage of data, and overall performance is made possible by AWD, which offers pre-designed layouts customized for various devices. To provide faster loading times and a smooth user experience, the mobile version may, for instance, have simpler animations and lower-resolution graphics, while the desktop version may include richer media and more sophisticated features.

- **Preserving Brand Consistency**

  By creating distinct designs for every screen size, adaptive design makes it possible to keep a consistent brand image across a variety of devices. With exact control over the display of trademark elements like typefaces, logos, and images, you can guarantee an optimal user experience while maintaining the uniqueness of your business.

  A luxury firm that places a high value on aesthetics, for instance, can opt for adaptive design to create a polished and elegant experience across all platforms, offering desktop and mobile consumers equally excellent aesthetics.

When it comes to updating an existing website, targeting certain devices, or creating unique layouts for different screen sizes, adaptive web design, or AWD, is the best option.

Compared to responsive design, it offers designers greater control and flexibility by concentrating on particular devices. AWD is excellent for updating outdated websites, preserving brand consistency, and enhancing performance. For companies that want a tailored strategy for various devices without requiring an entirely adaptable design, it's a sensible choice.

When to Use the Responsive Web Design

The best situations to use responsive web design (RWD) are when you're building a website from the ground up or need a flexible solution that works on every device. The following situations call for responsive design to be used:

- **Building a New Website**

  When beginning from scratch, responsive design works wonderfully. Its flexible layout conforms to various screen sizes, eliminating the need for you to build separate versions of the same website. The layout of the design dynamically adjusts to match several screen sizes, including desktop, tablet, and phone. This makes it a wise option for newly created websites where adaptability and flexibility are crucial.

  For example, responsive design guarantees a seamless purchasing experience for users on desktop and mobile devices while setting up an e-commerce site. There is no longer a need for distinct designs for every device because the layout adapts to various screen sizes.

- **Easier Development and Maintenance**

  Compared to adaptive design, responsive web design (RWD) is easier to create and maintain. Developers only need to maintain one version of the site because RWD relies on a single layout that uses CSS media queries to automatically resize to multiple screen sizes. Businesses with limited resources will find this especially helpful as it reduces the time and effort needed to update or correct numerous versions.

  Making responsive websites has become simpler thanks to content management systems (CMS) like WordPress, Drupal, and Joomla. Since many themes and templates are already responsive, designers don't have to start from scratch when working with pre-built alternatives. RWD is becoming a popular option for new web projects because of its accessibility.

- **Future-Proofing Your Website**

  You won't need to worry about creating designs for every new gadget or screen size that hits the market when using responsive design. It can accommodate a wide range of devices, from smartphones and tablets to TVs and novel form factors like foldable phones, thanks to its flexible and adaptive layout. Because of this, RWD is a future-proof solution that guarantees your website will appear beautiful on gadgets that are still years away from being created.

For example, your flexible website will be ready for every new tablet or wearable gadget that gains popularity and has a different screen resolution. This means that you won't have to revamp it every time a new piece of technology comes out.

- **Growing Mobile Usage**

  Responsive design is more important than ever due to the steady increase in mobile internet usage. A website that functions properly on mobile devices is essential, as mobile devices account for almost half of all web traffic worldwide as of 2021. Because it adjusts to all screen sizes and offers a consistent user experience across all platforms, responsive design is especially well-suited for this.

  Consider the scenario where a consumer tries to browse your website while commuting on a mobile device. They're probably going to depart if the website is hard to use. This is avoided with a responsive design, which enhances usability and engagement by making sure that the navigation, pictures, and text all immediately adapt to the smaller size.

- **SEO Benefits**

  Search engines like Google give preference to mobile-friendly websites, especially with Google's shift to mobile-first indexing. Responsive design enhances SEO by making sure your site is optimized for mobile devices, improving its chances of ranking higher in search results. On the other hand, websites that aren't responsive may rank lower since search engines favor those with better mobile experiences.

  For instance, if you manage a blog or online business, using responsive design can improve your search rankings and help drive more organic traffic to your site.

- **Cost-Efficiency**

  Over time, responsive design turns out to be more cost-effective since it eliminates the need to create and manage different versions of a website for different devices. It may require more planning and testing during the initial setup, but the lower maintenance expenses make it a more cost-effective option for companies.

  Responsive design allows you to create a single website that adjusts to all devices, saving you the time and money associated with building a separate mobile site. Due to its ability to reduce development costs, this strategy is especially beneficial for startups or smaller companies with tighter resources.

- **When Adaptive Design is Less Suitable**

  While adaptive design might be useful for making updates to an already-existing website, it is not the ideal option when creating a brand-new one. Responsive design is the best choice if you want to create a fresh, contemporary website that is free of outdated website structures. It eases the procedure, offers more flexibility, and readily adapts to new devices without requiring regular updates. On the other hand, flexible design demands the development of several layouts, which can be more expensive and time-consuming, particularly for a new website.

When creating a new website, responsive web design is the best option, especially if you want a versatile, future-proof solution that functions on a range of devices. It guarantees uniformity across devices, is simpler to manage, helps with SEO, and caters to the increasing trend of mobile traffic. Although it might not provide the same degree of device-specific flexibility as an adaptable design, most current websites prefer this more economical and flexible approach.

Importance of Responsive Design

Responsive web design is crucial for several reasons in the present digital world when users access websites on a variety of devices with different screen sizes. Here's a detailed breakdown of why it's important:

- **Broader Reach:** Assures a broader audience by keeping your website operational and accessible on desktop and mobile devices.
- **Cost-Effective:** Lowers development and maintenance expenses by eliminating the need for several versions of your website.
- **Better User Experience:** Offers faster load times and flexible layouts for a seamless surfing experience.
- **Benefits of SEO:** Improves search engine position since Google rewards sites that load quickly and are mobile-friendly.
- **Future-proofing:** This feature makes sure your website will still be relevant in the future by adjusting to new screen sizes and devices.

Building Blocks of Responsive Web Design

In this section, we will explore the core principles behind responsive web design, delving into the essential components that make it effective. From flexible grids and layouts to media queries and responsive images, we will break down each building block that contributes to creating a seamless, adaptive user experience across various devices and screen sizes.

CSS and HTML

HTML (HyperText Markup Language) provides the structure and content of web pages, defining elements like headings, paragraphs, and images. CSS (Cascading Style Sheets) is used to control the visual presentation of those elements, including layout, colors, fonts, and spacing, allowing for a more visually appealing, responsive design.

Figure 9.2: *HTML and CSS*

HTML

Any webpage is structured by HTML, which effectively organizes its content. Semantic HTML elements such as **<header>, <nav>, <main>,** and **<footer>** are used to designate distinct sections in responsive design. These components support flexible layout as well as accessibility. Well-structured HTML makes it easier to apply responsive CSS, which guarantees that information displays correctly on various devices.

CSS

The way HTML elements look is handled by CSS (Cascading Style Sheets). CSS adjusts the layout and styling of responsive design to fit various screen sizes, devices, and orientations. For instance, CSS can be used to make a desktop layout with multiple columns on mobile devices into a single-column layout. Fluid grids, media queries, and adaptable pictures are important strategies. A CSS rule such as **`@media (max-width: 768px) {.container { width: 90%; } }`** modifies the width of the container according to the screen size, ensuring that the design looks good on both big and small displays.

Media Queries

With the use of a CSS feature called media queries, you may apply different styles based on the device's screen width, height, or orientation. By enabling developers to specify distinct stylistic guidelines for different devices, they aid in the creation of responsive designs. This guarantees that the information is well-suited to various screen sizes and formats, offering the best possible user experience on PCs, tablets, and mobile devices. Media queries provide flexibility and ease of use to web designs by allowing layouts and styles to be adjusted for any device.

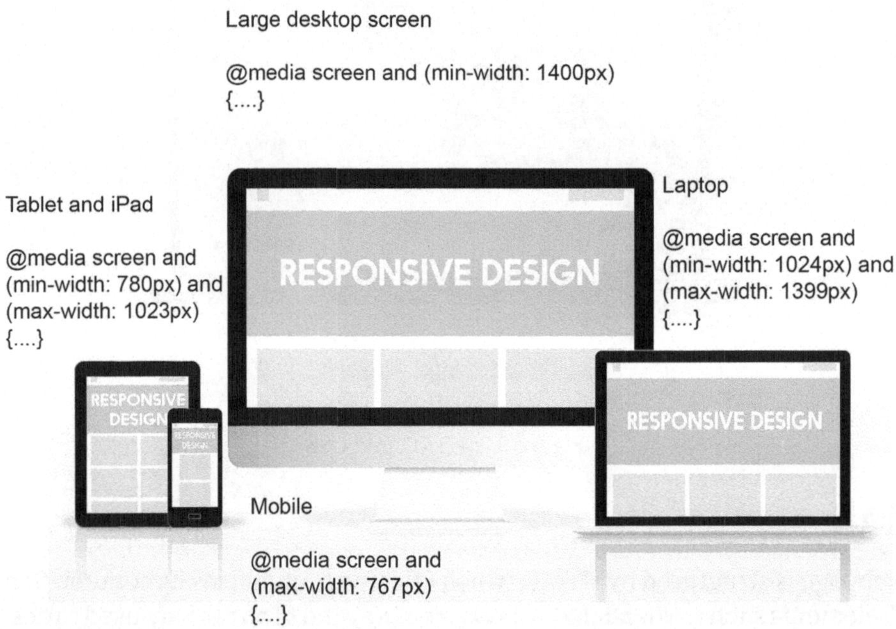

Figure 9.3: *Media queries for large screens, desktops, tablets and smartphones*

Example:

Here are some code samples for media queries used in creating responsive layouts.

```
/* Styles for devices with a screen width of at least 768px */
@media screen and (min-width: 768px) {
  .container {
    width: 75%;
    padding: 20px;
  }
}

/* Styles for devices with a screen width up to 767px */
@media screen and (max-width: 767px) {
  .container {
    width: 95%;
    padding: 10px;
  }
}
```

In this example, the **`.container`** class will have a width of 75% and additional padding on screens wider than 768px, while on narrower screens, the width is reduced to 95% with less padding. This approach ensures that the layout remains effective and visually appealing across different devices, from desktops to mobile phones.

In this case, the **`.container`** class will have a width of 75% with extra padding on devices larger than 768px, and a width of 95% with less padding on displays smaller than 768px. This method guarantees that the layout will continue to be functional and aesthetically pleasing on a variety of platforms, including smartphones and desktop computers.

Fluid Grid Layouts

With fluid grid layouts, items can scale proportionately to the size of the screen or container because relative units, like percentages, are used instead of fixed ones, like pixels. Unlike fixed grids, which can lead to layout problems or require users to scroll horizontally on smaller displays, this method makes sure that the layout adapts easily to different device sizes. More flexibility is provided by fluid grids, which dynamically resize content to keep the design accessible and adaptable on a range of platforms, including computers and mobile phones. This makes the design more responsive and user-friendly.

Figure 9.4: *Example of fluid layout*

Example:

Here are some code samples for Fluid Grid Layouts:

```
.container {
  width: 100%;
  max-width: 1200px;
  margin: 0 auto;
}

.column {
  float: left;
  width: 50%; /* Each column takes up half of the container's width */
  padding: 10px;
}
```

Here, the **`.column`** class uses a width of 50%, meaning it will take up half the width of the **`.container`**, regardless of the container's overall width. This adaptability guarantees columns shrink appropriately and retain a balanced layout on smaller screens without requiring fixed dimensions.

Flexbox Layout

A CSS module called Flexbox was created to help with responsive and flexible layout design. It allows items to automatically resize and reposition themselves inside a container based on available space. Flexbox removes the need for floats and manual positioning by effectively aligning and allocating space among elements, simplifying the design of layouts. Because of this, it's the perfect tool for creating intricate, responsive layouts that work perfectly on a variety of screens and devices.

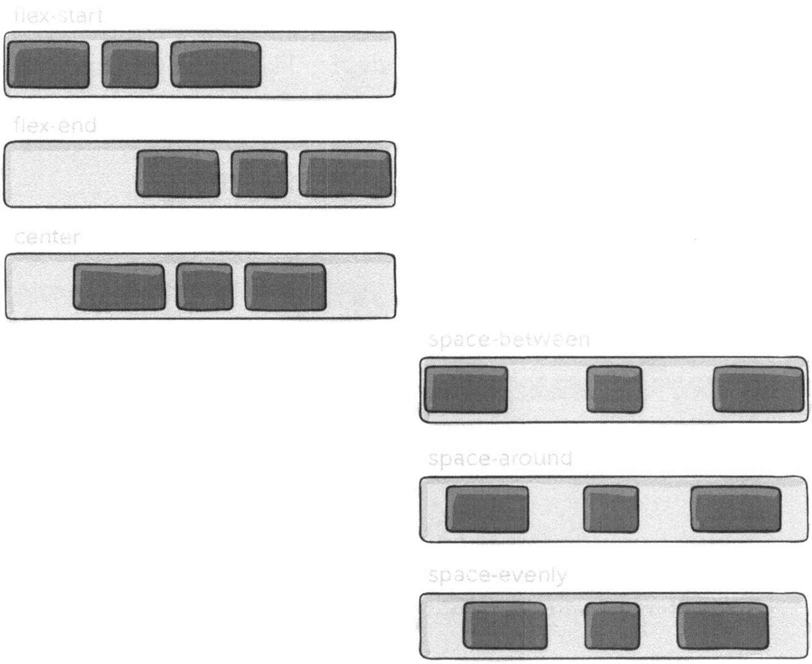

***Figure* 9.5**: *Unique properties of Flexbox container*

Example:

Here are the Code Samples for Flexbox Layouts:

```
.container {
  display: flex;
  flex-wrap: wrap;
}

.item {
  flex: 1 1 200px; /* Grow, shrink, and base size */
  margin: 10px;
}
```

The Flexbox layout is activated in this example by using **`display: flex`** on the **`.container`**. The **`.item`** elements are flexible, with **`flex: 1 1 200px`** indicating that they will expand and contract to fill the available space, beginning at a base width of 200px. It is simpler to create responsive designs with this style since it automatically modifies things to fit varying screen sizes without requiring complicated calculations.

Responsive Images

Images that are responsive change size to fill the available screen area and their containers. This avoids problems like overflowing or pixelation and guarantees that photos are displayed appropriately on devices of all sizes. Performance and visual quality can be preserved by employing strategies like employing responsive image formats and establishing a limited width.

***Figure 9.6:** Example of responsive images*

Example:

Here is the code example for responsive images:

```
img {
  max-width: 100%;
  height: auto; /* Maintain aspect ratio */
}
```

Images can be made to scale down to suit the container without losing aspect ratio by setting **`max-width: 100%`** and **`height: auto.`** This method makes sure that images stay inside the width of their container and adjust to fit various screen sizes and resolutions without any issues.

Responsive Typography

From giant computers to smaller smartphones, responsive typography ensures readability and visual appeal across all platforms by adjusting font sizes and line spacing based on the screen size or viewport width. Text scales proportionately when relative units like **ems** or **rems** are used, preserving consistent design. By maintaining proper text size and spacing across screen widths, media queries can be used to apply specified font sizes, improving user experience. This method guarantees that material will always be readable and available, irrespective of the device or screen size.

Example:

Following are code snippets for implementing responsive typography.

```
body {
  font-size: 16px; /* Base font size */
}

@media (max-width: 768px) {
  body {
    font-size: 14px; /* Smaller font size for smaller screens */
  }
}
```

For larger displays, the base font size is set to 16px here. The font size is 14px for displays that are 768px or smaller. This improves the overall user experience across various devices by ensuring that content stays readable and scaled appropriately.

Adaptive Layouts

Adaptive layouts change their content and structure according to the device being used. Adaptive layouts use pre-established breakpoints to transition between different fixed designs, in contrast to responsive layouts that change dynamically. By using this method, the layout is guaranteed to be customized for particular screen sizes, offering the best possible experience on any device. Adaptive layouts provide content a unique look and feel by emphasizing important breakpoints. This makes information accessible and easy to interact with across a range of platforms, including desktops and smartphones.

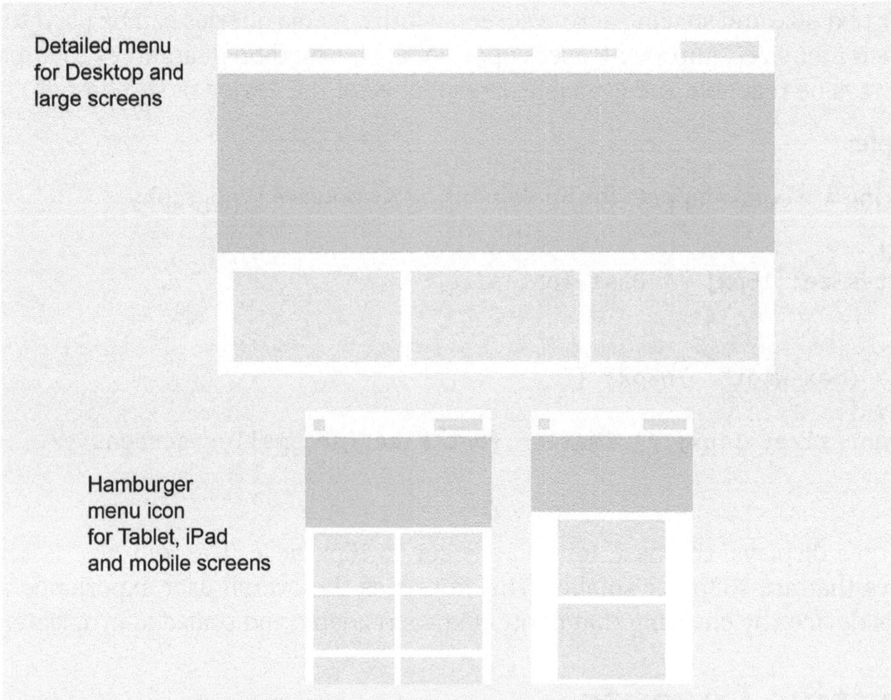

Figure 9.7: *Example of responsive images*

Example:

Here are the code snippets for creating adaptive layouts:

```
.nav-menu {
  display: none; /* Hide menu by default */
}

@media (min-width: 768px) {
  .nav-menu {
    display: block; /* Show menu on larger screens */
  }
}
```

In this illustration, the **`.nav-menu`** is visible on larger screens and hidden on screens that are smaller than 768 pixels. By using an adaptable strategy, you can improve usability and accessibility for various user scenarios by providing distinct navigation options dependent on the size of the device.

Mobile-First Design

The mobile-first design strategy is a responsive web design methodology that places emphasis on creating websites for mobile devices as a priority, with larger screens, such as tablets and desktops, coming later. This method's basic idea is to start with the smallest screen size and work your way up, making sure that mobile devices can access and use the most important features and content first.

Key Aspects of Mobile-First Design

- **Prioritize Essential Content**: To begin, build a condensed version of your website that highlights its main features and essential material. This guarantees a quick and effective experience that is concentrated on what matters most for mobile users, who are frequently multitasking or on the go.
- **Gradual Enhancement**: After the mobile version is finished, add features one at a time and make the design better for bigger screens. This technique creates a solid base that works well on all platforms and lets you add more sophisticated designs and features as screen sizes grow.
- **Performance Optimization:** Performance optimization is a key component of mobile-first design since mobile devices typically have slower internet connections and less processing power. You may make sure that the website loads swiftly and effectively on all devices by starting with mobile design.
- **Improved User Experience:** By prioritizing mobile design, you respond to the requirements of the biggest and fastest-growing internet user demographic. This method frequently results in a better user-friendly and intuitivc experience on every single device.
- **CSS Media Queries:** Media queries are used in mobile-first design to apply styles according to screen size. Your design seamlessly adjusts as screen sizes increase by starting with mobile styles and adding styles for larger screens using @media (min-width:...).

Example:

This section provides an overview of mobile-first design principles and their implementation.

```
/* Mobile-first styles */
body {
  font-size: 14px;
}

.header {
  display: block;
}

.nav-menu {
  display: none;
}
```

```
/* Tablet and larger screens */
@media (min-width: 768px) {
  body {
    font-size: 16px;
  }

  .nav-menu {
    display: block;
  }
}

/* Desktop and larger screens */
@media (min-width: 1024px) {
  .header {
    display: flex;
  }
}
```

The foundation styles in this illustration are made for mobile devices. Additional styles are applied when the screen width grows in order to modify the functionality and layout for tablets and desktops. This methodology guarantees that the essential features are tailored for mobile users, all the while offering a better viewing experience on bigger displays.

Linking Mobile-First with Responsive Design

Responsive Web Design (RWD) and Mobile-First Design are closely connected, as both focus on delivering a good user experience across different devices and screen sizes. However, they use distinct strategies to achieve this goal.

Key Connections:

	Mobile-First Design	**Responsive Web Design**
Design Philosophy	Emphasizes creating for small screens first, then expanding it to larger ones. The plan is to gradually improve the design for tablets and desktops while giving priority to the features and information that are most important for smaller devices.	Focuses on using flexible grids, graphics, and media queries to create a layout that is versatile and functions well on any screen. It guarantees that the layout adapts and changes according to various screen sizes.

Implementation Techniques	Frequently applies styles for smaller displays first using CSS media queries with a mobile-first strategy, and then adds styles for larger screens using `@media (min-width:...)}.	Creates a design that fluidly changes to fit different devices by using media queries, responsive pictures, and flexible grids. It can be implemented using a desktop-first or mobile-first approach, albeit the latter is increasingly common.
Performance Optimization	Usually takes performance into account right away because mobile devices frequently have slower connectivity and fewer computing power. A thinner, more efficient design results from this.	Includes speed optimization as well, but does so by ensuring that all components—including scripts and images—are effectively maintained across various platforms.
User Experience	The goal of both approaches is to ensure that content is responsive and user-friendly across a range of devices. Responsive web design ensures that content flows fluidly across all screen sizes, while mobile-first design gives priority to mobile users, who frequently have slower connections and smaller screens.	

Table 9.1: *The key relationships between mobile-first design and responsive web design*

Example of How They Work Together

A website that follows the guidelines of Mobile-First Design may begin with a simple layout that highlights the material that mobile consumers need to see. Flexible grids and media queries are two examples of responsive web design strategies that you may use to modify the layout and add more features as you scale up to larger displays. Together, these strategies guarantee that the website functions and looks great across all platforms, including computers and smartphones.

Balancing Mobile-First and Responsive Design for Adaptive Components

Using both mobile-first and responsive design approaches depending on the component can create a more adaptable, user-centered experience. Mobile-first prioritizes essential elements for smaller screens, while responsive design adjusts layouts dynamically across devices.

For example, a responsive navigation bar could adapt from a full horizontal menu on desktops to a collapsible "hamburger" menu on mobile, ensuring smooth usability across screen sizes.

Conclusion

Responsive Web Design (RWD) has become a fundamental practice for creating websites that adapt smoothly across various devices and screen sizes. By understanding the key elements like flexible grids, media queries, and responsive images, designers can ensure a consistent user experience. Additionally, the distinction between Adaptive Web Design and RWD highlights the flexibility in design approaches, depending on the project's needs. Finally, with the rise of mobile users, the Mobile-First Design strategy has proven to be a critical component, prioritizing smaller screens to ensure seamless scalability. Together, these concepts form the foundation of effective and future-proof web design.

The process of mastering design handoff, which is essential to bridging the gap between developers and designers, will be covered in the upcoming chapter. You may easily translate design thoughts into fully functional products by knowing efficient collaboration strategies, tools, and best practices. This will ensure accuracy and efficiency in the product's implementation.

Key Terms

- **Responsive Web Design:** A web design approach where websites automatically adapt to various screen sizes, ensuring a seamless user experience across devices.
- **Adaptive Web Design:** A different approach to web design that creates distinct layouts tailored for specific screen sizes rather than automatically adjusting like responsive design.
- **Desktop-Focused Websites:** Websites originally designed for large desktop screens that became less effective as mobile browsing increased, leading to missed opportunities for businesses slow to adapt.
- **Design Philosophy:** A principle emphasizing the creation of designs for small screens first, expanding to larger screens while prioritizing key features for mobile devices. Responsive design focuses on flexible grids and media queries for adaptable layouts across various screen sizes.
- **Implementation Techniques:** The use of CSS media queries in a mobile-first strategy to apply styles for small screens, later adding larger screen styles. Techniques like flexible grids and responsive images allow fluid changes for different devices.
- **Performance Optimization:** Ensuring fast performance on mobile devices by minimizing design complexity due to slower connectivity and lower computing power. Responsive design also includes optimizing images, scripts, and elements across platforms.

- **User Experience:** Both mobile-first and responsive web design ensure content is accessible and user-friendly on any device. Mobile-first prioritizes users on slower connections, while responsive design adapts content fluidly to various screen sizes.
- **Mobile-First Design:** A web design approach that starts with a simple layout for mobile users, adding complexity as screen sizes increase.
- **Portrait Mode:** A screen orientation where the height is greater than the width, commonly used on mobile devices.
- **Personalized Experience:** A tailored user experience based on individual preferences, behaviors, or demographics, enhancing user engagement and satisfaction.
- **Framework:** A pre-built structure or platform, like Bootstrap or React, that simplifies web development by providing reusable components and tools.
- **E-commerce Site:** A website that facilitates online buying and selling of products or services, often including payment processing and customer support features.
- **Pre-designed Layouts:** Ready-made web page designs that can be customized to fit specific needs, speeding up the design process.
- **Flexible Layout:** A web layout that adjusts dynamically to fit various screen sizes and devices, ensuring a responsive user experience.
- **SEO (Search Engine Optimization):** Techniques used to improve a website's visibility on search engines, increasing traffic and ranking.
- **Mobile-First Indexing:** A Google indexing approach that prioritizes mobile versions of websites for ranking and indexing, reflecting the growing dominance of mobile web traffic.
- **HTML (HyperText Markup Language):** The foundational coding language used to structure and format content on web pages.
- **CSS (Cascading Style Sheets):** A stylesheet language used to control the visual appearance of a website, including layout, colors, and fonts.
- **Media Queries:** A CSS technique used to apply different styles based on device characteristics, like screen size, ensuring responsive design.

Chapter 10
Mastering in Design Handoff

Introduction

This chapter explores the critical process of design handoff, whereby UX designers provide the development team with digital assets and comprehensive documentation to help in the development of the product vision. Together with file transfers, a smooth handoff requires close coordination and communication between developers and designers. This partnership ensures that the design is executed accurately, enhancing the user experience and resulting in a project that is successfully completed. To effectively complete this critical stage, a strong working connection between the designer and developer is required.

Structure

In this chapter, we will discuss the following topics:

- Understanding Design Handoff
- The Role of Collaboration in Design Handoff
- Strategies for Better Collaboration
- Design handoff checklist
- Tips for Effective Design Handoff

Understanding Design Handoff

Once UX designers finalize their designs, UX designers create a comprehensive document that includes all the requirements and digital resources the development team will need. The design handoff procedure is essential to turning the concept into a working product. Even though it might seem easy, a successful handoff needs close consideration. At this point, poor communication might cause serious problems in the development process. A common issue is the misconception that once the design is complete, the responsibility shifts entirely to the developers. Strong cooperation between designers and developers is the first step towards a good handoff since it guarantees transparent communication and a seamless transition.

Example:

Consider a UX designer who has recently completed the UI of a mobile application. The designer creates a document that includes every design element, including fonts, color schemes, button styles, and spacing. During the design handoff, this document is given to the development team.

However, the developers can misunderstand or overlook certain features if the designer does not provide clear instructions on how a specific animation should function or does not include responsive design specifics. For instance, if a button's hover effect is intended by the designer but is not adequately documented, the developer may implement an alternative interaction, which would negatively affect the user experience.

This demonstrates how misunderstandings during the handoff can lead to inconsistent output. Close cooperation between the designer and developer is necessary for a seamless handoff; they must evaluate the design together to make sure all the details are understood and the product is constructed according to the plan. Errors are avoided, and the successful realization of the design objective is ensured by clear communication and teamwork.

The Role of Collaboration in Design Handoff

Any product's success and a seamless design handoff depend on collaboration. When developers and designers collaborate closely, both teams are aware of the needs, technical limitations, and objectives of the project. A seamless transfer from design to development is ensured by effective communication, which also helps to avoid misunderstandings. Crucially, a designer must continue to be involved throughout the development process to guarantee that their vision is appropriately carried out. Both teams may address problems early, make changes, and guarantee that the finished product adheres to the original plan while leaving opportunities for ongoing improvement by keeping an open feedback loop.

Strategies for Better Collaboration

It is essential to first go over collaborative concepts before getting into the details of carrying out a Design Handoff. Since every project is different, these guidelines should be modified to fit your team's particular requirements and objectives. Better communication is fostered by effective teamwork, which helps to avoid misunderstandings and ensures a smoother and more streamlined workflow. Teamwork is the key to optimizing the handoff process, which facilitates creative problem-solving and guarantees alignment between engineers and designers. This method leaves flexibility for future modifications while producing a final result that follows the original design idea and produces fewer errors and clearer expectations.

- **Designing with Developers in Mind**

  Making designs that are both aesthetically pleasing and technically achievable for developers is the main goal of designing with developers in mind. It is important to keep developers' demands in mind because they depend on your designs, wireframes, and documentation to translate concepts into working code. This means asking questions like, "Which file format works best?" and "How detailed should the design instructions be?" For example, a UX designer can provide scalable assets and clear guidelines to avoid confusion. By understanding technical limits and improving communication, the handoff process becomes faster, leading to smoother collaboration and a better final product.

- **Embrace Flexibility and Adaptability**

  Even though the general procedure is the same, every project is different. Comparable to making a cake, the results might vary depending on ingredients, oven temperature, and even the baker's attitude. Because of this, designers need to consider potential obstacles and modify their strategy accordingly. Using the same documentation style that produced successful results in the past is an easy trap to slip into.

  However, no two projects are alike, just as no two cakes are. It is possible that what worked for the last documentation won't work for this one. In order to create design handoff documents that satisfy the requirements of a project, flexibility is crucial. Additionally, keep in mind that various developers work in different ways, some thrive in tight collaboration, while others are best left alone. Adapting to these differences ensures smoother collaboration and better project outcomes.

- **Design Continues Beyond the Handoff**

  When a designer transfers the design to developers, their work is not finished. This is known as "Design Continues Beyond the Handoff." Your plans are brought to life by developers, however, throughout execution, adjustments, feedback loops, and technical limitations frequently occur. By staying involved, you can make sure the final product matches your original vision.

  For instance, you may change some components or work together to overcome unforeseen difficulties. Design and development collaborate continuously to improve the product and make sure it functions well for the consumer. This highlights how design is a continuous process.

Design Handoff Checklist

A design handoff checklist is a vital tool that designers should use to ensure that developers have all the materials and data needed for a seamless transition from design to development. A thorough guide detailing the essential components of a design handoff checklist can be found here:

Design Files

Make sure that every design file is arranged correctly and is easily accessible by developers. This covers both the finished products and any revisions that show how the design has evolved.

- Deliver finished design files in Adobe XD, Sketch, or Figma formats.
- To show iterations, provide any relevant design revisions.

Figma Dev Mode: Streamlining Design Handoff for Developers

By providing developers with direct access to important specifications within design files, Figma's Dev Mode streamlines the design handoff procedure. This mode lowers the possibility of errors by enabling developers to easily inspect measurements, styles, colors, typography, and component information. Dev Mode also generates code snippets for CSS, Swift, and Android, helping developers replicate exact designs more efficiently. Dev Mode facilitates seamless, cooperative collaboration between designers and developers by ensuring consistent, transparent communication of design details, which eventually speeds up the development process and improves the quality of the final product.

Documentation

A good design handoff depends on thorough documentation. Make sure developers have precise instructions on how to implement the design, including how the functionality and aesthetics should be done.

- Provide design specifications such as padding, size, and spacing.
- Offer style manuals that address component usage, typography, and color schemes.
- To illustrate user navigation, share travel maps or user flow diagrams.

Interactive Prototypes

For the purpose of communicating how your design should work in practice, interactive prototypes are crucial. They provide a clear picture for developers of how users will interact with various components.

- Showcase user interactions and component activity.
- Draw attention to transition animations to provide a seamless user experience.

Assets

Ensure that developers have access to all necessary resources for a seamless implementation. This comprises photos, icons, and graphics in the proper forms.

- Provide resources in SVG, PNG, and other formats.
- Make shared folders or download links available for convenient access.

Design System or Style Guide

To keep consistency, share your design system with developers if you have one. It should include clear rules on component usage.

- Give components do's and don'ts.
- Exchange information about reusable parts for more efficient development.

Feedback and Revisions

To keep everyone informed during the design process, be sure to record all comments and changes. This makes it clearer what has to be changed and where developer participation is needed.

- List any conclusions from the design review and any upcoming changes.
- Indicate which areas want developer input.

Functionality and Features

To help developers, clearly define the main features and functions of your design. This guarantees that they are aware of how things should be done.

- Explain how the component behaves in various states (such as hover, active, and so on).
- Emphasize any APIs or integrations that are required for the finished product.

Technical Specifications

To prevent any surprises during implementation, make sure that developers are informed of all technical specifications. This makes it more likely that your design will function as intended on all platforms.

- Provide a compatibility list of the supported browsers and devices.
- Bring up any performance restrictions or issues that developers should take care of.

Contact Information

Ensure the right contacts are available for developers to communicate with during development. Share key team members' information so they can get help quickly if needed.

- Make designers reachable for inquiries while the project is being developed.
- Create a list of interested parties to stay updated on concerns or progress.

Project Timeline

To keep the development moving forward, be sure to include a clear project timeline that identifies important milestones.

- Provide significant dates for the various stages of development.
- Distribute the dates of any review meetings or feedback loops.

By using this checklist, you may minimize the possibility of misunderstandings and inefficiencies during the development process by ensuring that designers and developers are in sync and have all they need for a successful handoff.

Tips for Effective Design Handoff

An efficient design handoff is essential to a productive working relationship between developers and designers. Teams may guarantee a more seamless transition from design to development and, eventually, a better final product by adhering to best practices.

Here are some pointers for an improved handoff in design:

- **Involve Developers Early**

  Early developer involvement in the design process can facilitate more seamless collaboration and reduce the likelihood of later technical roadblocks. You can ensure your concepts are implementable by getting their essential opinion on technical constraints early on in the dialog.

  For example, if developers point out limitations, a complex animation can be simplified early, avoiding extra work later. By working together to align design goals with what is possible, delays are reduced, and teamwork improves.

- **Provide Clear and Detailed Documentation**

  Make sure the documentation you hand off for your design is organized and comprehensive. Important design components including color schemes, typography, space, and component details should be covered in this. To ensure there is no confusion, combine written explanations with visual aids.

  For example, including annotations on button functionality makes it easier for developers to precisely implement the design. Thorough documentation speeds up development, minimizes the need for frequent clarification, and guarantees that the finished product adheres to the original idea.

- **Provide Interactive Prototypes**

  Give developers access to interactive prototypes rather than simply static designs. Developers may see how elements behave by using tools like Figma or InVision, which makes it easier for them to understand user flows and animations.

  For example, to prevent misunderstandings and guarantee that the final product fulfills the functional requirements of the design, a prototype showcasing hover effects or transitions provides a clearer picture of the desired user experience.

- **Emphasize Design Consistency**

  Use uniform components, grid systems, and patterns to keep the project's design structure constant. This facilitates the implementation of designs by developers without interfering with the visual flow. To lower the likelihood of deviations, developers can guarantee they have a clear reference by adhering to a design system or style guide. In addition to increasing coding productivity, consistency guarantees that the finished result adheres to the overall design concept.

- **Establish a Continuous Feedback Loop**

  After the handoff, stay in touch to discuss any concerns or difficulties that may arise between the designers and developers. Development may highlight the need for clarifications or changes to the design.

  For example, frequent check-ins or collaborative meetings enable both teams to make sure the design is moving forward, making necessary adjustments on time, and averting major issues as the project gets closer to completion. This continuous feedback guarantees a more seamless procedure and avoids misalignments.

- **Have a Flexible Mindset**

  When unexpected issues or technical constraints surface during development, designers should be ready to make adjustments. It could be necessary to change some design components under technological requirements.

For example, coordinating with developers to change animations or layouts while retaining the overall design goal is vital. This adaptability ensures that the design objective is maintained without interfering with the development process and fosters a collaborative atmosphere.

- **Use Collaborative Design Tools**

  Make advantage of tools like Figma, Zeplin, or Sketch to facilitate the design handoff. These platforms let developers directly inspect elements, view specifications, and stay updated on any design changes in real-time.

  For example, organizing all design materials and specs makes it easier for developers to find what they need quickly, which reduces confusion and ensures a better workflow with fewer mistakes made during development.

Conclusion

Mastering the design handoff process is essential for successful project execution. By understanding the intricacies of design handoff, fostering collaboration between designers and developers, and implementing effective strategies and checklists, teams can significantly enhance their workflow. The emphasis on clear communication and shared responsibility ensures that both parties remain aligned throughout the development process. Ultimately, adopting these practices leads to a smoother transition from design to implementation, resulting in higher-quality products that meet user needs and expectations. A well-executed design handoff is not just a process, it is a foundation for collaborative success.

In the next section, we will explore how to effectively showcase your skills as a UI/UX designer. You will learn to navigate common interview questions, highlight your portfolio, and gain insights into industry trends and best practices. This guide will equip you to confidently approach your job interview and secure your ideal position.

Key Terms

- **Responsive Web Design:** A web design approach where websites automatically adapt to various screen sizes, ensuring a seamless user experience across devices.
- **Collaboration:** Close teamwork between designers and developers ensures both teams understand the project's needs, technical limitations, and goals, leading to smoother communication and fewer misunderstandings.
- **Seamless Design Handoff:** The smooth transfer of design elements from the design team to the development team, ensuring the design is properly implemented while maintaining its original vision.

- **Feedback Loop:** Continuous communication between designers and developers during the development phase to address issues, make adjustments, and ensure the final product aligns with the original design vision.
- **Technical Constraints:** Limitations imposed by technology or coding frameworks that may require design adjustments during the development process to ensure functionality.
- **Ongoing Improvement:** The idea that design is an evolving process, allowing for tweaks and enhancements during and after the development phase to better meet user needs and project goals.
- **Technical Specifications:** Detailed requirements that outline how a design should function across different platforms, helping developers ensure compatibility during implementation.
- **Compatibility List:** A documented list of browsers and devices that a design is intended to support, ensuring the design works correctly across various platforms.
- **Performance Restrictions:** Limitations or issues that may affect the speed or efficiency of the product, which developers must address during implementation to ensure optimal performance.
- **APIs (Application Programming Interfaces):** Tools that allow different software systems to communicate with each other, often required for adding advanced functionalities to the final product.
- **Integrations:** The process of connecting different software systems or tools to work together within the final product.
- **Milestones:** Key stages or deadlines in a project timeline that mark significant progress points. Milestones help track the completion of essential tasks and ensure the project stays on schedule.
- **Components:** Reusable building blocks of a design, such as buttons, input fields, or icons, that maintain consistency across a project. Components are essential for creating cohesive and efficient design systems.

CHAPTER 11
Interview Preparation for UI/UX Designer

Introduction

Discover essential tips and strategies to ace your first UI/UX designer job interview. Learn how to showcase your skills effectively, navigate common interview questions, and highlight your portfolio. Gain insights into industry trends and best practices to impress potential employers. With this guide, you will be well-prepared to confidently tackle your UI/UX designer job interview and land your dream role.

Structure

In this section, we will discuss the following topics:

- Interview Preparation
- Preparing and Polishing Your Portfolio
- Practicing Common Interview Questions
- Mastering Design Challenges and Soft Skills
- Mastering UI/UX Design Principles
- Staying Up-to-Date with Industry Trends
- Future Trends in UI/UX Design

Interview Preparation

There is more to preparing for a UI/UX designer interview than just having a well-designed portfolio. You must exhibit a solid understanding of design ideas, show that you can solve practical difficulties, and make sure that your abilities are in line with the objectives of the business if you want to stand out. From tackling design issues to presenting your portfolio, this guide provides essential advice and techniques to help you succeed. You will be prepared to leave a memorable impression and get your ideal job, whether it is demonstrating your creative process or handling typical interview questions.

This thorough guide contains all the necessary pointers and techniques to help you win your UI/UX interview.

Preparing and Polishing Your Portfolio

Imagine the recruiter opening your portfolio while you are seated in an interview room. At that point, your portfolio tells the story of your personality as a designer, not just a sample of your work. From the initial idea to a finished design that had an influence, every project narrates a journey. Your most significant asset is your portfolio, which should not only highlight your finest work but also show off your versatility and capacity to take on a variety of tasks.

Example

Demonstrate this by incorporating a case study in your portfolio, structured to tell the full story of a project. Start with an eye-catching cover image that represents the final design, then break down the project into sections: problem statement, research insights, design iterations, and final results. Each section should have visuals and brief captions to explain your decisions and thought process. This narrative format, complete with real-world challenges and solutions, lets recruiters quickly understand your approach, adaptability, and the value you bring as a designer.

How to Craft a Standout Portfolio

Consider your portfolio to be a self-contained design challenge. Similar to any product you would work on, it must be organized, understandable, and easy to use. A well-structured portfolio will show the recruiter your ability to think creatively, solve problems, and walk them through your work.

- **Structure it Clearly**

  Give a quick synopsis of the issue, difficulty, and user at the beginning of every project. After that, go over your procedure, emphasizing user flows, wireframes, and research. Provide the ultimate solution at the end, demonstrating how your efforts resolved the issue.

- **Showcase Your Process**

  Your design journey is what recruiters want to see. Talk about your ideas, difficulties, iterations, and criticism. To demonstrate how you improved the design, including wireframes, sketches, and previous iterations.

- **Make it Visual**

  Keep your portfolio simple yet eye-catching. To make your designs and explanations stand out, use clear font, high-quality photos, and a simple layout. Keep your writing readable by avoiding clutter.

Ensure that your portfolio can be accessed online. The secret to making sure recruiters can quickly browse your work is to have a well-designed website with easy-to-use navigation. Recall that your portfolio is a narrative that demonstrates your development, creativity, and problem-solving skills rather than merely a static presentation of your work. Every project should be a chapter that shows how you address design issues, work together, and produce meaningful outcomes.

Practicing Common Interview Questions

Preparing for behavioral and situational questions is just as crucial as addressing design difficulties and going over your portfolio during the interview process. These inquiries often focus on your design methodology, teamwork dynamics, how you handle constructive criticism and specific technical abilities.

Depending on the organization's size, your interview could be led by a panel of team members or just a single hiring manager. One of the first questions you will likely encounter is the classic icebreaker:

"Can you tell us about yourself?"

Although this inquiry may seem basic and friendly, it is actually your best chance to make a good first impression. Create a succinct narrative that emphasizes your enthusiasm for UX design, your pertinent experiences, and your motivations for being here today rather than just restating your CV.

Tip: *Remind yourself of how you fell in love with UX, what makes you stand out from the competition, and how these relate to the position you are applying for.*

Use a positive remark to close out your introduction, such as "I'm excited to demonstrate how my background and perspective on UX can be a valuable asset to your team."

Next, the core questions you are bound to encounter are:

"Can you take us through your design process?"

or

"What methods do you follow in your workflow?"

This allows you to explain your methodology and demonstrate how you use your own methods and techniques to turn design problems into solutions. Be ready to explain your procedures and the rationale behind them!

Keep in mind that different designers and teams may have rather different UX and UI procedures. Interviewers are interested in your critical thinking and approach to design difficulties. Begin by describing your procedure and the importance of each stage. Next, illustrate how your procedures result in successful outcomes by using real-world examples from your case studies to bring your process to life. This demonstrates your abilities and highlights your careful approach to design.

Preparing for a Series of Questions

Many frequently asked questions and suggested answers specific to UX and UI responsibilities can be found with a quick online search. Here is a list of common interview questions for UI/UX designers, categorized for easier reference:

General Questions

1. What inspired you to pursue a career in UI/UX design?
2. How do you stay updated with industry trends and design tools?

Design Process

1. Describe your design process from research to final implementation.
2. How do you approach user research, and what methods do you use?
3. Can you explain the difference between UX and UI design?

Tools and Technologies

1. What design tools do you prefer and why? (for example, Sketch, Figma, and Adobe XD)
2. How do you manage version control and collaborate with developers?

Problem Solving

1. Describe a challenging design problem you faced and how you solved it.
2. How do you prioritize user needs when designing a product?

Portfolio and Projects

1. Can you walk us through a project in your portfolio? What was your role?
2. What metrics do you use to measure the success of your designs?

Collaboration and Communication

1. How do you handle feedback from stakeholders or team members?
2. Describe a time when you had to advocate for a design decision. How did you approach it?

User Experience Focus

1. How do you ensure your designs are accessible and inclusive?
2. What techniques do you use to create user personas?

Trends and Future

1. What emerging trends in UI/UX design are you most excited about?
2. How do you envision the future of UI/UX design?

Behavioral Questions

1. Describe a time when you failed on a project. What did you learn from it?
2. How do you handle tight deadlines and multiple projects?

You will feel more confident and prepared to have meaningful discussions during your interview if you prepare your answers in advance and expect these types of questions.

Preparation Strategy

To keep situational inquiries focused and clear, use the STAR approach (Situation, Task, Action, and Result). Your responses will be stronger and more effectively demonstrate your abilities if they are detailed and backed up with examples from your prior work experiences.

Mastering Design Challenges and Soft Skills

In a lot of UI/UX interviews, you will be asked to solve an issue or create a feature as part of a design challenge. This is a crucial step in the interview process since it demonstrates your ability to solve problems and think under pressure.

The following advice will help you tackle a design challenge:

- **Understand the Problem:** Take your time coming up with a solution. Asking questions will help to define the challenge. Recognize the user, their objectives, and any limitations.
- **Describe Your Procedure:** Talk aloud about your ideas as you draft wireframes or sketches. In addition to the final design, employers want to know how you came up with the solution.
- **Focus on the User:** When resolving an issue, keep the user's needs in mind.
- **Display Your Work:** Whether you use a digital mockup or a sketch, make sure to go over your selections and provide justifications for them.

- **Be Receptive to Criticism:** Throughout the challenge, you can get criticism. Show that you are able to take constructive criticism well and modify your designs accordingly.

Employers value technical design talents, but they also seek soft qualities that demonstrate teamwork. UI/UX designers must be able to communicate, collaborate, and adapt because they frequently work directly with developers, product managers, and stakeholders.

Here are a few essential soft skills to highlight:

- **Collaboration:** Describe how you have produced a design solution in conjunction with cross-functional teams.
- **Adaptability:** Give examples of how you have managed deadline pressure or changing requirements.
- **Problem-Solving:** Display your capacity for critical thought and user-centered problem-solving.
- **Communication:** Emphasize your ability to convey design concepts and feedback to stakeholders who are not involved in the design process.

This method not only displays your proficiency in design but also your ability to interact with others, which is essential in any team setting.

Mastering UI/UX Design Principles

Making wise design choices requires a firm understanding of UI/UX design principles. During your interview, be prepared to talk about crucial subjects including design systems, accessibility, and usability. It is crucial to confidently explain your design decisions because interviewers frequently ask questions to test your knowledge of user-centered design.

Make use of everything you have learned from this book as well as your overall learning journey. In addition to assisting you in providing insightful answers, your experience will show that you are dedicated to developing user experiences that have a purpose. Prove to them that you are aware of the complexity of design and how it affects actual users.

Staying Up-to-Date with Industry Trends

The field of UI/UX design is always changing. Maintaining current knowledge of the newest tools, technologies, and trends will help you in interviews and enhance your design abilities. Candidates who exhibit a desire for lifelong learning are valued by employers.

Here are some ways to stay updated:

- Follow design influencers and read blogs on sites like Behance, Dribbble, and Medium. Networking on LinkedIn is also a great way to stay connected and informed.
- Take part in online communities such as Reddit's design threads or UX Stack Exchange.
- To maintain your abilities, take part in online courses, webinars, or seminars.

Be Confident and Authentic

Lastly, never forget to be who you are. Finding a good cultural match is just as important in interviews as your technical abilities. Have faith in your skills, but be genuine as well. Do not be afraid to admit if you don't know something–show that you are eager to learn.

Future Trends in UI/UX Design

Future developments in UI/UX design will emphasize immersive technologies like virtual reality (VR) and augmented reality (AR), as well as personalization and AI integration. Hyper-personalized user experiences that change in real-time according to user activity are becoming more and more popular among designers. Automation and AI-powered design tools expedite procedures, while voice and gesture interfaces are growing in popularity. Additionally, accessibility is becoming more important, guaranteeing inclusive designs for all users. Furthermore, motion design and micro-interactions keep improving user engagement by making interfaces more responsive and dynamic. The increasing emphasis on sustainability is also having an impact on UI/UX, promoting environmentally friendly digital product design solutions.

Final Thoughts

Landing your dream UI/UX design job is more than just luck–it is about blending your skills, communication, and portfolio into one powerful package. Picture yourself stepping into that interview room, armed with deep knowledge of the company, confident in answering questions, and ready to showcase your problem-solving genius. With preparation, you are already one step ahead of the game. Follow these tips to crush your interview and secure your dream role!

As you wrap up this book, we hope it boosted your passion for UI/UX design and equipped you with the tools to grow. But the journey doesn't stop here– continue to explore, experiment, and apply these insights in your projects.

Keep Creating!

Index

Symbols

<footer> 327
<header> 327
<main> 327
<nav> 327
<url> 196
<video> 196
4 Cs 39
4 Cs, concepts
  Complementary 45, 46
  Consistency 39, 40
  Context 43, 44
  Continuity 41, 42
4 Cs, implementing 47
4 Cs, wrap-up 47

A

A/B Testing 109
A/B Testing, challenges
  limit scope 111
  time/traffic, requirements 111
A/B Testing, methods
  Effective Technique 110
  Effective Timing 110
A/B Testing, steps
  audience, dividing 111
  best version, implementing 111
  hit, testing 111
  objective, setup 111
  results, analyzing 111
  variations, creating 111
A/B Testing, tools
  Abobe Target 111
  Google Optimize 111
  Optimizely 111
  Unbounce 111
  VWO 111
Adaptive Web Design (AWD) 318
Adobe Firefly 309
AI, impact 307
AirBnb 20
AirBnb, achievement 22
AirBnb, fundamentals
  defining 21
  Empathize 21
  Ideate 21
  Iterate 22
  Prototype 21
  Test 21
AI, tools
  Adobe Firefly 309
  Khroma 307, 308
  Uizard 308, 309
  Visily 310
Amazon's Checkout 119
Amazon's Checkout, key implementing 120
Amazon's Checkout, methods 120
Amazon's Checkout, outcomes 121
AWD, aspects
  content presentation 321
  Device-Specific Layouts 319
  Faster Load Times 319, 320
  fixed layouts, predictability 321
  legacy systems 320
  Specific Feature, optimizing 320

AWD, circumstances
brand consistency 323
devices, focusing 322
gradual design, upgrading 323
performance, optimizing 323
viewports, creating 322
website, redesigning 322
AWD/RWD, comparing 321

C

Card Sorting 94
Card Sorting, challenges 96
Card Sorting, methods
Effective Technique 96
Effective Timing 95
Card Sorting, types
closed card 95
hybrid card 95
open card 94
Card Sorting, ways
Moderate/Unmoderate 95
Paper, configuring 95
CJMs, elements
mindsets/emotions 152
ownership, insights 153
point of view 152
scenarios 152
Touchpoints 152
CJMs, importance 149, 150
CJMs, stage
awareness 150
consideration 151
decision stage 151
loyalty 151
retention 151
CJMs, steps
customer journey, improving 158
examine, finding 158
map over time, updating 158
map's goals, defining 154
objectives, personalities 154
personas, highlights 155
resources, accessing 158
Touchpoint 155-157
CJMs, tools
Canvanizer 168
smaply 168
UXPressia 168
Complementary, advantages
brand identity 46
engagement, improving 46
greater, memorability 46
user, experience 46
user happiness 46
CPS, purpose 53
CPS, step
Action Plan, draw up 52
action, taking 52
formulate, challenge 50
ideas, exploring 50, 51
problem, identifying 49
problem, researching 50
Creative Problem Solving (CPS) 47, 48
Customer Journey Maps (CJMs) 149

D

Dark UI Design Patterns 276
Dark UI Design Patterns, key points
Bait, trick 276
Confirmsharing 277
forced continuity 276
misdirection 277, 278
privacy, zuckering 277
roach motel 276
sneak, basket 277
Design Handoff 340, 341
Design Handoff, checklist
assets 344
contact, information 345
design files 343
Design System 344
documentation 343
feedback, revisions 344
functionality, features 344
project, timeline 345
prototypes, interactive 343
technical, specifications 344

Design Handoff, roles 341
Design Handoff, strategies
continues beyond 342
developers mind, designing 342
embrace, flexibility 342
Design Handoff, tips
Continuous Feedback, loop 346
Design Tools, collaborative 347
developers, involve 345
documentation, detail 346
Emphasize Design, consistency 346
mindset, flexibility 346
prototypes, interactive 346
Design Thinking 4
Design Thinking, benefits 31
Design Thinking, components
Define 9-12
Empathize 8, 9
Ideate 12
Prototype 14
Test 16
Design Thinking, considerations
age, appropriateness 28
inclusivity 29
long-term, engaging 28
safety 28
Design Thinking/CPS, comparing 53
Design Thinking, importance
assumptions, validating 6
Empathy, building 7
insights, gaining 6
iterative, improving 6
pain points, identifying 6
Design Thinking, industries
Agility/Iteration, utilizing 29
AI Digital, transformation 29
augmente, reality 30
comprehensive, integrating 30
Design Education, evolution 30
diversity, collaboration 29
Human-Centered, solutions 29
social, impact 29
Design Thinking, key points
Brainstorming 31
Empathy Maps 31
Personas 30
user, mapping 31
Design Thinking, methodology
AirBnb 20
UberEats 18
Design Thinking, methods
Brainstorming 13
Mind, mapping 13
Rapid, prototyping 13
SCAMPER 13
Six Thinking 13
Worst Possible Idea 13
Design Thinking, tools
Canva 32
Empathy Map, template 32
MindMeister 32
Miro 32
Design Thinking/UCD, comparing 60
Design Thinking, workflow 5, 6
Diary Studies 97
Diary Studies, challenges 98
Diary Studies, methods
Effective Technique 98
Effective Timing 97
Diary Studies, steps
data, analyzing 98
format, structure 98
instruction, providing 98
monitor, progressing 98
objective, defining 98
pilot test 98
recruit, participants 98
report, finding 98

E

Empathy Maps 159
Empathy Maps, aspects
actions 160
feelings 160
observations 160
Thought 160

Empathy Maps, benefits 161
Empathy Maps, goals 161
Empathy Maps, importance 161
Empathy Maps, optimizing 161, 162
Empathy Maps/Personas, comparing 163
Empathy Maps, structure 160
Empathy Maps, tools
- Canvanizer 169
- Mural 168
- Stormboard 169

Engaging Personas
- about 140
- benefits 141
- key elements 140
- structures 140

Experience Maps 163
Experience Maps, benefits 165
Experience Maps, components 164
Experience Maps, concepts
- actions 165
- mindset, feelings 165
- Phase 165
- thoughts 165

Experience Maps, tools
- Abobe XD 169
- Lucidchart 169
- Miro 169

Eye Tracking 106
Eye Tracking, elements
- Blind Spots 107
- read, patterns 107
- stumbling 107

Eye Tracking, fundamentals
- Heat Maps 107
- Saccade Pathways 107

Eye Tracking, limitations 109
Eye Tracking, methods
- Effective Technique 108
- Effective Timing 107

Eye Tracking, steps
- data, analyzing 108
- equipment, set up 108
- objectives, defining 108
- participants, selecting 108
- report, finding 109
- test, building 108
- test, perform 108

F

Fictional Personas
- about 138
- benefits 139
- key elements 138
- structures 139

Field Studies 101
Field Studies, challenges 104
Field Studies, methods
- Effective Technique 103
- Effective Timing 102

Field Studies, stage
- follow-up, questions 104
- insights, reporting 104
- iterate, implementing 104
- learn objective, identifying 103
- location, selecting 103
- participants 103
- plan, observations 103
- project, developing 104
- take notes, observe 103
- transcripts, analyzing 104

Five-Second Tests 112
Five-Second Tests, challenges 114
Five-Second Tests, key questions 113, 114
Five-Second Tests, methods
- Effective Technique 113
- Effective Timing 112

Five-Second Tests, steps
- goals, defining 113
- question, creating 113
- recruit, test 113
- results, analyzing 113
- test, setup 113

Focus Groups 90
Focus Groups, advantages 92
Focus Groups, types
  Effective Technique 91
  Effective Timing 90

G

Gift Dilemma, scenarios
  Empathize 23
  Ideate 25
  Iterate-Iterate 27, 28
  Prototype 25
  stage, defining 23, 24
  Test 26
Goal-Directed Personas
  about 136
  benefits 136, 137
  key elements 136
  structures 136

H

High-Fidelity Prototype 231
High-Fidelity Prototype, advantages
  design validation, enhancing 233
  detail, feedback 233
  precise, specification 233
  realistic user, experience 233
  risk, misalignment 233
  stakeholder, communicating 233
  usability, testing 233
  user engagement, improving 233
High-Fidelity Prototype, disadvantages
  details, overemphasis 234
  high cost 234
  limit, flexibility 234
  misleading, feedback 234
  resource, intensive 234
  scope, creep 234
  time, consuming 234
High-Fidelity Prototype, types
  Coded Prototypes 232
  Digital Prototypes 232
  Interactive Prototypes 231

I

IA, architecture 174-176
IA, fundamentals
  document, everything 189
  Goals, defining 186
  Hierarchy, navigation 187, 188
  Lable/Content, optimizing 187
  stay, flexibility 190
  User Test, iterating 189
IA, history 176, 177
IA, importance
  availability, enhancing 177
  content, managing 177
  Lessens Clutter, redundancy 178
  Overall Design, improving 178
  productivity, increasing 177
  SEO, encourages 177
  User Interface, improving 177
IA, principles
  choices 178
  disclosure 179
  exemplars 180
  front doors 181
  multiple classification 181, 182
  objects 178
IA, systems
  labeling 183
  navigation 184
  organization 183
  Search 183

IA, tools
Diagram.net 190
FigJam 190
MindMup 190
Mirp 191
Pencil Project 190
XMind 190
IA/UX, comparing 185
Information Architecture (IA) 174
Instagram 306

K

Khroma 307

L

Low-Fidelity Prototype 226
Low-Fidelity Prototype, advantages
communication, improving 229
cost-effective 229
encourage, creativity 229
focuses, functionality 230
promotes, teamwork 230
rapid, iteration 229
risk, reducing 229
user test, facilitates 229
Low-Fidelity Prototype, disadvantages
detail, insufficient 230
inadequate, visualizing 230
limit, interactivity 230
potential, misunderstandings 230
short, lifecycle 230
user, feedback 230
Low-Fidelity Prototype, types
Click-Through Prototypes 228
Paper Prototypes 227, 228
Sketches 227

M

MFD, key aspects
CSS Media, queries 335
gradual, enhancement 335
performance, optimizing 335
prioritize essential, content 335
user experience, improving 335
MFD/RWD, key strategies 336, 337
Microcopy 299, 300
Microcopy, impact
action, inviting 302
behavior, encourages 303
encourage, exploration 302
feedback, reassurance 302
personal touch 302
sense, progressing 302
tone, conversation 303
Microcopy, importance
Brand Voice, enhancing 301
Empathy Trust, building 301
friction confusion, reducing 301
reassurance 301
user action, guides 301
User Engagement, encourage 301
Microinteractions
about 303
benefits 304
Instagram 306
Pull-to-Refresh, preventing 306
seamless interactions 304, 305
Spotify's, configuring 305
UI/UX, optimizing 305
Mobile-First Design (MFD) 334, 335
Mobile UI Pattern, libraries
Ant Design Mobile 275
Google Flutter 275
Google Material Design 275
Human Interface Guidelines (HIG) 275
Ionic 275

Mockups 283, 284
Mockups, breakdown
 color, scheme 286
 content layout 285, 286
 element, interactive 286
 image, icons 286
 margins, spacing 287
 typography 286
 userflow, branding 287
Mockups, phases
 Mockups 298
 Prototypes 299
 UI, sketching 298
 Wireframes 298
Mockups, purpose
 consistency, ensuring 285
 design variations,
 exploring 285
 feedback, gathering 285
 precision, clarity 285
 product, visualizing 285
 time/money,
 resources 285
Mockups, steps 289-291
Mockups, tips 297, 298
Mockups, tools
 Adobe XD 293
 Axure RP 296, 297
 Figma 292
 InVision Studio 295
 Sketch 294
Mockups, types
 High-Fidelity 288
 Interactive 288
 Low-Fidelity 288
 Responsive 289
 Static 287

N

Non-Linear Process 17
Non-Linear Process, ways
 cake, planning 17
 decorating 17
 final touches, presentation 18
 Friends Taste 17
 mix, testing 17

P

Portfolio, ability
 showcase, process 350
 structure, clearly 350
 visual, making 351
Portfolio, polishing 350
Prototype 14
Prototype, methods
 3D, printing 16
 Apps 15
 Digital 15
 Oz Wizard 15
 Paper Prototypes 15
 role, playing 15
Prototypes 222, 223
Prototypes, benefits
 cost-effectiveness 225
 development,
 streamlining 225
 feature, validating 225
 risks, reducing 225
 technical feasibility,
 evaluating 225
 visualization,
 improving 225
Prototypes, key reasons
 communication,
 tool 224
 decision-making 224
 iterative, improving 224
 problem, detecting 224
 user-center,
 designing 224
Prototypes, qualities
 Evolution 224
 Interactivity 223
 Precision 223
 Representation 223
Prototypes, tools 235
Prototypes, types
 High-Fidelity Prototype 231
 Low-Fidelity Prototype 226
Prototypes/Wireframes,
 comparing 235
Prototype, ways 15

R

Responsive Web Design (RWD) 316, 317
Role-Based Personas
- about 137
- benefits 138
- key elements 137
- structures 137

RWD, breakdown
- broader reach 326
- cosr-effective 326
- future-proofing 326
- SEO, benefits 326
- user experience 326

RWD, evolution 317, 318
RWD, importance 326
RWD, key points
- adaptive, layouts 333, 334
- CSS 327
- flexbox, layout 330, 331
- fluid grid, layouts 329, 330
- HTML 327
- imagc, rcsponsivc 332
- media queries 328, 329
- Typography, responsive 332, 333

RWD, situations
- cost-efficiency 325
- development, maintenance 324
- future-proofing 324
- less, suitable 326
- mobile usage, growing 325
- SEO, benefits 325
- website, designing 324

RWD, structure 317

S

Service Blueprints 165
Service Blueprints, benefits
- comprehensive, view 167
- customer, insights 167
- opportunities, improving 167
- staff, training 167

Service Blueprints, key components
- backstage, interacting 167
- customer actions 167
- frontstage, interacting 167
- physical, evidence 167
- support, processing 167

Service Blueprints, tools
- ServiceDesignTools 169
- smaply 169
- Touchpoint 169

Sitemaps 191
Sitemaps/IA, comparing 204
Sitemaps, importance 192
Sitemaps, reasons 192
Sitemaps, steps
- code accuracy, ensuring 201
- page structure, reviewing 199, 200
- Root, integrating 202
- submit 203
- URLs, optimizing 201

Sitemaps, types
- HTML 192-194
- Image 197, 198
- Mobile 198
- News 198
- Video 195-197
- XML 194

Stakeholder, conducting 79
Stakeholder, guide
- assessment, impact 79
- concerns, challenges 79
- insights 79
- interview 79
- project, importance 79
- question, feedback 79
- role, responsibilities 79
- success, criteria 79

Surveys 92
Surveys, categories
- closed-ended, questions 92
- open-ended, questions 92

Surveys, challenges 94

Surveys, fundamentals
  Effective Technique 93, 94
  Effective Timing 93
Surveys, key points
  clarity 92
  neutrality 92
  respect 92
  variety 92

T

Tree Testing 104
Tree Testing,
  disadvantages 106
Tree Testing, methods
  Effective Technique 105
  Effective Timing 104
Tree Testing, steps
  activities, developing 106
  adjustment, making 106
  conduct, testing 106
  objective, defining 105
  participants, selecting 106
  results, analyzing 106
  retest, necessary 106
  structure, building 105
  tools, selecting 106

U

Uber 306
UberEats 19
UberEats, achievement 20
UberEats, concepts
  Empathize 19
  Ideate 19
  inconvenient 19
  Prototype 19
  test 19
UCD, benefits 58
UCD, concepts
  community, supporting 58
  experience, personalizing 57
  feedback, tracking 58
  food, database 57
  user-friendly, interface 57
  user objectives,
  recognizing 57
UCD, fundamentals
  continuous, improving 57
  convenience 57
  personalization 57
  reviews, ratings 57
  user, comprehending 56
  user-friendly, interface 56
UCD, points
  accessibility 56
  language 56
  legibility 56
  visibility 56
UCD, process
  Align 60
  Build 60
  Iterate 60
  research 60
  Test 60
UI Design AI, tools 311, 312
UI Design Patterns 259
UI Design Patterns, guide
  correct pattern, selecting 268
  issue, defining 268
  mind, usability 268
  pattern, implementing 268
  stay, updating 268
  test, iterate 268
UI Design Patterns,
  importance 260
UI Design Patterns,
  key aspects
  Content Display Patterns 272
  Feedback Patterns 273
  Input Patterns 273
  Interaction Patterns 274
  Navigation Patterns 272
  Onboarding Patterns 274
UI Design Patterns, key points
  action buttons 262
  Breadcrumbs 263
  card layouts 267
  Disclosure, progressive 264
  format, forgiving 262
  infinite scroll 266
  instant, suggestions 267
  lazy, registration 264
  leaderboard 266

modal windows 267
Sneak Peek 265
sticky, navigation 267
subscription plans 265
through, process 263
UI Design Patterns, libraries
Ant Design 269
Bootstrap 269
Carbon Design System 270
Fluent UI 270
Foundation 270
Material Design 269
Semantic UI 270
UI Design Patterns, reasons
across interfaces, consistency 261
across platforms, adaptability 261
design process, efficiency 261
learn curve, reducing 261
usability, improving 261
UI/UX 2
UI/UX Design, future trends 355
UI/UX Design, principles
confident, authentic 355
industry trends 354
UI/UX, history 2
UI/UX Interviews, challenges
criticism 354
display, work 353
problem, recognizing 353
procedure 353
user, focus 353
UI/UX Interviews, skills
adaptability 354
collaboration 354
communication 354
problem-solving 354
UI/UX, key difference 3, 4
Uizard 308
Usability Testing 99
Usability Testing, forms
assessment 99
comparative 99
explorative 99
in-person 99
moderate 99
remote 99
unmoderate 99
Usability Testing, limitations 101
Usability Testing, methods
Effective Technique 100, 101
Effective Timing 100
User-Centered Design (UCD) 56
User Experience Design (UX Design) 3
User Experience (UX) 36
User Interface Design (UI design) 3
User Interviews 88
User Interviews, concepts
downsides 90
effective, techniques 89
effective, timing 89
User Persona 134
User Persona, benefits 134
User Persona, character
boost, empathy 135
clear, direction 135
communication, enhancing 135
user, engaging 135
User Persona, fundamentals
background 144
behavior, patterns 145
goals, comprehensing 144
information, conversations 144
motivations 146
pain points, challenges 145
quotes 146
scenarios 146

User Persona, tools
Canva 135
HubSpot 135
Xtensio 135
User Persona, types
Engaging Personas 140
Fictional Personas 138
Goal-Directed Personas 136
Role-Based Personas 137
User Testing,
methods
A/B 17
interviews 16
Observational 16
prototype 17
surveys 16
usability 16
UX Design 36, 37
UX Design, architecture 37
UX Designer 54, 55
UX Designer, roles
Information Architect 55
Interaction Designer 55
UI Designer 55
User Researchers 55
UX Designer 55
UX Writer 56
UX Design, importance 37
UX Design, key points
costs, cutting 38
impression, making 38
intuitive experience,
offering 38
positive experiences 38
relationships, building 38
ROI, increasing 38
User Needs,
satisfying 38
UX, factors
accessible 68, 69
credible 66, 67
desirable 67, 68
findable 65, 66
usable 64, 65
useful 62, 63
valuable 70, 71
wrapping up 71
UX Mapping
about 126
focus 128
format, selecting 129
fundamentals 127
importance 126, 127
point of view 128
scope 128
structure 129
UX Mapping, scenarios
Chronological 129
Hierarchical 129
UX Mapping, steps
customer, interacting 132
issues, resolving 133
journey stages 131
Persona, developing 130
pinpoint friction, points 133
User Research,
performing 131
UX Mapping, tools
Customer Journey Maps
(CJMs) 168
Empathy Maps 168
Experience Maps 169
Service Blueprints 169
UX Mapping, types
Customer Journey Maps 149
Empathy Maps 159
Experience Maps 163
Service Blueprints 165
UX Research 75
UX Research, benefits 77
UX Research, case studies
Eye-Tracking 117
key changes,
implementing 118, 119
mobile, optimizing 117
UX Research, goal 75, 76
UX Research, key reasons
design,
improving 77
happy users, creating 77
problems, solving 77
targets,
comprehensions 77
time/money, saving 77

UX Research, methods
Behavioral/Attitudinal 86
Generative/Evaluative 87, 88
Qualitative/Quantitative 86
UX Research, process
opportunities, exploring 83
participants, recruiting 82, 83
research, findings 84
research goals, setting up 78
research methods, selecting 79, 80
results, integrating 84
user research, preparing 80
UX Research, tools 116

V

Visily 310
Visual Hierarchy 241-243
Visual Hierarchy, components
Consistency 255, 256
Contrast Color 249-251
Layout 256
Texture/Style 257, 258
Typography 253-255
White Space 251-253
Visual Hierarchy, factor
brand message, conveys 244
cognitive load, reducing 244
conversion rates, increasing 244
credibility trust, building 245
engagement, enhancing 244
Guides User, attention 243
User Experience, improving 244
Visual Hierarchy, strategies
F-Pattern 246, 247
Read Patterns 245
size, scaling 247-249
Z-Pattern 245, 246
Visual Hierarchy, tips
clear path, creating 259
consistent alignment 258
contrast, using 258
elements appropriately 258
prioritize, content 258
visual cues, using 258
white space 258

W

Wireframes 209, 210
Wireframes, benefits 215-217
Wireframes Desktop/Mobile, comparing 214
Wireframes, importance 210
Wireframes, key points
colors, establishing 218
image, creating 218
text, creating 218
Wireframes, purposes
cost-effective, iteration 210
features, clarifying 210
User-Focused Screen, planning 210
Wireframes, steps
draft sketches, identifying 219
iterate, feedback 220
refine 219
Wireframes, tools
Adobe XD 221
Balsamiq 221
Figma 220
InVision 222
MockFlow 221
Pencil Project 220
Sketch 221
Wireframe.cc 220
Wireframes, types
High-Fidelity Wireframes 213, 214
Low-Fidelity Wireframes 211, 212
Mid-Fidelity Wireframes 212
World Wide Web Consortium (W3C) 69